W9-BOA-295

THE NEW RIGHT, 1960-1968 WITH EPILOGUE, 1969-1980

Jonathan Martin Kolkey

UNIVERSITY PRESS OF AMERICA

LIBRARY
BRYAN COLLEGE
DAYTON, TENN. 37321

78732

Copyright © 1983 by **Jonathon Martin Kolkey**

University Press of America, Inc.

P.O. Box 19101, Washington, D.C. 20036

All rights reserved

Printed in the United States of America

ISBN (Perfect): 0-8191-2994-1
ISBN   (Cloth): 0-8191-2993-3

LIBRARY
BRYAN COLLEGE
DAYTON, TENN. 37321

To Peggy: I owe her everything

CONTENTS

ii

ACKNOWLEDGEMENTS

Special thanks go to all of the original members of my Ph.D. Committee who made my nine years at U.C.L.A. the most enjoyable period of my life: my Chairman, Professor of History Robert Dallek; my Vice-Chairman, Professor of History Richard Weiss; Professor of History John S. Galbraith; Professor of Political Science Robert Jervis; and the late Professor of Political Science Bernard Brodie. Several other friends also deserve mention including Professor of History Morris Schonbach of California State University, Northridge; and Professors of History Conrad Kinstad and Donald Schmidt of Los Angeles Valley College. I also appreciate suggestions furnished by U.C.L.A Professor of History Ronald Mellor, and by California Political Consultant Joseph R. Cerrell. In addition, let me extend my gratitude to Arizona Senator Barry M. Goldwater, who kindly gave me permission to quote from his various published works; to Mr. Gordon Gipson, Editor of Caxton Printers, Ltd., who kindly gave me permission to quote from James T. Hunter's, Our Second Revolution; and to Mr. Charles O. Mann, Editor of Western Islands Publishers, who kindly gave me permission to quote from Robert Welch's, The New Americanism, and The Blue Book of the John Birch Society. Finally, let me take my hat off to the entire staff of the U.C.L.A. Graduate Research Library for their unsung efforts, without which, doctoral candidates like myself would be unable to pursue our studies.

INTRODUCTION

"The political phenomenon of our time"

"A specter is haunting American Liberalism," newspaper editor M. Stanton Evans announced in 1960, "the specter of conservative revival." Three years later Evans concluded proudly, "The outstanding fact of American political life today is the resurgence of conservatism." At the same time, Arizona Republican Senator Barry M. Goldwater predicted that this "wave of Conservatism...could easily be the political phenomenon of our time." Likewise, the Reverend Gerald L.K. Smith, a familiar campaigner for the Radical Right since the 1930's, noted with satisfaction that "Everywhere we look, grass roots movements are sprouting from ground where the veteran patriots, through the years, have sown the seeds."1/

The rapidly growing strength of radical Conservatism in the United States during the early 1960's impressed political observers. Syndicated newspaper columnists Roland Evans and Robert Novak called this conservative tide "the closest thing to a spontaneous mass movement in modern American political history." In the same fashion, Professor Eugene V. Schneider writing in The Nation in September, 1961 warned, "In spite of optimistic predictions following the demise of McCarthyism, the voice of the right-wing radical is heard loud and clear in our land once more." 2/

As expected, the American Left watched the rise of radical Conservatism during the early 1960's with great alarm. In an expose entitled Men of the Far Right, Richard Dudman reported, "The most spectacular political phenomenon in the United States today is the growing power of the extreme conservative - the 'Far Right'." Dudman pointed out in 1962 that, "A powerful tide of right-wing thought and action has been running through the country as a whole for about two years. It has yet to reach a high water mark." Similarly, Socialist Worker's Party leader Eric Hass stressed that "the ominous character of the extreme right-wing organizations that have proliferated in this country in the past several years can scarcely be exaggerated." 3/

Democratic Party leaders also voiced grave concern over the surprising strength of the Radical Right. Wisconsin Senator William Proxmire told an audience in Hartford, Connecticut that "the great political phenomenon of today is the onrush of a conservative movement that would repeal many of the Woodrow Wilson and Franklin Roosevelt reforms of the past 50 years." Ohio Democratic Solon Stephen A. Young took to the Senate floor on August 15, 1963 to denounce the Radical Right. Senator Young blasted the "nearly 1,000 radical right-wing organizations in the nation," many of which were "well financed, and reach millions of Americans through their propaganda and radio and television programs." Referring to his enemies as "home-grown fascists," Senator Young believed "that the radical right today is an even deadlier threat to our democratic traditions and institutions than are American adherents to communism." Even President John F. Kennedy speaking before the Young Democrats Convention in Miami Beach, Florida in December of 1961 quipped, "For all I have been reading in the last three, four, or five months about the great Conservative revival sweeping the United States, I thought perhaps no one was going to show up today." 4/

Observers have agreed that America's radical Conservative revival during the early 1960's represented just the most recent episode in a long series of extreme right-wing movements which have erupted periodically throughout the course of American history. Thus one commentator traced a direct line "from the Know-Nothings of a hundred years ago to the American Protective Association of the eighties to the Ku Klux Klan of the twenties and the native fascists movements of the thirties: to McCarthyism and the so-called 'Radical Right' among current phenomena." 5/

Yet observers who have studied this revival of radical Conservatism within the United States during the early 1960's have been uncertain as to the exact significance of the movement and its place in American history. To add to the confusion, commentators have applied various terms to describe this resurgence of radical Conservatism, including: "Radical Right," "Extreme Right," "Far Right," "Reactionary Right," Rampageous Right," "Lunatic Fringe," "Ultra Conservatism," "Pseudo Conservatism," "Super Patriotism," Neo McCarthyism," "Goldwaterism," "John Birchism," or even "Neo-Fascism." Henceforward, for the sake of uniformity and convenience I shall simply call the radical Conservative renaissance of the early 1960's, the "New Right."

By far the most significant interpretations of the New Right came from such scholars as Daniel Bell, Richard Hofstadter, Seymour Martin Lipset, David Riesman, and Arthur Schlesinger, Jr. -- men dedicated to the so-called "consensus" approach to the study of American history and politics. (This "consensus" school held sway roughly between the late 1940's and the mid 1960's.) These "consensus" scholars stressed an underlying unity running through American life. They saw both American Liberals and Conservatives competing against one another as honorable adversaries, pursuing common goals while differing only as to the best means to achieve these goals. Most "consensus" writers never went so far as Louis Hartz who seriously argued in his book, The Liberal Tradition in America (1955) that the United States has never had a "real Conservative tradition" and that the only American political tradition is the Liberal one. Nevertheless, "consensus" scholars did emphasize the comfortable, almost symbiotic, relationship between American Liberalism and American Conservatism. 6/

Thus, these writers refused to grant any sort of legitimate status to the New Right of the 1960's. Instead, scholars like Richard Hofstadter viewed the Movement as both an aberration from the American tradition as well as a dangerous attempt at "subverting the whole pattern of our politics of coalition and consensus." Hofstadter characterized New Rightists as "pseudo-Conservatives" who overreacted with a display of "heated exaggeration, suspiciousness, and conspiratorial fantasy...," while claiming to uphold tradition in the face of a whole flock of largely imaginary enemies. Thus Hofstadter detected a kind of "paranoid style" running through the New Right, while Seymour Martin Lipset and Earl Raab depicted them as practicing "The Politics of Unreason." 7/

My study, therefore, takes issue with these "consensus" scholars by accepting the premise that the United States of America does indeed have a legitimate, longstanding "radical Conservative" political tradition. The term "radical" describes its tactics -- a bold activism stressing drastic solutions to problems while rejecting a "consensus" approach to American politics. The term "Conservative" describes its purpose -- to defend values closely identified with the so-called, traditional "American Way of Life" such as Anglo-Saxonism, Christianity, civic morality, fiscal integrity in government, free enterprise, individualism, male chauvinism, sexual chastity, and White supremacy.

Next these "consensus" writers have questioned the link between the New Right and traditional Conservatism. First, the New Right's "pseudo-Conservative" philosophy, as Hofstadter calls it, seemed to be based heavily upon a defunct, nineteenth century economic individualism, which had once been identified with Liberalism. And second, the New Right seemed to make the fundamental mistake of equating Conservatism with what sociologist Karl Mannheim has called "Traditionalism" -- i.e. an attachment to an older way of life. 8/

Now I would agree that a great deal of New Rightism was, in fact, nostalgia rather than a systematic expression of a true Conservative ideology. Nevertheless, in terms of its overall effect upon American society during the 1960's, this distinction is unimportant. For New Rightists consciously thought of themselves as Conservatives, and thus voted and acted accordingly.

Finally, these "consensus" scholars have suggested that the New Right fashioned its ideology, in large measure, to express its anxiety over its current social position in American society. Hence, the New Right contained a curious collection of "dispossessed" White Anglo-Saxon

Protestant elites unhappy over the nation's growing political and cultural pluralism and the Irish and German arrivistes determined to defend their newly won status while still "tormented by a nagging doubt as to whether they are really and truly and fully American." Like the McCarthy movement of the early 1950's Richard Hofstadter characterized the New Right of the 1960's as "a product of the rootlessness and heterogeneity of American life and, above all, of its peculiar scramble for status and its peculiar search for secure identity." 9/

No doubt, such sociological interpretations of the New Right do serve to explain part of the Movement's appeal. But to take the New Rightists at anything less than at face value would be to deprive ourselves of the opportunity to appreciate them for what they really are, and to listen carefully to exactly what they had to say.

The first chapter of my book describes the composition of the New Right, while the second traces the origins and examines the basic nature of the Movement. Chapters Three through Six serve as a compendium of the New Right's economic, political, and social philosophy. Lastly, chapters Seven through Twelve place the New Right within the overall context of American history during the 1960's with special emphasis upon the central events of the decade: the assassination of President John F. Kennedy, the Civil Rights struggle coupled with the emergence of the White Backlash, the Johnson-Goldwater Presidential Election of 1964, the passage of the Great Society, the rise of the New Left, the Vietnam War, climaxed by the turbulent year 1968. In addition, a three-chapter Epilogue has been added which follows the Movement right up through the election of Ronald Reagan as President in November, 1980, and assesses the long range impact of the New Right's recent revival.

INTRODUCTION - Notes

1. National Review, (January 30, 1960), p. 81;
Paul A. Sexson and Stephen B. Miles, Jr., The Challenge of Conservatism
(New York: Exposition Press, 1963), Preface p. XV;
New Guard, (July, 1963), p. 6;
Cross and the Flag, (April, 1962), p. 4.

2. New Guard (July, 1963), p. 6;
The Nation, (September 30, 1961), p. 199.

3. Richard Dudman, Men of the Far Right (New York: Pyramid
Publications, Inc., 1962), p. 1;
Ibid, p. 9;
Eric Hass, The Reactionary Right (New York: Labor News Company,
1963), p. 5.

Leftist Irwin Suall emphasized that "Radical reaction is on the
march in the United States." Irwin Suall, The American Ultras (New
York: New America, 1962), p. 3.

4. Human Events (April 28, 1961), p. 258;
U.S. Congress, Senate, Congressional Record, 88th Cong., 1st Sess.,
August 15, 1963, vol. 9, p. 15179;
Ibid., p. 15178;
Bill Adler, ed., The Kennedy Wit (New York: The Citadel Press, 1964),
p. 46.

5. Edwin S. Newman, The Hate Reader (Dobbs Ferry, New York:
Oceana Publications, 1964), p. 6.

Authors Arnold Forster and Benjamin Epstein writing in 1964
pointed out:

Today's Radical Right is the direct lineal descendant of ultra-
Rightist organizations that flashed across the national scene in the
1930's and the 1940's - from the Liberty League to the isolationist
America First Committee and the Constitutional Education League, and
thence to the whole amorphous carload of patrioteers and Communist-
hunters that came to be called the McCarthy movement, or
McCarthyites, after the late senator from Wisconsin. Arnold Forster
and Benjamin R. Epstein, Danger on the Right (New York: Random
House, 1964), p. 5.

Ohio Senator Stephen Young echoed the same theme:

The influence of early American rightist hatemongers has remained
in robust good health for a century. Their heirs of the past few decades

have been legion. They wore hoods and lynched Negroes as Ku Klux Klan members in the 1920's. They goosestepped among the fascistic Silver Shirts and Fritz Kuhn's German-American Bund and joined Father Coughlin's Christian front in the 1930's. Today they read as gospel Gerald L.K. Smith's hate sheet, The Cross and the Flag, or have been swept into the John Birch Society...U.S. Congress, Senate, Congressional Record, 88th Cong., 1st Sess., August 15, 1963, vol. 9, p. 15179.

6. In the words of Louis Hartz, "The ironic flaw in American liberalism lies in the fact that we have never had a real conservative tradition." Louis Hartz, The Liberal Tradition in America (New York: Harcourt, Brace, 1955), p. 57.

Examples of "consensus" scholarship on the New Right are...

Daniel Bell, ed., The Radical Right (Garden City, New York: Doubleday & Company, Inc., 1963) containing important essays contributed by Daniel Bell, Richard Hofstadter, Seymour Martin Lipset, Talcott Parsons, David Riesman, Peter Viereck, and Alan F. Westin;
Richard Hofstadter, The Paranoid Style in American Politics and Other Essays (New York: Alfred A. Knopf, 1965);
Seymour Martin Lipset and Earl Raab, The Politics of Unreason (New York: Harper and Row, 1970); and
Arthur M. Schlesinger, Jr., "The 'Threat' of the Radical Right." New York Times Magazine, (June 17, 1962).

7. Hofstadter, The Paranoid Style in American Politics and Other Essays, p. 103;

Lipset and Raab, The Politics of Unreason.

8. Hofstadter, The Paranoid Style in American Politics and Other Essays, p. 3;

Karl Mannheim, Essays on Sociology and Social Psychology (London: Routledge & Kegan Paul, Ltd., 1953), pp. 94-95.

9. Bell, ed., The Radical Right, p. 1;
Ibid., p. xi;
Ibid.;
Hofstadter, The Paranoid Style in American Politics and Other Essays, p. 51.

THE NEW RIGHT, 1960–1968

CHAPTER ONE

THE MEMBERSHIP OF THE NEW RIGHT

The various members who composed the New Right agreed upon most fundamental political and philosophical questions. (Chapters Three through Six examine the New Right's interesting ideology in depth.) Nevertheless, this basic doctrinal unity appears quite remarkable considering the Movement's great diversity. For the broad coalition which I call the New Right actually drew support from widely different sources: competing economic and occupational interests, countless religious sects and ethnic groups, several different geographic regions of the nation, and from both Democrats and Republicans as well as from citizens associated with minor parties. The New Right received inspiration from a number of American political traditions.

The following brief survey (which contains some unavoidable overlapping) analyzes the composition of the New Right, and explains why each group joined the Movement. Furthermore, the next section draws a distinction between groups which more or less permanently supported the American Radical Right throughout the twentieth century and those groups temporarily driven into the ranks of the New Right by the extraordinary events of the 1960's.

Reactionary Wealth

To begin with, reactionary wealth has represented, by and large, the mainstay of radical Conservatism in the United States throughout the twentieth century (if not well before). For instance, reactionary wealth acting through the American Liberty League provided the initial serious opposition to the New Deal's social and economic reforms during the 1930's. Likewise, reactionary wealth furnished both leadership and financial backing for many New Right organizations during the 1960's such as the American Conservative Union, Americans for Constitutional Action, Christian Freedom Foundation, the Intercollegiate Society of Individuals, the John Birch Society, Liberty Lobby, and the Young Americans for Freedom. Large corporations with significant connections to the New Right included General Electric (which employed Ronald Reagan as its traveling spokesman during the late 1950's and early 1960's), Republic Steel, and the Schick Safety Razor Company. Wealthy reactionary publications like American Opinion, Christian Economics, Economic Council Letter, Human Events, Liberty Letter, New Guard, and News and Views among others presented the New Right viewpoint. Key leaders of the Movement closely identified with reactionary wealth were Ohio Republican Congressman John M. Ashbrook, former Navy Secretary Charles Edison, newspaper publishers William F. Knowland and William Loeb, radio broadcaster Fulton Lewis, Jr., California G.O.P. Congressman John Schmitz, candy manufacturer Robert Welch, and Colorado brewer Joseph Coors.

1

The tradition of reactionary wealth in the South stretches back to the pro-slavery, states' rights "Fire-eaters" before the U.S. Civil War. Then during the 1930's Virginia Senator Harry F. Byrd furnished Southern reactionary wealth with the most effective opposition to Franklin D. Roosevelt and his New Deal. Accordingly, the New Right of the 1960's obtained strong support from reactionary Southern planters, mill owners, lumber and tobacco firms as well as utility companies. Another Virginian, via Oklahoma, James J. Kilpatrick, Editor of the Richmond News-Leader, North Carolina television commentator Jesse Helms (a future U.S. Senator), and South Carolina Solon J. Strom Thurmond stood out as the foremost defenders of Southern reactionary wealth during the Sixties.

Business and financial leaders sympathetic to the New Right viewpoint held high positions with major corporations all across the United States. Yet most New Rightists came from small and moderate size companies--especially family owned and operated firms. (Indeed a significant portion of the National Association of Manufacturers supported the Movement.) Concerned above all else with the protection of their economic and social position these representatives of wealthy reaction bitterly opposed labor unions, denounced government regulation of business, and grumbled loudly about their tax burden. Thus these New Rightists poured their energies into the fight to preserve and extend state right to work laws (National Right to Work Committee), demanded rigid economy in government (Liberty Amendment Committee), warned against the frivolous expense of the government's foreign aid program (Citizens Foreign Aid Committee), and sought to repeal the progressive Federal Income Tax (We, The People !). These wealthy reactionaries proudly referred to themselves as "constitutional Conservatives" and frequently spoke about "protecting private property" and, in the South, "States' Rights." 1/

Interestingly enough, the vast majority of wealth reactionaries supporting the New Right came from the Southern and Western Sunbelt and from the Middle-Western Farmbelt. Few prominent Northeastern industrialists or financiers joined the Movement. In fact, a genuine hostility existed between the New Right and the so-called Eastern Liberal Establishment (i.e. Wall Street, the New York banking community with its international monetary connections, and the giant corporations headquartered out of Manhattan). By the 1960's these professionally managed firms associated with the Eastern Liberal Establishment had long since accepted labor unions, favored a government regulated and subsidized economic system (the welfare state), and felt at least some degree of social responsibility to both consumers and the poor.

As expected, reactionary wealth wielded considerable power and influence. Besides contributing large sums of money to sympathetic Republican Party politicians and, on occasion, to Democrats (primarily in the South) reactionary wealth lobbied the corridors of the Congress and state legislatures across the nation. By patiently operating through well-established political channels these wealthy reactionaries often earned themselves the title of "Respectable Right."

Reactionary Community Elite

Next, a reactionary community elite composed of successful, but not necessarily rich professionals and small businessmen made up the backbone of the New Right in hundreds of small towns and cities, and in high income suburbs of great metropolitan centers throughout the land. These reactionary community elites provided the rank and file membership for organizations such as the John Birch Society, the Daughters of the American Revolution, and the White Citizens Councils, while their college age children joined the Intercollegiate Society of Individuals and the Young Americans for Freedom. Moreover, these reactionary community elites formed the core of grass-roots volunteer workers in Barry Goldwater's 1964 Presidential campaign. For the most part these New Rightists toiled in relative obscurity content to fire off angry letters to the editor or speak out at local P.T.A. meetings, yet once in a while a person such as pamphleteer Phyllis Schlafly attracted national attention.

These self-appointed "pillars of the community" staunchly defended traditional American middle-class culture. They preached civic virtue and joined "decency" crusades designed to clean up red-light districts, or jail narcotics dealers and smut peddlers. Indeed an auxiliary of the 1964 Goldwater for President campaign proudly called itself the "Mothers for a Moral America." (See Chapter Nine)

Descended predominately from "solid" WASP or German stock, these reactionary local elites (as with reactionary wealth in general) supported America's immigration laws which heavily favored admitting Northern Europeans into the United States while simultaneously restricting the flow of newcomers from other parts of the world. Of course, reactionary wealthy WASPs in the Southern states opposed the integration efforts of Negroes. However, wealth reaction outside of Dixie sympathized overwhelmingly with Southern attempts to retain Anglo-Saxon racial purity, law and order in the face of civil rights protests, and high standards of political morality. (See Chapter Seven)

Sunbelt Nouveau Riche

The tremendous economic expansion throughout the Sunbelt after World War Two created a new class of wealth based upon oil and cattle, land development and tourism, retailing, electronics and aerospace. (Indeed the Sunbelt economy became heavily dependent upon defense

3

contracts and payrolls from military installations.) The New Right philosophy found a receptive audience in Sunbelt boom towns, such as Dallas, Houston, Las Vegas, Los Angeles, Miami, Phoenix, and San Diego. The principle spokesmen for this new Sunbelt wealth were Arizona Republican Senator Barry Goldwater; cattleman J. Evetts Haley, author and founder of "Texans for America"; oil billionaire H. L. Hunt and his son Nelson Bunker Hunt; California G.O.P. Congressman John Rousselot; California industrialist J. Robert Fluor; television broadcaster Dan Smoot; and the Republican Senator from the Lone Star State John Tower.

The South and West had once reverberated with the colorful, old Populist denunciations of evil corporate wealth—a political tradition continued with success by the Progressives and the New Dealers. In truth, Northeastern based firms did exert a powerful influence over the Sunbelt economy before the Second World War (some angry citizens would describe this control as a virtual stranglehold). At any rate, many Sunbelters naturally associated great corporate wealth with the sinister Eastern Liberal Establishment.

However, a new homegrown corporate wealth suddenly sprang up in the South and West after World War Two. Yet these native Sunbelt millionaires still used the classic Populist rhetoric to condemn the old line Eastern Establishment as decadent, flabby, and infected with Liberalism (hence the name Eastern Liberal Establishment), while characterizing the new Sunbelt wealth as young, vigorous, and dedicated to Conservative principles. Worst of all, the Eastern Liberal Establishment wielded national political power by virtue of its inherited money. Thus the up-and-coming Sunbelters demanded a fair share of political power based upon their strong entrepreneurial talents and their recent achievements.

Consequently, the New Right's philosophy of "rugged individualism" and economic "laissez-faire" fitted perfectly the Sunbelt wealth's "nouveau riche" mentality. Obviously, these new Sunbelt aristocrats lacked the refinements and sense of social responsibility (noblesse oblige) found in genteel third or fourth generation Eastern Wealth. Accordingly, Sunbelters fought governmental restrictions on their entrepreneurial spirit and disliked paying heavy taxes to assist the "lazy" poor.

Southern Rednecks

The Poor Whites from the Deep South, often referred to as the "Rednecks," represented yet another Sunbelt group supporting the New Right during the 1960's. In truth, these Poor Whites have always possessed a dual political personality: a Liberal tradition on economic issues coupled with violent reactionary opinions on racial questions. On

4

the one hand, the Rednecks joined the Populist crusade of the 1890's, Woodrow Wilson's New Freedom, Franklin D. Roosevelt's New Deal, and even fell under the spell of Huey Long's "Share the Wealth" movement during the Great Depression. Leaders who championed the Poor Whites favored government spending for public works and social welfare (at least for the benefit of the Whites) and had long since mastered the delicate legislative art of logrolling pork barrel programs through Congress. Thus on the vital bread-and-butter issues the Rednecks supported the national Democratic Party.

On the other hand, while economics turned the Poor Whites leftwards, the Southern racial dilemma turned them towards the Right. The Rednecks have produced the Ku Klux Klan, and the frightening assortment of "Nigger-baiting" Dixie demagogues who have plagued Southern politics since the 1890's. This racist-Redneck tradition spawned the pro-segregation mobs and the nightriders of the 1960's as well as rabble-rousing politicians such as George Wallace of Alabama and Lester Maddox of Georgia.

As expected, the integration crisis of the 1960's sent the Poor Whites temporarily scurrying into the ranks of the New Right. The deep Southern states, which opened the tumultuous decade by voting for Liberal Democrat John F. Kennedy for President in 1960, abruptly switched to the New Right G.O.P. candidate Barry Goldwater by 1964, and then to American Independent Party nominee George Wallace in 1968.

The Forgotten Right

Millions of lower-middle-class or elderly poor New Rightists usually with Middle-Western roots reside in small towns and hamlets all across the United States. These members of the "Forgotten Right" lead a marginal existence outside the mainstream of American economic and cultural life. Politically the Democrats ignore the Forgotten Right while the Republicans simply take their votes for granted. New Right publications directed at the Forgotten Right included, America's Future, American Mercury, Beacon-Light Herald, Common Sense, and Cross and the Flag.

Unlike the economically Liberal Southern Redneck Democrats, these Forgotten Right Republicans remain faithful to the self-help tradition of their childhood and thus utterly reject the welfare state. And unlike the "hell-raising" Southern Rednecks these Forgotten Rightists take elaborate pains to cloak themselves in respectability.

Unfortunately, these church-going, law-abiding citizens of the Forgotten Right have traditionally supported all sorts of disreputable (one would say "quack") causes. Such cranky people during the mid-

5

1930's provided the rank and file for Dr. Francis Townsend's incredible Old Age Revolving Pensions scheme. During the 1960's the members of the Forgotten Right comprised the New Right's most active remaining pocket of anti-Semitism. (See Chapter Five) They also denounced fluoridated drinking water (See Chapter Four), fought running battles with the Food and Drug Administration in defense of various patent medicines, and pushed for legalization of a dramatic new "miracle" cure for cancer known as Laetrile.

Evangelical Protestantism

The Evangelical Protestant tradition has remained a profoundly reactionary force in twentieth century American politics. WASP Fundamentalists made up the backbone of the Prohibition crusade during the Progressive era as well as providing the impetus behind the passage of moral legislation designed to control urban vices such as gambling, narcotics, pornography, and white slavery (prostitution). The 1920's featured the Fundamentalist clash with Darwinism and academic freedom at the infamous Scopes Trial. The Twenties also witnessed the height of the WASP offensive against Catholicism in the United States while the following decade saw Fundamentalist anti-Semitism reach a crescendo. After the Second World War Evangelical Protestantism gave Biblical sanction to the efforts of the White supremacists in the Southern states to prevent integration, and by railing against "Godless Communism" has helped perpetuate an extreme Cold War mentality in American foreign policy. No wonder America's cultural and racial revolution of the 1960's turned Fundamentalism, once again, towards radical Right-wing political activities in earnest.

Evangelical Protestantism, especially strong throughout the Southern and Western states, represented an extremely important influence upon the New Right. Politically active ministers who blended the gospel of Christianity with the New Right ideology included Billy James Hargis, Carl McIntyre, Frederick Schwarz, and Gerald L. K. Smith. Public officials such as Ezra Taft Benson, the Secretary of Agriculture (1953-1961) and Minnesota Republican Congressman Walter Judd also brought their evangelical spirit into government. (Benson served as an Elder of the Mormon Church while Judd had done missionary work in China.) In addition, Sunbelt Fundamentalist sponsored academic institutions like Ambassador College and Pepperdine University in Southern California, Bob Jones University in South Carolina, and Harding College in Arkansas became prime focal points for New Right political efforts.

The Evangelical Protestant churches, once relatively poor and stagnant, suddenly grew and prospered in the years immediately after World War Two. In fact, a major Fundamentalist renaissance financed and directed by the new Sunbelt wealth swept through the Southern and

Western states. The New Right leadership (many still faithful to their Fundamentalist upbringing) looked upon this Evangelical revival as an effective means for politicizing the Sunbelt masses. With strong support from the New Right laymen, ministers like the Reverend Billy James Hargis (Christian Crusade) and the Reverend Frederick Schwarz (Christian Anti-Communism Crusade) successfully translated this Fundamentalist religious fervor into New Right politics.2/

Catholic Radical Right

The Roman Catholic Church has played a central role in the European Reactionary tradition for centuries stretching back to the Inquisition. Nevertheless, American Catholics before the Great Depression had never joined the American Radical Right -- rather American Catholics had often served as the Radical Right's favorite target. However, during the 1930's Father Charles Coughlin, the famed "Radio Priest," became the key figure in ending a century of mistrust as he cemented a Catholic-WASP Radical Right alliance with organizations such as the National Union for Social Justice (1934), the Union Party (1936), and the Christian Front (1939). Coughlin's vehement anti-Communism won him support from lower-middle-class Catholics living in big cities all across the country while his Populist-style denunciations of Eastern wealth and international bankers coupled with his anti-Semitism attracted many Sunbelt and Farmbelt WASPs.

Wisconsin Republican Senator Joseph R. McCarthy during the early 1950's continued the Catholic Radical Right tradition of Father Coughlin. However, McCarthy renounced anti-Semitism entirely, preferring instead to confine his activities to anti-Communism. In addition, the Wisconsin Senator dropped Father Coughlin's Populist style rhetoric, no doubt reflecting the greatly improved economic and social position of American Catholics after the Second World War. By the 1960's the Catholic leadership of the New Right, which included columnist William F. Buckley, Jr. and his brother James (soon to be elected U.S. Senator from New York in 1970), radio broadcaster Clarence Manion, International Affairs' Analyst Richard V. Allen (eventually President Ronald Reagan's National Security Advisor) and California G.O.P. Congressman John Schmitz, identified closely with the interests of reactionary wealth, as did Catholic members of the Cardinal Mindszenty Foundation, the Young Americans for Freedom, and the John Birch Society.

Catholic Isolationism

A Catholic "Isolationist" tradition on questions of United States foreign policy has also played an important role in shaping the American Radical Right since the 1930's. German and Irish Catholics who had bitterly opposed United States entry into the First World War constituted the core of Isolationist sentiment during the decade of the Great Depression. In truth, far from showing indifference to international events these so-called Catholic Isolationists followed world affairs quite closely: their non-interventionism reflected tacit approval as the forces of Fascism marched across Europe. Many Catholics especially savored General Francisco Franco's victory over the Communists in the Spanish Civil War (1936-1939). American participation in World War Two in alliance with the Soviet Union angered the Catholic Radical Right since the complete Axis defeat in 1945 paved the way for a Communist triumph throughout Eastern Europe and China.

Finally, these Irish and German Catholics, sensitive to hints of disloyalty to the United States during both World Wars and obviously anxious to prove their 100% Americanism, exploded in a self-proclaimed, super-patriotic frenzy during the early 1950's. Fueled, as Samuel Lubell has pointed out, by a strong desire for "revenge" against decades of mistreatment at the hands of snobbish Eastern WASPs, this burst of Catholic flag-waving found its classic spokesman in Senator Joseph McCarthy. The clever Wisconsin Solon succeeded in tapping forty years of Catholic resentment against the conduct of American foreign policy - a policy which they charged had led, ultimately, to the Communist conquest of one-third of the globe.3/

In addition, some Americans of Eastern European descent such as Catholic Czechs, Hungarians, and Poles as well as Eastern Orthodox Bulgarians, Romanians, and Yugoslavians, who had seen their ancestral homelands fall under Communist control during and immediately after World War Two, also supported Senator Joseph McCarthy. And a stream of refugees who fled to the United States in the wake of the Hungarian Uprising of 1956 and the Cuban Revolution of 1959 also joined this group. Thus these recent emigres from Red Tyranny plus angry native Americans of Eastern European heritage played a role in the New Right of the 1960's.

Protestant Isolationism

A somewhat different "Isolationist" tradition emanating from WASPs and German Protestants has also contributed to the American Radical Right since the Great Depression. Most frequently found in the Middle-Western states, this Protestant Isolationism has flourished for the past four decades among reactionary businessmen, reactionary community elites, and the lower-middle-class "Forgotten Rightists." Long-time leaders of this Protestant Isolationist tradition still active in the New Right up until the 1960's included author William Henry Chamberlain, columnist Westbrook Pegler, and General Robert Wood.

Protestant Isolationists provided the backbone for the America First Committee just prior to Pearl Harbor. Firmly convinced that United States entry into World War One back in 1917 had been a great mistake, these Protestant Isolationists, drawing upon the old Populist rhetoric, blamed the international bankers, Wall Street, the Jews and especially Great Britain for having dragged America into the European conflict. Indeed Protestant Isolationists hated the British nearly as much as they hated the Communists, President Franklin Roosevelt, or the New Dealers. When World War Two finally reached American shores on December 7, 1941, C.B.S. radio broadcaster Elmer Davis placed the sentiments of these Protestant Isolationists in proper perspective:

> There are some patriotic citizens who sincerely hope that America will win the war, but they also hope that Russia will lose it; and there are some who hope that America will win the war, but that England will lose it; and there are some who hope that America will win the war, but that Roosevelt will lose it ! 4/

Curiously, while Protestant Isolationists have often turned their backs on European events in disgust, they have always remained extremely interested in Far Eastern developments -- notably in China and the Philippines. In fact, many New Rightists had personal contact with the Orient. Nearly every Evangelical Protestant sect sponsored church activities in the Far East; and New Rightists like National Program Letter publisher Dr. George S. Benson and Minnesota Republican Congressman Walter Judd had once done missionary work inside China. Other members of the New Right including Barry Goldwater had served in the Pacific Theater during the Second World War or in Korea. Robert Welch had even named the John Birch Society after a zealous Fundamentalist U.S. Army Captain murdered by the Chinese Communists not long after V-J Day.

When the United States entered World War Two these Protestant Isolationists favored defeating the Japanese first, thus liberating our friends the Chinese and the Filipinos rather than assisting the hated British and Russians against the Germans. In addition, Samuel Lubell has pointed out that General Douglas MacArthur, already enormously popular with the Radical Right for his rout of the Bonus Army back in 1932, later won the affection of Protestant Isolationists "as our Pacific commander during World War II." For General MacArthur, in the words of Lubell, "became a symbol of the strategy which proposed defeating Japan rather that Germany first."5/

Protestant Isolationists continued to ignore Europe and concentrate their attention upon Asia even after 1945. Protestant Isolationists grumbled about the expense of the Marshall Plan designed to reconstruct war-ravaged Western Europe and wondered aloud whether the creation of N.A.T.O. in 1949 had militarily overcommitted the

9

United States abroad. Yet they fumed over the loss of Mainland China to the Communists that same year, enthusiastically supported American intervention in Korea in 1950, and then denounced the firing of Douglas MacArthur by President Harry Truman when the outspoken General called for a total victory. (See Chapter Two) Likewise, these Protestant Isolationist, New Rightists during the 1960's remained cool towards our European allies but took a hawkish position on Vietnam.

The Military

Retired United States military officers played a prominent role in the leadership of the New Right. Out of uniform and thus free at last to speak out on controversial public issues, these former career soldiers blasted America's Liberal foreign policy as "cowardly" and "flabby" and denounced attempts by the Kennedy-Johnson Administration to extend civilian controls over the armed forces. (See Chapter Six) As expected, they lobbied for increased national defense appropriations. (Indeed many ex-admirals and generals found post-service employment as executives or special consultants with firms bidding for lucrative defense contracts.)   These retired military officers lent their talents and contributed their money primarily to the Christian anti-Communist crusades and to the New Right organizations fostering the interests of reactionary wealth. Key ex-military men included General Curtis Le May, Captain Eddie Rickenbacker, General George E. Stratemeyer, General Nathan Twining, General Edwin A. Walker, and Admiral Chester A. Ward.

For a nation such as the United Stated founded upon the Anglo-Saxon dislike of large standing armies and professional soldiers, the militarization of American life after the Second World War represented a radical departure from the American tradition. In truth, the armed services became a powerful force in American political life during the Cold War.   Military themes dominated the political debate and the popular culture, and helped condition the public into accepting peacetime conscription and a swollen defense budget as somehow normal and healthy.

The New Right philosophy also flourished in veterans groups such as the American Legion and the Veterans of Foreign Wars; in organizations which operated on the fringes of the military like the Boy Scouts and the National Rifle Association; in some police departments, especially in Sunbelt cities and towns; in J. Edgar Hoover's F.B.I.; and in para-military self-defense forces such as the Minutemen.   Lastly, a handful of severly maladjusted ex-servicemen together with a few lower-middle-class social misfits with a taste for street fighting joined extreme para-military bands like James Madole's National Renaissance Party or George Lincoln Rockwell's American Nazi Party.

Hollywood Celebrities and Intellectuals

Two final New Right groups, famous Hollywood celebrities and intellectuals deserve brief mention. The first, consisting of motion picture stars such as Gene Autry, Shirley Temple Black, Pat Boone, George Murphy, Lloyd Nolan, Ronald Reagan, and John Wayne contributed their time and energies to various political candidates, and to the causes of anti-Communism and 100% Americanism.

The second, composed of New Right intellectuals represented a virtual potpourri of self-styled Libertarians devoted to individualism and free enterprise (but not Libertarian on many personal freedom issues); upholders of traditional Christian religious and moral values; and repentant ex-Communists who joined with other anti-Communists to preserve Western Civilization against the Red menace. New Right intellectuals included those associated with the National Review (William F. Buckley, Jr., L. Brent Bozell, James Burnham, M. Stanton Evans, and Frank S. Meyer) and American Opinion (Taylor Caldwell, Revilo P. Oliver, and E. Merrill Root).6/ (See Chapter Five)

The New Right and Traditional Republican Conservatism

At this point an important question arises: What was the exact relationship between the New Right of the 1960's and the kind of traditional, mainstream Republican Conservatism found primarily throughout the Middle-Western states? How did Conservative G.O.P. Farmbelt politicians such as Senators Everett Dirksen of Illinois, Robert Dole of Kansas, Roman Hruska of Nebraska, Karl Mundt of South Dakota, or Indiana Representative Charles Halleck differ from New Rightists like Barry Goldwater or Ronald Reagan?

To begin with, authors Arnold Forster and Benjamin Epstein have noted that "the two factions are difficult to separate at times, particularly when they sit at the same rallies and applaud the same ideas." Indeed Conservative Republicans and New Rightists often worked together closely, as for example during Richard Nixon's Presidential races of 1960, 1968, and again in 1972, and during Barry Goldwater's 1964 run for the White House, and, of course, during Ronald Reagan's 1980 Presidential Campaign. Moreover, Conservative politicians frequently accepted campaign contributions from New Right sources and vice versa. Forster and Epstein have even likened the collaboration between Republican Conservatives and New Rightists of the 1960's to the connection between Liberals and Communists in the 1930's and 1940's. Forster and Epstein go so far as to label G.O.P Conservatives "fellow travellers" of the New Right.7/

11

The leaders of the 1964 Goldwater Movement selected the interesting election year slogan "In your heart you know he's right" to describe an emotion which many Conservative voters must have undoubtedly felt when face-to-face with Barry Goldwater's rhetoric. For the Arizona Senator's political advisors realized that a great part of Goldwater's New Right message struck a responsive chord with traditional mainstream Republican Conservatives. In the words of the late historian Richard Hofstadter, "The great middle band of the party, which is by far its largest portion, is conservative enough to be susceptible to some of the right-wing notions, even though it does not share the partisan rage and the conspiratorial suspicions of the Goldwaterites."8/

Richard Hofstadter's perceptive pair of phrases "partisan rage" and "conspiratorial suspicions of the Goldwaterites" draw attention to the major differences separating New Rightists from Conservative Republicans. Without question, the New Rightists were extremely angry, deeply distrustful people quite disturbed by the collapse of the traditional American way of life during the decade of the 1960's. Most New Rightists lived in Southern and Western states, the section of the nation most infected with Evangelical Protestantism -- a militant, crusading brand of Christianity emphasizing a stern Fundamentalist morality which subsequently spilled over into New Right politics. In addition, the wide-open Sunbelt type of boom-town entrepreneurism fostered a "rugged individualism," anti-government economic philosophy. Then too, the South experienced the tremendous shock of racial integration during the 1960's. Finally, California's many New Rightists witnessed first-hand the political, sexual, and social revolution of the New Left-Hippie Movement. (See Chapter Ten)

In contrast, mainstream Republican Conservatism -- a Conservatism of comfortable apathy--really demanded very little sacrifice from its members, called for no great crusades, and while grumbling at a social change remained basically inert. (Even the Middle-Western religious style was sedate as opposed to the highly emotional Fundamentalism of the Sunbelt.) As a matter of fact, the Farmbelters of the 1960's had no burning issue to rouse them from their usual lethargy. Unlike the Southern states, the Middle-West lacked a strong anti-Negro tradition. Moreover, the prosperous Farmbelters might denounce the welfare state for everyone--that is--except for the farmers themselves. They had no desire whatsoever to return to a laissez-faire farm policy, as New Rightist Ezra Taft Benson discovered to his chagrin while serving as President Dwight D. Eisenhower's Secretary of Agriculture during the 1950's. Certainly, Barry Goldwater's campaign speeches of 1964 revived some wonderful memories of an earlier era as he thrilled Farmbelters with a dramatic appeal for a glorious reaffirmation of Conservative principles. Yet Richard Nixon in 1960, 1968, and again in

1972, as well as Gerald Ford in 1976 also won the confidence of Farm-belt voters by simply manipulating a few hackneyed Conservative symbols.9/

The New Right in Perspective

One final interpretive problem deserves mention: How did the New Right of the 1960's compare with the other, major American Radical Conservative movements which had previously erupted from time to time during the course of the twentieth century?

First of all, the New Right of the 1960's differed quite significantly from its immediate predecessor -- the Radical Right of the early 1950's commonly known as "McCarthyism." The Radical Right of the early 1950's lacked formal organization and structure. Sociologist Seymour Martin Lipset wrote, "McCarthyism was not a political movement. It never had members, organized chapters, offered candidates, or formulated a platform." Daniel Bell came to the same conclusion that McCarthyism "was never an organized movement; it was primarily an atmosphere of fear, generated by a one-man swashbuckler cutting a wide swath through the headlines." Likewise, Irwin Suall remarked, "McCarthy had a huge following, but he did not have an organization. Those who shared his fears and hates were never actually mobilized to go out and do battle."10/

In contrast, the New Right during the early 1960's concentrated a great deal of attention upon careful planning and organization. As Alan F. Westin observed, "Unlike Senator McCarthy and the loose apparatus of McCarthyism, the radical right is fervently organizational today." This organizational ability also impressed Daniel Bell: "the radical right of the 1960's has been characterized by a multitude of organizations that seemingly have been able to evoke an intense emotional response from a devoted following." Even Richard Hofstadter, who doubted whether "extreme rightists in the 1960's are any more numerous than they were in the McCarthyist period," did suggest that "the right wing has learned the secret of organization, which largely accounts for its greater success."11/

The New Right printed and distributed tens of millions of pamphlets, and organized thousands of anti-Communist seminars and study groups at the grass roots level. As New Right activist James T. Hunter explained, "Thousands, perhaps millions, of individuals were exposed to this grass roots program in one way or another." Indeed this vast grass roots effort made the New Right the most politically successful radical Conservative movement in modern American political history, a fact later confirmed by Ronald Reagan's 1980 nomination and

13

subsequent election. The New Right first gained control of a major American political party -- the G.O.P -- in 1964, and nominated Arizona Senator Barry Goldwater for President.12/

More importantly, as David Danzig pointed out, "McCarthyism was virtually devoid of social and economic content as well as religious inspiration...," in sharp contrast with the New Right. Wisconsin Senator Joseph McCarthy directed the brunt of his attack upon the Roosevelt-Truman foreign policy ("Twenty years of treason") which had supposedly led to Communist conquests in Eastern Europe and Asia. Thus McCarthy drew the bulk of his support from bitter Catholic and WASP Isolationists and from American citizens of Eastern European descent whose ancestral homelands now lay behind the Iron Curtain.13/

While reactionary wealth backed the Wisconsin Senator's anti-Communist activities as a convenient means of discrediting Liberalism at home, McCarthy, himself, never attempted a full-scale assault upon the welfare state. Indeed a significant portion of McCarthy's Catholic constituency vigorously favored the New Deal's domestic policy. As David Danzig noted:

> McCarthy managed to attack New Deal liberalism for allowing itself to be infiltrated by Communists, without directly challenging the policies and practices of reformed capitalism that had been achieved by the Democratic coalition and had come to be supported by the middle-of-the-road consensus in America.14/

In addition, unlike the New Right of the 1960's, McCarthyism lacked a strong Evangelical Protestant base, failed to cement an alliance with Southern White Supremacists, and never faced the breakdown of traditional American morality and culture. Senator McCarthy's coalition did not include as many different economic, ethnic, and religious groups as did the New Right, nor covered as wide a geographic area of the nation. Thus Irwin Suall correctly observed in 1962 that "what we are experiencing today is not merely the revival of McCarthyism."15/

The Radical Right and Senator Robert A. Taft

Senator Joseph McCarthy and the Radical Right worked diligently for Ohio Senator Robert A. Taft for the 1952 G.O.P. Presidential nomination. What then was the relationship between Robert Taft and the Radical Right, and how does Taft compare with New Rightist Presidential aspirants Barry Goldwater in 1960 and 1964 or Ronald Reagan in 1968, 1976, and 1980?

14

To begin with, as Richard Hofstadter observed, the Ohioan Robert Taft never adopted the same, extreme, laissez-faire economic position which Radical Rightists traditionally took. Senator Taft, who represented long-established, urban, industrial Ohio, appreciated the need for the welfare state. Consequently, Taft favored Federal Government assistance to the poor in areas such as education, health, and housing. He also supported farm subsidies, social security, and acknowledged a legitimate role for organized labor.16/

Conversely, Barry Goldwater took a step backwards from Robert Taft. The Arizonan Goldwater hailed from a frontier-oriented Southwestern state controlled by nouveau riche businessmen devoid of any sense of corporate responsibility to the working class or to the public or any sense of social obligation to the poor. Indeed Barry Goldwater in 1964, by campaigning upon an anti-welfare state philosophy of "rugged individualism," revived an economic idea which most Conservatives probably still secretly favored but had astutely abandoned thirty years before as politically unproductive.

Nevertheless, the gulf between Taft and Goldwater should not be overestimated. Robert Taft had reluctantly acquiesced in the building of a very limited national welfare state as a bitter necessity during the Great Depression only as an alternative to revolution. Then during the uncertain post World War Two period (1945-1953) when Taft dominated Republican Party politics the fear of another Depression hung over the United States. However, Goldwater celebrated the return of "rugged individualism" during the prosperous 1960's when the memories of the Great Depression had finally faded away. Perhaps the welfare state had once saved people in the midst of America's worst economic crisis but it had long since outlived its usefulness and had become quite counterproductive. Taft would have agreed wholeheartedly with Goldwater that the welfare state circa 1964 had become destructive of both personal character and civic morality. (See Chapter Three) Had Robert Taft been alive in 1964, he would surely have endorsed Barry Goldwater for President.

Of course, the true successor to Robert Taft was California Governor Ronald Reagan rather than Barry Goldwater. Both Taft and Reagan won election in urban, industrial states where they constructed a much more ethnically and socially diverse political base than the Arizona Senator ever enjoyed. Taft and Reagan tailored their Rightist philosophy in such a way as to obtain significant working-class support, which always eluded Goldwater. (See Chapter Nine)

In foreign affairs Robert Taft often sounded like a typical, Radical Right WASP Isolationist. Taft joined the America First Committee before World War Two and even after the War ended objected to America's continuing over-commitment in Europe. As with most WASP Isolationists who, on occasion, turned their backs upon

15

Europe, Taft retained a strong, life-long interest in Asia. Indeed, Taft had spent three years in the Orient (1900-1903) as a boy when his father William Howard Taft served as Governor of the Philippines. Thus Robert Taft mourned the loss of Mainland China to the Communists in 1949, applauded American military intervention in Korea the following year, and passionately defended Douglas MacArthur during the controversy surrounding the General's abrupt dismissal by President Harry Truman in 1951.

Yet Robert Taft represents the last great American Conservative spokesman to ponder the dilemma: how to defend the United States against foreign enemies abroad without, at the same time, resorting to the establishment of big government at home. Robert Taft along with most Radical Rightists still talked about cutting the defense budget during the early 1950's as part of an overall program for drastically reducing government spending.

However, the New Right by the 1960's had learned how to live, quite comfortably, with America's global military commitment requiring an expensive defense establishment. (In effect, the New Right accepted the Catholic-McCarthyite, world-wide, anti-Communist strategy of confrontation over the more limited, "Asia-first", WASP Isolationist tradition.) Then too, Soviet technological progress in the field of advanced weaponry had escalated the arms race. Finally, New Rightists in the Sunbelt had become dependent upon lucrative government aerospace contracts as well as upon large payrolls from military installations.

Futhermore, Robert Taft represented, in some sense, an heir to an older American Libertarian tradition. For the Ohio Solon had repeatedly voiced fears that the bloated defense budget, the peacetime draft, and the armed-camp mentality of the World War Two-Cold War years would foster an unwelcome, permanent militarization of American life coupled with a decline in respect for civil liberties. Many Radical Rightist of the Taft era agreed with the Ohio Senator. Yet the New Rightists of the Sixties moved away completely from a Libertarian position as they heartily applauded the repression of unorthodox social, sexual, and cultural ideas, denounced the Vietnam War draft protesters as traitors, and deliberately stoked the fires of the military-industrial complex.

The Great Depression Radical Right

Nor did the New Right of the 1960's closely resemble the American Radical Right-wing movement of the 1930's. The Great Depression Radical Right did contain a sprinkling of reactionary wealth (American Liberty League) and reactionary community elites, Catholic and Protestant Isolationists (Father Coughlin, America First

16

Committee), as well as para-military groups (German-American Bund, Silver Shirts). Yet the Great Depression Radical Right still lacked a powerful, diverse base of popular support and never developed a national political leader even remotely within reach of capturing the Presidential nomination of a major party. A third party organized in 1936, the Union Party, also failed miserably.

Fundamental issues also separated the two movements since the New Right flourished in the midst of the most prosperous decade in American history (1960's) while the Great Depression Radical Right emerged during the country's worst economic catastrophe (1930's). Then too, the Great Depression Radical Right never faced a revolution in cultural, moral, and sexual values.

Next the Great Depression Radical Right featured a vehement anti-Semitism. Reactionary wealth (American Liberty League) and reactionary community elites resented the arrival of Jews into positions of considerable power and influence in American life; Catholic and Protestant Isolationists (Father Coughlin, American First Committee) charged the Jews with trying to lead the United States into another war against Germany, this time in order to save their persecuted Jewish brethren from Adolph Hitler's wrath; while street-fighting goons joined para-military groups (German-American Bund, Silver Shirts) which imitated the vicious anti-Semitism of European Fascism. In contrast, the New Right of the 1960's has almost totally abandoned anti-Semitism. (See Chapter Five)

On the opposite side of the coin, the Great Depression Radical Right lacked the same widespread Southern Redneck contingent which played such an important role in the 1960's New Right. The urgent need for Liberal social reforms during the Thirties had kept the Southern Poor Whites securely behind the New Deal. In addition, the Blacks remained rather quiet during the decade of the 1930's; thus Southern Rednecks felt little need to rally in defense of White supremacy. However, when the Blacks, at long last, challenged the Jim Crow system during the 1960's the Southern Poor Whites turned sharply towards the Right politically.

The WASP Inquisition

The twentieth century American radical Conservative movement which most closely resembles the New Right held center stage roughly during the years 1914-1925. This frequently overlooked flurry of Radical Right-wing activity is often erroneously identified as an offshoot of the Progressive Movement. In truth, this burst of Radical Rightism between 1914 and 1925 represents a grand "WASP Inquisition" (my own phrase). As with the New Right of the Sixties this earlier "WASP Inquisition" strove, above all else, to protect and preserve traditional American culture and morality.

17

Superbly documented by historian Henry F. May in his masterpiece, The End of American Innocence, this "WASP Inquisition" battled disturbing new ideas which appeared around the time of the First World War concerning art, dancing, drama, literature, motion pictures, and music as well as birth control, economics, education, lady's fashions, politics, psychology, religion, science, sex, and women's rights. Thus in defense of the traditional American way of life, this "WASP Inquisition" goaded Congress and the states into passing laws directed against liquor, narcotics, pornography, and white slavery. Deeply alarmed over Anglo-Saxon "race suicide" (a la Madison Grant's Passing of the Great Race) the Movement successfully lobbied the Federal Government into restricting the flow of non-WASP immigrants into the United States. The "WASP Inquisition" also resurrected the Ku Klux Klan, produced the Red Scare, and the Scopes Trial.17/

Therefore, this "WASP Inquisition" served as the real predecessor to the modern day New Right. For nearly every alarming trend which had corrupted American life during the period 1914-1925 suddenly reappeared with a vengeance during the incredible decade of the 1960's.

CHAPTER ONE - Notes

1. Donald Janson and Bernard Eismann, The Far Right (New York: McGraw-Hill Book Company, Inc., 1963), p.47.

2. John Harold Redekop, The American Far Right (Grand Rapids, Michigan: W.B. Eerdman's Publishing Company, 1968), p. 22.

3. Samuel Lubell, Revolt of the Moderates (New York: Harper & Brothers, 1956), p. 52.

4. Robert E. Sherwood, Roosevelt and Hopkins (New York: Harper & Brothers 1948), p. 437.

5. Lubell, Revolt of the Moderates, p. 77.

6. For a thorough but not altogether convincing analysis of New Right intellectuals, see George Nash, The Conservative Intellectual Movement in America Since 1945 (New York: Basic Books, Inc., 1976).

7. Forster and Epstein, Danger on the Right, p. 175; Ibid., pp. 63-64; Ibid., p. 176.

8. Hofstadter, The Paranoid Style in American Politics and Other Essays, p. 139.

9. Lubell, Revolt of the Moderates, p.159.

10. Lipset and Raab, The Politics of Unreason, p. 220; Bell, The Radical Right, p. 4; Suall, The American Ultras. p. 18.

11. Alan F. Westin, "The John Birch Society: 'Radical Right' and 'Extreme Left' in the Political Context of Post World War II." in Bell, The Radical Right, p. 222; Bell, The Radical Right, p. 4; Hofstadter, The Paranoid Style in American Politics and Other Essays, p. 71.

12. James T. Hunter, Our Second Revolution (Caldwell, Idaho: The Caxton Printers, Ltd., 1968), p. 26.

13. David Danzig, "The Radical Right and the Rise of the Fundamentalist Minority," Commentary, (April, 1962), p. 296. Danzig's perceptive article deals with the influence of fundamentalist religion on the New Right.

14. Ibid.

15. Suall, The American Ultras. p. 18.

16. Hofstadter, The Paranoid Style in American Politics and Other Essays, pp. 97-98.

17. Henry F. May, The End of Americn Innocence (New York: Alfred A. Knopf, 1959).

CHAPTER TWO

THE ORIGINS OF THE NEW RIGHT

The Korean War and General Douglas MacArthur

From their vantage point in the early 1960's the New Right surveyed the scandalous events of the previous decade with a deep sense of betrayal. To begin with, the 1950's had opened with the tragic Korean War. Television broadcaster Dan Smoot pronounced the Korean conflict "the worst disaster in American history: it cost us the lives of over 50,000 American soldiers...and it ended on enemy terms, as the first war America ever lost..." In the same vein, an angry Arizona Senator Barry Goldwater pointed out that "Until 1950, America had never lost a shooting war." 1/

Futhermore, the United States' debacle in Korea had resulted from our own inexplicable reluctance to defeat our Communist enemies upon the battlefield. Despite the possession of overwhelming air and naval superiority, the United States Government refused to win a clearcut military victory. Barry Goldwater denounced, "the spectacle of Korea, where, with victory in our hands, we chose instead the bitterness of stalemate." Likewise, Human Events noted, "Had MacArthur been allowed to send his bombers into Chinese territory, undoubtedly the war would have been won and countless lives saved." Thus during the Korean conflict, as The Defender lamented sadly, "victory was not permitted."2/

The abrupt firing of General Douglas MacArthur by Democratic President Harry S. Truman in April, 1951 coincided with the failure of the United States to win a military victory during the Korean War. The New Right strongly supported MacArthur's famous dictum "there is no substitute for victory." (See Chapter Six) The Defender declared, "General MacArthur epitomized the principle that once a nation is engaged in war, it must have the will to win." Barry Goldwater wrote, "If we have learned anything from the tragic lesson of Korea, if we can draw any guidance from the life of one of history's great military figures, Douglas MacArthur, it might well be this -- that in war there is no substitute for victory."3/

President Harry Truman's decision to relieve MacArthur of his high command during the Korean conflict thus represented a conscious move on the part of the United States Government to reject a military victory. As the Reverend Gerald L. K. Smith explained, General MacArthur "was fired by Harry Truman because he insisted on winning the Korean War." 4/

The untimely dismissal of MacArthur occurred at a crucial moment in American history. In the opinion of Captain Eddie Rickenbacker, "General MacArthur, with victory within his grasp, was fired, and we lost the only war in our history." Flamboyant Major General Edwin A. Walker told a Dallas, Texas audience in December, 1961 that "the recall of MacArthur from Korea" was "a turning point in our country's history and an obvious censorship of the determination to win."5/

It goes without saying that the New Right held General Douglas MacArthur in the highest esteem. Columnist William F. Buckley, Jr., praised MacArthur as "the last of the great Americans." Nazi leader George Lincoln Rockwell openly "worshipped" the general. Actor John Wayne named MacArthur his favorite American of the century, while television broadcaster Dan Smoot called MacArthur "the greatest man of the twentieth century."6/

Senator Robert A. Taft

Hundreds of fervent Radical Rightists, sick of both the humiliating retreat before Communism in Korea and the treacherous firing of their beloved General Douglas MacArthur, assembled in Chicago at the Republican National Convention of 1952 prepared to help nominate Ohio Senator Robert A. Taft for President. Robert Taft, the brilliant, Right-wing Republican leader of the United States Senate, and son of the former G.O.P. President William Howard Taft had been the Conservative's bridesmaid at the Republican National Conventions of 1940, 1944, and 1948. However, 1952 finally looked like Robert Taft's golden opportunity. As John Birch Society founder Robert Welch recounted, "by 1952 a revulsion had set in, and that revulsion had a powerful, courageous, patriotic and tremendously popular leader, Robert A. Taft."7/

The Taft candidacy of 1952 constituted the greatest challenge to the vested interests controlling the Republican Party. Since 1940 G.O.P. Presidential nominees Wendell Willkie (1940) and Thomas E. Dewey (1944 and 1948) had cemented close ties with a coalition of interests known as the "Eastern Liberal Establishment." The key "Establishment" men who shaped the destiny of the Republican Party included attorney Herbert Brownell, Jr., diplomat John Foster Dulles, Massachusetts Senator Henry Cabot Lodge, Jr., many Eastern corporation leaders and public opinion moulders connected with the influential Eastern publications such as the New York Herald Tribune, the New York Times, and Time Magazine.

Finally, the Aldrich-Rockefeller family, using the awesome financial power of New York City's Chase Manhattan Bank, funded the political activities for the Eastern Liberal Establishment. No wonder Senator Robert A. Taft complained after his 1952 defeat that "Every Republican candidate for President since 1936 has been nominated by the Chase Bank." A dozen years later another Right-wing G.O.P. Presidential aspirant Barry Goldwater echoed these same sentiments:

"the Eastern money interests -- the large banks, the financial houses -- have most always been able to control the selection of the Republican candidate."8/

In order to continue their domination of the Republican Party the Eastern Liberal Establishment handpicked General Dwight D. Eisenhower as their Presidential candidate in 1952 to counter the Right-wing hopeful Senator Taft. As Taft himself noted, "it was the power of the New York financial interest and a large number of business men subject to New York influence, who had selected General Eisenhower as their candidate." In retrospect, Robert Taft had a better claim to the nomination since he represented the choice of the Republican Party at the grass roots level. However, Eisenhower, a popular, non-partisan war hero looked more like a winner, and after twenty long years in the political wilderness the G.O.P. desperately wanted an electable Presidential nominee.9/

Thus the Eastern Liberal Establishment attempted to derail the Ohio Senator's bandwagon with the argument that "Taft can't win." Even the firm Taft supporters realized that their candidate sported a lackluster image. As editor M. Stanton Evans concluded many years later, Senator Taft's "balding head, wire-frame glasses, and Midwestern twang were not the stuff of which popular dreams are made or political ground swells manufactured." In contrast, Ike the war hero had a big grin and a pleasing personality.10/

Furthermore, M. Stanton Evans suggests that Taft fell victim to subtle changes in American politics only dimly perceived at the time. Evans call Taft "the first notable casualty of the age of the image." For the advent of television, still in its infancy, placed a premium upon candidates with attractive visual images. And, of course, a Robert Taft could never compete with a Dwight Eisenhower.11/

"The Texas Steal"

Nevertheless, despite his obvious handicaps and the stubborn array of forces pitted against him, Senator Taft came to the 1952 G.O.P. National Convention with a slim lead over General Dwight D. Eisenhower, the Eastern Liberal Establishment candidate. However, Taft's enemies refused to surrender control of the party to the Right-wing without a fight.

Consequently, according to the New Right, the Eastern Liberal Establishment then engineered the infamous "Texas Steal" whereby the regular Texas delegation pledged to Taft found itself unseated and replaced by a rival Eisenhower delegation. Generous transfusions of Rockefeller family money allegedly bribed wavering conventioneers to vote to seat the Eisenhower supporters from Texas. As the Beacon-

Light Herald complained, young Nelson Rockefeller poured thousands, perhaps millions of dollars "to put Ike in the White House" by depriving Senator Taft of his duly selected Texas delegates.12/

Thus the Eastern Liberal Establishment wing of the Republican Party captured the Presidential Nomination for its own favorite candidate, General Dwight D. Eisenhower. Political analyst Morris A. Bealle commented that Eisenhower's "nomination was bought, stolen, bribed and blackmailed from the popular choice" Senator Taft. Moreover, the New Right held no illusions about General Eisenhower as the G.O.P. standard-bearer. He remained a very poor substitute for their beloved Senator Taft. In addition, even as a military hero Eisenhower ranked well below the stature of the legendary General Douglas MacArthur. The National Review decided, "We in America...never felt the need to reach beyond a mediocrity so we elected the affable Eisenhower... and let MacArthur... fade away."13/

The Lessons of 1952

After years of reflection, the New Right drew three important lessons from the events surrounding the Republican National Convention of 1952. To begin with, now that the age of televised politics had dawned, never again could their candidates afford to project a lackluster image. Henceforth, every New Right Presidential contender must master the techniques of television campaigning. Indeed both Barry Goldwater in 1960 and 1964 and, of course, Ronald Reagan in 1968, 1976, and 1980 represented a vast improvement over the unexciting Robert Taft of 1952.

Secondly, the New Rightist men and women chosen to attend future G.O.P. conventions must be immune to the bribes and threats emanating from the Eastern Liberal Establishment. Accordingly, the carefully selected, tough-as-nails Goldwater delegates at San Francisco in July , 1964 intended to support their candidate until hell froze over.

Lastly, Southern states like Texas which were growing increasingly Conservative with the passage of time should have automatically backed Senator Taft for President in 1952. However, the pathetically weak Republican Party throughout Dixie consisted of little more than "rotten boroughs" bankrolled by and therefore beholden to the Eastern Liberal Establishment. Isolated from the mainstream of Southern political life and existing solely for occasional rewards of federal patronage (whenever the G.O.P. happened to capture the White House), these Southern state Republican parties remained in virtual ideological and political bondage to the Eastern Liberal Establishment. Thus the New Right devised a "Southern Strategy" during the 1960's which transformed the once Liberal-oriented Southern G.O.P. into an effective vehicle of expression for a heretofore untapped Dixie

Conservatism. (See Chapter Eight) For without additional Southern votes at future G.O.P. national conventions the New Right had no chance whatsoever of capturing control of the Republican Party and nominating their own Presidential candidate.

Richard Nixon

To soothe the ruffled feathers of the irate Taft delegates, the 1952 Republican National Convention added the young California Senator Richard M. Nixon to the G.O.P. ticket as the Vice Presidential nominee. Senator Nixon had gained the reputation for vigorous opposition to Communism during his slashing campaigns for Congress in 1946 against Democrat Jerry Vorhees and again in 1950 for U.S. Senate against Democrat Helen Gahagan Douglas. Furthermore, while in Washington Richard Nixon had engineered the downfall of Communist spy Alger Hiss. At first glance, the New Right should have felt quite satisfied with the selection of Richard Nixon.

Yet the New Right had never really felt comfortable with Richard Nixon. The youthful Senator from the Golden State attended the 1952 Republican Convention in Chicago as a member of the California delegation technically pledged to vote for favorite son Governor Earl Warren. However, Nixon helped General Eisenhower defeat Senator Taft by backing the Eastern Liberal Establishment during the controversy surrounding the seating of the Texas delegation. Indeed in the years after 1952 support for Robert Taft became a sort of litmus test of true Conservatism; and Richard Nixon had obviously flunked the test.

Finally, the New Right never trusted Richard Nixon; he always remained an outsider to their Movement. The Economic Council Letter concluded that "Nixon had never been a Conservative," while a Californian Herbert Ellison Smith pointed out that "millions of people, especially here in California, are firmly convinced that Mr. Nixon did everything possible to destroy the conservative movement here and nationally." In fact, the New Right saw Richard Nixon as a man energized by an overpowering, all-consuming, personal ambition. Gerald L. K. Smith labelled Nixon "a prostituted politician" who "was never really right wing." The Reverend Smith called Nixon's sleazy politics "pseudo Conservatism". In the same manner, Robert Welch considered Nixon a "slippery politician" and doubted whether "Nixon is committed to anything other than the career of Richard Nixon."14/

Senator Joseph McCarthy

Alongside the treacherous dismissal of General MacArthur in 1951 and the sabotaging of Senator Taft's Presidential candidacy the following year, the sudden political downfall of Wisconsin's anti-Communist

Senator Joseph McCarthy in 1954 embittered the New Right. As the Reverend Billy James Hargis lamented, "The brave Senator from Wisconsin won censure from his fellow Senators and went to an early grave, broken in heart, as a reward for his patriotism." Likewise, Gerald L. K. Smith wrote that McCarthy "was virtually murdered by abuse, disillusionment, smear and misrepresentation although he was the man who more courageously than any other dared put his finger on the traitors inside Government, industry and culture."15/

In the eyes of the New Right, the same Eastern Liberal Establishment which had approved when Truman had fired MacArthur and which had deprived Senator Taft of the 1952 G.O.P. Presidential nomination, then decided to destroy Senator McCarthy as a viable political force. Thus the Eastern Liberal Establishment, in the opinion of the Cross and the Flag, "annihilated MacArthur, smeared the great Senator Taft and demanded the liquidation of McCarthy." With regard to Joseph McCarthy, once again, the Eastern Liberal Establishment unceremoniously ended the promising career of yet another dedicated patriot who dared to call for a total victory over Communism both at home and abroad. As William O. Lay, Jr. remarked, "A decade ago the late Senator McCarthy warned that subversives and perverts in departments of the Washington Government imperilled American security. For his pains he was hooted at, pilloried and hounded to his death."16/

The New Right always defended the ultimate aims of the late Joseph McCarthy. Arizona Senator Barry Goldwater frequently praised the Wisconsin Solon. Speaking before the 1957 Wisconsin Republican State Convention Goldwater expressed his thoughts concerning the recently deceased McCarthy: "Joe...made a contribution to his country-men that will forever redound to the credit of the people of Wisconsin and to your Republican organization." Common Sense Editor Conde McGinley proclaimed that "McCarthyism is Americanism," while Robert Welch justified Senator McCarthy's controversial means of exposing Communism in the United States Government: "Basically, and with very minor exceptions indeed, there was nothing wrong with McCarthy's methods from the point of view of the patriotic American." Mrs. George Peck observed that Joe McCarthy's so-called "great crime was in not being 'nice' in his methods." While campaigning in the 1964 Wisconsin Democratic Presidential Primary Alabama Governor George C. Wallace quipped, "Many of his warnings about left-wingism and communism have proved valid. Maybe he was just a little ahead of his time." Even American Nazi Fuehrer George Lincoln Rockwell paid a supreme compliment to Senator McCarthy: "I made it a point to go through Appleton, Wisconsin, Joe McCarthy's hometown, and practically worshipped the ground where this great American grew up and lived."17/

The Frustration of the Eisenhower Years

The New Right never accepted the rather leisurely tempo of the Eisenhower Administration. As Sociologist Daniel Bell explained, "After twenty years of Democratic power, the right-wing Republicans hoped that the election of Dwight Eisenhower would produce its own utopia: the dismantling of the welfare state, the taming of labor unions, and the magical rollback of Communism in Europe. None of this happened." Thus as Daniel Bell concluded, "eight years of moderation proved more frustrating than twenty years of opposition."18/

After General Eisenhower had defeated Senator Taft for the 1952 G.O.P. Presidential nomination the two men ostensibly reached an understanding. Eisenhower promised a true Conservative administration in return for Taft's blessings. Thus the New Right expected at least some satisfaction from President Eisenhower. As Barry Goldwater stated, "Dwight Eisenhower was elected on a conservative platform in 1952 because the American people were eager for a return to those governmental principles and practices which have survived the buffeting of chance and the testing of time."19/

Unfortunately, Eisenhower as President greatly disappointed the New Right. As Dan Smoot lamented, "In 1952, the American people, voting for a promised change in federal policy, elected Dwight D. Eisenhower. They waited in vein (sic) for eight years." For the popular Ike refused to steer the nation towards a genuine Conservative direction. William F. Buckley, Jr. charged that "Eisenhower did nothing whatever for the Republican Party; nothing to develop a Republican philosophy of government; nothing to catalyze a meaty American conservatism." In short, "what a miserable President he was!"20/

Worse yet, the wasted Eisenhower years granted the Left-wing forces an eight-year respite. As Frank S. Meyer complained, Eisenhower's two Presidential terms gave "the New Deal revolution an eight-year period to consolidate itself and prepare for the next leap forward towards socialism." Similarly, the National Review added, "Under Eisenhower the forces that gnaw at the strength of our country grew stronger — the bureaucratic parasites, the labor union monopolists, the centralizers." Consequently, as Herbert Ellison Smith observed, Ike "pushed America farther left into state socialism" than "Truman was able to accomplish in the years he occupied 1600 Pennsylvania."21/

"Modern Republicanism"

The Republican Party drifted away from its longstanding Conservative principles during the Eisenhower years towards "Modern Republicanism." Indeed the Eisenhower Administration itself represented the fullest flowering of "Modern Republicanism". The G.O.P.

27

gracefully accepted the social and economic innovations of the Democratic New Deal, and finally came to terms with the newly enlarged role of the Federal Government.

Under "Modern Republicanism" Dwight Eisenhower left the New Deal essentially intact while restricting his opposition to peripheral problems of cost and excessive bureaucracy. In other words, "Modern Republicanism" favored a cheaper, better-managed welfare state. No wonder Arizona Senator Barry Goldwater blasted the Eisenhower Administration as a "dimestore New Deal."22/

As expected, the New Right thoroughly loathed "Modern Republicanism." William F. Buckley, Jr. referred to "Modern Republicanism" as "a day-to-day conservatism of expediency." Barry Goldwater, likewise, rejected the entire "Modern Republican" philosophy. Goldwater challenged his own party to return to its traditional Conservative principles, for under the misguided notion of "Modern Republicanism," the G.O.P. acquiesced in the dangerous expansion in the size and scope of the Federal Government. Accordingly, the Arizona Senator accused the Republicans of failing to fulfill their historic mission as America's Conservative party: "If the Republican Party is to lead this nation forward to a restoration of freedom, to progress and to a better tomorrow, we must once again become the Republican Party. We must be ourselves."23/

The Radical Right felt disenfranchised and homeless during the Eisenhower years. As Frank S. Meyer noted early in 1956, "Millions of Americans followed Taft's leadership; millions admired MacArthur; millions supported McCarthy's drive against Communism; and millions exhibit a desire for an alternative to the dominant Liberal control of both political parties."24/

The Radical Right During the Eisenhower Years

The Radical Right limped along sluggishly during the Eisenhower years. Barry Goldwater suggested that...

> Though we Conservatives are deeply persuaded that our society is ailing, and know that Conservatism holds the key to national salvation -- and feel sure the country agrees with us -- we seem unable to demonstrate the practical relevance of Conservative priniciples to the needs of the day.

Moreover, the American Right, in the words of Robert Welch, failed to grasp the initiative: "In the worldwide ideological struggle which divides mankind today, we conservatives fight always on the defensive. The very name by which we identify ourselves defines our objective."25/

Other factors contributed to the weak position of the Radical Right during the middle and late 1950's. As George Lincoln Rockwell explained, "The times were wrong. The American people were sound, sound asleep." Furthermore, "the Right Wing were all playing 'king-of-the-hill' with each other....They seemed more interested in attacking each other than the enemy." Finally, "morale in the so-called 'right-wing' was close to zero" during the Eisenhower years.26/

The Right-wing of the G.O.P. wielded very little influence in party circles by decade's end. Senators Taft and McCarthy had died while General MacArthur had meanwhile faded away. The mid-term elections of 1958 proved disastrous to Republicans in general and Right-wingers in particular. Californian William F. Knowland, the U.S. Senate Minority Leader and the Radical Right's best prospect for the 1960 G.O.P. Presidential Nomination, became the chief casualty of the November, 1958 debacle. The departure of Knowland from the national political scene marked the end of an era in Republican Party politics. Reflecting upon the passing of the old guard, former Notre Dame University Law School Dean Clarence Manion remarked, "When Eisenhower prepared to leave office, the conservative Republican leadership that had flourished so militantly with such bright promise in 1952 had all but disappeared."27/.

"Fifth Avenue Compact"

The defeat of Senator Knowland in November, 1958 removed the last major, Right-wing obstacle from the path of Vice President Richard Nixon's triumphant march towards the 1960 G.O.P. nomination. With his Right flank now secured Nixon moved leftwards to court Republican Moderates and Liberals. As Nixon shifted toward the Left, he collided with New York's Liberal Republican Governor Nelson A. Rockefeller. Indeed, the New York Governor provided the only real opposition to Nixon in 1960. Interestingly enough, the presence of the New York Governor on the Left greatly improved relations between the Vice-President and the G.O.P. Right. For the Right hated Rockefeller so much that it made even Nixon palatable to them.

Nixon ultimately out-maneuvered Rockefeller for the 1960 G.O.P. Presidential nomination. Nevertheless, Rockefeller forced the Vice President to reach an accommodation with the Liberal wing of the party. The two men made peace at a dramatic face-to-face meeting held in Rockefeller's Midtown Manhattan apartment building on Friday evening July 22, 1960 just prior to the opening of the G.O.P. National Convention. In exchange for Rockefeller's unqualified support in the upcoming General Election against the Democrats, Nixon pledged to modify his positions leftward on several issues.28/

29

Angry Radical Rightists denounced this private agreement as the "Fifth Avenue Compact" and Barry Goldwater characterized this "surrender" as the "Munich of the Republican Party." In truth, while the Right could have easily swallowed Rockefeller's modest demands this "Fifth Avenue Compact" demonstrated the utter weakness of their position. For without even notifying the Right-wing, Richard Nixon had made a pilgrimage to Nelson Rockefeller, the hated bankroller of the Eastern Liberal Establishment. As a result of the "Fifth Avenue Compact" Nixon lost his remaining credibility with the Right.29/

Of course, even before the July, 1960 "Fifth Avenue Compact" most Radical Rightists entertained few illusions about Richard Nixon. Frank S. Meyer offered a shrewd analysis of the Vice President: When compared with the Liberal Democrats, Richard Nixon...

> Like Eisenhower...is undoubtedly less obnoxious than the alternatives....And he has made it clear, no less unmistakably than Eisenhower, that he regards the reversal of the Roosevelt revolution as equally unthinkable. He stands for the welfare state and has proposed no substantial modification of it....On the record, he is no conservative. All the arguments urging conservatives to support him boil down to the argument that there is nothing else for them to do.

Likewise, Harold Lord Varney, Political Editor of the American Mercury warned that "November will find many trusting conservatives voting for Nixon under the impression that they are voting for a new Robert Taft." They are dead wrong.30/

Until the drafting of the "Fifth Avenue Compact" the G.O.P. Right still held out some hope for the redemption of Richard Nixon's soul. After all, Nixon, as he himself kept reminding everyone, had exposed the Communist agent Alger Hiss back during the late 1940's. Moreover, every once in a while the Vice President actually sounded like a Conservative. Finally, nobody ever accused Nixon of being an inflexible ideologue. Nixon always responded to political pressures and checked the direction of the wind before venturing outside. Therefore, Nixon would adopt Conservative positions if pushed hard enough. Thus Robert Welch spoke for the disgruntled rank and file of the John Birch Society when he announced in July, 1960, "Many of our members feel that our best present course is to support Richard Nixon, while working hard to make Nixon less 'liberal' as a candidate, if nominated and less 'modern' as a Republican if elected."31/

John F. Kennedy vs. Richard Nixon

The Presidential Election of November, 1960 between Democrat John F. Kennedy and Republican Richard Nixon created a major dilemma for the Radical Right: Should they support the hated Richard Nixon or boycott the election entirely, thus insuring the victory of a Liberal Democrat? This difficult question stimulated a lively discussion among members of the Radical Right.

To begin with, the most compelling argument advanced in favor of Nixon's candidacy revolved around the necessity of keeping the White House safely in Republican hands. For while a "Modern Republican" like Nixon would basically mark time, a Democrat like Kennedy would once again release the rampant Liberalism of the Roosevelt Revolution. Thus as one observer commented, "the alternative to the victory of Nixon in November is much too horrible to envision..." Another wrote, "It is absolutely suicidal for conservatives deliberately to aid Kennedy's cause on election day by refusing to vote for Nixon." A third pleaded, "For heaven's sake, conservatives, don't stay home now !"32/

Then too, many Radical Rightists saw no reasonable alternative to Richard Nixon. Arizona Senator Barry Goldwater sensed this fact as he reaffirmed his support for the 1960 G.O.P. nominee: "I summon Conservatives of both parties...to get behind Nixon and work tirelessly to give him the victory America needs....What other choice have we?....In short, for Conservatives there exists no alternative to Nixon."33/

Finally, since the G.O.P. remained America's only realistic political vehicle for a radical Conservative revival, the Radical Right could not risk jeopardizing its good standing within the Republican Party by failing to support its duly-selected Presidential nominee. Indeed Barry Goldwater's call for party harmony coupled with his intensive lobbying on behalf of the entire G.O.P. ticket carried the day. Most members of the Radical Right kept quiet, held their noses, and voted for Richard Nixon. As author John Stormer later confided, "Under pressure for 'party unity' anti-communist Republicans remained silent."34/

On the other side of the coin, Richard Nixon's recent activities had deeply offended the Radical Right. The "Fifth Avenue Compact" represented in their eyes a cowardly surrender to the Eastern Liberal Establishment. Nixon had further aggravated the situation by selecting Henry Cabot Lodge, Jr., a key Eastern Liberal Establishment kingmaker, as his Vice Presidential running-mate. The Radical Right bitterly remembered Lodge for his work back in 1952 as General Dwight Eisenhower's National Campaign Manager. For Lodge "did quite a hatchet job on Taft" while masterminding the infamous "Texas Steal" which neatly deprived the Ohio Senator of his rightful G.O.P. Presidential nomination.35/

Then too, Richard Nixon ran a disappointing Fall campaign against John F. Kennedy by staunchly defending the record of the Eisenhower Administration. As John Stormer charged, Nixon deliberately ignored "crucial topics" such as "Communist infiltration of government and appeasement of world Communism" because "Richard Nixon was not likely to dredge up the record of failure and appeasement of the Administration of which he was part." In the domestic sphere Nixon embraced the welfare state and sounded indistinguishable from Democrat John F. Kennedy on many issues. As L. Brent Bozell pointed out, "Nixon's Liberal tendencies in domestic affairs...had never been well-disguised."36/

Thus a few members of the Radical Right welcomed a Nixon loss in November, 1960 as punishment for his sins; and from the ashes of defeat a new Republican Party would emerge purged of all traces of "Modern Republicanism." As Human Events reported, "some conservative constituents...welcome a GOP defeat in a belief that such is the necessary prelude to renaissance of a 'real conservative party' in '64." Most Radical Rightists rejected this approach and worked for Richard Nixon. However, as Chapter Eight explains, the Radical Right expected a Kennedy victory on election day and prepared to seize control of the G.O.P. afterwards.37/

The Rise of the New Right

No sooner had the despised Eisenhower Administration left town than the New Right quickly erupted into full public view. An alarmed Irwin Suall wrote, "It was in the Spring of 1961 that the nation first began to realize that a new wave of rightism had begun to descend on the land." Likewise, veteran observers Harry and Bonaro Overstreet pinpointed the Spring of 1961 as the date when the American people suddenly took notice of the sharp upsurge in activity on the New Right.38/

Arnold Forster and Benjamin Epstein in their book Danger on the Right posed the following important question: "Why did the Radical Right, which in various forms had been kicking and screaming about for many years, emerge around 1960 as a force to be reckoned with in American life?" In answer to this question, a combination of factors definitely contributed to the rapid growth of the New Right after 1960. These included the fact that the subtle restraining influence imposed by G.O.P. President Dwight D. Eisenhower ended, at long last, on January 20, 1961; the new Democratic President John F. Kennedy attempted to advance the cause of Liberal social reform at home; and the United States suffered a series of spectacular disasters in foreign affairs during the years 1960-1961.39/

32

First of all, many commentators noticed the apparent soothing effect which the relaxed Eisenhower Administration had upon the American Radical Right: "The presence of a benign and popular General of the Army in the White House had a calming influence on people and kept the Rightists' audience small." Likewise, historian Arthur Schlesinger, Jr., wrote, "In conservative periods, the radical Right is characteristically disorganized and dormant. Its members are soothed by the eternal hope that a conservative administration may do something they will like."40/

However, the election of Liberal Democrat John F. Kennedy to the White House in November, 1960 changed the entire outlook of the Radical Right. Sociologist David Riesman observed that "Kennedy's victory released the Republican right wing...and the fundamentalist Democrats North and South from many of the mild restraints that Eisenhower's presence had imposed." Arthur Schlesinger, Jr. added, "it was wholly to be expected that the extremists of the Right would raise their voices precisely when the national mood is moving in a progressive direction." The New Right could no longer afford to grumble from the sidelines as they did during the status-quo Eisenhower years: "But the election of a progressive administration had a galvanizing effect. The radical right grows desperate." In other words, "The thunder on the right," as the American Mercury noted, "is the result of the lightning on the left."41/

Moreover, American foreign policy problems in 1960-1961 fostered the growth of the New Right. The long list includes the U-2 Spy Plane Incident followed by the abortive Paris Summit Conference between President Eisenhower and Premier Khrushchev; the wave of anti-American riots around the globe in 1960; the Congo Episode; the neutralization of Laos; and the construction of the Berlin Wall. In addition, the American response to these Communist advances infuriated the New Right. Dean Clarence Manion warned, "The deadly disease of Communism is ravaging mankind today and sentencing Christian civilization to death precisely because four successive Presidents of the United States and eight successive Congresses have refused to say, and mean it, that Communism is intolerable." Robert Welch demanded to know, "Just what on earth does it take to make the American people...recognize the Communist steamroller at work?" Welch wondered if "our country" would "soon become just another group of provinces in a Communist empire."42/

But in the eyes of the New Right, the crowning Cold War humiliation occurred right in America's very own backyard on the island of Cuba, where the Communists had established an advanced outpost from which to spread revolution and subversion. U.S.A. Associate Editor Newton H. Fulbright stressed that "International communism -- armed to the teeth and dedicated to burying us -- has marched to within 90 miles of our shores." In the same strident tone, former California Senator

33

William F. Knowland announced, "Somewhere, somehow, at some time, the right place must be found for the free world to say to Communism: 'You have gone far enough,' and for Americans to say: 'Indeed, you have gone too far when you have established your bases 90 miles from our shore."43/

America's half-hearted attempt to remove Fidel Castro from power ended ignominiously in April, 1961 at the Bay of Pigs. Human Events spoke for the entire New Right when it called the invasion a "debacle." Similarly, William F. Buckley, Jr. denounced the Bay of Pigs "where we left, rather than offend World Opinion, seven hundred brave Cubans to die, and six million others to live in slavery. If the people of the world look upon us with contempt, it is because we have been contemptible."44/

Without a doubt, the New Right considered the loss of Cuba the single, most serious setback of the Cold War. As Frank S. Meyer explained, "The American people, with instinctive common sense, realize that in the seventeen years of the Cold War this is the turning point." Likewise, Barry Goldwater added:

> The average American citizen, preoccupied with earning a living and with family responsibilities, can with some justification ignore the establishment of a Communist government in, say, Laos. But no American can ignore the deadly serious situation resulting from the establishment of a Communist-dominated government on the island of Cuba.45/

America's numerous foreign policy defeats made the New Right impatient and angry. As South Carolina Representative William Jennings Bryan Dorn insisted, "We should stop backing up in Berlin, in Cuba, in Laos, in Vietnam -- and all over the world. We have yet to win a major victory since World War Two, and so I'm tired of backing up..." Barry Goldwater called the fact that "we are losing the cold war...tragically apparent," and Major General Edwin A. Walker charged that "We are at war....We are losing that war every day." Not surprisingly, Thomas L. Hughes, a State Department official during the Kennedy Administration, noted the growing frustration of the nation with our indecisive foreign policy and suggested that the American people suffered from a severe case of "cold war battle fatigue."46/

The increasing militancy of the New Right surfaced everywhere. Rear Admiral Chester Ward (retired) declared, "Americans are tired of defeats. They are tired of surrenders covered up as 'negotiated settlements.' They are, indeed, tired of so much talk and little action by our leaders." Thus "For the first time in sixteen years of the cold war a demand for victory is beginning to roll into Washington." Arkansas

Democratic Senator J. William Fulbright sensed the mood of the New Right during the early 1960's. In a secret memorandum to the Defense Department, inadvertently made public, Fulbright, acknowledging the rising tide of Conservatism and anti-Communism among the American public, wondered if the Kennedy Administration would be able "to restrain the desire of the people to hit the Communists with everything we've got, particularly if there are more Cubas and Laos." Furthermore, the Arkansas Senator pointed out that similar circumstances had inflamed the Radical Right during the early 1950's: "Pride in victory, and frustration in restraint, during the Korean war, led to MacArthur's revolt and McCarthyism."47/

The Nature of the New Right

A gut feeling told the New Right that something drastic had to be done soon to reverse the appalling decline in the quality of American life. Marilyn R. Allen warned that "America is rapidly becoming a lawless, insecure, unsavory place in which to live." Thus as Paul Sexson and Stephen Miles, Jr. concluded, "Americans want tightly enforced measures against communism, crime, immorality, vice, pornography, not simply because these are bad ideas, but because, if unchecked, they will corrupt the people."48/

Indeed Clarence Manion best summed up the sentiments of the New Right when he suggested that "it is easier and perhaps better to feel this conservatism than attempt to define it." For he noted the intense emotional reaction of the New Right: "Basically, this movement is logical but its momentum is psychological and its across-the-board push can be identified as unapologetic, old-fashioned American patriotism that is angered beyond words." Dean Manion added that "the common denominator of the big mobilization is the determination to protect the American republic from a variety of assaults now being made against it," because, "if American freedom falls,...Christian civilization will be suffocated in the resulting ruins."49 (See Chapter Four)

Next the New Right deeply regretted the disappearance of personal morality, the absence of chastity and sobriety, the shirking of responsibility, the end of self-reliance, and the neglect of thrift and industriousness among far too many American citizens. A disturbed F.B.I. Director J. Edgar Hoover asked, "What has happened to our sense of values? Where is the strong sense of individual responsibility by which a self-governing nation retains its freedom?" Along the same lines, former Navy Secretary Charles Edison lamented that...

For a people who proudly held honor among the basic tenets of individual national life, we have become a

35

people where, more and more, honesty and honor are looked on as being old-fashioned. A country where self-reliance, pride, hard work and thrift are being replaced by ideas of dependence on government, pleasure before duty, higher pay for less work and the right to government handouts.50/

In the New Right's eyes, this sad decline of individual responsibility contributed to America's rampaging crime, political corruption, and moral decay. And either the United States would return to its traditional values or face certain destruction. Ezra Taft Benson spoke for the Movement when he asserted, "We must square our actions and our policies with eternal principles if this nation is to be preserved and not go the way of Rome and other dead civilizations."51/ (See Chapter Three)

The New Right also pictured itself as the last line of defense against encroaching collectivism. The premier issue of New Guard magazine announced, "We are sick unto death of collectivism" which has "poisoned the minds, weakened the wills and smothered the spirits of Americans for three decades and more." Likewise, Dan Smoot warned that "The longer we wait to abandon collectivism and return to individualism...the harder our task will be. If we do not act quickly, we will soon reach the point of no return to freedom and decency in an organized society." Thus New Rightists such as Robert Welch tried to rally the troops in the battle against collectivism: "We must oppose the collectivists in every way, because both their methods and their purposes are diametrically contrary to our own."52/

Lastly the New Right viewed itself as a youthful movement riding the wave of the future. Walter Trohan pointed out in 1961 that "Youth is in revolt, which is its right, but the curious thing about the current revolt is that it is on the right." In the same fashion, Paul Sexson and Stephen Miles, Jr. remarked, "While age has always been conservative, youth, which is traditionally the exponent of liberalism, is today becoming a hot-bed of conservatism." Sexson and Miles bragged that the "Liberals are being thrown back on the defensive for the first time in a generation." Barry Goldwater agreed: "I find that America is fundamentally a Conservative nation. The preponderant judgment of the American people, especially of the young people, is that the radical, or liberal, approach has not worked and is not working. They yearn for a return to Conservative principles."53/

Therefore, the college campuses, particularly those institutions of higher learning located throughout the economically booming, Evangelical Protestant Sunbelt, became prime focal points for the New Right during the early 1960's. In fact, the New Right leadership made a concerted effort to attract as many enthusiastic, hard-working, young students as possible into the Movement. On the whole, this widespread campus recruitment drive proved successful. The results gratified New Rightists like Barry Goldwater: "Young people are discovering that, contrary to what they might have been told in school, conservatism is not dead."54/

A fresh wave of radical Conservatism swept across the United States during the Spring of 1961 as the nation finally awoke from the sleepy Eisenhower years. This Movement, the New Right, stressing youth, careful attention to organization, and dedicated to political activism reverberated with a deep sense of mission: to save America from the threat of International Communism abroad and from cultural and moral decadence at home.

1. Dan Smoot Report, (April 1, 1963), p. 102;
Barry M. Goldwater, Why Not Victory? (New York: McGraw Hill Book
Company, Inc., 1962), p.33.

2. Goldwater, Why Not Victory?, p. 45;
Human Events, (January 28, 1960), p.3;
The Defender, October, 1962), p. 24.

3. The Defender, (September, 1962), p. 8;
Barry M. Goldwater, Where I Stand (New York: McGraw Hill Book
Company, Inc., 1964), p.28.

4. Beacon-Light Herald, (August-September, 1962), p. 52.

5. Cross and the Flag, (June 1963), p.34;
Common Sense, (February 1, 1962), pp. 3-4.

6. J. Allen Broyles in his excellent doctoral dissertation on the
John Birch Society discovered that many of the top leaders of the John
Birch Society had previously served in the United States Army under the
command of General Douglas MacArthur. See J. Allen Broyles, The John
Birch Society, (Anatomy of a Protest) (Boston: Beacon Press, 1964);
National Review, (April 5, 1964), p. 310;
Rockwell Report, (September 1964), p.2;
Human Events, (August 25, 1960), p. 3;
Dan Smoot Report, (May 4, 1964), p.137.

7. Robert Welch, The New Americanism (and Other Speeches and
Essays) (Belmont, Massachusetts: Western Islands Publishers, 1966),
p.71.

8. Edwin McDowell, Barry Goldwater: Portrait of an Arizonan
(Chicago: Henry Regnery Company, 1964), p. 16;
New York Times, July 9, 1964.

9. Robert A. Taft, privately circulated memorandum written late
in 1952 published in Human Events, (December 2, 1959), p.7.

10. M. Stanton Evans, The Future of Conservatism (New York:
Holt, Rinehart and Winston, 1968), pp. 258-259. Robert Taft's image
problem taught the New Right a valuable lesson. Indeed by the early
1960's the New Right had become quite media conscious. Barry
Goldwater and later Ronald Reagan stressed electability while both
presented a rugged image. Goldwater was good--Reagan even better.

11.   Ibid., p. 257.

12.   Clarence Manion, The Conservative American (New York: The Devin-Adair Company, 1964), p. 71;
Beacon-Light Herald, (July, 1960), p. 9;
The Radical Right's almost pathological hatred of Nelson Rockefeller undoubtedly stems from his family's financing the destruction of the Taft candidacy in 1952.

13.   Morris A. Bealle, 1960 Washington Squirrel Cage (Washington, D.C.: Columbia Publishing Company, 1960), p. 72;
National Review, (April 21, 1964), p. 309.

14.   Economic Council Letter, (December 1, 1962), p. 1;
Beacon-Light Herald, (September–October, 1964), p. 22;
Cross and the Flag, (June, 1963), p. 24;
Robert Welch, The Blue Book of the John Birch Society 1st ed. (Belmont, Massachusetts: The John Birch Society, 1959), pp. 121-124 as quoted in Janson and Eismann, The Far Right, pp. 37-38.

15.   Billy James Hargis, Communist America--Must It Be? (Berne, Indiana: Economy Printing Concern, 1960), p. 26;
Beacon Light Herald, (August-September, 1962), p. 52.

16.   Cross and the Flag, (June, 1963), p. 23;
Destiny, (September, 1963), p. 187.

17.   A strong defense of Senator Joseph McCarthy can be found in William F. Buckley, Jr. and L. Brent Bozell, McCarthy and His Enemies (Chicago: Henry Regnery Company, 1954);
Speech to the Wisconsin Republican State Convention delivered June 8, 1957 quoted in Arthur Frommer, ed., Goldwater from A to Z (New York: Frommer-Pasmontier Publishing Corporation, 1964), p. 61;
Common Sense, (February 1, 1961), p. 2;
Welch, The New Americanism, p. 73;
Beacon-Light Herald, (January, 1962), p. 26;
George C. Wallace, Hear Me Out (Anderson, South Carolina: Droke House Publishers, 1968), p. 94;
George Lincoln Rockwell, This Time the World (New York: Parliament House, 1963), p. 160.

18.   Bell, The Radical Right, p.3.

19.   Human Events, (February 18, 1960), p.1.

20.   Dan Smoot Report, (June 22, 1964), p. 194;
National Review (December 3, 1963), p. 487;
Ibid., (January 14, 1961), p.8.

21. National Review, (February 28, 1959), p. 556;
Ibid., (January 14, 1961), p.9;
Beacon-Light Herald, (September-October, 1964), p.18.

22. "Issues and Answers", A.B.C. telecast, June 4, 1961 as quoted in Edward Paul Mattar III, Barry Goldwater (A Political Indictment) (Riverdale, Maryland: Century Twenty-One Limited, September, 1964), p.40.

23. William F. Buckley, Jr., Up from Liberalism (New York: McDowell, Obolensky, 1959), p. 161; Human Events, (February 18, 1960), p.1.

24. National Review, (February 8, 1956), p. 23.

25. Barry M. Goldwater, The Conscience of a Conservative (New York: MacFadden-Bartell Corporation, 1960), Foreword, pp.4-5; Welch, The New Americanism, p. 11.

26. Rockwell Report, (April 15, 1964), p. 2.

27. Manion, The Conservative American, p. 104.

28. For an account of the Nixon-Rockefeller meeting see Theodore H. White, The Making of the President, 1960 (New York: Atheneum Publishers, 1961), p. 109.

29. Ibid.

30. National Review, (December 19, 1959), p. 555; The American Mercury, (April, 1960), p.4.

31. John Birch Society Bulletin, (July, 1960), p.7.

32. Douglas Caddy, "Letter to the Editor," National Review, (August 27, 1960), p. 125; Tim Terry, "Letter to the Editor," Ibid., (October 22, 1960), p. 253; Nancy B. Johnson, Ibid.

33. Human Events, (August 4, 1960), p. 333.

34. John Stormer, None Dare Call It Treason (Florissant, Missouri: Liberty Bell Press, 1964), p. 54.

35. Human Events (April 21, 1960), p. 3.

36. Stormer, None Dare Call It Treason, p. 54; National Review, (October 8, 1960), p. 204.

37.   Human Events, October 27, 1960), p. 516.

38.   Suall, The American Ultras, p.11;
Harry and Bonaro Overstreet, The Strange Tactics of Extremism (New York: W.W. Norton & Company, Inc., 1964), p. 27.

39.   Forster and Epstein, Danger on the Right, p. 5.

40.   Janson and Eismann, The Far Right, p. 6;
New York Times Magazine, (June 17, 1962), p. 10.

41.   David Riesman, "The Intellectuals and the Discontented Classes: Some Further Reflections - 1962," in Bell, ed. The Radical Right, p. 117;
New York Times Magazine, (June 17, 1962), p. 10;
The American Mercury, (September-October, 1962), p. 16.

42.   Manion Forum Network broadcast, (December 23, 1962); Welch, The New Americanism, p. 58.

43.   U.S.A., (April 5, 1963). p. 1;
Manion Forum Network broadcast, (July 7, 1963).

44.   Human Events, (April 28, 1961), p. 257;
National Review, (May 6, 1961), p. 269.

45.   National Review, (November 6, 1962), p. 352;
Goldwater, Why Not Victory? p. 70.

46.   Human Events, (July 28, 1962), p. 568;
New York Times Magazine, (September 17, 1961), p. 17;
Human Events, (November 10, 1961), p. 763;
Dudman, Men of the Far Right, p. 7.

47.   Bell, ed., The Radical Right, p. 3; U.S. Congress, Senate, Congressional Record, 87th Cong., 1st Sess., August 2, 1961, vol. 107, part II, pp. 14433-14434.

48.   Marilyn R. Allen, Kingdom Digest, (August 1960), as quoted in the Beacon-Light Herald, (March-April, 1961), p. 34;
Sexson and Miles, The Challenge of Conservatism, p. 139.

49.   Manion, The Conservative American, p. 3; Ibid., p.6; Ibid.; Ibid., p. 4.

50.   Human Events, (August 4, 1961), p. 501;
Manion Forum Network broadcast, (April 5, 1964).

41

51.   New York Times, September 11, 1964; Ezra Taft Benson, The Red Carpet (Salt Lake City, Utah: Bookcraft, Inc., 1962), p. 298.

52.   New Guard, (March, 1964), p. 9;
Dan Smoot Report, (July 7, 1965), p. 183;
Welch, The New Americanism, p. 150.

53.   An interesting book on this subject is Edward Cain, They'd Rather Be Right: Youth and the Conservative Movement (New York: The MacMillian Company, 1963);
Human Events, (April 14, 1961), p. 235;
Sexson and Miles, The Challenge of Conservatism, p. 170;
Ibid., p. 130;
Goldwater, The Conscience of a Conservative, Foreword.

54.   Goldwater, Why Not Victory?, p. 14.

CHAPTER THREE

THE LESSONS OF HISTORY

"Those who learn nothing from the past are
condemned to repeat it."

The New Right firmly believed that the history of civilization always repeats itself. The long and varied record of man's past contained countless examples of difficult problems arising again and again. Unfortunately, whenever man searched for satisfactory solutions to these challenging problems he invariably committed the same disastrous blunders time after time. Alas, man would never see the light ! And foolish men who insisted upon ignoring the obvious lessons of history suffered the bitter consequences. As author James T. Hunter observed, "History is a harsh teacher." The New Right frequently quoted the Spanish-born, American-educated philosopher George Santayana to this effect: "In a general way history repeats itself," Robert Welch, founder of the John Birch Society explained, "For as George Santayana so brilliantly pointed out, those who will learn nothing from history are condemned to repeat it."1/

Clearly, history had many valuable lessons to teach modern man. Destiny concluded that "the shores of time are strewn with the wreckage of the great empires of the past. History reveals their birth, growth and final decadency, ending in the extinctions of powerful governments." Likewise, in the words of another member of the New Right, history describes "the repeated agonies of repeated tyrannies, the consuming poison of unremitting hatred, the price of faithlessness."2/*

Thus modern man must grasp this golden opportunity to profit from the crucial lessons of ancient history by carefully examining the chronicles of antiquity. The Beacon-Light Herald announced that "the greatest errors we could make today would be to ignore or fail to utilize the invaluable lessons of history which are now available to us," while Robert Welch urged young people to "study the past,..." and not to ignore the experience accumulated by two hundred generations of your ancestors."3/

---

*Note--The New Right believed that history books, just like the Holy Bible, contained important ethical lessons. Indeed the rejection of great historical truths was as much a sin as the rejection of the scriptures. Furthermore, history as an academic discipline should provide modern man, above all else, with sound moral instruction. Thus New Rightists enjoyed reading heroic biographies and dramatic narratives with their easily understood lessons rather than the more sophisticated types of historical analysis based upon extensive economic, political or social research.

Therefore, a sound understanding of the lessons of history became the most vital tool in diagnosing the current condition and future prospects for our civilization. History provided the answer whether the modern world would follow in the tragic footsteps of the ancient world. As Destiny pointed out, "A study of the causes of the decline of these great empires in the past will reveal whether or not the seeds of destruction are already germinating in the midst of modern civilization today."4/

After a thorough examination of the evidence, a disheartened New Right unanimously concluded that the modern world headed inexorably towards the same catastrophe which had ruined the ancient world. Consequently, the various speeches and writings of the New Right contained references to the decay and disappearance of the great empires of antiquity such as Egypt, Babylonia, Assyria, Greece, and Carthage. However, ancient Rome stood out as the best single example of the decline and fall of a once flourishing civilization. For alongside its epic quality most Americans possessed at least a smattering of knowledge about ancient Roman history.

Hence when the New Right suggested that history repeats itself they usually compared ancient Rome with the United States of the 1960's. Novelist Taylor Caldwell stressed the strong similarities between both great civilizations:

> Nearly two thousand years stand between us and Rome. Never before the rise of Rome, and never since, did two nations so remarkable resemble each other, in history, in splendid rise in civilization, in magnificent communication between nations, in grandeur and wealth. In strange and amazing ways, we are the counterpart of ancient Rome. Her history, almost step by step is our history.5

The New Right learned a great deal from the tragic fate of ancient Rome. The once stable and free Roman Republic degenerated into imperial tyranny under the pressure of the irresponsible street mobs in the capitol demanding "bread and circuses" while clamouring for a Caesar to lead them. Jenkins Lloyd Jones, Editor of the Tulsa Tribune described how "the Roman mobs, flabby with free bread and bemused by free circuses, cheered for the unspeakable Nero and the crazy Caligula."6/

In turn, the mighty Roman Empire, already weakened by internal decay fell before the onslaught of the barbarians. The declining Empire had suffered from debauched leadership, bloated bureaucracy, and excessive taxation which sapped the strength of the people and stifled individual initiative. In addition, personal morality plummeted to new

depths as sexual perversion and promiscuity spread. The Reverend
Gerald L. K. Smith declared:

> Alaric's Goths finally poured over the walls of
> Rome. But it was not that the walls were low. It was
> that Rome itself was low. The sensual life of Pompeii,
> the orgies on Lake Trasimene, the gradually weakened
> fibre of a once self-disciplined people that reduced them
> at last to seeking safety in mercenaries and the payment
> of tribute—all these brought Rome down. She went down
> too early. She had much to teach the world.7/

In various books, pamphlets, periodicals, and speeches the New
Right drew the logical conclusion: since Roman society had ultimately
collapsed, the lessons of history pointed toward a similar decline and fall
for the United States of America. The New Right believed that the
United States of the 1960's stood upon the very brink of destruction.
Educator E. Merrill Root asserted, "We dwell today amid the peril of the
Republic, the trample of the barbarians, the rage of the heathens, the
bread and circuses and legions of Caesar, the new Dark Ages."8/

In the view of the New Right, contemporary America reeked with
the overpowering stench of decay. Corrupt government officials
wallowed in luxury at the expense of the hard-working, over-burdened
taxpayers. An oppressive bureaucracy crushed the rights of individuals
and hampered the operation of the free enterprise system. Demagogic
politicians, who promised fat welfare handouts to the unruly masses,
rose to high positions by placing the lazy and the depraved on the public
dole. Sexual degeneracy increased and illegitimacy multiplied.
Pornography filled the bookstores, libraries, and motion picture theaters
across the land. Children indulged in sex and drugs and joined juvenile
gangs. Muggers, rapists, perverts, and murderers roamed the city
streets at will terrorizing honest, law-abiding citizens.

Indeed, history repeated itself as the United States of America of
the 1960's emulated the fate of both the Roman Republic and the Roman
Empire. In order to save their beloved nation from the impending doom,
the New Right felt a strong obligation to awaken their fellow
countrymen to the dangers ahead.

America and the Fall of the Roman Republic

The New Right had enormous admiration for the ancient Roman
Republic. Robert Welch considered the Republic the most glorious
chapter in the entire history of mankind, surpassed only recently by the
rise of the United States. To New Rightists, the Roman Republic
epitomized the well-governed society. The conduct of the affairs of
state rested securely in the capable hands of the Senate. This small

band of tough, dedicated leaders steered the Republic on a true course, eschewing the treacherous shoals of imperial tyranny or the brutality of democratic mob rule. The Senators governed Rome, not as a selfish elite, content only to protect the narrow interests of the upper class, but as enlightened, selfless patriots always serving the greater good of Rome.9/

Of all the outstanding members of the Senate the New Right singled out the great Roman orator Cicero for special commendation. He exemplified the ideal of an ancient republican statesman. Before his assassination Cicero had bravely defended the integrity of the crumbling Republic against both the blood-thirsty, urban mobs, on the one hand, and the vicious tyrants Julius Caesar and Mark Antony, on the other. Author Taylor Caldwell praised Cicero as "A Pillar of Iron" making him the central character in her historical novel of the same name, and Revilo P. Oliver, a distinguished Classics professor and the John Birch Society's most celebrated intellectual, paid tribute to Cicero as "one of the world's greatest men."10/

The wisest Romans like Cicero, who struggled in vain to preserve their faltering republic, realized the shortcomings of popular democracy. Robert Welch noted that "by the beginning of the Christian era the most intelligent Romans had learned...that an unbridled democracy was the worst of all forms of government." He quoted the Roman philosopher Seneca: "Democracy is more cruel than wars or tyrants." For democracy simply meant the dreadful spectacle of ignorant masses of people participating directly in affairs of government.11/

The unruly populace always supported the wily demagogues who made the most extravagant pledges to the greedy people. Television broadcaster Dan Smoot announced: "When the emperors of ancient Rome discovered that they could win popular support by using public funds to buy food, entertainment, and pensions for the people, candidates for the office of emperor vied with each other to see who could promise most." Clever demagogues heavily taxed the wealth of the prosperous, hard-working citizens in order to feed and amuse the lazy lower classes. Cicero himself, while referring to the charismatic, crowd-pleasing Julius Caesar, acknowledged that the populace invariable chose for its leader "someone bold and unscrupulous...who curries favor with the people by giving them other men's property."12/

The people's clamour for "bread and circuses" eventually destroyed the Roman Republic and paved the way for the Empire. In return for free food and exciting entertainment the masses of ancient Rome gladly surrendered all of their political freedom to the tyrants. Without question, this fear of "bread and circuses" leading the United States towards despotism haunted the New Right during the 1960's. With obvious reference to contemporary America, 1964 G.O.P. Presidential candidate Barry M. Goldwater (who clearly enjoyed playing the role of a modern day Roman Senator a la Cicero) told a Madison Square Garden campaign rally:

> You know, once before a great and self-governing people gave up their liberty--a liberty far less than ours. They put themselves in the hands of their leader, asking only to be fed and entertained. They traded their votes for 'bread and circuses'. They traded their Senate for an Emperor.
> We call them Romans. They lost their nation when they traded away their freedom.13/

Thus in the New Right's view, ancient history pinpointed the fatal weakness of the Republican form of government. Excessive popular participation by the ignorant masses always introduced an unfortunate element of democracy into the political system; and tyranny soon came on the heels of democracy. The people themselves welcomed despotism with a sense of relief. Food and entertainment in exchange for liberty seemed like an excellent bargain, certainly worth the price of appeasing their appetite and their boredom with "bread and circuses."

"America is a Republic, not a Democracy !"

The momentous decision by the Founding Fathers to endow the United States of America with a well-designed Republican Constitution in 1787 signified a rejection of the excesses of both monarchy and privilege, on the one side, and democracy, on the other. The newsletter Report to America commented that "For countless centuries the pendulem sic of government has swung back and forth from aristocracy to mobocracy, until the creation of the Republic of the United States by our forebears." Of course, the Founding Fathers recognized the relatively fragile nature of all previous republican experiments. In truth, republicanism remained a very difficult type of government to establish and a perilous type of rule to maintain. John Birch Society member Robert Montgomery relates the story of old Benjamin Franklin leaving the Pennsylvania State House after finishing the drafting of the United States Constitution. When an interested bystander inquired what form of government the Convention had given to the new nation, Franklin replied with a twinkle in his eye, "A Republic, if you can keep it."14/

Yet the wise and patient Founding Fathers proved equal to this mighty task by writing a magnificently resilient Federal Constitution for the young republic. The New Right praised the Founding Fathers highly for their noteworthy achievements. Ronald Reagan called them "that little band of men so advanced beyond their time that the world has never seen their like since." In the same vein, Robert Montgomery

47

believed, "In the field of government and statecraft the eighteenth century is the greatest of all the centuries and the founding fathers who met to draft our Constitution had the greatest minds of that century."15/

While the Founding Fathers created a constitutional republic they never had the slightest intention of establishing a democracy. New Right spokesman Thurman Sensing pointed out that the Fathers "made a very marked distinction between a republic and a democracy...and said emphatically that they had founded a republic....They knew full well the dangers of a democracy." Barry Goldwater asked, "Was it then a Democracy the framers created?" He answered, "Hardly." The New Right often noted that the Declaration of Independence and the Constitution do not mention the word "democracy" anywhere. Mrs. J. J. McLaughlin, Chairman of the Defenders of American Education wrote, "There is no mention of Democracy in the historical documents of the United States of America." An editorial in the Richmond News-Leader observed, "Surely it is no accident that the word 'democracy' is nowhere found in the Constitution, that Article IV declares 'The United States shall guarantee to every State in the Union a Republican form of government.' " Likewise, American Nazi Fuehrer George Lincoln Rockwell asserted that the term "Republic is mentioned prominently in the Constitution -- 'democracy' not once!"16/

Without a doubt, the Founding Fathers wanted nothing to do with popular democracy. The John Birch Society Bulletin noted, "Although our republic was established before the French Revolution had supplied this horrible example, our founding fathers were well aware of the faults and dangers of a democracy. They wanted no part of one for our national government." The Founding Fathers also knew that "when an elected government succeeds in attracting and maintaining an overwhelming majority behind it for any length of time, its mob instincts make it the most tyrannical of all forms of social organization." Dan Smoot remarked that the Founding Fathers had learned from the example of Roman history how the poor masses under a democratic system of government jumped at the first opportunity to confiscate the property of the rich. Power-hungry demagogues whipped the populace into a state of frenzy by promising to redistribute the wealth, in the name of equality: "The Founding Fathers were well aware of this danger in 'democracy'. They had studied the record of how it had destroyed ancient civilization."17/

Since the New Right believed that history repeats itself, it expected the United States of the 1960's to follow in the footsteps of the ancient Roman Republic -- degeneration into the tyranny of democratic despotism. E. Merrill Root comparing Rome and the United States noticed "the terrible parallels between the Republic of Rome and our Republic." The Roman Republic was "worm-eaten with welfare," destined to "collapse into democracy," and then "the inevitable collapse

48

of democracy into dictatorship." Moreover, Revilo P. Oliver believed that "Our efforts to restore and preserve the Republic are futile, because the United States, like Rome, has reached a stage of such irreversible moral decay that the only form of government now possible for us is an authoritarian one." The urgent question of whether the United States should remain a republic or become a democratic dictatorship constituted "the real intellectual issue that divides Americans today. We are either Ciceronians or Caesarians."18/

Most New Rightists firmly denied, however, that the United States had already become a popular democracy. Refusing to concede defeat they took their message straight to the American people. Senator Goldwater told a nationally broadcast news interview program that "we are not a democracy, and that's a mistake that too many people make. We are a republic." Likewise, the John Birch Society sold automobile bumper stickers echoing the slogan of its founder Robert Welch: "This is a Republic, not a Democracy. Let's keep it that way !" 19/

"There is not tyranny as bloodthirsty or destructive as that of the mob"

Democracy with its policy of majority rule seemed to New Rightists to be an extremely dangerous form of government. The ignorant, unpredictable lower classes appeared utterly incapable of passing judgment upon the important issues of state. American Nazi leader George Lincoln Rockwell maintained "that the mass of people... are gullible, unthinking, little guided by facts, and largely emotional." As a hard and fast rule, "The masses are moved always and only by basic emotions." Universal suffrage quickly became a ghastly farce. Robert Welch declared that "the idea that the vote of the people, no matter how nearly unanimous, makes or creates or determines what is right or just becomes as absurd and unacceptable as the idea that right and justice are simply whatever a king says they are."20/

Indeed a system of democracy invariably led to tyranny and mob rule. H. W. Norman writing in the American Mercury pointed out, "History proves that majority rule in so-called democracies can be used to impose a ruthless dictatorship." No wonder radio newscaster Paul Harvey denounced democracy as "little more than mob rule," while Timothy McInerny decided, "there is no tyranny as bloodthirsty or destructive as that of the mob."21/

Unsophisticated citizens often fell prey to sly, unprincipled rabble-rousers. Columnist William F. Buckley, Jr. complained, "Too many countries in the democratic world have gone down into totalitarianism because some demagogue or other has persuaded everyone who can stagger to the polls to go there, and vote: usually to give power to himself." These political agitators promise the people bread and circuses and then confiscate the property of the wealthy to pay for it. Timothy McInerny lashed out against the crowd-pleasing politician who "finds it beneficial to advocate plunder of the rich to benefit the poor." Along the same lines, Barry Goldwater decried, "the assumption by the state of the obligation to keep men in a style to which demagogues encourage them."22/

The New Right contended that America's Left-wing demagogues have allowed the populace to enjoy bread and circuses at taxpayer's expense ever since the early 1930's. A steady stream of Democratic party leaders from Franklin D. Roosevelt through John F. Kennedy have gladly fed and entertained the poor through various government welfare programs in exchange for their votes at election time. However, this blatant appeal to the mob reached a new plateau under President Lyndon B. Johnson's "Great Society" during the middle of the 1960's. (See Chapter Eleven) As Robert Welch lamented:

> On January 15, 1964, in a speech at the White House, President Lyndon B. Johnson said: We are going to try to take all of the money that we think is unnecessarily being spent and take it from the "haves" and give it to the "have-nots" that need it so much.' Now Lyndon Johnson is hardly a Julius Caesar, but maybe he ought to get some ghost writers who have read a bit more history.23/

Ironically, the politicians often lost control of the mobs. Rather than leading the people, the frightened government officials became virtual prisoners continually forced to cajole and appease the unruly populace with ever more expensive bread and circuses. Presidential candidate Barry Goldwater discussed this serious problem during September, 1964, just as the United States emerged from its first "Long Hot Summer" of racial turmoil in the cities. Goldwater charged that the Black ghetto rioters and Civil Rights agitators held the Johnson Administration hostage. In return for the promise of expanded welfare programs the Blacks reluctantly curtailed their bombings, burnings, and lootings until after the upcoming presidential election had safely passed. Goldwater predicted. "Choose the way of this present Administration and you will have the way of mobs in the streets restrained only by pleas that they wait until after election time to ignite violence again."24/

The Democratic Tragedy Awaiting the United States

In the eyes of the New Right, a blind worship of democracy infected the American political culture during the 1960's. On the one hand, misguided Left-wing politicians and pundits erroneously equated the quality of government with the increasing popular participation of

50

the masses. On the other hand, the basic motives of the elites were seen as devious and selfish; for the Left always associated elite leadership with corruption, privilege, rule by "special interests", and the cynical manipulation of the innocent, trusting people. In contrast, the Left found the basic motives of the masses noble and unselfish. Consequently, democracy translated these laudable popular sentiments into impartial and enlightened government. Indeed this glorification of the proletariat reached its fullest flowering during the turbulent late Sixties as the New Left cried, "Power to the people !"

This dreamy idealization of the "people" annoyed the New Right. The lessons of history quickly and convincingly dispelled any illusions that truth and justice flowed from mass rule. The people often welcomed corruption and tyranny and gladly surrendered their liberty to demagogues in return for bread and circuses. Thus the New Right, deeply committed to republicanism and limited constitutional government, saw absolutely no redeeming civic virtue in democracy. In the words of Barry Goldwater, "We have gone the way of many a democratic society that has lost its freedom by persuading itself that if 'the people' rule, all is well."25/

Moreover, democracy contradicted the American political tradition. As Robert Montgomery pointed out, democracy "was not a reasoned, debated, political decision. It had no roots in economic nor in social conditions in the United States." Thus the New Right viewed democracy as a dangerous foreign ideology which had quietly crept into the American political culture. Barry Goldwater commented, "This nation has always been a conservative nation. The radical ideas of Europe gained no supporters in this land of freedom and opportunity."26/

"The great evils of Welfarism..."

The lessons of ancient history demonstrated yet another pitfall associated with democratic politics: the masses demanded and received expensive government favors. Dan Smoot cautioned that "we are headed toward a disastrous condition prevalent in ancient Rome during the latter days of its decline; when soldiers and veterans became such powerful groups that they could empty the public treasury with their demands for bonuses and benefits." This plight ruined the integrity of the government by undermining the electoral process (not to mention the state finances). "At Rome, as with us," Revilo P. Oliver explained, "the kind of political corruption that is invariably fatal began, of course, when the public treasury was used to bribe voters."27/

The New Right denounced the Johnson Administration for placing millions of poor, easily suggestible voters on the public dole. The New Right considered this gambit a naked attempt to buy votes at the taxpayer's expense. An angry Dan Smoot warned, "The criminals and the

51

drones feed and flourish on the bounty which productive citizens are forced to provide. When tax consumers so overwhelmingly outnumber tax producers that they control all elections and politicians, it will be too late to save our civilization."28/

The New Right noted that whenever the welfare rolls expand, the quality of life abruptly declines. Ezra Taft Benson claimed that "History teaches that when individuals have given up looking after their own economic needs and transferred a large share of that responsibility to the government, both they and the government have failed." Likewise, Senator Barry Goldwater stressed "the great evils of Welfarism...it transforms the individual being into a decadent animal creature without his knowing it." Thus "government policies which create dependent citizens inevitably rob a nation and its people of both moral and physical strength." He predicted, "The effects of Welfarism on freedom will be felt later on--after its beneficiaries have become its victims, after dependence on government has turned into bondage and it is too late to unlock the jail." Goldwater outlined how "man's political freedom is illusory if he is dependent for his economic needs on the State." He then announced, "The Welfare State is not inevitable, as its proponents are so fond of telling us." But examining the decline of the long-standing American principles of hard-work and individual self-reliance he commented sarcastically:

> Perhaps it is time for government by decree. Perhaps it is time to mold public opinion rather than ask for it. Perhaps it is time for the people to come straggling back inside the protective walls and settle down to squabbling over their share of the public dole. As long as they're fed three times a day, they can always be reminded that they enjoy 'freedom' from hunger.29/

Not surprisingly, the New Right utterly detested the entire idea of the modern welfare state. For the lessons of history demonstrated beyond question the folly of the welfare state. Destiny wondered:

> Will the American people continue on down the road to national and economic oblivion, a road traveled by many civilizations in the past who also decided to adopt the Welfare State? One has only to read history to mark the awful price exacted from the nation whose people followed a course that destroyed individual initiative and ambition. The shores of time are strewn with the wreckage of civilizations which succumbed to the so-called blessings of a Welfare State. To be pampered and cared for by government is not worth such a price.30/

The New Right found numerous faults with the welfare state. For instance, the system fostered all sorts of immoral, non-productive activities. The John Birch Society Bulletin listed "the subsidation of illegitimacy, laziness, and political corruption" as the end result of "government welfare programs," while the industrious citizenry paid the cost. Thus the system discouraged hard work and sobriety, in the eyes of Gerald L. K. Smith, because the welfare state "taxes away the rewards for responsible behavior." Consequently, society "is building on a foundation of jelly." Along the same lines, 1964 G.O.P. Presidential nominee Barry Goldwater linked welfare state social theories with the skyrocketing crime rate. Such misguided theories encouraged the notion that the "have-nots" can take from the "haves".31/

Another major criticism of the welfare state concerned the need for progressive taxation to finance the costly social services given to the masses. Thus the graduated tax drew the ire of the New Right. They viewed the graduated tax as an unnatural attempt to penalize the frugal and talented for the benefit of the incompetent and the slovenly. Robert Welch observed that the graduated tax transfers money from the thrifty to the thriftless. And Barry Goldwater, concluding that "The graduated tax is a confiscatory tax," emphasized:

Its effect, and to a large extent its aim, is to bring down all men to a common level. Many of the leading proponents of the graduated tax frankly admit that their purpose is to redistribute the nation's wealth. Their aim is an egalitarian society--an objective that does violence to both the charter of the Republic and the laws of Nature.32/

History demonstrated the folly of progressive taxation. The New Right pointed out that the progressive tax "was not a new idea--its record of failure goes back almost as far as the history of civilization." Destiny asserted that "Modern civilization cannot endure the oppressiveness of an unjust tax system any more than Rome was able to do so."33/

The United States of America adopted the principle of progressive taxation with the passage of the Sixteenth Amendment to the Federal Constitution in 1913. The New Right deeply regretted this action. Therefore, the future health of republicanism in the United States rested with the quick repeal of this unfortunate addition to our nation's basic charter. As Dean Clarence Manion concluded, "constitutional government cannot be restored while the Sixteenth Amendment is intact."34/

Finally, the immoral sexual practices of the "growing horde of lazy Negroes" living off the public dole represented the ultimate horror of the welfare state. Degenerate personal conduct, once regarded as a sin against God now received government blessings. Christian Economics stressed that under the welfare system "Desertion and illegitimacy are rewarded handsomely" and "are already out-of-bounds and increasing." Gerald L. K. Smith cried, "Relief is gradually becoming an honorable career in America.... The politicians will weep over you. The state will give a bonus for...illegitimate children." Marilyn R. Allen criticized, "the unmarried Negro women who make a business of producing children ...for the purpose of securing this easy welfare money."35/

Huge waves of Black babies threatened to engulf the White majority. Common Sense pointed out that "The Negro population in this country is increasing 38% faster than the white population, and a great percentage of this increase is due to illegitimacy...promoted by the politicians through welfare payments."* The entire welfare system invited the Blacks to reproduce while the Whites paid the bills. Marilyn R. Allen commented, "The white race...is being exploited and its tax money used to support and encourage a Negro welfare state for the benefit of this race which is rapidly out-breeding the whites at their expense." Nazi leader Rockwell announced that the welfare system forced the industrious Whites to limit their own population "while every miserable herd of half-animal blacks with no more morals than a troop of monkeys is encouraged to breed as fast as possible." He grumbled that "every welfare program is rigged so that the moral and increasingly sterile whites support and subsidize the immoral proliferating blacks."36/

Accordingly, the welfare state lowered the intellectual, physical, and racial character of the American people. Christian Economics deplored the "Long range effect of welfare statism...an alarming population growth from the lower strata while levying the cost upon the wiser, more prudent and more competent portions of society." The finest elements in society "are inordinately taxed...limit the number of their children and then find themselves paying for the large families of the imprudent, the unwise, the incompetent, the substandard wasters and chiselers."37/

In summation, ancient Roman republicanism had succumbed to the assorted pressures of democracy: the wily demagogues using the

---

*Note--Because of strong religious convictions New Rightists categorically rejected the most practical solution to the growing problem of Negro illegitimacy--abortion and birth control. Instead the New Right recommended total sexual abstinence for all non-married men and women. (See Epilogue, Chapter Thirteen.)

public treasury to buy votes; the ignorant masses willing to surrender their freedom in exchange for bread and circuses; and a welfare state financed by progressive taxation encouraging and rewarding immorality and laziness. The New Right believed that, once again, history illuminated the simple truth: the Roman Republic had never survived such a vicious assault, and neither could the United States of the 1960's.

America and the Fall of the Roman Empire

Just as the collapse of the Roman Republic haunted the New Right so, too, did the subsequent decline and fall of the Roman Empire. The once-mighty, ancient Roman Empire had come crashing to the ground and the obvious lessons of history promised a repeat performance for the United States of America. "The rise and fall of the United States is being written," author Malcolm Knight announced, "What part are you playing in this great drama? Are you...floating along without seeing the obvious handwriting on the wall of time...?" In the same vein, Dan Smoot warned, "The end for Rome had been a long time in coming. How far from the end is America? No one can tell but everyone who has studied the facts knows we are on the way."38/

Sadly American society had acquired the same problems and vices which had plagued the decaying Roman Empire. Novelist Taylor Caldwell asked, "Shall we continue along the path which led to the extinction of Rome? We have made her terrible mistakes, we have duplicated her crimes and stupidities almost to the letter." Common Sense reminded its subscribers of the striking similarities between the United States of the 1960's and the deteriorating Roman Empire:

In 1787 Gibbon completed his notable work 'The Decline and Fall of the Roman Empire.' Have you read it lately? Here is the way Gibbon accounted for the fall of the Empire:

1) The rapid increase of divorce; the undermining of the dignity and sanctity of the home, which is the basis of human society.
2) Higher and higher taxes and the spending of public monies for free bread and circuses for the populace.
3) The mad craze for pleasure; sports becoming every year more exciting and more brutal.*

---

*Note—Yet the Sunbelt nouveau riche helped transform professional football into contemporary America's version of the brutal, exciting, ancient Roman games. Apparently, even the solemn warnings of Edward Gibbon took a backseat to the thrills of the Dallas Cowboys!

55

4) The building of gigantic armaments when the real enemy was within, in the decadence of the people.

5) The decay of religion--faith fading into mere form, losing touch with life and becoming impotent to warn and guide the people.39/

In short, the decadence of the Roman people rather than the pressures applied by foreign enemies caused the demise of the Roman Empire: "ancient Rome after 700 years of glorious history was destroyed, not by the military power of the Huns but by the decay within." In the same manner, Common Sense had no doubts that "Before Rome Fell--It Decayed From Within."40/

Thus the teachings of history left yet another indelible imprint upon the mind of the New Right: "It is not the strength of the barbarians but the moral and intellectual weakness of the civilized that is usually their undoing." As Ezra Taft Benson remarked:

> History reveals that rarely is a great civilization conquered from without until it has weakened or destroyed itself within.... At least twenty great civilizations have disappeared. The pattern of their downfall is shockingly similar. All, before their collapse, showed a decline in spiritual values, in moral stamina, and in the freedom and responsibility of their citizens.41/

Therefore, the same danger of domestic decay threatened the very soul of the United States in the Sixties. According to Barry Goldwater, "Like so many other nations before us, we may succumb through internal weakness rather than fall before a foreign foe." In the same vein, James H. Jauncey pointed out, "What has happened to Rome could and might happen to the United States."42/

"The moral fiber of the American people is
beset by rot and decay"

The outward signs of serious moral decay among the American people alarmed the New Right. "The nation has become too corrupt and demoralized," declared Revilo P. Oliver. Barry Goldwater during his 1964 Presidential campaign noticed that "something basic and dangerous is eating away at the morality, dignity, and respect of our citizens, old as well as young, high as well as low." He added, "the moral fiber of the American people is beset by rot and decay." F.B.I. Director J. Edgar Hoover also detected "a dangerous flaw in our Nation's moral armor. Self-indulgence--the principle of pleasure before duty is practiced across the length and breadth of the land."43/

The blame for this sorry state of public morality, in large measure, could be traced directly to corrupt leadership. Former Texas

Congressman Martin Dies suggested that "a public servant's life should be like Caesar's wife--above suspicion....One of the first clear signs of a nation's decadence is the peoples' acceptance of immorality on the part of its leaders." During an election rally at Boston's Fenway Park Republican Presidential nominee Barry Goldwater echoed the same theme: "Nothing is more clear from history than that moral decay of the people begins at the top. It seeps down from the highest offices into all walks of life." Senator Goldwater, a self-proclaimed student of history and political philosophy, did not speak solely in abstract terms. He savagely attacked President Lyndon B. Johnson for contributing to the moral decay of the United States. Referring to L.B.J. and his corrupt, one-time associates Bobby Baker and Billy Sol Estes, Goldwater admonished his audience, "And when men use political advantage for personal gain we can understand the decline of moral strength generally." The Arizona Solon often discussed the detrimental effects of high government corruption upon the rest of society: "The example this sets can be traced, tragically, through the easy morals and uneasy ethics which in private life disturb so many parents and lure so many young people." It behooves those in positions of power to exercise sound moral leadership because "if the tone of America is not set by men in public service it will be set, as unfortunately it is being set too often today, by the standards of the sick joke, the slick slogan, the off-color drama, and the pornographic book."44/

Washington, D.C., the seat of government for the world's greatest republic, had become the New Rome. Alabama Governor George Wallace deplored the "repulsive stench rising from the shores of the Potomac. It is occasioned by the crime, the corruption, the moral decay, the debauchery, the drunken revelries, and moral degeneracy commonplace in the Nation's Capital." The Reverend Kenneth Goff wrote, "Our national capitol should be made safe for all citizens: yet today, it has become a mecca for crime, rape, murder, robbery and homosexuality--even in the highest offices, these sex depravities occur."45/

The startling disclosures of sex scandals within the highest councils of the British Government, known as the 1963 "Christine Keeler Affair," heightened apprehensions that similar mischief commonly occurred in Washington. Indeed Revilo P. Oliver pointed out the intimate connections between London and Washington: "some specialists in vice and crime shuttle back and forth from one country to the other." Furthermore, he decried "the hundreds of known nests of drug-addicts, perverts, and degenerates in Washington." He predicted sensational new disclosures of widespread debauchery, this time within the highest American echelons: "There are rumors of an even more filthy scandal, involving both sadistic perversions and the use of government powers for the importation and distribution of hallucinatory narcotics."46/

The fear and detestation of homosexuality in the government represents another thread running throughout New Right thought. American Nazi leader George Lincoln Rockwell blasted "pansies" and "queers," labelling them as "the ultimate disgrace of civilization." He continued: "the most unhealthy, most un-wholesome cancer in any civilization is homosexualism. Whenever it appears and gets the upper hand, as it did in Greece and Rome, civilization, rots and dies." Another observer called homosexuality "a world-wide conspiracy against society" which has "infiltrated into the press, the movies and the cabinets; and it all but dominates the arts, literature, theater, music and TV." Destiny lamented that "It no longer merely stalks back alleys and infests filthy garrets. It has crept into high society; it has invaded the citadels of government."47/

Long before the major sex perversion scandals came to light, the New Right noted an alarming rise in homosexual activity in Washington. Gerald L. K. Smith warned that "homosexuals have gravitated to positions of great power and influence in the affairs of our Government, including the State Department, the Armed Services, and even the Senate and the Congress of the United States." But in the estimation of the New Right, the final proof of homosexual perversion in high places occurred with the shocking arrest of a top Presidential aide on a lewd conduct charge in October, 1964. Incredibly, the Washington, D.C. police apprehended L.B.J.'s closest personal advisor, Walter Jenkins in a public restroom only a few blocks away from the White House itself. Afterwards, the New Right castigated "the nests of homosexual degenerates like sweet Walter Jenkins, that dominates high administration circles in Washington." Meanwhile, President Johnson, in the midst of his bitter reelection campaign against Senator Goldwater, came under personal attack as the result of his intimate friendship with Walter Jenkins. Placards at Republican Party campaign rallies read "L.B.J. For Moral Decay" and "Lyndon Baker Jenkins". The American Nazis even picketed the White House with signs demanding to know "Is L.B.J. Queer?"48/

"Are we to go the way of...Sodom and Gomorrah?"

"Flesh worship is the mood of the moment," cried Gerald L. K. Smith, "Any student of history knows that the perversion of sex constitutes one of the most alarming symptoms of degeneration in the life of a people, or a Nation, or an Empire." Indeed the lessons of the past proved conclusively the dangers of sexual misconduct. As the Reverend Bruce W. Dunn asserted, "No civilization, no empire, no nation has survived obsession with sex and impurity." Likewise, The Defender added, "Sexual immorality, they say, has destroyed more nations than any other single sin."* Thus the speeches and writings of the New Right contain admonitions against nudity, masturbation, pre-marital as well as extra-marital relations, homosexuality, lesbianism, and other disturbing sexual practices.49/

Unfortunately, many Americans by the 1960's seemed absolutely unable to control their own sexual passions anymore. The Defender spoke for the New Right when it complained that "Pornographic literature, indecent films, filthy dialogue, improper dress, idleness of youth, and educational trends have given impetus to sexual license that defies description."50/

In the eyes of the New Right, this growing sexual deviation in the United States resulted, in large part, from pornographic books, magazines, and motion pictures. Robert Welch blamed the trouble on "the filling of half the drugstores in America with blasphemous and pornographic books...,"and described its serious effects: "the pornography now being rammed down the throats of our youth is none the less harmful simply because it has become so common place." Gerald L. K. Smith voiced his wrath against magazines "devoted to sex, pornography, perverted relationships, and a study of sex violations..." "Is our Nation degenerating," he queried, "Are we to go the way of Rome, Assyria, Carthage, and Sodom and Gomorrah?"51/

The New Right believed that pornography contributed to the growing crime wave sweeping the United States during the early 1960's. J. C. Drummond wrote in the American Mercury: "Again and again, the investigation of juvenile robbery, extortion, embezzlement, forgery, rape and murder reveals that those guilty were or had been collectors of obscene pictures and films." The shocking increase in violent, sex-related crime especially disturbed the New Right. And, once again, pornography played a leading role. F.B.I. Director J. Edgar Hoover stated, "We know that in an overwhelmingly large number of cases sex crime is associated with pornography." Thus he concluded that "pornography is a major cause of sex violence."52/

The New Right directed its greatest ire at the producers of the pornography itself. George Lincoln Rockwell found those men offensive "who advance their 'private enterprise' by selling...filthy literature to kids." Common Sense held that "The penalty for writing, publishing, distributing and retailing pornographic books, magazines, pictures, films,

---

*Note--Edward Gibbon in his Decline and Fall of the Roman Empire does mention sex perversion as a minor reason for the fall of Rome, but considers sex far less important than the spread of Christianity! Of course, the New Right never repeats Gibbon's anti-Christian views; which proves to me at least, that most New Rightists never actually bothered to read Gibbon's book.

etc. should be execution..." The spread of such smut could not be halted with lenient courts and immoral politicians reluctant to enforce the obscenity statutes by actually prosecuting cases and punishing violators. As Common Sense complained, "How can we expect sanity in our government when high places are filled with mentally ill perverts?"53/

The motion picture industry also contributed to the decline of decency. Timothy McInerny asserted, "Low people of animal morals and no taste started and maintained the motion-picture industry and brought mass debasement to the world scene." Hollywood had long offended the American Radical Right. Marilyn R. Allen grumbled that for years the nation's film capitol had produced a steady stream of movies "many of them lurid, licentious, crime-filled, race-mixing and shocking to sane sensibilities." Furthermore, the well-publicized marital escapades of Hollywood personalities irritated the New Right: "The lustiest sluts in Hollywood are glorified and made into heroines when as a matter of fact, they haven't a shred of decency or morality."54/

Thus motion pictures constituted a prime factor in the appalling decline of American moral standards, particularly among the young. California State Superintendent of Public Instruction Dr. Max Rafferty told a nationwide radio audience:

> We have a situation now where it's almost unsafe to take a child to the movies anymore. We are parading for them on the silver screen a dismal, dreadful succession of themes ranging from sodomy to prostitution and rape, with the possibility every now and then of a little old-fashioned cannibalism thrown in just to keep us on our toes apparently. No generation in all the world, even including Restoration England, has wallowed so in filth as ours has done today.

Likewise, Common Sense, while deploring "Adultery, prostitution, sodomy, incest, frigidity, and nymphomania" in motion pictures, condemned contemporary films for "depicting life's basest aspects."55/

In addition to motion pictures, television contributed to America's moral and spiritual decline. Gerald L. K. Smith proclaimed, "There is no greater problem in American life than the problem of television." It "brings crime, burlesque shows, murder, sex perversion,...free love, and marital infidelity into the living room of the American home without restraint."56/

Yet excessive violence rather than explicit sex remained the major complaint against television. J. Edgar Hoover observed that "The continuous diet of mayhem, murder and violence served daily to our TV audiences constitutes a monumental insult to the genius that developed this mass medium." Tulsa Tribune Editor Jenkins Lloyd Jones warned, "We are drowning our youngsters in violence, cynicism and sadism piped into the living room and even the nursery." Finally, Nazi leader George Lincoln Rockwell, of all people, complained bitterly of excessive bloodshed and violence on the tube. He felt that television glorified hoodlums. The tube exalts "the slum type, depraved, despicable city hood and his degenerate rapes, robberies, and murders -- to say nothing of thrill killings and beatings."57/

Modern art both bewildered and disturbed the New Right. To begin with, they found modern art utterly incomprehensible, as critics frequently commented after visiting art exhibitions. Cross and the Flag reported that "our museums are filled with daubs being stared at by confused citizens who haven't the guts to admit they are confused." The New Right enjoyed reciting the story of the modern art painting accidentally hung upside down on a gallery wall. Since "you could not tell which was the top and which was the bottom....It was days before it was discovered."58/

Moreover, modern art mirrored the lowering of the cultural standards of the American people. According to Christian Economics, modern art "reflects the decay of our values and standards, a loss of faith in God and the dignity of man, and the Communist infiltration of our cultural life." Thus alongside motion pictures and television, modern art abetted the destruction of civilization. With his usual highly imaginative flair for words George Lincoln Rockwell placed his finger on the problem: "We see our Western Christian culture reduced almost to the point of utter idiocy, as paintings made by the tails of donkeys, or by gorillas or by women crawling over canvas coated with warm chocolate win art prizes..."59/

Music played a vital role in the general decline of the culture. The frenzied Beatles craze which swept across the nation during the early months of 1964 irritated the New Right. An article entitled "Subversion by Music" appearing in Report to America warned, "the spirit of the American people is being systematically subverted by the substitution of a new... and corrupting kind of 'music' for the music they once enjoyed." Report to America then added, "Perhaps a decline in the quality of its music is a symptom that a civilization has passed its peak." The tumultuous reception accorded to those youthful, shaggy English rock singers during their highly successful 1964 American tour sickened observers such as Rockwell: "The heroes used to be Sam Houston, Daniel Boone, Tom Mix, General MacArthur" but today "our kids grovel at the feet of scum."60/

Furthermore, the Beatles arrived in the United States soon after the sensational Christine Keeler Scandal had exposed how morally decadent England had become. Next, the Beatles' longer hair styles suggested homosexuality. Finally, the amazing power of the Beatles to induce mass hysteria among American teenage girls frightened New Rightists who feared that the Communists might use similar techniques for political purposes.

The state of native American music equally disquieted the New Right. College campuses and sleazy night clubs abounded with "barefooted beatniks with long hair strumming guitars and reciting sick poetry." The growing popularity of Negro music replete with heavy sensual overtones infuriated the New Right. According to Gerald L. K. Smith, "jazz music originated in the jungles of Africa, promoted by the sex mad worshippers of the sex acts." Rockwell outlined the fatal consequences of the spreading "Negroid-jungle music": "our White Youth is utterly captivated and hypnotized by the Cannibal 'music' and the savage, brutal 'beat' of apelike Negroes, who have no faint perception, let alone understanding or love, of the subtleties or beauties of White Man's Music." He also deplored the intrusion of "Degenerate Negro 'bop' talk" into White folk music: "The language is something else. Filthy Nigger-talk sprinkled with Mother F.- -, every third word or so, simply cannot be tolerated."61/

"Our greatest asset is our youth..."

While the New Right gave up all hope of any moral regeneration among America's elders they fervently believed that the nation's young citizens might still lead the country back to virtue one day. Ezra Taft Benson remarked, "Our greatest asset is our youth--our boys and girls-- the future leaders and fathers and mothers of this great country." Regrettably, America's children had acquired their parents' vices. Observers watched an alarming rise in teenage suicide, illegitimacy, along with juvenile delinquency, alcoholism, and drug addiction. The Defender even denounced teenage "glue-sniffing" for "kicks".62/

Dr. Max Rafferty led the chorus of New Right anger by naming the educational system as the basic source of the moral decay of American children. For schools produce "booted, sideburned, ducktailed, unwashed, leather-jacketed slobs, whose favorite sport is ravishing little girls and stomping polio victims to death." Taylor Caldwell charged that young students "were corrupted in many of our secular schools, given 'sex education' and by implication were taught that chastity and self-control and modesty were somehow 'square' and beneath contempt." She blamed elected officials and educators for subverting traditional American values:

> I accuse our politicians, and especially our public
> school boards, of breaking down the morals of our
> children, of indolently teaching children...that they owe
> their allegiance to the state only, that religion is foolish

and patriotism is somehow shameful and that 'sex enlightenment' is sophisticated.

Likewise, Robert Welch told a Culver City, California audience, "Today a grade school teacher is not allowed to have the children say a prayer or read Bible verses in her classroom, while letting them shoot dice or stomp on the American flag is considered permissible, and in some high educational circles even praiseworthy."63/

"Progressive education", in the opinion of Barry Goldwater, lay at the root of the problem: "In our attempt to make education 'fun' we have neglected the academic disciplines that develop sound minds and are conducive to sound character." In an attempt to set a national trend back towards old-fashioned, "readin', writin', and 'rithmetic" as taught in the "good old days" of the little-red schoolhouse, the John Birch Society republished the late nineteenth century McGuffey Readers and heavily lobbied with many local school boards for their adoption as text books."64/

"Our city streets are jungles of terror"

The New Right cringed in horror as America's major urban centers degenerated into jungles of crime. James Burnham asserted, "In the parks of our great cities, exactly as in all jungles, honest men may no longer move at night; when the sun goes down they must stay near the fires, while the beasts prowl." Decrying "this senseless sadism," J. Edgar Hoover testified, "Our city streets are jungles of terror. The viciousness of the rapists, murderers and muggers who attack women and young girls seem to know no bounds." In the same vein, Frank S. Meyer lamented, "Our great cities are becoming jungles where no man can go about his business or stroll in the public park in safety, and even inside the schools themselves our children are terrorized, knifed, and raped."65/

New York City loomed as the foremost example of this ugly urban brutality. Common Sense warned, "Today, New York City is a veritable 'jungle town' and white females are attacked and raped on streets in residential areas, in their apartments and on the waiting platforms of the subways." George Lincoln Rockwell, a frequent critic of "criminal mobs of teenagers", damned "the evil depraved and vicious murders such as the thrill-killings by teenage gangsters in Central Park."66/

Unfortunately, soft-hearted humanitarians thwarted the vital war against street crime. The New Right especially disliked the kid-glove treatment accorded to youthful offenders. J. Edgar Hoover was "disgusted by the misguided sentimentalists who want to pamper and excuse teen-age thugs." Hoover continued: "We misname brutal crimes committed by vicious young thugs as 'juvenile delinquency.' " Jenkins Lloyd Jones recommended a "swift kick on juvenile delinquency....We've

63

tried Big Brother clubs, and palsy-walsy cops—and still the young hoods multiply."67/

Furthermore, while sympathy and misplaced compassion for the law breakers increased, the prestige and respect for peace officers plummeted. Robert Welch complained that the bleeding-heart, do-gooders have made "criminals out of local police and heroes out of our criminals." American Nazi leader Rockwell stressed the ineffectiveness of law enforcement officials because "the enemies of society constantly howl about 'police brutality.' "68/

Finally, the breakdown of law and order epitomized the shocking condition of American life and the lessons of the past clearly pointed the way towards disaster. "History demonstrates," Barry Goldwater explained, "that nothing prepares the way for tyranny more than the failure of public officials to keep the streets safe from bullies and marauders."69/

"The society will wind up mongrelized,
as did Rome"

The horrors of race mongrelization represented the last historical lesson gleaned from the study of the downfall of the once-proud Roman Empire. Common Sense outlined how "In every case where there has been integration, mongrelization has been the result....Every civilization that has been destroyed was first integrated; and history has a way of repeating itself."70/

The New Right believed that the Negro Revolution, gaining momentum during the early 1960's, threatened to integrate and then ultimately mongrelize the United States. Discussing Negroes, Gerald L. K. Smith warned:

> these untrained and underdeveloped people will infiltrate our whole race. They will degenerate and dissipate our bloodline, and we will...go down with the destroyed civilizations of centuries past. Invariably the first symptoms of decay and degeneracy in these other civilizations was when the bloodline was degenerated by mongrelization and intermarriage.

In the same fashion, George Lincoln Rockwell announced that "as long as there is sex and black and white are mingled closely geographically...lust will have its way, and the society will wind up mongrelized, as did Rome."71/

64

Thus, the specter of ancient Rome haunted the New Right, for they saw the bread and circuses and moral decay tragically reappearing in America during the 1960's. Just like declining Rome, the United States had become corrupt, debauched, and lazy. In vain, New Rightists attempted to alert their fellow citizens to this danger. History was indeed repeating itself right before their very own eyes.

1. Hunter, Our Second Revolution, p. 139;
John Birch Society Bulletin, (June, 1962), p. 5;
Robert Welch, The Blue Book of the John Birch Society 7th ed. (Belmont,
Massachusetts: The John Birch Society, 1959), p. 10.

2. Destiny, (May, 1960), p. 118;
William F. Rickenbacker as quoted in the National Review, (December
31, 1960). pp. 407-408.

3. Beacon-Light Herald, (May-June, 1961), p. 17;
Welch, The New Americanism, p. 15.

4. Destiny (May, 1960), p. 118.

5. Dan Smoot Report, (October 19, 1964), p. 334.

6. Ibid., (October 12,1964) p. 322.

7. Cross and the Flag, (September, 1962), pp. 3-4.

8. American Opinion, (March, 1964), p. 62.

9. Welch, The New Americanism, p. 94.

10. Taylor Caldwell, A Pillar of Iron (Garden City, N.Y.: Doubleday
& Company, Inc., 1965). E. Merrill Root enthusiastically calls her novel
"the greatest historical novel in American Literature." American
Opinion, (April, 1965), p. 97;
American Opinion, (May, 1965), p. 57.

11. Welch, The New Americanism, p. 119;
Ibid., p. 95.

12. Dan Smoot Report, (March 1, 1965), p. 67;
Welch, The New Americanism, p. 115.

13. New York Times, October 27, 1964.

14. Report to America, (December, 1963), p. 3;
Welch, The New Americanism, Foreword, p. xi.

15. America's Future, (June 8, 1962), p. 6;
Welch, The New Americanism, Foreword, p. x.

16. Report to America, (March, 1965), pp. 2-3;
Goldwater, The Conscience of a Conservative, p. 18;

Common Sense, (April 15, 1961), p. 3;
Editorial, Richmond News-Leader as quoted in Human Events, (May 19, 1961), p. 316;
Rockwell Report, (June 15, 1962), p. 3.

The New Right cited several other examples of American republicanism. Discussing the federal structure of our government Lt. General George E. Stratemeyer (retired) said, "We are a Republic of fifty sovereign states, not a Democracy." Common Sense, (November 15, 1962), p. 1.

Thurman Sensing stated that "Our pledge of allegiance refers to the flag and to the Republic for which it stands." Report to America, (March, 1965), pp. 2-3.

17. John Birch Society Bulletin, (January, 1961), p. 22;
Welch, The New Americanism, p. 8;
Dan Smoot Report, (July 1. 1963), p. 202.

Other nations in the Western world during modern times have also suffered from the egalitarian plague of democracy. Mrs. J. J. McLaughlin commented that "Democracy caused the downfall of France at the end of the 18th century." Common Sense, (April 15, 1961), p. 3.

Barry Goldwater, in his book The Conscience of a Conservative described the French " 'democratic' Jacobins" as "a mob tyranny that paraded under the banner of egalitarianism." Goldwater, The Conscience of a Conservative, p. 13.

Likewise, "The British Empire, once the mighty balance wheel in the world," in the words of Revilo P. Oliver, "fell apart when its aristocracy abdicated to the vulgar mob." American Opinion, (April, 1965), p. 69.

18. American Opinion, (April, 1965), p. 97;
Ibid., (November, 1963), pp. 46-47.

Taylor Caldwell proclaimed that democracy "was too deep in the heart and body of the ancient world, as it is now so deep in ours. Cicero delayed the days of final collapse, but only delayed it. He was assassinated. Rome then declined into despotism,...just as America is now declining." American Opinion, (June, 1965), pp. 71-72.

19. "Face the Nation," C.B.S. telecast, January 26, 1961;
Welch, The New Americanism, p. 114.

20. Rockwell Report, (June 15, 1963), p. 5;
Ibid., (December 1962), p. 5;
Welch, The New Americanism, p. 113.

Dan Smoot believed that "America was founded as a Republic. In a Republic, law and the Constitution prevail, not the current whim of a majority." Dan Smoot Report, (April 22, 1963), p. 121.

21. American Mercury, (January, 1962), p. 62;
National Defender, (September, 1964), p. 6;
Timothy A. McInerny, The Private Man (New York: Ivan Obolensky, Inc., 1962), p. 87.

22. National Review, (July 14, 1963), p. 574;
McInerny, The Private Man, p. 8;
New York Times, September 11, 1964.

23. Welch, The New Americanism, p. 115.

24. New York Times, September 4, 1964.

25. Goldwater, The Conscience of a Conservative, p. 22.

26. Welch, The New Americanism, Foreword, p. xi;
Human Events, (February 18,1960), p. 1.

27. Dan Smoot Report, (March 25,1963), p. 92;
American Opinion, (May, 1965), p. 65.

Likewise, Timothy McInery insisted, "an irresponsible electorate is to invite looting of the treasury..." McInerny, The Private Man, p. 87.

28. Dan Smoot Report, (July 7, 1965), p. 183.

In the same spirit, the Economic Council Letter pointed out how the hordes of government bureaucrats on the public payroll were forced to cast their ballots for the Democrats in order to keep their jobs. Economic Council Letter, (August 15, 1964), p. 1.

29. Benson, The Red Carpet, p. 168;
Goldwater, The Conscience of a Conservative, p. 75;
Human Events, (February 18, 1960), p. 1;
Goldwater, The Conscience of a Conservative, p. 72;
Ibid., p. 12;
Ibid., p. 76;
New York Times, October 27, 1964.

30. Destiny, (May, 1961), pp. 101-108.

31. John Birch Society Bulletin, (September, 1961), p. 6;
Cross and the Flag, (September, 1962), p. 25;
New York Times, September 11, 1964.

32. Welch, The New Americanism, p. 109;
Goldwater, The Conscience of a Conservative, p. 64.

33. Fred G. Clark and Richard Stanton as quoted in Human Events,
(January 20, 1961), p. 46;
Destiny, (July-August, 1963) p. 151.

34. Manion, The Conservative American, p. 179.

35. Rockwell Report, (February 1, 1963), p.4;
Christian Economics, (July 10, 1962), p. 2;
Cross and the Flag, (September, 1962), p. 25;
Kingdom Digest, (August, 1960), as quoted in the Beacon-Light Herald,
(March-April, 1961), p. 33.

   Along these lines, Barry Goldwater added, "I don't like to see my
taxes paid for children born out of wedlock." New York Times, July 19,
1961.

36. Common Sense, (June 15, 1962), p. 3;
Kingdom Digest, (August, 1960), as quoted in the Beacon-Light Herald,
(March-April, 1961), p. 33;
Rockwell Report, (December 1, 1962), p. 5.

37. Christian Economics, (July 10, 1962), p. 2.

   A thoroughly dismayed Revilo P. Oliver observed that...

   The United States is now engaged in an insane, but terribly
   effective, effort to destroy the American people and Western
   civilization by subsidizing, both at home and abroad, the breeding
   of the intellectually, physically and morally unfit; while at the
   same time inhibiting by taxation and in many other ways, the
   reproduction of the valuable parts of the population--those with
   the stamina and the will to bear the burden of high civilization.
   American Opinion, (December, 1964), p. 68.

38. Common Sense, (January 1. 1963), pp. 2-3;
Dan Smoot Report, (March 1. 1965), p. 68.

39. Dan Smoot Report, (October 19, 1964), p. 334;
Quoted from the Glenwood Hills News in Common Sense, (April 1. 1963),
p. 4.

40. James H. Jauncey, "The Key to Greatness," American Mercury,
(January, 1961), p. 6;
Common Sense, (February 1, 1965), p. 4.

41. Dr. Wilhelm Roepke in America's Future, (May 11, 1962), p. 8; Benson, The Red Carpet, p, 236; Ibid., p. 169.

42. Goldwater, The Conscience of a Conservative, pp. 22-23; American Mercury, (January, 1961), p. 6.

To many observers, not simply the United States but the entire Western World suffered from the cancer of domestic decay. Classical scholar Revilo P. Oliver asserted that Western civilization was not declining as "the result of a mysterious destiny or an irreversible historical process" but rather "If we perish, our epitaph will be that Gibbon wrote for the decadent Romans. They themselves decreed their fall." American Opinion, (September, 1964), p. 44.

Professor Anthony Bouscaren summed up the position of the New Right succinctly:

If some future Gibbon should write the history of the decline and fall of Western civilization, he will have to record that in the 20th century the West seemed to have lost its instinct for survival; its will to resist. And he can demonstrate that the democracies--strong, rich, highly cultured--were defeated not by superior force, but by spiritual decay. News and Views, (February, 1963), p. 2.

43. American Opinion, (November, 1963), p. 47; New York Times, October 11, 1964; Remarks by J. Edgar Hoover to the 1962 American Legion National Convention quoted in the Cross and the Flag, (December, 1962), p. 29.

F.B.I. Director J. Edgar Hoover also wondered:

What has happened to the time-honored precepts of hard work and fair play which influenced the American scene during the all-important formative years of this great Republic? Where is the faith in God which fortified us through our past trials? Have our national pride, our moral conscience, our sensitivity to filth and degradation , grown so weak that they no longer react to assaults upon our proud heritage of freedom. Remarks to the 1962 American Legion National Convention quoted in the Cross and the Flag, (December, 1962), p. 32.

44. American Opinion, (October, 1964), p. 24; New York Times, September 25, 1964; Ibid., September 4, 1964.

45. Cross and the Flag, (November, 1964), p. 8; Beacon-Light Herald, (October, November, December, 1965), p. 10.

46. Cross and the Flag, (September, 1963), p. 9;
American Opinion, (February, 1964), p. 75;
Ibid., p. 22.

47. Rockwell, This Time the World, p. 407;
Rockwell Report, (July 15, 1964), p. 7;
R.G. Waldeck, "Homosexual International," Human Events, (September 29, 1960), p. 453;
Destiny, (September, 1964), p. 182.

48. Cross and the Flag, (June, 1962), p. 28;
American Opinion, (November, 1964), p. 30;
New York Times, (October 29, 1964);
Storm Trooper, (November, 1964), p. 23.

49. Cross and the Flag, (October, 1963), p. 21;
Ibid., (June, 1962), p.28;
Destiny, (January, 1965), p. 20;
The Defender, (August, 1962),p. 18.

50. The Defender, (August, 1962), p. 18.

51. Welch, The New Americanism, p. 173;
John Birch Society Bulletin, (September, 1961), p. 6;
Cross and the Flag, (June, 1962), p. 19.

52. American Mercury, (June, 1961), p. 70;
James J. Kilpatrick, The Smut Peddlers (Garden City, N.Y.: Doubleday & Company, Inc., 1960), p. 7.

53. Rockwell Report, (December 15, 1962), p. 7;
Common Sense, (February 1, 1965), p. 4.

54. McInerny, The Private Man, p. 34;
Marilyn R. Allen, Beacon-Light Herald, (May-June, 1961), p. 43.

55. Manion Forum Network broadcast (May 10, 1964);
Common Sense, (January 15, 1963), p. 4.

Cross and the Flag argued with sarcasm, "Can anyone deny that movies are dirtier than ever. But they don't call it dirt. They call it 'realism'." Cross and the Flag, (September, 1962), p. 25.

56. Cross and the Flag, (July, 1962), p. 8.

Likewise, Ezra Taft Benson echoed the sentiments of the New Right when he denounced "salacious and suggestive TV programs." Ezra Taft Benson, A Nation Asleep (Salt Lake City, Utah: Bookcraft, Inc., 1963), p. 11.

57. Human Events, (September 22, 1961), p. 636;
Ibid., (November 24, 1961), p. 795;
Rockwell Report, (January 1. 1963), pp. 4-5.

58. Cross and the Flag, (September, 1962), p. 24;
Destiny, (October, 1963), p. 207.

59. Christian Economics, (January 21, 1964), p. 2;
Rockwell Report, (December 15, 1962), p. 6.

60. Report to America, (February, 1964),p. 6;
Rockwell Report, (February 15, 1964), p. 7.

61. The Defender, (February, 1963), p. 13;
Cross and the Flag, (March, 1963), p. 24;
Rockwell Report, (June 15, 1963), p. 2;
Ibid., (April 15, 1963), pp. 9-10;

Curiously, both Communism as well as Fascism deplored modern art and jazz music. For example, Stalin's henchman in cultural affairs, Andrei Zhdanov, once described modern music as reminding him of the whirring of the dentist's drill ! Adam B. Ulam, Stalin: The Man and his Era (New York: Viking Press, 1973), p. 647.

62. Benson, The Red Carpet, p. 279;
The Defender, (February, 1963), p. 13.

63. Dr. Max Rafferty, "What's Happened to Patriotism?" Reader's Digest, (October, 1961), p. 109;
Look,(October 22, 1963), p. 56;
American Opinion, (September, 1964), p. 70;
Welch, The New Americanism, p. 166.

64. Goldwater, The Conscience of a Conservative, pp. 85-86;
Broyles, The John Birch Society, p. 119.

Christian Economics endorsed "A McGuffey Reader in Every School" Christian Economics, (February 20, 1962), p. 1.

65. James Burnham, Suicide of the West (New York: The John Day Company, 1964), p. 286;
Cross and the Flag, (December, 1962), p. 29;
National Review, (January 17, 1959), p. 462.

66. Common Sense, (June 1, 1963), p. 4;
Rockwell Report, (May 15, 1964), p. 6;
Ibid., (January 1, 1963), p. 4.

67. Cross and the Flag, (March, 1963), p. 26;
Human Events, (August 4, 1961), p. 501;
The Defender, (August, 1963), p. 8.

68. Welch, The New Americanism, p. 173;
Rockwell Report, (September 1, 1963), p. 8.

69. Goldwater, Where I Stand, p. 11.

70. Common Sense, (March 15, 1964), p. 1.

71. Cross and the Flag, (June, 1962), p. 6;
Rockwell, This Time the World, p. 260.

CHAPTER FOUR

THE "INTERNATIONAL COMMUNIST CONSPIRACY"

"Our enemy is the International
Communist Conspiracy"

The New Right concluded that the sinister International Communist Conspiracy represented the greatest single threat to the United States. Revilo P. Oliver summed up this consensus when he asserted flatly: "Our enemy is the International Communist Conspiracy." Furthermore, the American people must never forget that the International Communist Conspiracy remains the true adversary: "For our enemy is the Communists," Robert Welch reminded readers in his famous Blue Book of the John Birch Society, "and we do not intend to lose sight of that fact for a minute. We are fighting the Communists-- nobody else."1/

The International Communist Conspiracy assumed many different shapes and forms. Nevertheless, the New Right considered Communism a single entity. Dr. Gerhart Niemeyer, a political science professor at Notre Dame University, decided that "we have only a single enemy. That enemy is not Russia, not China, nor any particular country, but the world enterprise of Communism, which uses these other countries as its power resources, and the base for its military, and political operations." Senator Barry Goldwater agreed: "We are at war with an evil and the evil is communism--all kinds and varieties."2/

The development of various types of nationalistic Communism failed to impress the New Right. Barry Goldwater warned, "The enemy is Communist ideology and power, and must be opposed with a total concept, whether it exists in Yugoslavia, Moscow, East Berlin, or North Vietnam."3/

The New Right recognized the existence of a major schism between Red China and the Soviet Union by the early 1960's. Both superpowers vied for the top position within the International Communist Movement while differing only over the precise timetable and methods of world revolution. Thus "the struggle between Red China and the Soviet Union," in the opinion of The Weekly Crusader, centered not around the basic goals of global conquest but "primarily over techniques and tactics of destroying us."4/

Consequently, the Sino-Soviet split did not diminish the danger of International Communism to the West. Communism, according to America's Future, "is a world-wide conspiracy whose sworn enemy is freedom....This is a fact all communists, regardless of their differences or who runs the parts of their slave empire, never forget."5/

75

The New Right felt that this intense competition between Peking and Moscow made International Communism much more dangerous to the West. As they battled for world Communist hegemony both the Red Chinese and the Soviets devised new programs for infiltration and conquest of the Free World. Kenneth de Courcy pointed out that "since each of the Communist giants is laying claim to the leadership of the world revolution, they will attempt to outdo each other both in outright propaganda and in subtle subversion."6/

Furthermore, the New Right rejected the notion that the United States could capitalize upon the growing Sino-Soviet rift by helping one Commununist power against the other. As Barry Goldwater commented, "the last thing we should do is assist the enemy be sending money, weapons, food, and other goods to Communist nations regardless of whether they have had a falling out with the power clique in the Kremlin."7/

Thus after examining the Sino-Soviet split the New Right concluded that "the conflict between Peking and Moscow will be of little advantage to the West." Both Communist superpowers agreed that the Free World must be destroyed. The Chinese and the Russians simply quarrelled over the best method to subvert and conquer the West. Therefore, as Barry Goldwater noted, "we can take no comfort from their differences." The apparent rift represented a mere tactical dispute between two branches of an international conspiracy totally dedicated to world revolution. Indeed the basic hostility of Communism to the Free World forever precluded the West from exploiting the Sino-Soviet split. Those Americans foolish enough to try suffered from what James Burnham called a "narcotic illusion."8/

"By 1970 the world will be all slave or all free"

The ultimate goal of the International Communist Conspiracy remained nothing short of complete world conquest. Robert Welch stressed that "the objective of these conspirators is to increase their power and extend it downward until the international Communist hierarchy has established a rigid and absolute tyranny over the total population of our planet." Welch outlined "the three-step program laid out by Lenin for the Communist conquest of the world: First, eastern Europe, then the masses of Asia, and last the final bastion of opposition, the United States of America." Former Texas Congressman Martin Dies emphasized that "the Communists are playing for keeps. They intend to conquer the world and they will not settle for anything less than complete conquest." Along the same lines, Dr. Max Rafferty cried out, "A race of faceless, godless peasants from the steppes of Asia strives to reach across our bodies for the prize of world dominion."9/

The well-designed Communist program for absolute global domination unfolded right on schedule. Barry Goldwater asserted that

"Forty years ago a handful of Communists began to implement their plans to destroy the social, economic, and political establishments of the free world." The Arizonan deplored the astonishing success of the enemy: "Today the Communist masters rule a billion people--a third of the world." Texas insurance man W. P. Strube echoed the same admonition: "Communism...is conquering the world in accordance with a definite blueprint and time schedule."10/

Unfortunately, the sands of time had nearly expired for the Free World. The conquest of our planet by the International Communist Conspiracy lay but a few scant years in the future. Robert Welch predicted that "Unless we can reverse forces which now seem inexorable in their movement, you have only a few more years before the country in which you live will become four separate provinces in a world-wide Communist dominion ruled by police-state methods from the Kremlin." He disclosed that "The map for their division and administration is already drawn." Granville F. Knight, M.D. regretted that "There are too many who still laugh at the timetable of Communist world conquest, which has been advanced from 1975 to 1967." Motion picture actor Ronald Reagan pointed out that "one of the foremost authorities on communism in the world today has said, we have 10 years. Not ten years to make up our minds, but ten years to win or lose--by 1970 the world will be all slave or all free."11/

The Communists possessed a wide variety of resources at their disposal in order to implement their diabolical plans for world conquest. The National Review noted that "the communist enterprise... has consolidated as its base the most powerful strategic situation on earth; extended its rule over a billion human beings and a fifth of the world's land surface; neutralized half and infiltrated all of the remainder." Senator Barry Goldwater also examined the assets available to the International Communist Conspiracy:

> ... a military power that rivals our own, political warfare and propaganda skills that are superior to ours, an international fifth column that operates conspiratorially in the heart of our defenses, an ideology that imbues its adherents with a sense of historic mission; and all of these resources controlled by a ruthless despotism that brooks no deviation from the revolutionary course.12/

"The greatest peril that Christian civilization has ever faced"

According to the New Right, Communism represented the greatest threat to Western Christian Civilization since the onset of the Dark Ages. Placing the Communist menace in historical perspective Classics Professor Revilo P. Oliver announced, "This is Chalons or Tours,

77

and the issue, quite simply, is whether the world's most hated minority, the Christian West, shall be forever obliterated by the infinite barbarism of irrational hordes." A Communist victory in the Cold War would plunge the Western world back into the Dark Ages once again. Gerald L. K. Smith elaborated: "Nearly a thousand years elapsed between the fall of Western Rome and the rise of the Renaissance, and in between we had the Dark Ages....I don't want my children's children to go through a couple of centuries of dialectic materialism before the sun comes up again."13/

Thus the International Communist Conspiracy plotted the extermination of Western Civilization. J. Edgar Hoover labelled Communism "a systematic, purposive, and conscious attempt to destroy Western civilization and roll history back to the ages of barbaric cruelty and despotism..." Likewise, Frank S. Meyer saw Communism "as an armed and messianic threat to the very existence of Western civilization..."14/

The specter of the Western world crumbling before the Communist onslaught haunted the New Right. Barry Goldwater wondered, "whether Western civilization is due to survive or will pass away." In the same vein, Nazi leader George Lincoln Rockwell warned that "White, Western, Christian civilization is racing to utter catastrophe in the immediate future."15/

Atheistic Communism posed a grave threat to Christianity as well. Indeed Clarence Manion characterized the International Communist Conspiracy as "the greatest peril that Christian civilization has ever faced." For "the overall plan" of Communism, in the opinion of the Beacon-Light Herald, "is to destroy christian civilization."16/

A world-wide, winner-take-all battle existed between Communism and Christianity. Robert Welch pronounced this contest "a struggle from which either Communism or Christian-style civilization must emerge with one completely triumphant and the other completely destroyed." Charles Kenneth Clinton, President of the American Coalition of Patriotic Societies, claimed, "the future of Christian civilization itself depends upon how clearly we recognize the stark alternatives to victory in this conflict." Likewise, Gerald L. K. Smith emphasized that "The over-all supreme issue in the world today is: The forces of Christian civilization versus the forces opposed to Christian civilization."17/

The New Right frequently associated Communism with the forces of Satan. Cross and the Flag announced that "Christian Civilization is in the process of being crucified, destroyed and disillusioned-not, by accident, but as the purposeful result of a well organized satanic conspiracy." The Reverend Kenneth Goff revealed that "The secret of communism is that it is the religion of Satan and receives its power from

78

Lucifer himself." The Reverend Billy James Hargis exhorted his disciples to "choose Christ, for Christ loves America. Communism, which is of Satan hates America."18/

The clash between Christianity and Communism assumed epic proportions. Robert Welch described this contest as "a world-wide battle, the first in history, between light and darkness; between freedom and slavery; between the spirit of Christianity and the spirit of anti-Christ for the souls and bodies of men." In the same manner, Clarence Manion viewed the struggle as an "all-out, full dress, winner-take-all confrontation between spirit and matter, good and evil, God and anti-God..."19/

Many members of the New Right clearly enjoyed participating in this grand battle on behalf of Western Civilization and Christianity since the struggle gave a sense of drama and mission to their lives by casting them as important actors upon the stage of history.

> "The inclination of the Left at its deepest
> levels is to destroy, to overturn
> civilization and morality"

The New Right believed that Communism represented the most ghastly form of social organization ever devised by man. Robert Welch remarked that "For the first time in all history...we have the forces of evil openly and brazenly setting up their precepts and values and codes as the acceptable and preferable mores of mankind." Ezra Taft Benson declared that America's fight against "godless Communism" was "a fight against slavery, immorality, atheism, cruelty, barbarism, deceit, and the destruction of human life through a kind of tyranny unsurpassed by anything in human history."20/*

The New Right never considered Communism as simply an alternative social system. Senator Barry Goldwater cautioned that "We must not think of the international Communist conspiracy as a 'system' that merely sees things differently from us." Kenneth Goff agreed: "To understand Communism you must realize it is not a political party or an economic order..."21/

---

*Note--The American Radical Right has traditionally looked upon Left-wing Communism as a much worse social system than Right-wing Fascism. Thus although Radical Rightists, on the whole, have despised Fascism, when forced to choose between the lesser of two evils (as during the Spanish Civil War--1936-1939) they invariably selected Fascism over Communism. As Alabama Governor George Wallace explained, "I'd rather be a Fascist than a Communist. At least a Fascist believes in God !" New York Times Magazine (April 24, 1966), p. 94.

Rather than a legitimate social system, Communism resembled a fatal disease infecting the entire world. Barry Goldwater called Communism "a disease attacking and eating away at human society and human freedom." Karl Baarslag referred to Communism as "the new Black Plague of human intellect," while Timothy McInerny suggested that Communism "Like a disease...must eventually be killed or it will kill the human race." New Rightists also advocated placing a strict "quarantine" around subversive Communist regimes and described how Communism spreads like a contagion by infecting its victims after a brief exposure.22/

As the Communists achieve their ends they deliberately destroy civilization and morality in the process. Revilo P. Oliver pointed out that "The Communist is driven by an insatiable hatred of Western civilization, and of everything that we esteem: truth, honor, decency, mercy, integrity, learning, culture. He is driven by an overwhelming lust to defile and destroy, to desecrate and maim, to torture and kill." Indeed the Richmond News-Leader concluded that "The inclination of the Left at its deepest levels is to destroy, to overturn civilization and morality."23/

Communism perverted man's basic nature in order to gain absolute power. Under the Communist system, as J. Edgar Hoover explained, "Evil is depicted as good, terror as justice, hate as love, and obedience to a foreign master as patriotism." Likewise, Robert Welch discovered in Communism "a conscious, deep-rooted, long range, deliberate, incredibly determined and diabolically cunning attempt to have the evil in man's nature become revered instead of the good." Welch described how...

The Communists have been striving for the past fifty years to destroy, utterly and permanently, the three basic human loyalties. These are loyalty to God, loyalty to country, and loyalty to family. They simply must do so in order to become and remain victorious, for no permanent and completely totalitarian regime could possible permit any loyalty other than to itself.24/

"The real danger is not Russian rockets but internal Communist subversion..."

While the Communists intended to conquer the Free World they discovered that internal subversive activities are much more subtle and effective than purely military tactics. Robert Welch pointed out that "the history of the Soviet Union is not military aggression but safer, surer conquest by internal subversion," and, therefore, "The real danger is not Russian rockets but internal Communist subversion heading towards Communism."25/

Thus while the Soviet Union rarely employs overt military force anymore, this hardly signals an abandonment of its ultimate goal of destroying the West. Irene Corbally Kuhn writing in Christian Economics noted that "world domination...is the ultimate objective of Soviet policy. It always has been. It has never changed and it never will..." In the same vein, Ezra Taft Benson found "no real evidence" that the fundamental Communist aim of complete world conquest "has changed in the last forty years."26/

Hence the New Right rejected the idea that the Soviet Union "mellowed" as time passed. Irene Corbally Kuhn strongly emphasized that "As time goes on it becomes clearer that instead of mellowing the USSR is getting tougher." In response to the question, "Is the Soviet Union Mellowing?" the Economic Council Letter answered, "Anyone who really observes the Soviet state today cannot rest in the hope that it is mellowing. It has merely replaced force with guile."27/

The Communists wage a relentless campaign of psychological warfare against the West with great success. According to South Carolina Senator J. Strom Thurmond, "World communism has made its biggest gains through use of the powerful art of psychological warfare and propaganda." The Weekly Crusader agreed: "The communist conspirators are already at war with us even though the major battlefield is in the area of psychological or political warfare." While "it is an undeclared war," nevertheless, "psychological war is still war, even though bullets and bombs are not killing large numbers of Americans."28/

However, the tactics of internal subversion and gradual infiltration remained the most potent weapons in the Communist arsenal. An alarmed August W. Brustat wondered, "When before in human history has a would-be conqueror succeeded in organizing fifth columns, schooled in termite tactics, on every continent and in every country of the globe?" Indeed the Communists certainly knew how to infiltrate and sabotage their adversaries. Eventually their enemies lost the ability and the will to resist. Entire nations fell to the Communists with surprising ease.29/

"A patient gradualism," in the estimation of Robert Welch, "has been the most important key to the Communists' overwhelming success." At a slow, nearly imperceptible pace, the Communists and their American allies have sought "to erode the foundations of our Republic." News and Views noted:

> For more than 40 years, these totalitarian termites have been gnawing at the foundations of our Republic with little or no opposition from the great mass of U.S. citizens. Very carefully, with great cunning and

patience, these enemies infiltrated our churches, government, schools, and mass communications media.30/

Worst of all, the bulk of the American people seemed completely oblivious to the danger. "Communism is winning World War III without firing a single shot or losing a single soldier," Billy James Hargis exclaimed, "And the apathy and lethargy of God's people are responsible." Likewise, James H. Jauncey warned that "This world could enter the greatest dark ages...because of the complacency of its citizens..."31/

"Communism ceaselessly pursues the disintegration of the American way of life"

The International Communist Conspiracy had skillfully undermined nearly every vital aspect of American life. California Congressman John H. Rousselot warned that the Communists "work to infiltrate our churches, to disarm us spiritually, to destroy our system of government, to destroy our currency and to downgrade our ability to remain a stable, financially sound nation." According to J. Edgar Hoover, the Communists have "infiltrated every conceivable sphere of activity; youth groups, radio, television and motion picture industries; church, school and educational groups; the press, nationality minority groups and political units."32/*

The International Communist Conspiracy considered the youth of America a prime target. Therefore, disruption of the nation's educational system received the highest priority. Raleigh, North Carolina TV commentator Jesse Helms, a future United States Senator, announced that the Communists "seek to destroy freedom...through poisoning the intellectual climate and the educational system." Billy James Hargis outlined how "A California school girl, for example, received an 'A' for an essay suggesting that America surrender to the Kremlin." The enemy subtly brainwashed high school and college students, yet, as Hargis pointed out, "the Communist strategy goes much deeper than that--even into the kindergarden of the American public schools."33/

In addition to education, the International Communist Conspiracy used rock music to subvert America's youth. As Report to America disclosed, "Music especially, which so directly affects the habits and attitudes of the young, is a prime target for those who would confuse

---

*Note--Catholic members of the New Right viewed the Communist threat primarily on the international level while Protestants focused most of their attention upon the domestic dangers of Communism. (See Chapter One)

and weaken a nation as a preliminary to its conquest." The Weekly Crusader spoke out against the Communist plan to use rock music "to render a generation of American youth mentally sick and emotionally unstable." In a pamphlet entitled Communism, Hypnotism and the Beatles, Baptist minister David Noebel referred to the popular British rock group as part of "an elaborate, calculating and scientific technique directed at rendering a generation of American youth useless through nerve-jamming, mental deterioration and retardation."34/ (See Chapter Three)

The International Communist Conspiracy utilized folk music in addition to rock and roll in order to subvert America's children. In the opinion of The Weekly Crusader, Leftist folk singers "promote ideas tearing down the American way of life, and as always, it is done in a clever, subtle manner. The communists realize that music is a very effective weapon in helping to mold people's thinking." Music critic Jere Real cautioned that "the seemingly innocent revolution in popular music-from rock 'n roll to folk music--is most assuredly replete with political overtones." He emphasized that "the established Soviet line inserted into currently-popular folk music is designed to develop the following themes...

1) need for Peace, ban the bomb
2) civil rights
3) anti-capitalism
4) criticism of patriotic organizations
5) criticisms of contemporary American culture

Jere Real concluded: "No one who has been subjected to the performance of more than ten minutes of the contemporary folk music can fail to recognize the amazing extent to which the Reds now infect such music with the above ploys."35/

Pornography played a major role in the Communist program of preparing the United States for eventual conquest. Headlines in Common Sense read "Our Youth at Mercy of Fiends--Filthy Literature Breaking Down Youth for Communism." Kenneth de Courcy observed that "Key agents" of the International Communist Conspiracy "are placed in the publishing world to help to spread books and literature encouraging the breakdown of what are said to be 'social inhibitions.' This is a planned operation." This moral degeneration inevitably reduced a nation's ability to resist a Communist takeover. As Robert Welch remarked, "The Communists are able to use this lack of moral stamina among their enemies in a thousand ways to make their own progress easier and the conquest of those enemies more rapid."36/

The New Right cried out with alarm that the Communists had even infiltrated a significant segment of the American religious community. In the estimation of William Kullgren, "The so-called religious world is saturated with anti-Christ elements but carrying a Christian label." Robert Welch, while emphasizing that "the largest single body of Communists in America is in our Protestant clergy," stressed that the Reds "infiltrate the clergy of various denominations." Welch explained that even though the Communists intend to destroy all religions once they have seized power, in the meantime "they make as much use as they can of the organizational structure of religious bodies as a means of reaching large numbers of good men and women with subtle propaganda most favorably presented."37/

The Communists hoped to sap the strength of the American people by tampering with the public drinking water system. Indeed J. Edgar Hoover felt compelled to alert the nation against the "poisoning of water supplies." Moreover, Revilo P. Oliver disclosed that powerful drugs "if introduced into the drinking water, could convert the whole urban population of the United States into...docile and almost mindless zombies..." Oliver discussed new experimental, mind-altering chemicals such as LSD which if "thrown into one of the reservoirs that supply water to New York City would suffice to reduce the entire population of the city to a temporary insanity in which they would be incapable of resisting a Bolshevik or other takeover."38/

The New Right also denounced the fluoridation of public drinking water. According to the Reverend Lyle F. Sheen, "Adoption of fluoridation by any community would provide our enemies with a perfect weapon. A turn of a valve, and the city is at their mercy." Common Sense editor Conde McGinley called fluoridation "one of the most dangerous and diabolical methods of the enemy. They weaken our will to resist through the medication of our water." The deleterious effects of fluoridation even surfaced in the nation's capital itself: "Washington, D.C. has fluoridated water," Conde McGinley pointed out, "Is this what is wrong with our Congressmen?" he wondered.39/

The International Communist Conspiracy used both psychiatry and psychology to subvert the American people. John Stormer in his best selling expose None Dare Call It Treason warned that "Just as in the fields of education, religion, press, radio and TV, the collectivists have succeeded in infiltrating and twisting the honorable psychiatric and psychological profession to their own ends." Indeed the Communists skillfully practiced "psychopolitics"--"a technical term for brainwashing and thought control." Thus the Communists have transformed the government's rapidly expanding mental health programs into powerful vehicles for Communist brainwashing and mind control. The Weekly Crusader observed that "for years the communist conspirators" have advanced "their cause through the new and enlarged concept of mental health."40/*

Government mental institutions became places of horror to the New Right. Revilo P. Oliver lashed out against the United States Department of Health, Education, and Welfare for importing into the country "large numbers of diseased sadists, many of them known agents of the Communist Conspiracy, to staff our mental health institutions..." Moreover, honest American citizens fighting the International Communist Conspiracy (such as Major General Edwin A. Walker--See Chapter Six) found themselves suddenly branded as insane and mysteriously confined to mental health facilities against their will. As Destiny reported, "Men and women have already been railroaded into mental institutions as mentally disturbed or ill in order to silence them."41/

Finally, the Communists strove to undermine America's republican form of government by establishing a popular democracy in its place. The John Birch Society Bulletin explained that a basic change in our structure of government "from a republic, governed by laws, into a democracy, governed by men unchecked by law and precedent, is the most comprehensive and necessary part of the whole program of the Communists to bring us into their imperial system." Barry Goldwater agreed that a transformation in the power and scope of the government would pave the way for a Communist takeover: "We can be conquered by bombs or by subversion; but we can also be conquered by neglect--by ignoring the Constitution and disregarding the principles of limited government."42/

In conclusion, the New Right saw the International Communist Conspiracy as representing the most dangerous adversary that Western, Christian Civilization had ever faced. Driven by the power of Satan, and bent upon crushing all traces of culture and morality, Communism embodied everything brutal and evil. Having already gained control of nearly half the world since 1917, the Communists intended to master the

---

*Note--Since the days of the "WASP Inquisition" (1914-1925) the American Radical Right has accused both psychiatrists and psychologists of condoning free-love and all sorts of criminal behavior by encouraging people to shed their "prudish, old-fashioned" sexual and moral inhibitions. Thus the New Right had long associated psychiatry and psychology with dangerous avant-garde ideas. However, the publicity surrounding the so-called Communist "brainwashing" of U.S. prisoners of war during the Korean Conflict (1950-1953) alerted the Radical Right to the connection between "psychopolitics" and the designs of the International Communist Conspiracy.

globe totally by 1970. The United States, of course, remained the major roadblock. Yet internal Communist subversion gradually weakened the United States. Communist agents had infiltrated schools, churches, the mass communications industry, and the government. The New Right predicted that within a few short years the American people would lose the ability and the will to resist a Communist takeover. And when the United States fell, the entire world would enter the Dark Ages once again.

Socialism

The New Right considered Socialism as nothing more than an unholy ally of International Communism. Francis E. Mahaffy dubbed Socialism "Communism's Winning Weapon." Indeed Socialism frequently came under attack as simply a rest stop along the highway leading to Communist control. Ezra Taft Benson, while labelling "creeping Socialism" as "the Red Carpet" announced, "it is high time that we recognize creeping Socialism for what it really is--a Red Carpet providing a royal road to Communism." Moreover, Socialism resembled Communism in many ways. Professor Anthony Bouscaren observed that under both systems "government becomes the master of the people. Individual and collective freedom and opportunity are eliminated or suppressed and individuals become servants or even slaves to an all powerful governmental bureaucracy."43/

The New Right listed the baneful effects of Socialism. In the estimation of the Report to America, "Socialism kills incentive, stifles initiative, and destroys ambition," and unfortunately, "Socialism drags everybody down to a low level of mediocrity." Christian Economics concurred: "Socialism denies individual responsibility and freedom. It destroys initiative. It stifles free and original thought."44/

However, Socialism remained a very elusive enemy, as the New Right quickly discovered. The Left understood the traditional American antipathy to the word "Socialism." Consequently, the proponents of Socialism use different terms to advance their programs. The Arizona Republic concluded, "Socialists realize that the average person's distaste for socialism--that is, socialism sold under its proper name--is so strong that it is necessary to merchandise Socialist policies under other labels." Fred De Armand agreed: "No political or economic measure offered the people ever bears the honest label 'socialism' or 'socialistic.' Invariably these reforms are disguised in the sheep's clothing of humanitarianism, social justice or some other misleading brand name."45/

According to the New Right, the American Left, by not using the repugnant word "Socialism" to describe its programs, cleverly avoided the stigma which the term evokes. Instead, the Left favored something

86

called the "Welfare State"—an assortment of various government welfare schemes coupled with government supervision and stimulation of the economy. Despite repeated disavowals of any socialistic intent, the Welfare State increases the power and scope of the government enormously. Private property and free enterprise suffocate under the heavy hand of bureaucracy, and over-regulation.

The New Right maintained that by sugar-coating Socialism, the Welfare State made big government seductively attractive to the American people. The New Right noted the effectiveness of this tactic. Barry Goldwater decided that "Socialism-through-Welfarism poses a far greater danger to freedom than Socialism-through-Nationalization precisely because it is more difficult to combat."46/

Thus the expansion of the Welfare State meant increasing socialization and ultimate communization of the United States. Dan Smoot equated "the growth of the welfare state with Socialism and Socialism with Communism." The Weekly Crusader pointed out that "The Communist conspirators consider the welfare state-type of government which we now have as a preliminary step to socialism which is the immediate preceding step to communism." Christian Economics called "Fabian Socialism, alias welfare statism...the peaceful, pleasant road to the death of freedom and totalitarian government."47/

Liberalism

The New Right also believed that a decadent Liberalism infected the entire Western World. This Liberal ideology perverted "our religion, ethics, political and economic thought, and virtually every other aspect of our civilization," and thus represented a grave danger to the West. Frank S. Meyer warned that "the corrosive ideology of American Liberalism...eats away at the foundation values of our civilization and our Republic." Likewise, James Burnham pronounced Liberalism "the ideology of Western suicide."48/

The New Right felt a special obligation to confront and challenge American Liberalism. William F. Buckley, Jr. emphasized that "we must bring down the thing called Liberalism, which is powerful, but decadent; and salvage a thing called conservatism, which is weak but viable." Thus a revitalized American Conservatism clashed with Liberalism in every sphere of American life. As Frank S. Meyer explained, "In every field of national life, from academy and church, television and press, to school district and Congressional District, the battle between Liberalism and conservatism has become the central issue."49/

"Liberalism," in the words of Frank S. Meyer, "weakens the fiber of society..." Thus the New Right linked Liberalism with the breakdown of America's traditional moral values. For instance, Jim Lucier connected sex perversion with "the inner moral degeneracy of the 'Liberal' ideology," while Nazi leader Rockwell noted that "Liberals never tire of belittling our cries of alarm over the deteriorating morals of our times." Along the same lines, Paul Sexson and Stephen Miles, Jr. commented sarcastically that Liberals often lecture the public concerning the question of "rights":

> The right of writers to write whatever they want and readers to read whatever they choose, no matter how pornographic; the right of homosexuals to practice their persuasion; the right of suspected communists and fellow travelers to be immune from 'persecution'; the right of hardened criminals to escape capital punishment; the right of romantically inclined (but not wedded) couples to be furnished with birth control information and aids...the right of mothers to receive aid-for-dependent-children allotments for their illegitimate offspring.50/

The New Right, however, focused the bulk of its attention upon what it considered the two most conspicuous failings of modern American Liberalism. First of all, in domestic affairs Liberalism encouraged the rapidly expanding crime wave which swept across the nation beginning in the early 1960's. Secondly, in the realm of foreign policy Liberalism prevented the United States from effectively confronting the menace of International Communism.

Liberalism and Crime

The Liberal ideology, in the eyes of the New Right, stimulated the rising crime wave of the Sixties, especially juvenile delinquency. The Liberal theories of progressive education discourge strict student discipline while neglecting moral instruction and character building. As a result of this permissive attitude which permeates the schools, the youth gain no respect for authority and often turn to crime. James Burnham contended that "Liberalism even fosters new sorts of crime through its permissive approach to education and discipline..."51/

Furthermore, the "provocative egalitarianism" of Liberalism contributed to the alarming increase in crime. The problem stems from the Liberals' beloved Welfare State, and the progressive tax system used to finance the various social services. In effect, the government assumes the role of a Robin Hood. Money taken from the rich winds up subsidizing the poor. The government itself sets a bad example by confiscating private property from those who own it and then giving it to someone else. Barry Goldwater discussed this dangerous trend at length during his 1964 Presidential campaign. By its redistribution of society's wealth through progressive taxation the government legitimizes the notion that the "have-nots" can take from the "haves". The government simply tempts the poor to turn to crime and help themselves to another man's property whenever they wish.52/ (See Chapter Three)

The New Right held that Liberalism placed sole responsibility for lawless behavior upon society rather than upon the criminal himself. In short, a bad environment created criminals. Frank S. Meyer noted that "The Liberal theory is that criminal violence is the product of 'under-privileged' environments, and that the only thing to do about it is to improve the environment." Another observer commented that "when the criminals are caught" the public is "told that as 'culturally handicapped' victims of white society the criminals had every justification for committing their crimes."53/

On the other hand, the New Right refused to sympathize with the criminal on the grounds that he had a bad childhood or grew up on the wrong side of the tracks. Paul Sexson and Stephen Miles, Jr. pointed out that "the liberal excuses the criminal because of his environment, his parents, his heredity, or just because he 'didn't have a chance.' The Conservative excuses nobody."54/

The New Right strongly believed that crime reflected the failure of the individual rather than the failure of society. An unwholesome environment did not create criminals; in point of fact, criminally inclined citizens create an unwholesome environment. As Dan Smoot explained, "Slums do not breed crime and juvenile delinquency. It is the other way around. People make slums. Slums do not make people." William Henry Chamberlain concurred, "It is not so much slums that make people as people who make slums."55/*

Since crime remained, to the New Right's way of thinking, an individual rather than a social problem, the Liberals' elaborate welfare programs could never halt the spreading lawlessness. The real solution to crime, in the New Right's eyes, included improved personal morality coupled with more respect for authority. Increasing the welfare handouts, as the New Right explained, would never work. During his Prescott, Arizona speech kicking-off his Presidential campaign Barry Goldwater maintained that "on our streets we see the final, terrible

---

*Note--The New Right continued this line of reasoning as they strongly opposed gun control legislation: "Guns don't kill people; people kill people." Yet the New Right abruptly reversed its position when demanding a crackdown against drugs, gambling, or pornography. Logically, all true-blue New Rightists should have uttered slogans like, "Pornographic books don't commit sex crimes; people commit sex crimes." However, the New Right saw no need for perfect philosophical consistency when dealing with dangerous vices such as drugs, gambling and pornography.

89

proof of a sickness which not all the social theories of a thousand social experiments has ever begun to touch."56/

Liberalism and Communism

According to the New Right, the second great failure of modern American Liberalism occurred in the sphere of foreign affairs. Liberalism has never been able to adequately oppose the menace of International Communism. As Ohio Congressman John M. Ashbrook stated:

> Surely, world Communism of today must stand as a monument to the ineptness and the color-blindness of the so-called Liberals who nurtured its growth, winked at its steady parade of crimes and atrocities, bristle at the thought of defeating it and attack those of us who point out its evil and monstrous design. On the issue of Communism alone, Liberalism has failed so significantly that it should be soundly defeated wherever it now prevails.57/

America's foreign policy under Liberal stewardship, in the eyes of the New Right, has been a total disaster. William F. Buckley, Jr. complained that our statesmen "drink deeply in liberalism, and Liberalism makes for the worst and most ineffective foreign policy in the history of diplomacy." M. Stanton Evans added that "Liberalism has given us a foreign policy whose major achievements have been the liquidation of Western hegemony in every quarter of the globe, the transfer of one billion people from the Western World to the armed camp of Communism, and the establishment of a Communist beachhead 90 miles from American shores."58/

The Liberal mind could never grasp the true dangers of International Communism. Frank S. Meyer called "This incapacity of the Liberal mind to understand Communism in its full horror...the essential tragic cause of the devastating retreat of the United States and the West before Communism." M. Stanton Evans denounced "the chronic inabilty of the Liberal to perceive the nature of the world we live in and" to parry "the thrust of Communist aggression." Likewise, The Weekly Crusader condemned "the left-wing liberals who continue to flounder hopelessly in a never, never land where the reality of communism is never faced..."59/

This problem, the New Right maintained, stems from the basic fact that Liberalism and Communism are both ideologies of the Left. Consequently, the Liberal cannot comprehend the dangers of Communism because the Left traditionally looks upon the Right as the true enemy. James Burnham emphasized that "The challenge of communism is from the Left" but "Liberalism can function effectively

90

only against the Right." The Liberal steadfastly refuses to classify Communism, an evil Left-wing extremism, in the same category as Nazism, an evil Right-wing extremism. The Liberal mind clearly understood the utter depravity of Nazism but seemed oblivious to the shortcomings of Communism. According to Frank S. Meyer, the Liberals "simply do not feel about Communism, as they did about Nazism, that this is an enemy so thoroughly alien and so threatening to Western civilization that it must be defeated if freedom and truth are to survive."60/

The Liberals hate everything even remotely connected with Nazism. But at the same time, Liberalism desperately searched for some redeeming qualities in Communism. As James T. Hunter explained, "Liberals have struggled mightily to find some 'good' in Communism."61/

Both Liberal and Communist alike share a common vision of the world turned into Utopia. This dream of a carefully planned, perfectly constructed society infects all ideologies of the Left. On the one hand, the Liberal builds his Utopia one brick at a time gently nudging all obstacles out of the way. On the other hand, the Communist boldly utilizes the awesome power of the state to ruthlessly crush all opposition and simply rams his version of Utopia down the people's throat. While the Liberal may dislike the rough-and-tumble tactics employed by the Communists, he invariably overlooks the brutalities and the atrocities. Indeed, the more impatient Liberals even secretly admire the brazen Communist for his daring and his vigor.

Both Liberalism and Communism sought to use government as an instrument to turn the earth into a paradise. Well-designed social engineering would tame the ravages of nature, make the deserts bloom, end poverty and disease, provide abundance for all, and insure equality and justice for every citizen. Therefore, the Liberal agreed with the ultimate goals (if not with the tactics) of Communism. As E. Merrill Root pointed out, the Liberals' "subconscious premise is: 'How can those whose desire is to make government serve man...(just as we do !) be really bad?"62/

In addition, the Liberals' warm feelings toward Communism spilled over into the conduct of foreign policy. The Liberals always disregards the aggressive nature of International Communism. Instead, he bends over backwards to accommodate America's enemy in the interests of world peace. M. Stanton Evans asserted that...

> The Liberal believes Communists are at bottom
> not too different from ourselves, and that the Cold War is
> the result of misunderstanding. If the Communists once
> were dangerous (which the Liberal doubts), they are now

91

'mellowing,' and the urgent necessity of the hour is to build bridges of mutual trust and association -- to establish contacts between East and West which will dissipate the misunderstanding and make the outbreak of war less likely.63/

Finally, the New Right found a striking resemblance between Liberalism and Communism. Thurman Sensing remarked that "Modern liberals and socialists deny that there is any similarity between their program and communism; but the objective of communism...is identical with that of modern American liberals and socialists..." E. Merrill Root concurred:

'Liberalism' is itself arbitrary and monolithic and even truculent; but Communism is even more openly and obviously ruthless, militant, total, comprehensive: it forces men to submit -- or else....And its modes and moods and manners, its no-nonsense militancy, its naked will, almost frighten the anemic 'liberal' and make him say, 'Gently please!' Yet the 'liberal' shares the goals and meaning of Communism.64/

In conclusion, the New Right saw the United States of the 1960's moving swiftly away from its traditional emphasis upon individualism towards collectivist social philosophies based upon big government: Communism, Socialism, and Welfare-State Liberalism. On the one hand, Communism brutally employed the awesome power of the state to crush the individual citizen. On the other hand, the more genteel forms of collectivism (Socialism and Welfare-State Liberalism) attained their goals under the guise of "humanitarianism," "social engineering," or "social reform." Yet the New Right felt instinctively that all forms of collectivism, no matter how mild, ultimately elevated the state while dehumanizing the individual. Thus until America finally renounced all types of collectivism the future of the Republic remained in grave danger.

1. American Opinion, (February, 1964), p. 69;
Welch, The Blue Book of the John Birch Society, p. 4.

2. Manion Forum Network broadcast (December 29, 1963);
Goldwater, Why Not Victory?, p. 172.

Robert Welch emphasized the basic unity of the International
Communist Conspiracy despite its various manifestations: "Communism
is not a political party, nor a military organization, nor an ideological
crusade, nor a rebirth of Russian imperialist ambition, though it
comprises and uses all of these parts and pretenses." In reality,
Communism was "a gigantic conspiracy to enslave mankind..." Welch,
The Blue Book of the John Birch Society, p. 26.

3. Goldwater, Why Not Victory?, pp. 172-173.

4. The Weekly Crusader, (January 17, 1964), p. 1.

5. America's Future, (December 7, 1962), p. 2.

Barry Goldwater agreed:

Inner differences between the parts of Communism do not
remove the threat of any of them to non-Communist nations, so
long as the overthrow of the present society remains their
common goal. The antagonism between the Soviets and Red
China is not based on any difference in ideas to their enemy (the
non-Communist nations, particularly the United States) and his
assigned fate (destruction of his society). Goldwater, Where I
Stand, p. 52.

6. Destiny, (October, 1963), p. 209.

7. Goldwater, Why Not Victory?, p. 173.

8. Kenneth de Courcy in Destiny, (October, 1963), p. 209;
Goldwater, Where I Stand, p. 52;
National Review, (February 23, 1965), p. 146.

9. Welch, The New Americanism, p. 179;
American Opinion, (April, 1958), p. 19;
Martin Dies, Martin Dies' Story (New York: Bookmailer, Inc., 1963), p.
205;
Max Rafferty, Suffer Little Children (New York: The Devin-Adair
Company, 1962), Foreword.

South Carolina Senator J. Strom Thurmond pictured the aim of Communism as "domination of the world under a totalitarian rule." Human Events, (January 27, 1962), p. 68.

10. Goldwater, Why Not Victory?, p. 26;
W.P. Strube, Communism-A Conspiracy (Houston, Texas, 1960), pp. 2-3.

11. Welch, The Blue Book of the John Birch Society, p. 9;
American Mercury, (September, 1961), p. 25;
Human Events, (July 21, 1961), p. 460.

12. "Bear and Dragon," Supplement to the National Review, (November 5, 1960), p. S-5;
Goldwater, The Conscience of a Conservative, p. 88.

13. American Opinion, (February, 1964), p. 78;
Cross and the Flag, (September, 1962), p. 3.

14. J. Edgar Hoover, Masters of Deceit (New York: Henry, Holt and Company, 1958), p. 319;
Frank S. Meyer, "Conservatism" ed. Robert A. Goldwin, Left, Right and Center (Chicago: Rand McNally & Company, 1965), p. 8.

15. Goldwater, The Conscience of a Conservative, p. 78;
Rockwell Report, (December, 1962), p. 4.

16. Manion Forum Network broadcast (December 23, 1962);
Beacon-Light Herald, (September 1960), p. 26.

17. Robert Welch, The Life of John Birch (Chicago: Henry Regnery Company, 1954) p. 76;
Report to America, (April 1964), p. 1;
Cross and the Flag, (June, 1962), p. 2.

18. Cross and the Flag, (May, 1963), p. 4;
Beacon-Light Herald, (October-November, 1962), p. 73;
Hargis, Communist America--Must It Be?, p. 171.

19. Welch, The Blue Book of the John Birch Society, p. 32;
Manion Forum Network broadcast (December 23, 1962).

20. Welch, The New Americanism, pp. 62-63;
Benson, The Red Carpet, p. 16.

21. Goldwater, Why Not Victory?, pp. 170-171;
Beacon-Light Herald, (October-November, 1962), p. 73.

94

22. Goldwater, Why Not Victory?, p. 171;
News and Views, (January, 1963), p. 1;
McInerny, The Private Man, p. 57.

23. American Mercury, (February, 1961), p. 7;
Richmond News-Leader, November 25, 1963.

24. Hoover, Masters of Deceit, p. 319;
Welch, The New Americanism, p. 63;
Ibid., p. 144.

25. American Opinion, (April, 1958).

26. Christian Economics, (April 6, 1965), p. 1;
Benson, The Red Carpet, p. 26.

27. Christian Economics (April 6, 1965), p. 1;
Economic Council Letter, (March 15, 1964), p. 2.

28. Human Events, (January 27, 1962), p. 68;
The Weekly Crusader, (June 28, 1963), p. 6;
Ibid., (March 19, 1965), p. 3;
Ibid., (April 24, 1964), p. 8.

29. American Mercury, (January, 1961), p. 94.

30. Welch, The Blue Book of the John Birch Society, p. 12;
News and Views, (September, 1963), p. 1.

31. Hargis, Communist America—Must It Be?, p. VII, p. 10;
American Mercury, (January, 1961), p. 7.

Robert Welch sensed the tragedy of the situation:

> If we do not wake up to the real facts fast, and wake up
> enough of our fellow citizens, it will be our children and
> ourselves living as enslaved subjects of the Kremlin--possibly
> within five years, and certainly within ten to fifteen years at
> the very most. Welch asked sarcastically, "Are we going to let
> our country and our whole civilization go under, and new 'Dark
> Ages' of serfdom be ushered in, while we happily play at our
> little games? Robert Welch, The Politician 5th ed. (Belmont,
> Massachusetts: Belmont Publishing Company, 1964), p. 300;
> Welch, The Blue Book of the John Birch Society, p. 32.

32. Manion Forum Network broadcast (October 21, 1962); Human Events, (July 21, 1961), p. 462.

Likewise, Lawrence Sullivan listed Communist penetration "in government, in education, in labor, in the Red-fringe clergy, in movies, radio and TV, in books and book clubs, newspapers, magazines, and all the Communist-front leagues of art critics and lecture forums." Christian Economics, (February 6, 1962), p. 3.

33. Human Events, (May 4, 1963), p. 77; Hargis, Communist America--Must It Be?, p. 61; Ibid., p. 55.

34. Report to America, (February, 1964), p. 6; The Weekly Crusader, (February 26, 1965), p. 5; David A. Noebel, Communism, Hypnotism and the Beatles (Tulsa, Oklahoma: Christian Crusade Publications, 1965), p. 1.

35. The Weekly Crusader, (March 26, 1965), p. 5; American Opinion, (December, 1964), pp. 19-20.

36. Common Sense, (December 25, 1963), p. 1; John Birch Society Bulletin, (September, 1961), p. 1; Welch The Blue Book of the John Birch Society, p. 52.

37. Beacon-Light Herald, (October, 1960), p. 4; Welch, The New Americanism, p. 79; Ibid., p. 144.

38. American Mercury, (February, 1961), p. 24; Beacon-Light Herald, (February-March, 1962), p. 13; American Opinion, (November, 1964), p. 31.

39. Beacon-Light Herald, (February-March, 1962), p. 13; Common Sense, (October 1, 1958), p. 3.

40. Stormer, None Dare Call It Treason, p. 155; Earl Livery, Jr. in the American Mercury, (August, 1961), p. 6; The Weekly Crusader, (October 25, 1963), p. 4.

41. American Opinion, (December, 1962), p. 31; Destiny, (September, 1962), p. 190.

42. John Birch Society Bulletin, (January, 1961), p. 6; Goldwater, The Conscience of a Conservative, p. 22.

43. Christian Economics, (January 9, 1962), p. 1; Benson, The Red Carpet, p. 65; Human Events, (December 8, 1962), p. 946.

44. Report to America, (January, 1964), p. 1;
Christian Economics, (March 6, 1962), p. 3.

45. Human Events, (January 9, 1965), p. 10;
Ibid., (April 27, 1963), p. 59.

46. Goldwater, The Conscience of a Conservative, p. 72.

47. Daniel Bell, ed., The Radical Right, p. 12;
The Weekly Crusader, (April 17, 1964), p. 6;
Christian Economics, (May 15, 1962), p. 2.

48. Hans Sennholz in American Opinion, (September, 1964), p. 58;
National Review, (April 10, 1962), p. 244;
Burnham, Suicide of the West, p. 35.

49. Buckley, Up From Liberalism, p. XVI;
National Review, (November 5, 1963), p. 386.

50. National Review, (May 6, 1961), p. 281;
American Opinion, (January, 1965), p. 23;
Rockwell Report, (May 15, 1964), p. 6;
Sexson and Miles, The Challenge of Conservatism, p. 106.

51. Burnham, Suicide of the West, p. 279.

52. Ibid.;
New York Times, September 11, 1964.

53. National Review, (May 17, 1966), p. 471;
John Wyndham in the National Review, (June 17, 1961), p. 375.

Likewise, the ultra racist George Lincoln Rockwell remarked:

In this society, which attempts to equate savage, stupid
cannibals with decent white men, nigger sex-killers, bandits and
robbers are always portrayed as innocent and misunderstood
souls, the victims of 'discrimination' and 'lack of
opportunity'...murderers and felons are treated with kid gloves
out of 'humanitarianism.' Rockwell Report, (September 1, 1963),
p. 8.

54. Sexson and Miles, The Challenge of Conservatism, p. 143.

55. Dan Smoot Report, (February 4, 1963), p. 38;
Human Events, (January 16, 1965), p. 8.

56. New York Times, September 4, 1964.

57. Manion Forum Network broadcast as quoted in the Beacon-Light Herald, (April-May, 1962), p. 24.

58. William F. Buckley, Jr., The Jeweler's Eye (New York: G.P. Putnam's Sons, 1968), p. 61;
M. Stanton Evans, The Politics of Surrender (New York: The Devin-Adair Company, 1966), p. 531.

59. National Review, (February 27, 1962), p. 131;
Evans, The Politics of Surrender, p. 521;
The Weekly Crusader, (June 28, 1963), pp. 5-6.

60. Burnham, Suicide of the West, p. 289;
National Review, (February 27, 1962), p. 126.

61. Hunter, Our Second Revolution, p. 31.

62. News, and Views, (September, 1964), p. 5.

63. Evans, The Politics of Surrender, p. 16.

64. Thurman Sensing, The Case Against the Welfare State (Nashville, Tennessee: n.d.), p. 3;
News and Views, (September 1964), p. 5.

CHAPTER FIVE

"OTHER ENEMIES OF THE REPUBLIC"

In the view of the New Right, the International Communist Conspiracy, along with its Socialist and Liberal allies on the Left, represented, without question, the greatest threat to the well-being of the United States. Yet the New Right believed that a host of other sinister forces gnawed away at the American Republic including the Intellectuals, the United States Supreme Court, and to a minor extent the Jews.1/

Intellectuals

A strain of anti-intellectualism surfaced within the New Right. For the lessons of history demonstrated to their satisfaction that intellectuals had contributed to the downfall of past civilizations. Karl Baarslag challenged the public to "Read any good history of Rome or Byzantium and you will learn that decadence first set in among the intellectuals." Then the decadence "spread like a subtle cancer to the economic and political organs of society, and finally from them to the military, which meant 'finis.' " The New Right also linked the intellectuals with the modern day degeneracy of International Communism. Richard M. Weaver disclosed that "today it is a notorious fact that intellectuals have been exceedingly active in the greatest subversive movement in history, whereby a doctrinaire Communism seeks to overthrow an order which has been the very basis of Western civilization."2/

The New Right's anti-intellectualism also grew out of rural America's traditional distrust of bureaucratic experts, specialists and technocrats, university professors and educated city dwellers in general. This phenomenon has been superbly documented by the late Professor Richard Hofstadter in his brilliant book, Anti-Intellectualism in American Life. The New Right of the 1960's did retain a definite anti-urban flavor coupled with a strong skepticism of most intellectuals.3/

However, the basic thrust of the New Right's attack centered not so much against intellectualism in general, but rather against Left-wing intellectuals in particular. For in the view of the New Right, Leftist intellectuals frequently endorsed unrealistic Utopian schemes, overemphasized theory at the expense of practical considerations, lacked any experience in the real world, relied too much on book knowledge, and failed to use simple common sense. Terms describing Left-wing intellectuals included "do-gooder," "dreamer," "fuzzy-headed," "impractical," and "Utopian."

Conversely, the New Right proudly paraded its own intellectuals in full public view. The National Review magazine served as the focal point for a sort of "Brain Trust" with men like William F. Buckley, Jr., L. Brent Bozell, James Burnham, and Frank S. Meyer producing a steady stream of books and articles reflecting the New Right perspective on a wide range of subjects. This National Review "Brain Trust" even found time to ghost write for Arizona Senator Barry M. Goldwater.4/

A rival intellectual crowd formed around the John Birch Society and its publication American Opinion. Robert Welch, the founder and inspirational leader of the John Birch Society, assembled an intellectual cadre composed of Taylor Caldwell, Revilo P. Oliver, and E. Merrill Root, among others.

In fact, many members of the New Right genuinely enjoyed the stimulating clash of ideas. The writings and speeches of the New Right aimed clearly at the public's head and rarely resorted to crude demagogic appeals to people's emotions. Furthermore, publications contained copious footnotes as if to underscore the New Right's careful devotion to meticulous scholarship. In the words of Richard Hofstadter, "The entire right-wing movement of our time is a parade of experts, study groups, monographs, footnotes, and bibliographies."5/

Yet critics labelled the New Right's "Brain Trusters" as "pseudo-intellectuals" and described their vaunted work as "mediocre," "superficial," or "extremely one-sided." Critics charged that the New Right often relied upon disreputable or outdated sources of information. In addition, many so-called New Right "experts" and "professors" were branded as "sophists" or "quacks."* Thus according to its enemies, the New Right's much heralded claim to impartial scholarship dissolves under closer scrutiny.

These critics make a number of telling points against the New Right. A pathetic simplicity runs through most New Right minds. Reared on a bland intellectual diet of homespun nostrums and corny, common-sense cliches, heavy doses of Bible reading, and taught to trust in the power of blind faith, New Rightists saw the world completely in terms of good or evil--right or wrong. The New Right mind categorically rejected all shades of gray, could not tolerate any ambiguity, nor fathom a complex answer to a difficult problem.

New Right thought exhibits an appalling ignorance of modern intellectual trends. Of course, this does not automatically discredit their positions on such issues as criminal justice, economics, or

---

*Note--Speaking of quacks, an inordinate number of New Rightists posing as "medical doctors" turn out to be chiropractors.

100

education. However, their unfamiliarity with recent intellectual developments leaves the New Right poorly informed on nearly every subject and wide open to the charge that they have failed to come to grips with the twentieth century.

For instance, although they often drew lessons from ancient history, the New Right does not seem to be acquainted (either personally or more likely second handed) with anything published more recently than Gibbon's Decline and Fall of the Roman Empire (1787).* To understand the nature of contemporary International Communism, the New Right ransacked the dusty texts of Marx and Lenin for clues. Their economic thought reflects pure nineteenth century American-style Laissez Faire. Ideas on warfare stem from a gross misreading of Clausewitz. Attitudes concerning the non-Western world sustain the old "White Man's Burden" complex. Education remains locked in the McGuffey Reader--"little red schoolhouse" mentality. F.B.I. Director J. Edgar Hoover reigns as the ultimate authority on all matters of criminal justice. Finally, when every other source fails, the New Right quotes Dale Carnegie, the Reader's Digest, or the Holy Bible.

United States Supreme Court

The New Right held the United States Supreme Court more responsible than any other single branch of government for the breakdown of the American way of life. The Reverend Billy James Hargis called the High Tribunal, "A Supreme Court Against America," while author Rosalie M. Gordon likewise assailed the Court as "Nine Men Against America." Moreover, the New Right denounced the various Left-wing ideologies infecting the Supreme Court's judicial philosophy, and often branded the Court as "Pro-Communist," "Socialistic," or as Rosalie M. Gordon so quaintly described it: a bunch of "left-leaning pincos."6/

The New Right heaped its greatest scorn upon the "ultra Leftist" Chief Justice Earl Warren. Barry Goldwater blasted the Chief Justice as "an out and out socialist." Earl Warren, the New Right also complained, had always taken orders directly from the Eastern Liberal Establishment. In particular, back in 1952 while serving as the Republican Governor of California, Warren had helped steal the G.O.P. Presidential nomination from Ohio Senator Robert Taft. As a reward for his assistance to the victorious Eisenhower forces, Governor Warren

---

*Note--Indeed, former University of Southern California Political Science Professor Michael Ban remarked to me in passing that the New Right got its views on ancient Rome "from watching old Cecil B. De Mille movies on television."

supposedly received the appointment to the vacant Chief Justiceship the following year. And, of course, anyone even remotely connected with the infamous "Texas Steal" of 1952 earned the undying enmity of the New Right.7/

Thus the New Right felt no qualms about removing the errant Chief Justice for his assorted Left-wing transgressions. Robert Welch led the chorus: "So Let's Impeach Earl Warren," and so his John Birch Society moved into high gear. A nationwide campaign featured outdoor billboards, automobile bumper-stickers, along with a student essay contest on the topic of exactly "Why Earl Warren Should Be Impeached."8/

A long series of controversial Supreme Court decisions infuriated the New Right. The Warren Court's rulings on the questions of search and seizure, right to counsel, and coerced confessions hampered the police and placed many violent criminals back upon the streets on "idiotic" legal technicalities. The landmark reapportionment cases ordering state legislatures and the Federal House of Representatives to adopt the principle of "one-man, one-vote" removed the last rural restraints upon unchecked urban political power. In addition, the High Court frequently failed to uphold convictions of Communists, anarchists, and other social agitators.

Yet three types of decisions aroused the most anger from the ranks of the New Right. These cases dealt with public school integration, religious prayers in the public schools, and pornography.

Even by the early 1960's the New Right had neither forgotten nor forgiven the 1954 Brown v. Board of Education ruling outlawing racial segregation in the public schools. This decision abruptly shattered the racial peace of the nation "with the ultimate purpose...of fomenting civil war in this country," as Robert Welch remarked. Texan Morris A. Bealle announced that what Chief Justice Earl Warren accomplished "will take a century for the nation to recover from. Not only is Segregation of the races the law as well as the fact in the South, it is the fact in the North, East and West. Bealle pointed out that in New York City, "the Negroes segregate themselves and enforce their edict with switch blade knives."9/

Another unpopular Warren Court ruling outlawed prayer in public schools. Gerald L. K. Smith labelled the 1962 School Prayer case (Engle v. Vitale) as "The New Crucifixion." David O. McKay, President of the Mormon Church, predicted that this decision would lead "the nation down the road to atheism." The Supreme Court had struck down school prayer at a particularly inappropriate moment in our nation's history. With moral standards crumbling and with crime and sexual degeneracy spreading, America's youth needed religious instruction in school more than ever before. As G.O.P. Presidential nominee Barry Goldwater asked during his 1964 campaign, "is this the time in our nation's history for our Federal Government to ban Almighty God from our school rooms?"10/

The educational system recoiled from what Report to America called the "assaults upon religion in the public schools." Indeed the Supreme Court's School Prayer ruling made it impossible to instill good moral values into the youth of America. The Defender warned that juvenile delinquency and teenage immorality would spread:

> The juvenile delinquency problem has well-nigh terrorized us and many cannot understand this lawlessness among the youth of the land. But is it to be wondered at when we have robbed them of the only Book which holds before them the standards of right living and which reminds them of their accountability to God?11/

Moreover, the Supreme Court's ruling had struck a devastating blow against Christianity itself. An editorial in the Garden Grove, California News stressed that "religious freedom does not mean we ought to repudiate the Christian faith which gave birth to America ! Religious freedom does not mean we must apologize for being a Christian nation -- and forget our Christian heritage." In the same spirit, Robert L. Sonfield, President General of the Sons of the American Revolution wrote, "Our forefathers were Christians. Has it come to pass that we must bow to the will of a mere handful of atheists and permit ourselves to become not only a pagan and unchristian nation, but a Communist welfare state."12/*

The New Right refused to accept passively the hated School Prayer decision. They wanted Chief Justice Earl Warren, seen by many as the major culprit, removed in due course by impeachment. Meanwhile, the New Right would simply disobey the Court's edict. As Alabama Governor George Wallace announced, "We are going to keep on reading the Bible in Alabama - I don't care what the Supreme Court says."13/

As a final incitement to the New Right, the Warren Court seemed to protect and encourage pornography. An angry Gerald L. K. Smith cried out that "The cynical majority in the high court seems to take a sadistic satisfaction in giving the green light to literary filth,

---

*Note--The United States Constitution, which New Rightists openly revered (see Chapter Three), specifically upholds the strict separation of church and state. The New Right skirted this sensitive issue by simply proclaiming "Christianity" in general as the unofficial American state religion.

pornographic journalism and rhetorical vulgarity." The Supreme Court's lenient obscenity decisions placed a dangerous weapon in the hands of the International Communist Conspiracy. Revilo P. Oliver emphasized the importance of "pornographic filth, now officially sanctioned and protected by the Warren Court in the International Communist Conspiracy's over-all strategy for corrupting and stultifying American children by exciting...precocious sexual lusts."14/

The New Right believed that these incomprehensible Warren Court rulings perverted many traditional American values. For instance, Common Sense, which contrasted the School Integration case with the School Prayer case, lamented that "The Supreme Court has placed Negroes in White Schools and Taken God Out." William F. Buckley, Jr. voiced a similar complaint as he compared the School Prayer ruling with the obscenity decisions. Buckley quipped that "Hell" was "the only 4 letter word that nowadays shocks the courts."15/

Jews

Anti-Semitism occasionally surfaced within the ranks of the New Right. This included traditional anti-Semitic themes featuring the Jews as Christ killers, Jews as international money manipulators (the Rothschilds), and Jews as loan sharks (Shylock) and racketeers. New Right anti-Semites also denounced Zionism, connected World Jewry with the International Communist Conspiracy, and blamed the American Jews for encouraging the Blacks to demonstrate and riot for "civil-rights".

The New Right's leading anti-Semites included George Lincoln Rockwell and his revitalized American Nazi Party, the Ku Klux Klan, James Madole's National Renaissance Party, Willis Carto of Liberty Lobby, and a few high ranking U.S. military officers, coupled with a handful of Fundamentalist Christian ministers, most notably Dr. Wesley Swift, and the Reverend Gerald L. K. Smith. The American Mercury, Beacon-Light Herald, Common Sense, and the Cross and the Flag represented the major anti-Semitic publications. Of the various groups composing the New Right, the Protestant Isolationists (especially members of the lower-middle-class "Forgotten Right" reared on the old Middle-Western Populist rhetoric) seemed most disposed to periodic outbursts of anti-Semitism. (See Chapter One)

However, no single individual matched American Nazi leader George Lincoln Rockwell as a hater of the Jews. Rockwell blamed the Jews for the world's problems: "Jewish-Communist-Race-mixing Zionist enemies of all mankind are literally destroying western civilization..." He accused the Jews of fostering "sex perversion" and frequently compared "Judeaized America" with "decaying Rome". Rockwell, who signed his personal correspondence "Heil Hitler," threatened to emulate Adolph Hitler's extermination policy of the Jews if and when he came to

104

power in the United States: "Bye, bye, Jews ! Us Nazis are coming....And the gas smells just as bad !"16/*

Nobody else on the anti-Semitic fringes of the New Right approached Rockwell's loathing of the Jews. Common Sense editor Conde McGinley did speak out concerning "the Communist-Jewish Conspiracy" and held the Jews responsible for America's social ills: "The white-slavery, prostitution, narcotics and liquor rackets are almost completely Jewish controlled." A few other individuals mentioned the link between Communism and Judaism. For example, Rear Admiral John G. Crommelin, Jr. (retired) decided that "The ultimate objective of the Communist-Jewish conspiracy is to use their world-wide control of money to destroy Christianity and set up a world government in the framework of the United Nations."17/

Nevertheless, when considering the New Right in its entirety, anti-Semitism remained a relatively minor issue restricted to a few isolated groups and individuals. As a general observation, most anti-Semites belonged to the older generation within the New Right. Indeed many had participated in anti-Semitic activities stretching back to the 1930's when hatred of the Jews dominated the Great Depression Radical Right.18/ (See Chapter One).

---

*Note--American Liberals simply dismissed George Lincoln Rockwell as a raving lunatic--a typical, Liberal reaction which avoids dealing with the actual substance of the New Right's message by conveniently explaining away the extreme Rightist viewpoint as somehow symptomatic of an underlying personality disorder.

As a matter of fact, when the police, on occasion, arrested Rockwell for disturbing the peace, or for some other minor infraction, he would undergo a thorough psychiatric examination which, to everyone's chagrin, he invariably passed. Consequently, the Nazi leader received a clean bill of mental health.

At any rate, why did this ordinary Taft-MacArthur-McCarthy vintage Republican suddenly convert to so bizarre and universally detested a philosophy as Nazism during the late 1950's? George Lincoln Rockwell's father had successfully performed upon the vaudeville stage for many years. Moreover, Rockwell himself had worked on Madison Avenue as an advertising and public relations executive. The Nazi leader clearly appreciated the values of both showmanship and gimmickry. Thus realizing the fierce competition among the various New Right groups for media attention, Rockwell probably adopted the Nazi image as his gimmick to gain publicity. For a further understanding of George Lincoln Rockwell see his interesting autobiography This Time the World (New York City: Parliament House, 1963).

However, the ugly events of the Second World War firmly associated anti-Semitism with Adolph Hitler's genocide program in the American public's mind. Henceforth, the Radical Right bent over backwards to avoid overt anti-Semitism since it revived the ghastly memories of the Nazi atrocities.19/

Therefore, Wisconsin Senator Joseph McCarthy's Catholic Radical Right Movement of the early 1950's abandoned Father Coughlin's earlier anti-Semitism entirely. (See Chapter One.) In fact, McCarthy placed his closest personal aides, Roy Cohn and G. David Schine--both Jews--on prominent display as if to underscore the Catholic Radical Right's rejection of anti-Semitism.

Among members of the New Right anti-Semitism had nearly vanished by the early 1960's. With the growth of the Civil Rights Movement, Blacks quickly replaced Jews as the most aggressive, disruptive minority group in American life. Meanwhile, Jews had assimilated to such a degree that a few actually joined the ranks of the New Right ! Jewish blood even flowed through the veins of several key leaders of the Movement including Barry Goldwater, Frank S. Meyer and Frederick Schwarz.

The amazing, June, 1967, Six-Day War fought between the Jewish state of Israel and the Soviet-backed Arab nations shattered forever in the minds of New Rightists the apparent link between Zionism and International Communism. Thus in the wake of the stunning, swift Israeli military victory, the New Right's attitude towards the Jewish people abruptly shifted from a grudging toleration to warm support and glowing admiration.

The overwhelming majority of New Rightists spoke out vigorously against anti-Semitism. Timothy McInerny wrote that "all Jewish people can take comfort from the truism that there is not... the slightest room for blind bigotry." Robert Welch agreed: "In this country so far, thank goodness, (except for Dr. Wesley Swift, and perhaps George Lincoln Rockwell), nobody has proposed putting the Jews in gas chambers, or rounding them all up and shipping them somewhere else, or even making them ineligible for any office."20/

Furthermore, the New Right considered anti-Semitism self-defeating in the battle against the International Communist Conspiracy. Kent and Phoebe Courtney labelled anti-Semitism a "built in booby trap." Those foolish enough to oppose Communism along the lines of religious bigotry "provide the Communists with a built-in weapon to smear respectable Americans who oppose the International Communist Conspiracy, and who are not anti-Semitic." In addition, a preoccupation with the Jews obscured the real enemy--the Communists. The linking of Communism with World Jewry, in the opinion of Robert Welch, replaces "positive intelligent, constructive

106

action against the Communists with a negative, simmering, futile, do-nothing hatred of the Jews."21/

Most members of the New Right flatly refused to connect Judiasm with Communism. J. Edgar Hoover stressed that "one of the most malicious myths that has developed in the United States is that persons of Jewish faith and communists have something in common." The F.B.I. Director pointed out that Communist members "are recruited from all nationalities, races, and areas of the country....Never can a communist be identified simply by his physical appearance, occupation or clothes." Robert Welch also denied the existence of a Jewish-Communist alliance: "when a Jew or a Catholic or a Protestant becomes a Communist he is no longer a Jew or a Catholic or a Protestant."22/

Finally, of course, a host of other dangerous enemies could be mentioned; indeed the list is almost endless. Footnote One of Chapter Five presents a potpourri of insidious individuals, groups, publications, social ideas, etc. cited by members of the New Right at various times as factors contributing to the decline of the American way of life.

1.   In addition, the New Right lashed out against all sorts of enemies. A partial list includes:

abortionists
abstract-artists
alcoholics
Steve Allen
American Civil Liberties Union
Americans for Democratic Action
American Federation of Labor (A.F.L.C.I.O.)
anarchists
atheists
beatniks
big spenders
bomb-fearers
Harry Bridges
David Brinkley
brotherly lovers
Lenny Bruce
bureaucrats
call girls
Fidel Castro
child molesters
collectivists
Council on Foreign Relations
criminals
Walter Cronkhite
Sammy Davis, Jr.
do-gooders
Dwight D. Eisenhower
Dr. Milton Eisenhower
Eastern Liberal Establishment
Fabian Socialists
family planners
feather-bedders
Federal aid to education
Federal Income Tax Amendment to the Constitution
fellow-travellers
fluoridation
folk-singers
foreign aid
free-loaders
Freedom Riders
J. William Fulbright
fun lovers
gangsters
Gus Hall

Harvard University
Hollywood
homosexuals
Hubert H. Humphrey
Humanists
Chet Huntley
Lyndon B. Johnson
Kennedy family
Nikita Khrushchev
Dr. Martin Luther King, Jr.
labor bosses
lesbians
Henry Cabot Lodge, Jr.
Madison Avenue
Mafia
marijuana
Mao Tse-Tung
Marxists
materialists
Robert McNamara
George Meany
Edward R. Murrow
narcotic addicts
National Council of Churches
National Labor Relations Board
New Republic
Newsweek
New York City
New York Times
Richard M. Nixon
One-Worlders
Jack Paar
pacifists
Peace Corps
pornography
Elvis Presley
probation and parole
progressive education
psychiatrists
psychologists
race-mixers
Walter Reuther
rock and roll music
Rockefeller family
Eleanor Roosevelt
Bertrand Russell
sado-masochists
Arthur Schlesinger, Jr.
Eric Severeid

Howard K. Smith
social workers
socialized medicine
sociologists
Dr. Benjamin Spock
State Department
Adlai E. Stevenson
Ed Sullivan
teenage hoodlums
television networks
Tennessee Valley Authority
think tanks
Marshal Tito
Trotskyites
Harry S. Truman
Unitarians
United Nations
Washington, D.C.
Whiz Kids
wife swappers
World Opinion

2.   News and Views, (January, 1963), p. 4;
National Review, (September 10, 1960), p. 153.

3.   Richard Hofstadter, Anti-Intellectualism in American Life
(New York: Alfred A. Knopf, 1963).

4.   Occasional contributors to the National Review included M.
Stanton Evans and James J. Kilpatrick among others.

5.   Hofstadter, The Paranoid Style in American Politics, p. 37.

6.   Hargis, Communist America-- Must It Be?, p. 106;
Rosalie M. Gordon, Nine Men Against America (New Rochelle, N.Y.:
America's Future Pamphlet, 1961), p. 6.

7.   Baltimore Sun, April 18, 1959 as quoted in Thomas Morgan, ed.,
Goldwater Either/Or (A Self-Portrait Based Upon His Own Words)
(Washington, D.C.: Public Affairs Press, 1964), p. 66.

8.   American Opinion, (February, 1964), p. 77.

9.   Welch, The New Americanism, p. 22;
Bealle, The Washington Squirrel Cage, p. 39.

10.   Cross and the Flag, (August, 1962), p. 2;
New York Times, October 11, 1964;
Ibid.

11.   Report to America, (August, 1963), p. 1;
The Defender, (February, 1963), p. 7.

12.   Garden Grove News as quoted in Common Sense, (June 15, 1962), p. 4;
The Sons of the American Revolution Magazine, (October, 1963), p. 1.

13.   Bill Jones, The Wallace Story (Northport, Alabama: American Southern Publishing Company, 1966), p. 248.

14.   Cross and the Flag, (December, 1964), p. 18;
American Opinion, (November, 1964), p. 37.

15.   Common Sense, (June 15, 1962), p. 3;
"On the Right", June 30, 1964.

The Weekly Crusader added:

> Thanks to our Supreme Court, it is now illegal to use God's Name reverently in our public schools but it is still legal to use it irreverently.... The Bible never harmed anyone but this vile literature does great damage to youthful minds. We suggest that the Court leave the Bible alone and turn its attention to some of these unspeakable books which are poisoning the minds of our youth. The Weekly Crusader, (November 1, 1963), p. 8.

16.   Rockwell Report, (February 15, 1963), p. 3;
Ibid., (December 1, 1962), p. 3;
Ibid., (April 15, 1964), p. 8;
Ibid., (February 15, 1963), p. 4;
Ibid., (March 15, 1964), p. 7.

17.   Common Sense, (February 1, 1965), p. 4;
Ibid., (November 15, 1962), p. 2.

18.   For an excellent account of the Radical Right in the United States during the 1930's see Morris Schonbach, "Native Fascism During the 1930's and 1940': A Study of its Roots, its Growth, and its Decline" (Doctoral Dissertation, University of California, Los Angeles, 1958).

19.   In this light, Robert Welch called the suggestion to gas all the Jews living in the United States "both so abhorrent and so ridiculous to the American people as to defeat the purpose of those who are doing all of the shouting." Robert Welch, The Neutralizers (Belmont, Massachusetts: The John Birch Society, 1963), p. 12.

In fact, Robert Welch suspected that American Nazi leader George Lincoln Rockwell was a Communist agent who adopted the Nazi garb in order to discredit the New Right Movement.

111

20.   McInerny, The Private Man, p. 55;
Welch, The Neutralizers, p. 12.

21.   Kent and Phoebe Courtney, The Case of General Edwin A. Walker (New Orleans: Conservative Society of America Publication, 1961), p. 172;
Welch, The Neutralizers, p. 12.

22.   Hoover, Masters of Deceit, p. 255;
Ibid., pp. 105-106;
Welch, The Neutralizers, p. 51.

CHAPTER SIX

AMERICAN FOREIGN POLICY

"There is no substitute for victory"

The New Right repeatedly underscored the need for a convincing Cold War victory over America's arch-rival--the International Communist Conspiracy. Texas Senator John Tower called a "victory over Communist tyranny...an imperative of American foreign policy." Tower's G.O.P. Senate colleague Barry Goldwater stressed that "This nation desperately needs an official statement that our objective is victory and a priority list of what is required to meet that objective." Goldwater pointed out that "In this mortal struggle there is no substitute for victory." Consequently, "Victory is the key to the whole problem; the only alternative is--obviously--defeat."1/

An American victory over International Communism consisted of two basic steps. First of all, the United States must stop retreating before the Communist onslaught. Barry Goldwater predicted that "As long as every encounter with the enemy is fought on his initiative, on grounds of his choosing, and with weapons of his choosing, we shall keep on losing the Cold War." Thus the United States must stand firm and refuse to surrender "a single inch of free territory anywhere in the world to Communist powers..."2/

Secondly, America must assume the initiative in the Cold War. As Barry Goldwater wrote, "In addition to parrying the enemy's blows, we must strike our own." Senator Goldwater, in his best-selling book Why Not Victory?, recommended that "the United States and her allies go on the offensive" not merely "to wage a struggle against Communism, but to win it."3/

A victory over Communism required a positive commitment on the part of the American people. Clarence Manion decided that "when our President and our Congress together proclaim officially that Communism is intolerable and proceed firmly to act accordingly, the big Red tide will roll back and disappear into the halls of Hell from which it came." Likewise, "a decisive victory over the Communists is possible," Barry Goldwater pointed out, since "Every time we have stood up to the Communists they have backed down. Our trouble is we have not stood up to them enough."4/

The New Right understood that tough tactics towards the Communists might lead to war. Barry Goldwater admitted that "Victories will not always come so easily for the West; we may not always be able to avoid shooting." Nevertheless, "our only hope today is to proclaim victory as our aim, accept the cost, rid ourselves of fear, and then press boldly forward on all fronts -- always prepared to fight and always making sure the Communists know we are prepared to fight."5/

The New Right accepted the risks of war. In the opinion of columnist William F. Buckley, Jr., "War is the second worst activity of mankind, the worst being acquiescence in slavery." Thus "Better to face the chance of being dead, than the certainty of being Red." Senator John Tower noted that "There are risks in the strategy of victory but they are less danger than the risks of unending defeat and retreat." Likewise, Barry Goldwater wrote, "We want to stay alive, of course, but more than that we want to be free." In short, "we would rather die than lose our freedom."6/

A few members of the New Right did advocate an all-out nuclear attack upon the Soviet Union. Air Force General Nathan Twining grumbled, "If it were not for the politicians I would settle the war in one afternoon by bombing Russia." Colonel Bluford H. J. Baltar allegedly said, "Bomb Russia ! Why did the Heavenly Father...give us the atomic bomb?....to use it judiciously to destroy Communism....Bomb Stalingrad and Moscow !" In the same vein, General Orvil A. Anderson added, "Give me the order to do it and I can break up Russia's five A-bomb nests in a week. And when I went up to Christ...I think I could explain to Him that I had saved civilization."7/

At the opposite end of the spectrum, nearly every member of the New Right comprehended the ultimate horror of nuclear war. Senator J. Strom Thurmond emphasized that "no sane man wants a nuclear war." The National Review concurred: "Only an ignoramus or a moral degenerate will talk loosely about pressing nuclear buttons."8/

Yet Barry Goldwater complained that "a craven fear of death is entering the American consciousness." Consequently, the American people might view a complete surrender to the Communists as the only possible means of avoiding a nuclear war. The Arizona Senator lamented that "There are, unfortunately, people among us who would crawl to Moscow on their hands and knees rather than run the risk of a shooting war with the enemies of freedom."9/

This all-pervasive fear of nuclear catastrophe paralyzed America's Liberal foreign policy makers, thus rendering it difficult to confront the menace of International Communism. The Weekly Crusader noted the "prevailing view in our nation today that a strong U.S. foreign policy against Communist aggression and subversion would throw our nation into a nuclear war." In the same fashion, William F. Buckley, Jr. outlined the Liberal mentality on the subject of nuclear war:

All the roads that lead to the recovery of freedom,
or to the diminution of Communist power, are closed to

us, because to follow them would mean to risk nuclear war. This is the clinching argument in all liberal rhetoric, by which they seek to paralyze all purposive action, everywhere in the world, that aims at the improvement of the position of the Free World.10/

The New Right refused to accept the Liberal premise that appeasing Communism represented the only way to avert mutual nuclear annihilation. The Weekly Crusader maintained that the Liberals' "foremost and over-riding objective is to stop nuclear war...by continuing piece-meal surrenders to communism." However, "left-wing liberals" should understand that "This will not stop nuclear war. It will eventually give us a horrifying choice of all-out nuclear war under conditions most unfavorable for us, or else, surrender to the communist conspiracy." Thus while "the Liberal establishment seems to shudder at any thoughts of victory," Ohio Republican Congressman John M. Ashbrook boasted that "Conservatives will talk in terms of victory over Communism. We are not afraid of the word."11/

Indeed an American foreign policy based upon victory over Communism in the Cold War remained the only realistic method of preventing nuclear war. As Senator John Tower explained, "A policy of victory over the enemy is not an extremist reaction born of wounded pride, hate, impatience, or frustration." Rather, "It is a plan calculated to offer the best chance of avoiding world-wide nuclear devastation and of yielding a secure peace." Barry Goldwater echoed the same sentiments: "In the final analysis the choice...is: win or fight a nuclear war. For a nuclear war we shall certainly have to fight, from whatever beleagured outpost we are reduced to occupying, if we continue to yield, piece by piece, all over the world."12/

The Illusion of Peaceful Co-existence

Instead of victory New Rightists complained that the American Liberal preached "peaceful co-existence" with the Communist world. The idea of "peaceful co-existence" consisted of a set of basic assumptions. Since civilization could never have survived under the shadow of Nazi brutality, the battle to destroy Adolph Hitler and his hideous Third Reich surely justified even the horrors of World War Two. However, unlike the tyranny of Nazism, the United States could easily learn to live alongside Communism. The overthrow of International Communism was simply not worth risking another World War. Both the United States and the Soviet Union possessed the awesome weapons capable of obliterating each other, thus making nuclear war quite "unthinkable"; indeed this delicate "balance of terror" paved the way for the relaxation of international tensions. The United States and the Communists must learn to settle their differences across the conference table. In fact, serious negotiations promised handsome dividends because the Communists really wanted world peace as badly as the Americans did.

Of course, two such antagonistic social systems still disputed nearly every conceivable subject. Nevertheless, under "peaceful co-existence" the competition between the United States and the Soviet Union shifted away from the perilous military and political fields towards the safer economic and cultural spheres. The East and West would henceforth boast about Gross National Products, Olympic Gold Medals, and International Chess Grandmasters.

The New Right rejected the entire notion of "peaceful co-existence." To begin with, Communism was not seen as a sufferable evil but rather the worst plague to infect mankind in all human history. Major General Edwin A. Walker quoted General Douglas MacArthur: "There can be no compromise with atheistic communism—no halfway in the preservation of freedom and religion. It must be all or nothing." Thus General Walker concluded that "There can be no co-existence on the battlefield." Another surprised observer wondered, "Why should we want to co-exist with the Communists any more than we wanted to co-exist with the Nazis?"13/

Secondly, history demonstrated the impossibility of settling disputes with dangerous adversaries like Communism. News and Views declared that "the bitter and irrefutable lesson of history from Carthage and Byzantium to Cuba and Laos is that compromise with a ruthless and determined enemy intent only upon total subjugation, is and always has been utterly futile."14/*

Finally, "peaceful co-existence" overlooked the fact that both the United States and the Soviet Union sought totally different objectives in world politics. Barry Goldwater outlined how "our avowed national objective is 'peace.' We have, with great sincerity, 'waged' peace, while the Communists wage war." Thus Goldwater pointed out that "we have sought 'settlements,' while the Communists seek victories. We have tried to pacify the world. The Communists mean to own it."15/

The Communists looked upon "peaceful co-existence" as yet another tool for bloodless advancement. In the opinion of the American

---

*Note—Curiously, the New Right rarely uses the celebrated 1938 Munich Agreement as an example of the folly of appeasement. I suspect that New Rightists remember with a great deal of embarrassment that the Great Depression Radical Right had once heartily applauded the now-infamous Pact. For the Great Depression Radical Right during the 1930's looked upon Nazi Germany as the citadel of Western Civilization against the threat of Soviet Bolshevism. (See Chapter One)

Mercury, "To Communists, 'peaceful coexistence' means Communist conquest without war." Likewise, the National Defender warned that the Communists "using 'peace' as their prime weapon...press their campaign for world hegemony."16/

"The United States has a no-win foreign policy"

In the New Right's estimation, the United States continued losing the Cold War because we failed to appreciate the dangers of International Communism and lacked the courage to strive for total victory. John Stormer noted that "most Americans refused to admit that we are at war. That is why we are rapidly losing--why America has yet to win its first real victory in 18 years of 'cold' war." Robert Welch summed up "the record of America from Eastern Europe to China to Korea to Vietnam to Laos. It is the record of a nation sick with...a fawning and cringing fondness for her foes."17/

During the entire Cold War the United States has pursued a "no-win" foreign policy. Senator J. Strom Thurmond suggested that "The phrase may be new, but the policy is not. When the Communists took over in China, we had a 'no-win' policy; only then, it was called a policy of 'letting the dust settle.' At various times since, it has been given many names: such as 'containment' or 'accommodation.' " In the same fashion, Senator John Tower characterized our foreign policy as "passive half-measures, designed only to hold on to the status quo, to appease the enemy, to retreat with dignity and good humor."18/

The government of the United States reflected this no-win attitude. Dean Clarence Manion wondered, "just what is our government trying to do about the war that the Communists are waging against us?....Are we deliberately trying to lose?" Barry Goldwater, Jr. remarked that "I have yet to hear a spokesman for the State Department say that it is our objective to win the Cold War." Illinois State Senator Paul W. Broyles demanded that we "get rid of misfits in all government.... those who plan ways to surrender or have a No Win policy. Replace them with men who believe in and love America. Men who would rather be dead than be red."19/

The New Right asserted that the Eastern Liberal Establishment, which effectively controlled both major political parties, favored this cowardly no-win foreign policy. Thus while the White House passed from Democrats Franklin D. Roosevelt and Harry S. Truman, to Republican Dwight D. Eisenhower, then back to Democrats John F. Kennedy and Lyndon B. Johnson, the United States continued to appease Communism and surrender American national sovereignty to international organizations. Captain Eddie Rickenbacker told a nationwide radio audience in 1963 that "For 32 years, this Communist-inspired Liberal Establishment has been gunning to destroy the nationalism of this once

117

great Republic." Rickenbacker denounced, "the stupid shenanigans of Ivy League Internationalist Liberals in Washington, who are nullifying our national traditions,...and steering us into One World chaos which, under Moscow's leadership, would reduce humanity to a condition of slavery."20/

"Muzzling the military"

The New Right contended that the Eastern Liberal Establishment sought to infect the American armed services with its no-win philosophy. President Truman had once fired General Douglas MacArthur at the height of the Korean War when that gallant soldier had dared to advocate a complete victory over Communism. However, the crisis reached a climax during the Kennedy-Johnson era. Under Secretary Robert McNamara the Defense Department underwent some drastic reorganization. Left-wing university professors, Rand Corporation "brain-stormers," armchair nuclear strategists, and "whiz kids" complete with computers and cost-effectiveness studies took charge of the nation's security. Many high-ranking military officers found themselves unceremoniously elbowed out of the way. As expected, the New Right reacted with anger. They believed that by ignoring expert military advice the Kennedy-Johnson Administration rejected the wisdom of some of America's most dedicated and knowledgeable anti-Communist patriots. As Barry Goldwater complained, "under the rigid civilian control instituted at the Pentagon by Defense Secretary Robert MacNamara, the nation's military voice is being muted, if not ignored."21/

The New Right outlined some of their objections to excessive civilian meddling in military affairs. Writing in American Opinion Slobodan M. Draskovich lashed out against...

> the Kremlinologists, Stalinologists, Sinologists, McNamara's 'whiz kids' and his 'Rand Corporation boys', to whom the idea of really fighting the Communists and winning the Cold War is just another chauvinistic 'spasm': whose overwhelming concern is just how to devise the most fantastic and unnatural ways, means, and philosophies for refusing not only to win but even to do battle.

Paul Sexson and Stephen Miles, Jr. remarked sarcastically that "Professors and whiz kids are supposed to know more about military strategy and tactics than generals and admirals."22/

Ostensibly, the Liberal Establishment simply wanted to tighten control over the nation's armed forces to eliminate waste and duplication, save money, and increase combat readiness. But the

Liberals also dreaded unchecked military power translated into unwarranted political influence. The New Right disagreed totally. Barry Goldwater echoed their sentiments when he wrote, "As for those who say fear military men, I say fear the civilians--they're taking over."23/

The American military, the New Right said, committed the unpardonable sin of warning the American public concerning the growing International Communist menace. An astonished National Review questioned, "Is it wrong for officers to say that international Communism is trying to conquer the world?" Barry Goldwater observed that...

> it is now becoming popular in the national government to investigate and censor military men who have any words of warning to say in public about Communist influence in American life. I cannot help but wonder what kind of struggle we are waging when it becomes a censorable offense to discuss the tactics of the enemy. Regardless of what the official policy might be, there can be no denying that communism is our enemy.24/

Military men with New Rightist leanings felt an obligation to speak out against the nation's no-win foreign policy. Six frustrated naval officers protested. "We can die for America, but we cannot speak out in her behalf." Walter Darnell Jacobs reminded the readers of the National Review that "our military leaders have a place in our society and have something to say." Furthermore, "Civilian control of the military command is good and blessed but it was never conceived as a device (before January, 1961) to silence completely any word from any person in uniform on any subject on which the Whiz Kids presume to have an opinion."25/

Yet most military men kept silent and avoided any public disagreement with their civilian superiors. As Phyllis Schlafly and Admiral Chester Ward pointed out, "A life-long habit of obedience, a genuine loyalty to superiors, and a true dedication to civilian supremacy under the Constitution of the United States, prevent military men on active duty from giving effective warning to the American people."26/

However, one Army officer, Major General Edwin A. Walker refused to remain silent. This native-born Texan became a cause celebre during 1961-62. While commanding U.S. troops stationed in Europe, General Walker decided to indoctrinate his soldiers against International Communism and in favor of the New Rightist brand of one-hundred percent Americanism. Under his prodding his troops conducted seminars and study groups and distributed New Right literature.

Civilian authorities saw General Walker as a dangerous, Right-wing crackpot. An official investigation resulted in the General's rebuking. The New Right exploded with anger. Just how on earth could a sincere, dedicated anti-Communist patriot like General Walker find himself reprimanded for educating his soldiers about the horrors of International Communism? The Economic Council Letter grumbled that "a powerful group within our government will not tolerate a vigorous anti-communist attitude among high military officers." Senator J. Strom Thurmond called the Walker Affair "a dastardly attempt to intimidate the commanders of U.S. Armed Forces and prevent these commanders from teaching their troops the nature of the menace of World Communism."27/

In the midst of this dispute General Walker resigned his commission and returned home to the United States to defend his name and to present his case to the American public. His voluntary decision to leave the Army spared the Kennedy Administration the embarrassment of firing the controversial General. At any rate, the New Right considered the Walker resignation more or less forced. Consequently, a bitter Barry Goldwater described the entire episode as "one of the most insidious and one of the most dangerous things that ever happened in the history of our country."28/

General Walker received a hero's welcome when he finally returned to the United States. The New Right lionized the former General and linked his fate with that of two other controversial American officers, General Douglas MacArthur and Colonel Billy Mitchell. As with the case of MacArthur, General Walker had infuriated the Eastern Liberal Establishment by advocating total victory over Communism. Similarly, after both men left the service they came back to America to receive the plaudits of their countrymen and renew their call for victory in the Cold War. Secondly, the prophetic Billy Mitchell had advanced far-sighted theories on air power which had utterly baffled his stodgy contemporaries. General Walker's warnings about the threat of International Communism, likewise placed him too far ahead of current government opinion. However, just as the passage of time ultimately vindicated Billy Mitchell, so, too, would future events vindicate General Walker.

Several members of the New Right urged General Walker to seek elective office once he severed his connections with the Army. California G.O.P. Congressman James B. Utt remarked, "It is my hope that General Walker will resign from the military service and enter the civilian political field where he could render great service to his country." Of course, Left-wing critics viewed General Walker as a clever demagogue and a prime candidate to lead a Rightist coup d'etat. Indeed, author Mark Sherwin characterized Walker as the New Right's eagerly awaited "man on horseback."29/

Yet many perceptive members of the New Right cautioned General Walker against a political career. To begin with, the unavoidable partisan squabbles might serve to overshadow his important message. Secondly, keen observers detected a streak of instability in General Walker's personality. While testifying before the Senate Special Preparedness Sub-Committee on April 4th and 5th, 1962 Walker became hysterical and incoherent. After leaving a particularly grueling Committee session he lost his composure and punched a newspaper reporter in the eye. Often abrasive, often inarticulate, he obviously lacked the finesse of a seasoned politician.

General Walker selected the Governorship of his native state of Texas as his initial political target and prepared to enter the Democratic Party Primary scheduled for spring, 1962. Since the General knew nothing about politics he sought advice from his staunchest supporters in Washington: Senators Barry Goldwater of Arizona, J. Strom Thurmond of South Carolina, and John Tower of Texas. Prior to announcing his candidacy Walker travelled to the nation's capital and met with this trio of Solons inside Senator Tower's office. They begged Walker not to run for Governor of the Lone Star State. Senator Thurmond warned Walker that his plunge into the political arena would only serve to distort his timely anti-Communist message since the General's enemies would surely brand him as a rank opportunist trying to capitalize upon Cold War tensions. Thus Thurmond told Walker, "You will be judged in a totally different manner if you get into politics." Ignoring the South Carolina Senator's sound counsel, General Walker entered the May, 1962 Texas Democratic Gubernatorial Primary, where he placed a dismal sixth in a contest won by John Connally.30/

Even after his election defeat, General Walker continued making headlines. By late September, 1962 he waltzed into strife-torn Oxford, Mississippi, where a Black student, James Meredith, sought to enroll at the previously lily-white University of Mississippi. What really occurred next remains unclear. According to some sources, Walker led a charge of rabid segregationists on a destructive rampage during the night of September 30, 1962. According to other reports, the General had done nothing of the sort and instead had tried to quell the disturbance by urging the Redneck mobs to avoid any violence. At any rate, one additional point must be emphasized: Walker had come to Oxford, Mississippi to generate publicity for himself and to salvage his political career. His presence on the scene hardly quieted the already tense situation.31/

Federal Marshals arrested General Walker on October 1st after a wild night of rioting and arson had swept through the sleepy little college town of Oxford. Quickly whisked out of troubled Mississippi the General landed at Springfield, Missouri as a prisoner in a mental

121

institution.   After Walker submitted to a complete psychiatric examination, the Federal authorities released the General and subsequently dropped all criminal charges.

Seven Days in May, Fail-Safe, and Doctor Strangelove

The New Right saw the muzzling of the military and the attacks upon General Edwin A. Walker as portions of a larger plan to downgrade the public image of the American soldier. As the Economic Council Letter lamented, "The devoted, patriotic, and law-revering American military men must be pictured as stupid, violent, barbarian, and fascist..." The Left described the American military leaders as either Munich Beer Hall conspirators plotting their Putsch or else crazed maniacs itching to press the nuclear button annihilating the world.32/

The New Right rejected the notion that American military officers represented a threat to America's Constitution and republican form of government. Barry Goldwater emphasized, "Those who warn against American military leaders as potential threats to our political process and civilian government do not understand the military mind." Likewise, Walter Darnell Jacobs pointed out that "a military leader, or anyone else for that matter, can disagree with the policies of the political leadership of the country without desiring--or even dreaming of--a forceful overthrow of the government."33/*

Along the same lines, the New Right challenged the Left's portrait of the American soldier as an unthinking, vicious killer. Barry Goldwater detected, "an erroneous assumption behind this downgrading of military men that...a general or admiral is 'nothing but a fighting man,' that he sees solutions to all international problems in terms of dropping bombs, that he is, in short, a tiger on a leash." Goldwater suggested that "The nuclear philosophers on the left who paint this distorted image must know better. The admirals and generals of today are hardly blood-thirsty pirates wearing black patches and gripping cutlasses in their teeth."34/

Furthermore, the Left insisted that the trigger-happy, Right-wing, American military leaders and not the International Communists represented the real threat to world peace. According to M. Stanton Evans, Left-wing politicians "tell us we must fear our own defenses more than we fear the Communists."35/

---

*Note--A fact conveniently forgotten by New Rightists themselves during the late 1960's when they denounced the anti-Vietnam War protesters as "traitors."

A pair of popular novels published during the early 1960's, Seven Days in May and Fail-Safe, and the motion picture Doctor Strangelove played a major role in creating a negative image of the American armed services. Walter Darnell Jacobs labelled them "political tracts designed to destroy whatever is left of American faith in the military." These books and movies implied that America's generals and admirals constituted the greatest danger to our system of government and our hopes for global peace.36/

Seven Days in May, in the words of M. Stanton Evans, focused upon "the danger of a military coup by fascist-minded generals." In the book a handsome, charismatic Chairman of the Joint Chiefs of Staff schemes to oust the Liberal President who has just negotiated an arms limitation agreement with the Soviet Union. The scheduled Putsch never materializes because a lone, brave Army colonel dedicated to civilian supremacy informs the President in the nick of time.37/

Both the book Fail-Safe and the film Doctor Strangelove featured the United States unleashing a nuclear first-strike against the unsuspecting Soviet Union. In Fail-Safe a technical malfunction in the electronic equipment accidentally sends American bombers on a deadly mission to Moscow. In Doctor Strangelove an insane, Right-wing general, obsessed with the creeping International Communist Conspiracy orders an American attack upon the Soviet Union. In both Fail-Safe and Doctor Strangelove America's civilian leaders desperately attempt to recall the errant bombers. However, the trigger-happy military leadership, excited at the prospect of World War Three, counsel against recalling the bombers and welcome the outbreak of full-scale hostilities with the Soviet Union. In both Fail-Safe and Doctor Strangelove the United States appears as the aggressor nation making unprovoked war upon the innocent, peace-loving Soviet Union. Finally, both depict the Commuist rulers joining America's politicians in a last ditch effort to avert mutual nuclear annihilation.

Fail-Safe and Doctor Strangelove created "nuclear hysteria" in the words of M. Stanton Evans. For the anxious American public might believe the Left's propaganda that the mere possession of nuclear weapons by the United States increased the likelihood of war. The panic-striken American people might find the specter of impending annihilation unbearable and opt for unilateral nuclear disarmament in the desperate hope of averting World War Three. As The Weekly Crusader observed, the Liberals "peddle the Communist line that nuclear war is so terrible that the U.S. should appease, retreat, and even surrender rather than risk it..."38/

Arms and Disarmament

The New Right underscored the importance of a strong national defense. In the judgment of William F. Buckley, Jr., "we view our atomic arsenal as proudly and as devotedly as any pioneer ever viewed his flintlock hanging over the mantel as his children slept and dreamed." Indeed the preservation of Western Civilization itself required sufficient weapons. Dan Smoot emphasized that "it behooves all...civilized Western nations...to maintain whatever weaponry is necessary to protect their civilization against all threats, within or without."39/

Thus the New Right rejected all plans for disarmament as impractical and dangerous. Barry Goldwater conceded that "The idea of disarmament is a beautiful one. No man can deny that." However, "at this moment in history, the disarmament concept is an effective weapon in the hands of the Communists and a danger to the freedom of mankind." Senator John Tower agreed: "At a time when Western civilization is confronted by an extreme militaristic threat looking forward to world conquest, I think it is naive and unrealistic to be preoccupied with the question of disarmament."40/

Furthermore, the proponents of disarmament failed to understand a simple truth: Rather than causing international tensions, an arms race only reflected already existing national rivalries. As Barry Goldwater stated, "History teaches us that armament races are no more than a symptom of international friction, not a cause of it." James Burnham pointed out that "Armaments do not, generally speaking, cause wars. Actually, it is wars, or conflicts threatening war, that cause armaments, not the reverse."41/

Therefore, Barry Goldwater concluded that "Easing the arms race will not ease tensions" because the expansionistic goals of World Communism remained the real source of international friction. Until the Communists renounce their policy of complete world conquest no meaningful relaxation of global tensions is possible. And until such time, only the military strength of the United States protected the Free World against a Communist takeover. Any program of American disarmament would simply "encourage the Communists to adopt increasingly reckless tactics."42/

Finally, the New Right wondered how on earth the United States could ever negotiate a disarmament pact with the Communists. For as Barry Goldwater wrote, "We can assume nothing where the Communist leaders are concerned...trust nothing that the Communist leaders say...accept nothing that the Communist leaders sign as a conclusive guarantee." In the same vein, The Weekly Crusader asserted that "anyone who has passed the equivalent of the kindergarten stage in studying the nature, methods and objective of the international communist conspiracy knows that no agreement with them is worth the paper upon which it is written."43/

The Communists sign treaties with the West as part of their program of world conquest. The Weekly Crusader called "negotiations, agreements, and treaties...merely weapons of psychological warfare to the communist conspirators." The Communists follow a specific strategy regarding treaties: "they cannot be trusted to keep any agreement unless such agreement serves to further the communist plot to enslave mankind." William F. Buckley, Jr. outlined the Communist theory of negotiations with the West:

> The Soviet Union does not 'honor' treaties, it 'observes' treaties, for so long as it finds it useful to do so. It honors only the imperatives of its own dynamic ideology, which laugh at the very concept of honor as applying to relations between socialist and imperialist countries: the sanctity of treaties is, for the Communist, merely one more bourgeois sentimentality that stands in the way of the conclusion of the world revolution.44/

In the eyes of the New Right, President Kennedy's 1963 Nuclear Test Ban Treaty with the Soviet Union compounded the foolishness of disarmament with the perils of trusting the Communists. Dean Clarence Manion called the Nuclear Test Ban Treaty, "A Covenant With Death and an Agreement with Hell." The Daughters of the American Revolution magazine feared "that the United States may be mousetrapped into unilateral disarmament, while the Soviet Union makes itself invincible." The Weekly Crusader emphasized that "Our nation has absolutely nothing to gain from the nuclear test ban treaty or any other treaty with murdering, lying communist conspirators."45/

As with disarmament, the New Right saw the Left erroneously associating the halting of nuclear testing with world peace. The National Review excoriated "the fetishists, who believe that cessation of tests has something to do with securing peace, which in fact it has not." Likewise, Jenkins Lloyd Jones observed that "One of the most pernicious illusions abroad in the world today is the fond hope that if nations will give up testing atomic weapons the threat of an atomic holocaust will vanish."46/

The New Right also discounted the dangers of radioactive fallout. As M. Stanton Evans stated, "the hysteria stirred up about fallout...is completely without foundation in fact." In the estimation of The Weekly Crusader," this propaganda fear line on nuclear fallout...is nothing but a phony scare which serves the communist drive to wreck the nuclear defense potential of our nation." Clearly, the New Right considered radioactive fallout a harmless waste-product of the atomic age.47/

Foreign Aid

The New Right thought that foreign economic aid represented yet another conspicuous Liberal failure in the realm of foreign policy. M. Stanton Evans described foreign economic aid as "Liberalism's principle surrogate for purposeful Cold War action" and called it "an attempt to formalize, through the medium of hard cash, the virtue of not being jingoist..." In Evans' estimation, the spineless Liberal always shuns direct military confrontations with our Communist enemies. Thus instead of flexing our muscles the generous distribution of American dollars would suffice to halt the spread of International Communism.48/

New Rightists chided the Liberals for expecting foreign economic assistance to purchase the friendship of our allies, subsidize the developing uncommitted nations of the world, and, on occasion, even bribe our Communist opponents. The Weekly Crusader labelled foreign aid "the refuge of those who...refuse to face up to the facts about communism and its aggressive designs upon our nation."49/

History itself, the New Right said, demonstrated the folly of foreign aid. The ancient Romans made the mistake of buying allies and bribing enemies. Dan Smoot reminded his television audience, "The emperors squandered the resources of Rome, giving military equipment, gold, and other goods (today we call it economic and military aid) to rulers of countries on the outer fringes of the empire." Thus "We should get out of all the far corners of the earth where we now stand as self-appointed--and, generally, unwelcome--guardians, and uplifters, and moralizers, and subsidizers of people who would rather be left alone."50/

The New Right criticized the entire foreign economic assistance program as an unconstitutional extension of the authority and scope of the Federal Government. According to Dan Smoot, "The government of the United States has no constitutional right to use the resources of the American people to support foreign nations." Likewise, Barry Goldwater stressed that "the American government does not have the right, much less the obligation, to try to promote the economic and social welfare of foreign peoples." He pointed out that the United States Constitution "does not empower our government to undertake that job in foreign countries, no matter how worthwhile it might be."51/

The New Right also disputed Liberal claims that foreign Communism, like domestic crime, resulted from poverty, hunger, and disease. At home, government welfare schemes--by improving social conditions--reduced the frustration and despair of the poor, thus eliminating the major causes of crime. Abroad, America's foreign aid program--by upgrading the living standards of Third World nations-- prevented starving peoples from embracing Communism out of sheer desperation. As Vollie Tripp noted, "It is widely claimed that

Communism is bred by poverty and misery, and can only be countered by raising the living standards of depressed peoples. This theory is used to justify massive foreign giveaway programs."52/

However, Revilo P. Oliver, speaking for the New Right denounced "the preposterous notion that Communism is somehow related to poverty." Billy James Hargis refuted the suggestion that the Communists conquer the world by "filling empty bellies"--"This is a false diagnosis of international communism, yet it has affected the thinking of our liberal political leaders for years." In the same vein, Barry Goldwater pointed out that "it does not help any to adopt the false notion that communism is spawned by poverty, disease, and other similar social and economic conditions." Moreover, "when we adopt the idea that the only way effectively to halt the spread of communism is to terminate social and economic conditions that do not make for universal ease and comfort, we are adopting defeat..." For Goldwater explained that "high standards of living have not, of themselves, saved nations from Communism, in the past and are not doing it today."53/

"Communism is not a disease of the stomach," Christian Economics insisted, "it is disease of the mind and soul." Herein lay the real source of Communism. For "Communism does not originate with the poor, the uneducated, the exploited or the working classes." In fact, most Communist leaders had comfortable bourgeois backgrounds and identified more with fellow intellectuals than with the downtrodden proletariat. As Christian Economics concluded, "It was not hunger for food that turned them to communism, but hunger for power." Thus the New Right blamed the spread of Communism not on poverty and disease but on Communist subversion. In short, Barry Goldwater announced, "Communism is spawned by Communists and Communists alone."54/

Unfortunately, the American Liberal erroneously believed that by simply raising living standards the United States could prevent the developing nations of the world from embracing Communism. Thus instead of confronting the "subversive, psychological, and political" challenge of Communism directly, Revilo P. Oliver complained that "we must set out, like Boy Scouts, to eradicate hunger, poverty, ignorance, and disease." In the same fashion, Barry Goldwater agreed:

> I certainly don't think for one minute that there is anything unworthy in a goal which envisions a world without poverty, disease, and filth, and where all international relations are humanized and conducted in good faith. But this is not the practical objective which we should be pursuing in the Communist War. It is a dream for the future of mankind, a dream which can never come to pass if we do not apply ourselves immediately to the first objective--the removal of Communist power.

127

Goldwater warned that when we concentrate solely upon improving the standard of living we merely "diffuse our strength and weaken our assault on the prime target, which is Communist power."55/

In the end, the much-heralded American foreign economic assistance program, in the eyes of New Rightists, failed to halt the spread of Communism, failed to end poverty and misery around the globe, and failed to purchase the allegiance of the "uncommitted nations". First of all, as The Weekly Crusader noted, "foreign aid programs have failed to stop communism." By the early 1960's Communist influence had extended into Africa, Asia, the Middle East, and Latin America despite the tens of billions of dollars in foreign economic assistance given to the developing nations. Barry Goldwater pointed out that "foreign economic aid cannot end poverty around the world," since poverty is a moral and spiritual sickness rather than a purely economic problem. (See Chapter Eleven) Finally, American generosity cannot "win the allegiance of the 'uncommitted' nations" because "we cannot, in the last analysis, buy friends."56/

Nevertheless, while the New Right opposed foreign economic assistance they did support limited military aid to a handful of anti-Communist allies. These recipients of U.S. military assistance included Greece, South Korea, South Vietnam, Taiwan, and Turkey. According to America's Future, "we can be really effective in the world struggle against communism with sane and very limited military aid to allies on whom we can depend when the chips are down." In the same vein, Barry Goldwater outlined how "military assistance has helped many nations, particularly those on the periphery of the Communist world, from being overrun." Consequently, "we should adopt a discriminating foreign aid policy. American aid should be furnished only to friendly, anti-Communist nations that are willing to join with us in the struggle for freedom."57/

Foreign Aid to Communist Nations

The New Right complained that the dreamy Liberals even expected to woo independent Communist regimes with the glittering promise of lavish economic assistance. A Communist nation estranged from Moscow might accept American aid thus moving further away from the Soviet bloc and closer towards the West. Hopefully, capitalistic Yankee dollars would destroy the unity of the World Communist Movement ! Perhaps the disciples of Marx and Lenin would be seduced by hard American cash !

The New Right totally rejected any thoughts of supplying economic assistance to Communist nations. Such madness, in the opinion of Senator J. Strom Thurmond, ignores "the singleness of purpose of the International Communist Conspiracy." Despite strong internal disagreements within the World Communist Movement, every red regime fully intended to destroy the capitalistic United States and her Free World allies. A quarrel with Moscow or Peking did not alter the basic hostility of any Communist country towards the West.58/ (See Chapter Four)

Therefore, in the eyes of the New Right, economic aid to Communist governments represented either treason or insanity. The Economic Council Letter demanded to know, "If Communism is our enemy, why isn't this treason?" Presidential candidate Barry Goldwater stated that, "if Communism intends to bury us let us tell [the] Communists loud and clear we're not going to hand them the shovel." Likewise, John Stormer asked sarcastically:

> Does aid to communism make sense? If, during World War II, anyone had suggested sending food or industrial materials to Nazi Germany, they would have been tried for treason, or carted off to a mental institution. Today, favoring aid to communism is, to some, evidence of good mental health.59/

Marshal Tito's Yugoslavia exemplified a so-called Independent Communist regime currently at odds with the Soviet Union. Thus some thought that abundant United States aid could lure Yugoslavia into the Western camp. The Kennedy Administration in particular favored supplying Yugoslavia with foreign aid in an effort to detach Tito further from the Soviet orbit.

Of course, the New Right considered economic assistance to Yugoslavia senseless, unproductive and humiliating. First of all, the United States should never subsidize our sworn enemies, the International Communist Conspiracy. As Robert Welch reported, "Our billions in money and materials delivered to Tito were used as completely to strengthen the international Communist conspiracy as if they had been delivered directly to the Kremlin."60/

Secondly, as Barry Goldwater noted, "United States aid to Communist countries helps them avoid paying the full price for being Communist. It provides a sort of economic sanctuary for the weakness and repressions of Communism." The faulty Communist economic system could never provide a decent standard of living for its own citizens. So why should United States dollars protect Tito from the wrath of his own under-nourished, ill-clad people?61/

Finally, New Rightist Julian E. Williams observed that "the United States has received no support from Tito in return for millions of dollars in aid given to him." The New Right demanded results: In exchange for assistance America should at least receive Yugoslavian friendship. Yet G.O.P. Congressman Richard Poff of Virginia wondered, "And what has Marshal Tito given us in return ?--the back of his hand !" Worst of all, subsidizing Yugoslavia humiliated the United States. The Manchester Union Leader grumbled that "we crawl on our bellies to Yugoslavia, and ask Tito, pretty please to take some more aid from us."62/

United Nations

The New Right maintained that the United Nations epitomized the American Liberal's basic approach to foreign policy. Indeed, M. Stanton Evans called the U.N. "Liberalism's Favorite Secular Institution." The United Nations symbolized world brotherhood, global cooperation, and the transformation of aggressive nationalism into more constructive peaceful internationalism. The United Nations also took the initial step in the direction of world government as mankind headed towards the Liberal Utopia of "One-World".63/

At the opposite end of the spectrum, the New Right detested everything associated with the United Nations. This dangerous organization, "founded and dominated by the Communist Conspiracy," reeked with the stench of "atheism" and "immorality". The U.N. advanced the absurd idea of "One-World" which would ultimately destroy all traces of American national sovereignty. The U.N. stood for the folly of democracy upon a global scale by creating a proto-World government controlled by the savage, backwards, non-White peoples of the earth.

To begin with, the International Communist Conspiracy designed the United Nations to further its program for global conquest. The American Mercury noted that "the United Nations was formed to take the place of the League of Nations" and both organizations "were lifted directly from the Communist Manifesto." Thus "both are merely an extension of world revolution, which was to be the prelude to World Government." Chesly Manly, longtime U.N. observer for the Chicago Tribune, declared that "the U.N. was the principal instrument of a gigantic conspiracy to control both the foreign and domestic policies of the United States, to subvert the Constitution and establish a totalitarian society." In the same fashion, California G.O.P. Congressman James B. Utt lamented that "we were sold the U.N. on a promise of peace, but we failed to realize that this peace was to be on Communist terms; in fact, it was to be a total victory for the international Communist conspiracy."64/

According to the New Right, well-placed Communist agents operating within the highest echelon of the United States Government had drafted the United Nations Charter back in 1945 upon direct orders from the Kremlin. These "key communist sympathizers" identified by

Congressman John Rousselot and other New Rightists included the infamous Alger Hiss, Secretary General of the San Francisco Conference and a close advisor to President Franklin D. Roosevelt; Dr. Leo Pasvolsky, Assistant U.S. Secretary of State; and Harry Dexter White, Assistant U.S. Secretary of the Treasury. Thus Mrs. M. Conan emphasized that "since the U.N. was drafted by our enemies it is silly to think for a moment it would benefit us in any way."65/

The basic charter of the United Nations itself reflected the influence and goals of the Communist Conspiracy. The American Mercury disclosed that "many of the Articles" appearing in the U.N. Charter "were lifted from the Constitution of the U.S.S.R." The Council on American Relations pictured the U.N. Charter as a device to bring "the United States into a world government" ruled by Moscow. Consequently, Howard Kershner warned, "The predominent sic philosophy of the U.N. is Marxist. Its whole ideology and operating technique is Marxist."66/

By the early 1960's the International Communist Conspiracy had assumed nearly total sway over the United Nations. According to Robert Welch, "The communists have now reached the point where they can count on just as complete control of the whole United Nations apparatus as they need."67/

The future promised ever increasing Communist hegemony over the United Nations. In the estimation of Hans F. Sennholz, "We must anticipate the day when the U.N. majority will vote consistently Communistic." And then, as Congressman James B. Utt predicted, "You can expect to see a one-world government, Communist controlled, under the United Nations."68/

The New Right considered atheism yet another strike against the United Nations. Ezra Taft Benson denounced the U.N. as "Godless" because "there is no mention of God in the United Nation's Charter," and without reference to Almighty God in its basic document the United Nations, in the words of another New Rightist, "is not a Christian organization. It is unashamedly Godless."* Thus the "utterly godless" United Nations typified "an Antichrist institution."69/

---

*Note--Incidentally, the venerated United States Constitution mentions God's name only one time (and probably as an afterthought). Article Seven refers to the date as "the Year of our Lord" 1787.

131

One World

The United Nations threatened to subvert America's national sovereignty. For instance, Barry Goldwater feared "that our involvement in the United Nations may be leading to an unconstitutional surrender of American sovereignty," while Christian Economics also expressed alarm that "little by little we are substituting loyalty to [the] U.N. in place of loyalty to our own country."70/

The New Right held that the American Liberal welcomed the wholesale destruction of United States sovereignty in the interests of his beloved "One-World" Utopian dream. Thus every trace of American national identity would vanish and each United States citizen would become just another "citizen of the world." War would disappear forever as nationalistic rivalries subsided altogether. The World's people would lay down their swords and embrace as true brothers.

As expected, the New Right totally rejected the entire concept of One-World. To begin with, world government led to the horrors of Communism, not utopia. As Job Brinton stressed, "World government must inevitably be equated with Communism and dictatorship." The One-Worlders sought to establish world government without considering the aggressive designs of the Communist Conspiracy—the Communists fully intended to use world government to control the earth. Yet the idealistic One-Worlders refused to permit the inconvenient fact from spoiling their beautiful plans for universal peace and brotherhood. Therefore, the National Review called world government "the last refuge of men unwilling to face the reality of messianic Communism, unwilling to accept their moral responsibility to beat it down."71/

Furthermore, "God didn't intend it to be One World," as New Right pamphleteer Stephen Nenoff emphasized. The good Lord created a diverse planet containing several races, dozens of religious sects, scores of ethnic and nationality groups with countless political creeds and philosophies. Consequently, all signs pointed away from One-World towards ever increasing fragmentation of the globe's swiftly multiplying population.72/

The New Right feared that "One-World" would destroy Western Christian Civilization. Indeed Charles F. Robertson wrote that "the grisley thought of a world government tyranny would not be so shocking and so chilling if a majority of the world was Christian." Unfortunately, the earth contained "a majority made up of pagans, atheists and Communists..."73/

One-World would place the White race at a distinct numerical disadvantage vis-a-vis the colored races. Marilyn R. Allen observed that "the white race is a world-wide minority of color. The coloreds are united and 'on the march' against the white race everywhere." George

Lincoln Rockwell outlined how "the dark races on the earth are uniting in a bloody mutiny against the white race which is outnumbered by more than 7 to 1."74/

Accordingly, any democratic system of world government automatically placed the minority White race under the control of the majority non-White peoples of the earth. As Dean Clarence Manion warned, "Any scheme for a 'democratic' international organization of the world would put" the United States of America "at the mercy of a predatory population pool in which we would be outnumbered at the rate of 16 to 1." Stephen Nenoff predicted, "Should this One World idea become a reality, such cities as Dallas, Fort Worth, or Chicago will be ruled by Asiatics because the bulk of the human race lives in Asia."75/

By the mid-1960's Hans F. Sennholz described the United Nations as "a family of Afro-Asian nations with a minority of Western observers." And any program of world government established under the United Nations framework would reduce the United States "to a mediocrity among the nations of the world, and subject to...foreign ideologies," to quote Congressman James B. Utt. Another publication summed up the New Right's strong opposition to United Nations sponsored world government quite succinctly: "Farwell sic to sovereignty, Farwell sic to the Republic, All hail the omnipotent U.N. world government, with the United States possessing one vote among 110, and with the number still growing."76/

"Bestial lust and savage hate"

The New Right heaped scorn upon the non-White peoples of the world, especially the Black Africans. Frequent terms used to describe Black Africans throughout New Right literature included: animalistic, barbaric, bestial, cannibalistic, heathen, rhythmic, satanic, sensual, and violent. For instance, Dan Smoot called Africa a continent "where millions of blacks will be under constant incitement to bestial lust and savage hate." George Lincoln Rockwell referred to the tropical peoples of the earth as "black and mongrel human garbage."77/

The New Right saw Black Africa standing at an incredibly low level of societal development. Stuart Cloete believed that "the African is still in an infantile stage of violence. He cannot think, argue or rationalize. His answer to any problem is the spear, the club or the witch doctor." James Burnham concluded that "for the most part the natives are...at the stage of primitive, pre-civilized barbarism; quite simply, savagery."78/

As a result, the New Right never looked down upon European imperialism as an absolute evil. Professor Anthony T. Bouscaren suggested that "the time has come to stop talking about Western colonialism as if it were an unmitigated evil. Western colonialism is no more an evil than adolescence." Timothy McInerny stated that "colonialism has many facets, only a few of them bad." In the same vein, James Burnham characterized "the colonial system" as "a reasonable solution for a transition period to civilization. The colonial system was abused, sometimes fearfully. It also accomplished much, and abuses can be corrected."79/

For the most part, European Imperialism brought the blessings of higher civilization to Africa. Robert Welch praised the imperial powers for their "enlightened and benevolent rule," while Destiny maintained that "Except for the establishment of law and order by the white race...in Africa, unabated barbarism, and all that it entails, would have continued to flourish there."80/

The New Right still accepted the "White Man's Burden." The superior White race had an obligation to uplift the inferior races of the earth. Barry Goldwater emphasized "that the privilege of being born in the West carries with it the responsibility of extending our good fortune to others. We are the bearers of Western civilization, the most noble product of the heart and mind of man." Goldwater added that "if, in Africa, the West has failed in the past to do the full measure of its duty, then all the more reason for doing our duty now." Frank S. Meyer lamented that...

> It has become fashionable to laugh at the phrase, 'the white man's burden,' but in the laughter what is forgotten, perhaps purposefully, is that the hegemony of Western civilization was indeed a burden, the assumption of which...represented high purpose, and confidence that the truth by which the West lived was the highest truth known to man. Behind all the self-congratulatory encomiums to which we treat ourselves about the 'dissolution of colonialism' and the 'end of imperialism,' is the hard truth: decay of belief, failure of nerve and confidence, an immoral casting aside of burdens, a sloughing of responsibility.81/

Thus the Black African still desperately needed the helping hand of the White man in order to make progress. As Stuart Cloete disclosed, "Without white direction and control" the Blackman "can do nothing. There are no African achievements." American Nazi leader Rockwell concurred: "In the darker races, slavery, cannibalism, brutality and tyranny still prevail, whenever the influence of the White Race is sufficiently removed.'82/

The New Right considered the liberation of colonial Africa during the 1950's and 1960's a total disaster. The American Mercury insisted that "Freedom is Rape; Independence is Murder." Robert Masters wondered, "What in the world...is to be gained by encouraging the premature independence of nations whose peoples are still largely superstitious witch-worshipers, cannibals and spear-throwing savages?" George Lincoln Rockwell lashed out, "Let's give these cannibals real 'freedom'--and they will soon be back to their natural state of nakedness, cannibalism, corruption, and filth." Then Rockwell howled, "The Game of 'Let's pretend That Niggers are People' produces More International Insanity in Africa !"83/

The gruesome spectacle of these newly liberated Black African states joining the United Nations appalled the New Right. The Economic Council Letter complained that "we have allowed the General Assembly of the UN to be stacked with African countries, many of them hardly out of savagery." Likewise, Destiny mentioned that "even cannibalism is reported as far from extinct in the land of African groups recently accorded UN membership."84/

The New Right denounced the anti-colonial frenzy sweeping through the Third World. J. Barry Gardnes regretted, "the bestialities committed in the name of self-determination and anti-colonialism." In an essay, "Satan Stalks the Earth in Jungle Darkness," Edith Essig expressed concern that this "dogged drive to expel the white man from Africa" will "wipe out the gains of colonialism" and will "rally the primitive blacks to join with the hordes of Asia in a rapidly-mounting assault upon white Christian civilization." She noted that "the beat of the tom-toms...ritual murder and cannibalism mark the...path of retrogression to the jungle."85/

The New Right believed that the International Communist Conspiracy stimulated this virulent anti-colonialism. In the opinion of Kenneth De Courcy, "The entire policy of all anti-colonial or pro-colored movements is motivated by Communist agents." Robert Welch recounted how the Communists have cleverly used the phrase "anti-colonialism" as "a slogan and a weapon to drive out of one 'underdeveloped' country after another the civilizing influences and stabilizing governments of the British, Dutch, French, and other leading powers."86/

The Communists create anti-Western imperialist sentiment in order to direct attention away from their own brutal imperialism. Kenneth De Courcy pointed out how "Communism encourages and fosters every hostile demonstration against Western colonialism with the aim of preventing people from seeing, understanding and opposing Soviet colonialism." Thus while International Communism enjoyed picturing itself as the best friend and benefactor of the earth's down-trodden, exploited peoples, Destiny reminded its readers that "it is the Communists, not the West, who hold whole nations in subjection through force and terrorism."87/

135

By the early 1960's the Third World had unwittingly become the prime focus of the Cold War rivalry between the Free World and the Communist bloc. E. H. Rawlings thought that "the main battleground in the struggle between freedom and totalitarianism is today in the underdeveloped countries, because the course of events in them will eventually decide the kind of political system that will become dominent sic in the world." Considering the enormity of the stakes, the United States could never accept the liberation of any country if this newly emancipated nation threatened to fall into the Communist orbit. Barry Goldwater emphasized that "We cannot acquiesce in independence movements where independence means Communist domination or a return to savagery."88/

In summation, the New Right advocated a vigorous American foreign policy based upon total victory in the Cold War over International Communism. Despite the risks of war, the United States must forge ahead fearlessly, proud of our great military tradition, confident in the strength of our armed forces, determined to protect American national sovereignty and American interests throughout the world.

Unfortunately, America's Liberal dominated foreign policy floundered in the face of this awesome Communist challenge. The American Liberal chased the illusion of peaceful co-existence with Communism while simultaneously appeasing the enemy in a cowardly attempt to avoid war. The Liberal downgraded the American armed services and pushed for a dangerous program of disarmament. Instead of actually confronting Communism with military force he relied solely upon foreign economic aid. While pursuing his One-World Utopian dream the Liberal surrendered American sovereignty to the Communist controlled United Nations. The Liberal ultimately sought a democratically organized world government ruled by the non-Christian, non-White, Third World peoples of the Earth hardly out of barbarism and cannibalism.

CHAPTER SIX - Notes

1. John Tower, A Program for Conservatives (New York: MacFadden-Bartell Corporation, 1962), p. 19;
New York Times Magazine, (September 17, 1961), p. 100;
Goldwater, Why Not Victory?, p. 163;
Ibid., p. 23.

Likewise, General William H. Wilbur (retired) favored "a campaign whose announced objective is victory, victory over Communism ..." Manion Forum Network broadcast as quoted in the Beacon-Light Herald, (December, 1960), p. 22.

2. Goldwater, The Conscience of a Conservative, p. 97;
Barry Goldwater as quoted in Human Events, (January 27, 1961), p. 64.

3. Goldwater, The Conscience of a Conservative, p. 122;
Goldwater, Why Not Victory?, p. 44;
Goldwater, The Conscience of a Conservative, p. 121.

Therefore, Goldwater suggested, "we look at America's foreign policy and ask whether it is conducive to victory," Goldwater, The Conscience of Conservative, p. 94.

4. Manion Forum Network broadcast (December 23, 1962);
Goldwater, Why Not Victory?, p. 154.

5. Goldwater, Why Not Victory?, p. 65;
Barry Goldwater as quoted in the New York Times Magazine, (September 17, 1961), p. 102.

6. "On the Right", April 1, 1965;
National Review, (December 4, 1962), p. 424;
Tower, A Program for Conservatives, p. 31;
Goldwater, The Conscience of a Conservative, p. 94;
Ibid., p. 93.

Barry Goldwater elaborated upon this point:

We do not, of course, want to achieve victory by force of arms. If possible, overt hostilities should always be avoided; especially is this so when a shooting war may cause the death of many millions of people, including our own. But we cannot, for that reason, make the avoidance of a shooting war our chief objective....We cannot, by proclamation, make war 'unthinkable.' Goldwater, The Conscience of a Conservative, pp. 92-93.

7.   Mike Newberry, The Yahoos (New York: Marzani and Munsell, 1964), p. 30;
Stanhope T. McReady, Birch Putsch Plans For 1964 (n.p.:   Damino Publications, 1963), p. 33;
Newberry, The Yahoos, p. 30.

8.   Manion Forum Network broadcast (April 1, 1962);
National Review, (November 6, 1962), p. 341.

9.   Goldwater, The Conscience of a Conservative, p. 90;
Speech by Senator Barry Goldwater before the American Legion Convention of the State of Texas delivered at Houston, Texas on July 28, 1961, as quoted in U.S. Congress, Senate, Congressional Record, 87th Cong., 1st Sess., July 31, 1961, vol. 107, part II, p. 14105.

Granville F. Knight M.D. pointed out that "we tremble in fear of atomic annihilation and are told surrender is the only alternative." American Mercury, (September, 1961), p. 26.

10.   The Weekly Crusader, (September 18, 1964), p. 1;
National Review, (February 27, 1962), p. 127.

11.   The Weekly Crusader, (June 28, 1963), p. 6;
Manion Forum Network broadcast (September 30, 1962).

12.   Tower, A Program For Conservatives, p. 20;
Goldwater, Why Not Victory?, p. 161.

13.   Human Events, (November 10, 1961), p. 764;
Ibid., p. 763;
J. Kesner Kahn in the American Mercury, (April, 1962), p. 8.

14.   News and Views, (April, 1963), p. 3.

15.   Goldwater, The Conscience of a Conservative, p. 92.

16.   American Mercury, (May, 1960), p. 63;
National Defender, (October, 1963), p. 1.

17.   Stormer, None Dare Call It Treason, p. 7;
American Opinion, (July, 1964), p. 49.

The New Right emphasized the historic boldness and courage of the American people coupled with our total commitment to victory. As J. Edgar Hoover announced, "Challenge, not compromise--victory, not defeat--these are words which have real meaning for true Americans ! " Cross and the Flag, (December, 1962), p. 31;

Likewise, Barry Goldwater declared that "the American people have never failed when freedom has been challenged." Goldwater, Why Not Victory?, p. 17.

18. Manion Forum Network broadcast (April 1, 1962); Tower, A Program For Conservatives, p. 19.

The Economic Council Letter added that "Peaceful coexistence and a no-win policy have brought the image of the United States to about the lowest point in history." Economic Council Letter, (January 1, 1965), p. 4.

19. Manion Forum Network broadcast (January 7, 1962); New Guard, (April, 1964), p. 6; News and Views, (August, 1963), p. 3.

20. Manion Forum Network broadcast (July 21, 1963).

Along the same lines, The Weekly Crusader attacked "the suicidal idiocy of policies towards communism followed by the ruling left-wing liberal clique." The Weekly Crusader, (June 28, 1963), p. 6.

21. Los Angeles Times, June 2, 1963.

22. American Opinion, (July-August, 1963), p. 67; Sexson and Miles, The Challenge of Conservatism, p. 15.

Likewise, Barry Goldwater protested...

I don't care how many computers this Administration has, or how many self-styled 'whiz kids' man them, the life-or-death decisions of national defense cannot wisely be made in an atmosphere that suppresses dissent, ignores experienced military advice, downgrades military men, and divides the Pentagon into a five-sided arena for the abuse rather than the development of ideas. Goldwater, Where I Stand, p. 71.

23. Washington Post, October 13, 1963.

24. National Review, (November 4, 1961), p. 292; Goldwater, Why Not Victory?, p. 183.

25. Memphis, Tennessee Press-Scimitar, July 26, 1961 as quoted in Kent and Phoebe Courtney, The Case of General Edwin A. Walker, p. 108; National Review, (December 4, 1962), p. 445.

26. Phyllis Schlafly and Rear Admiral Chester Ward (retired), Strike From Space (New York: The Devin-Adair Company, 1966), p. 79.

27.   Economic Council Letter, (May 1, 1962), p. 1;
Courtney, The Case of General Edwin A. Walker, p. 55.

28.   U.S. Congress, Senate, Congressional Record, 87th Cong., 1st
Sess., July 3, 1961, vol. 107, no. 11, p. 14174.

29.   Courtney, The Case of General Edwin A. Walker, preface;
Mark Sherwin, The Extremists, (New York: St. Martin's Press, 1963),
p. 128.

30.   Alberta Lachicotte, Rebel Senator (New York: The Devin-
Adair Company, 1966), p. 191.

31.   For an excellent account of the 1962 Ole Miss Riot see Russell
H. Barrett, Integration at Ole Miss (Chicago: Quadrangle Books, 1965).

32.   Economic Council Letter, (May 1, 1964), p. 2.

33.   Los Angeles Times, October 9, 1962;
National Review, (December 4, 1962), p. 445.

34.   Goldwater, Why Not Victory?, p. 180.

35.   Walter Darnell Jacobs, "Home-made Holocaust" National
Review, (December 4, 1962), p. 444;
Evans, The Politics of Surrender, p. 507.

36.   Fletcher Knebel and Charles W. Bailey II, Seven Days in May
(New York: Harper and Row, 1962);
Eugene Burdick and Harvey Wheeler, Fail-Safe (New York: McGraw-
Hill, 1962);
Doctor Strangelove, Hawk Films (Released by Columbia Pictures Corp.,
1963), produced and directed by Stanley Kubrick;
National Review, (December 4, 1962), p. 444.

37.   Evans, The Politics of Surrender, p. 507.

38.   Ibid., p. 508;
The Weekly Crusader, (April 24, 1964), p. 6.

Jack Moffitt noted that the spokesmen on the Left are "scaring
us into abandoning our nuclear weapons."   American Opinion, (April,
1964), p. 69.

39.   National Review Bulletin, (July 24, 1962), p. 1;
Dan Smoot Report, (May 20, 1963), p. 154.

40.   Goldwater, Why Not Victory?, p. 113;
Speech by Senator John Tower as quoted in U.S. Congress, Senate,
Congressional Record, 87th Cong., 2nd Sess., January 29, 1962, vol. 108,
Part I, p. 1043.

Likewise, Dan Smoot described the problems of nuclear
disarmament:

> Suppose non-communist nations could make an agreement
> with communist dictators which resulted in the actual world-
> wide elimination of all modern weapons of war. What would
> then prevent the hordes of Asia and Africa from overrunning
> the civilized world with butcher knives? Dan Smoot Report,
> (May 20, 1963), p. 153.

41.   Goldwater, Why Not Victory?, p. 121;
National Review, (January 30, 1960), p.67.

42.   Goldwater, Where I Stand, p. 51.

43.   Goldwater, Why Not Victory?, pp. 156-157;
The Weekly Crusader, (August 23, 1963), p. 4.

44.   The Weekly Crusader, (August 23, 1963), p. 7;
Ibid., (June 28, 1963), p. 4;
"On the Right", April 4, 1964.

45.   Manion Forum Network broadcast (September 1, 1963);
The Daughters of the American Revolution Magazine as quoted in The
Weekly Crusader, (August 23, 1963), p. 6;
The Weekly Crusader, (August 23, 1963), p. 7.

46.   National Review Bulletin (August 21, 1962), p. 3;
Human Events, (August 3, 1963), p. 13.

47.   National Review Bulletin, (September 17, 1963), p. 6;
The Weekly Crusader, (August 23, 1963), p. 5.

48.   Evans, The Politics of Surrender, p. 124.

49.   The Weekly Crusader, (January 22, 1965), p. 3.

50.   Dan Smoot Report, (March 1, 1965), p. 68;
Ibid., (April 29, 1963), p. 135.

51.   Dan Smoot Report, (April 29, 1963), p. 135;
Goldwater, The Conscience of a Conservative, p. 98.

52.   Destiny, (November, 1963), p. 234.

53.   American Mercury, (February, 1961), p. 4;
The Weekly Crusader, (May 24, 1963), p. 1;
Goldwater, Why Not Victory?, p. 171;
Goldwater, Where I Stand, p. 30.

   Christian Economics observed that "the single most important error about communism is the belief that it is caused by poverty, hunger and social injustice." Christian Economics, (June 9, 1964), p. 1.

54.   Christian Economics, (June 9, 1964), p. 1;
Goldwater, Why Not Victory?, p. 171.

55.   American Opinion, (December, 1962), p. 32;
Goldwater, Why Not Victory?, p. 171.

56.   The Weekly Crusader, (January 22, 1965), p. 1;
Goldwater, Where I Stand, p. 30.

57.   America's Future, (March 30, 1962), p. 1;
Goldwater, Where I Stand, p. 30;
Goldwater, The Conscience of a Conservative, p. 123.

58.   Human Events, (September 29, 1961), p. 647.

59.   Economic Council Letter, (December 15, 1961), pp. 1-4;
New York Times, September 20, 1964;
Stormer, None Dare Call It Treason, p. 9.

60.   Welch, The New Americanism, p.65.

61.   Goldwater, Where I Stand, p. 35.

62.   The Weekly Crusader, (November 1, 1963), p. 2;
Human Events, (July 14, 1961), p. 443;
Manchester Union Leader as quoted in The Citizen, (July-August, 1963), p. 11;

   For a further look at this strange man, William Loeb, the reader should consult, Kevin Cash's, Who the Hell is William Loeb? (Manchester, New Hampshire: Amoskeag Press, Inc., 1975).

63.   Evans, The Politics of Surrender, p. 136.

64.   American Mercury (April, 1963), p. 10;
Christian Economics, (March 6, 1962), p. 1;
Speech by Congressman James B. Utt, U.S. Congress, House, Congressional Record, 87th Cong., 2nd Sess., January 15, 1962, vol. 8, Part I, p. 215.

65.   Benjamin R. Epstein and Arnold Forster, Report on the John Birch Society 1966 (New York: Random House, 1966), p. 39.

Mrs. M. Conan stated, "The UN Charter was drafted by Leo Pasvolsky, Harry Dexter White and Alger Hiss, all three rabid Communists." Beacon-Light Herald, (May-June, 1961), p. 15.

66.   American Mercury, (April, 1963), p. 10; Letter from the Council on American Relations to the American Mercury, (March, 1961), p. 25; Christian Economics, (June 29, 1965), p. 1.

67.   Welch, The New Americanism, p. 77.

Welch's John Birch Society cohort John Rousselot concurred: "today the organization is controlled and administered by the Communists."   Epstein and Forster, Report on the John Birch Society 1966, p. 39.

Destiny magazine also agreed: "the UN is completely dominated by Communists and one-world conspirators." Destiny, (February, 1964), p. 42.

68.   Christian Economics, (March 3, 1964), p. 3; Ibid., (May 1, 1962), p. 1.

69.   Benson, The Red Carpet, p. 195; George Winder in Christian Economics, (August 6, 1963), p. 1; Billy James Hargis in Hargis, Communist America -- Must It Be?, p. 126.

Similarly, Mrs. M. Conan complained that at the signing of the U.N. Charter "the name of God was omitted so as not to offend the Russians..." Beacon-Light Herald, (May-June, 1961), p. 15.

In addition, the United Nations contained sinners and moral degenerates.   Cross and the Flag explained that "some of the most important persons in the United Nations are homosexuals, adulterers, and sex deviates." Cross and the Flag, (October, 1963), p. 21.

70.   Goldwater, The Conscience of a Conservative, p. 117; Christian Economics, (January 23, 1962), p. 2.

71.   American Mercury, (January, 1962), p. 73; National Review, (March 12, 1963), p. 197.

72.   Stephen Nenoff, Who Are the Fellow Travelers? (Denton, Texas: Southern Patriotic Breeze Publications, n.d.), p. 10.

73. Cross and the Flag, (April, 1962), p. 3.

Thus in the opinion of the Cross and the Flag, "The Western Christian nations...would be greatly in the minority and subject to this global majority under a United Nations World Government military dictatorship." Cross and the Flag, (June, 1962), p. 5.

74. Marilyn R. Allen from Kingdom Digest, (August, 1960), as quoted in the Beacon-Light Herald, (March-April, 1961), p. 32; Rockwell Report, (August 15, 1963), p. 2.

75. Manion, The Conservative American, p. 135; Nenoff, Who Are the Fellow Travelers?, p. 10.

76. Christian Economics, (March 3, 1964), p. 3; Manion Forum Network broadcast (March 4, 1962); Chicago Tribune Editorial, September 25, 1963 as quoted in the National Defender, (November, 1963), p. 1.

77. Dan Smoot Report, (April 15, 1963), p. 120; Rockwell Report, (May 15, 1964), p. 6.

78. Stuart Cloete as quoted in Carleton Putnam, Race and Reason: A Yankee View (Washington, D.C. Public Affairs Press, 1961), p. 81; National Review, (October 22, 1960), p. 240.

79. News and Views, (February, 1963), p. 3; McInerny, The Private Man, p. 75; National Review, (October 22, 1960), p. 240.

80. Welch, The New Americanism, p. 180; Destiny, (August, 1960), p. 173.

Timothy McInerny announced that since the White man...

> brought benefits to wild or backward peoples, he was entitled to the riches that the effort brought him. He brought justice where none existed before; he brought rules of sanitation and health to regions of superstition and witchcraft; he brought cultivation, mining and markets to areas wherein only barbarism and cannibalism had existed. McInerny, The Private Man, p. 75.

81. Goldwater, Why Not Victory?, p. 139; National Review, (April 8, 1961), p. 218.

82. Stuart Cloete as quoted in Putnam, Race and Reason, p. 81; Rockwell Report, (April 15, 1963), p. 4.

Timothy McInerny added that "By taking away the stability of colonialism, and putting irresponsible agitators in charge of huge sections of the world's population, we expose ourselves to the eventual dragging down of the human race." McInerny, The Private Man, p. 77.

83. American Mercury, (January, 1962), p. 19;
Ibid., p. 22;
Rockwell Report, (March 1, 1964), p. 5;
Ibid., p. 4.

84. Economic Council Letter, (February 1, 1962), p. 4;
Destiny, (January, 1962), p. 3.

85. New Guard, (April, 1965), p. 21;
Cross and the Flag, (May, 1962), p. 32.

86. Destiny, (October, 1961), p. 225;
Welch, The New Americanism, p. 64.

87. Destiny, (March, 1962), p. 64;
Ibid., (November, 1962), p. 223.

88. American Mercury, (July, 1961), p. 73;
Goldwater, Why Not Victory?, p. 138.

145

CHAPTER SEVEN

THE KENNEDY ASSASSINATION AND THE CIVIL
RIGHTS MOVEMENT

Fall, 1963: Tension in the Air

The mood of the American people grew increasingly tense and violent during the Fall of 1963. The Civil Rights struggle moved into a more militant phase. After an explosion ripped through a Negro church in strife-torn Birmingham, Alabama, killing four little Black girls, President John Kennedy sent a strong Civil Rights Bill to Congress for consideration. America's racial crisis reached many Northern cities. A rent strike directed against slum lords in Harlem soon spread to Newark and San Francisco. Frequent clashes between Negroes and the police dramatized the dangerous situation inside America's urban ghettos. And from far off Vietnam, as the United States slipped deeper and deeper into a quagmire, came the sudden, shocking military coup in Saigon followed by the brutal murder of President Diem.

American politics also reached an inflamed state during the Fall of 1963. New Right Senator Barry Goldwater of Arizona assumed the front-runner position in the pre-primary jockeying for the upcoming 1964 Republican Presidential nomination. The New Right worked busily for Goldwater at the grass roots level in an effort destined to prove successful the following July at San Francisco. Finally, a Kennedy-Goldwater Presidential race looming on the horizon for November, 1964 promised to be a classic Liberal vs. Conservative duel.

The tension between the Left and Right had already reached the breaking point in the state of Texas. United Nations Ambassador Adlai Stevenson, the very symbol of contemporary American Liberalism, found himself roughed up, spat upon and bumped on the head with picket signs wielded by an angry mob of New Rightists in the city of Dallas in October, 1963.*

---

*Note—The tragic assassination of President John Kennedy on November 22, 1963 injured, perhaps unfairly, the reputation of Dallas, Texas. The Liberal news media subsequently described Dallas as a city consumed with hatred, crawling with intolerant, trigger-happy, Right-wing Rednecks. However, Dallas has always been a rather peaceful, cosmopolitan Southern community. Houston, not Dallas was the real center of New Right activities in Texas which so deeply disturbed the Liberal press.

147

The Assassination of President John F. Kennedy

Thus despite expressions of grave concern for his personal safety, President John F. Kennedy travelled to Dallas a month later on November 22, 1963. The President hoped to halt the estrangement of the Conservative-oriented, Texas Democrats from the party's Liberal national leadership. Furthermore, Kennedy prepared to deliver a strong verbal blast at the "extremism" of the New Right and in a highly provocative gesture chose Dallas as his forum.

The New Right sympathized with the demonstrators who had attacked U.N. Ambassador Adlai Stevenson outside the hall. Dan Smoot believed that "the people who picketed Stevenson were not wild-eyed ignoramuses. The ignoramuses were inside applauding what Stevenson said." Smoot predicted that the picketing and demonstrating would continue to "grow in frequency, and become increasingly unmanageable. And there will be head bumpings that are not accidental, until Americans who believe in the traditions and principles of their society are allowed some better means of expression." In the same vein, George Lincoln Rockwell gloated, "In Dallas, a few weeks before the President arrived, right-wingers had bashed Adlai Stevenson with a picket sign and otherwise given plenty of evidence that there was a lot of right-wing hatred of the President in the area."1/

However, the New Right desperately wished to avoid another violent, ugly incident during President Kennedy's November 22nd visit to Dallas. Consequently, they approved of the actions of one opponent of J.F.K. who took out a full page newspaper advertisement in the Dallas Morning News denouncing the President, rather than risk staging another demonstration which might get out of hand.

Moreover, the New Right understood that the authorities diligently watched for any signs of possible Right-wing trouble. M. Stanton Evans pointed out that "In Dallas, Texas, federal agencies took careful measures to ascertain the whereabouts of right-wing agitators to forestall the possibility of violence." Likewise, Nazi leader Rockwell said that "before the President arrived every strong right-winger in Dallas was hunted down and kept under fantastic surveillance."2/

In the midst of this strained atmosphere, soon after the deadly rifle shots rang out in Dallas, the National News Media accused the New Right of ambushing the President of the United States. Television and radio commentators drew the apparent connection between the city of Dallas, the assault a month before upon Adlai Stevenson, the powerful Right-wing Texas opposition to J.F.K., and now the assassination.

The New Right bitterly resented these assertions. As Frank S. Meyer grumbled, "hardly had John F. Kennedy been officially pronounced dead than the Liberal Establishment broke forth in a nationwide

148

television and radio orgy of lynch incitement against the American Right." In the same vein, Gerald L. K. Smith noted that "The character assassins on the left and [the] news media mind-washers were itching for the chance to say, 'another symptom of right wing extremism.' "3/

No wonder a sense of panic spread through the ranks of the New Right immediately after J.F.K. had been slain in Dallas by an unidentified and as yet uncaptured gunman. Since most early news bulletins seemed to implicate the New Right in this shocking crime, the Reverend Billy James Hargis confided, "It may be difficult for my readers to understand my fear upon hearing the right-wing accused of participation in President Kennedy's death."4/

"Had Oswald escaped..."

Therefore, the New Right breathed a deep sigh of relief when the Dallas police apprehended Lee Harvey Oswald, an avowed Marxist, and charged this rootless, young ex-Marine with the murder of the President. It goes without saying that the New Right had narrowly escaped disaster. As The Weekly Crusader emphasized, "the revelation...that Lee Oswald, a communist, had killed the President of the United States, was the only thing that saved the leaders of the anti-communist movements of the United States." The New Right shuddered at the prospect of a successful getaway by Lee Harvey Oswald. In the opinion of General Edwin A. Walker, "Had Oswald escaped, as I believe was intended, anti-communists would have received full blame for this dastardly deed by a communist conspirator." Dan Smoot announced that "if the President had been murdered by a maniac who claimed to be a John Bircher or a racial segregationist, the vigilantes of liberalism would really be stalking the land."5/

The New Right believed that the Communists had murdered J.F.K. in Dallas hoping to pin the crime on the Right. As The Weekly Crusader stated, "communist Oswald hoped to assassinate the President and make a clean get-away, thus blaming it on the anti-communists or the conservative right-wing in the United States." Along the same lines, Harold Lord Varney listed the Communists' motives for shooting the President in Dallas:

1) Produce a violent national reaction against the Right-wing.
2) Pull the rug out from under the Goldwater movement by associating it with murderous 'extremists'.
3) Put a damper on all Right-wing 'extremist' ideas.
4) Deflect the masses away from anti-Communist 'extremist' leaders like Robert Welch and General Walker.

5) Place a moratorium on all criticism of Kennedy's Leftist policies and programs.6/

Of course, part of the Communist scheme backfired when Lee Harvey Oswald failed to elude capture after the assassination. The startled American public soon learned of Oswald's Communist connections. The International Communist Conspiracy naturally feared that Oswald might confess. So two days later, on November 24, 1963, Jack Ruby, owner of a sleazy, strip-tease joint, conveniently murdered Oswald himself right inside the Dallas Police Station. The New Right always maintained that Jack Ruby, a rather shady character, had participated in the Communist plot to kill the President and discredit the Right, and then acting upon orders from above forever silenced Lee Harvey Oswald.

The New Right stressed the irony of the situation: President John F. Kennedy had come to Dallas to denounce the so-called "extremism" of the far-Right only to be gunned down by the far-Left. As The Defender remarked:

> At the time he was killed the president was only a few minutes away from delivering a speech which contained some of the strongest words he had yet uttered against 'the extreme rightists' in American politics. He, of course, never delivered the speech. He was cut down by a bullet fired by the hand of an extreme leftist.7/

Moreover, American Opinion suggested that "the country has been so conditioned to believe that the danger of...violence comes from the Right, that it has completely overlooked that it is the left which preaches a philosophy of violence as a means to achieving its political ends." Indeed the American Liberal issued perennial warnings about "the danger of the far right" while completely disregarding the menace of domestic Communism. The Rockwell Report pointed out that "Kennedy and his gang did their damnedest to promote the illusion that all danger in America comes from the 'ultra-conservative,' 'radical-rightist' 'super patriots'--the racists, White Supremists, States Righters, etc."8/

In the eyes of the New Right, the Liberal's exclusive preoccupation with Right-wing violence probably cost John F. Kennedy his life. Human Events explained that the "Reports from Dallas indicate that the New Frontier's belittling of the internal Communist threat may well have been the chief reason Oswald was ignored, despite knowledge of his left-wing extremism." Thus as Human Events concluded, "the government's obsession with 'right wingers'--to the point of almost ignoring left-wing extremists--definitely contributed to...President Kennedy's untimely death."9/

The New Right quickly recovered from the trauma of the Kennedy assassination and adopted an "I told you so" attitude towards their Liberal foes. The Weekly Crusader wondered whether the myopic Liberals, at long last, had "learned the mistakes of their ways, that is, trusting the communists, appeasing the communists, co-existing with the communists?" Indeed after years of abuse the supposedly violence-prone New Right took grim satisfaction in describing how the far Left had murdered the President. Dean Clarence Manion reminded his nationwide radio audience that "what killed President Kennedy was Communism." The John Birch Society Bulletin for the month of December, 1963 contained decals proclaiming, "Communism killed Kennedy."10/

Yet the Left seemed unable or unwilling to accept the simple truth that a Communist, Lee Harvey Oswald, had slain the President. As James Burnham remarked, "In November, 1963, the liberals of all nations found themselves utterly unable to assimilate the fact that President Kennedy had been shot by a confirmed and long-time Marxist." The one-dimensional Liberal mind, apparently, could associate political assassination only with the Right, never the Left.11/

New Rightists complained that American Liberals had naturally assumed that the killing of J.F.K. represented the handiwork of Redneck bigots, trigger-happy Christian super-patriots, Fascist-oriented military officers, or Texas oil billionaires. Tocsin* pointed out that "the American left was greviously disappointed to learn that the murder of President Kennedy was not effected by a racist bigot." Likewise, America's Future noted that "it evidently came as a terrific shock to the left-wingers that so horrible a deed was perpetrated not by individuals and groups speaking out for traditional Americanism...but by an avowed left-wing Marxist." Finally, William F. Buckley, Jr. denounced those "who will not be satisfied until a commission comes along that proves Kennedy was struck down by General Walker while H. L. Hunt was passing him the ammunition."12/

"Hate mongers"

American Liberals felt a surprisingly small amount of bitterness towards Lee Harvey Oswald, the Marxist who had slain their beloved John Kennedy, but continued to savagely pummel the New Right. As

---

*Note—UCLA History Professor Richard Weiss has pointed out to me the striking nature of the magazine's name "Tocsin" which means, of course, an alarm bell. Published in the San Francisco Bay area Tocsin kept a close watch upon Left-wing political activities at the University of California, Berkeley and sounded warnings over any signs of Communist influence on campus.

Dan Smoot remarked, "Liberals, who idolized the President, expressed little resentment for the murderer but heaped venom on conservatives." The Left, Smoot asserted, refused to permit the inconvenient fact that a Communist had killed J.F.K. from side-tracking their smear campaign against the Right. The Left, therefore, proceeded to imply that since the New Right detested John Kennedy and probably wanted him dead anyway, many New Rightists would have also pulled the trigger if given the opportunity! Liberal author I. F. Stone stated that "there are hundreds of thousands in the South who had murder in their hearts for the Kennedys..." Similarly, Illinois Democratic Senator Paul Douglas insisted that "while the assassination of the President was undoubtedly carried out by a man of the extreme left...it is also true that the so-called radical right has been preaching hatred for some years."13/

Furthermore, the New Right objected to suggestions that the "right-wing extremists" and the "hate-mongers" had created an unhealthy climate in Dallas which had stimulated a crazed gunman to act. As Tocsin editorialized, "Irresponsibility continues to mark discussion of the assassination of President Kennedy....the blame continues to be placed on 'hate' groups for creating an atmosphere of tension." Dan Smoot complained that "Dallasites were accused of hate-mongering fanaticism, of having molded the twisted mind of Lee Harvey Oswald, a stranger in their midst."14/

Moreover, the New Right saw the Left spreading the preposterous notion that somehow all of the American people shared the collective guilt for the isolated act of a lone, over-zealous, Marxist gunman. According to California G.O.P. Congressman James Utt, "Following the assassination, there were four solid days of attempted brainwashing of the American people and the world into believing that all America must share the guilt. That is hokum and hogwash. The assassination was the work of a cool and calculating mind, steeped in communism..."15/

The Liberal gambit linking this so-called "extremism" and "hate-mongering' with the Kennedy assassination failed in the New Right's eyes on three counts. First of all, the good Right-wing citizens of Dallas, Texas may well have disliked J.F.K.; in truth, they probably hated him. Nevertheless, Dan Smoot quoted a sensible excerpt from the moderate Sacramento Bee: "The heat engendered by political conflict between liberals and conservatives had nothing to do with the fact that a communist shot the President."16/

Secondly, President Kennedy's killer, Lee Harvey Oswald, embraced Communism, which surely hates everything decent and humane found in Western Civilization. Thus as Wyoming Republican Senator Milward L. Simpson noted, "If hatred was a factor in the killing of John F. Kennedy the hatred was from the left - that hatred which would 'bury' America."17/

152

Finally, Lee Harvey Oswald acted because his Communist superiors ordered him to shoot the President. The Right-wing extremism in Dallas had nothing whatsoever to do with it. Harold Lord Varney explained that "Oswald, like every Communist who commits any crime having to do with the political world, was acting under orders from above." Likewise, The Weekly Crusader pointed out that "no communist does anything on his own. He waits for orders, and, like a robot, he obeys."18/

Nonetheless, the New Right objected that the American Left tried to exploit the Kennedy assassination for political advantage. The Congress found itself beseeched to pass everything from the Civil Rights Act to the tax cut in memory of the gallant, fallen, young President. The Left demanded a moratorium on partisan politics out of respect for the late Chief Executive, and insisted that all criticism of the Left coming from the New Right suddenly cease. The Left called for national unity behind the new Democratic President Lyndon B. Johnson who, in the same spirit, personally admonished the American people to stop "hating" one another during his November 27, 1963 address to a Joint Session of Congress:

> So let us put an end to the teaching and the preaching of hate and evil and violence. Let us turn away from the fanatics of the far left and the far right, from the apostles of bitterness and bigotry, from those defiant of law, and those who pour venom into our nation's bloodstream.19/

The New Right deeply resented these "attempts" to capitalize upon the Kennedy assassination. For instance, Tocsin acknowledged that "calls for unity are abroad in the land. But they ignore the real cause of disunity. There will be no unity until there is unity against communism." Moreover, in the opinion of Clarence Manion, this terrible tragedy was "being used to muffle debate" over important public issues. Perhaps most unfair of all, the Left asked the country to stop "hating" while continuing its savage attacks upon the New Right! As Tocsin explained, "All of the admonitions against hate which have been given since that fateful Friday [November 22, 1963] are basically concealed invitations to hate. It is all right to hate, they imply, as long as the hate is directed against those who feel that communism and Communists are despicable."20/

Kennedy vs. Goldwater

John F. Kennedy, Thirty-Fifth President of the United States, passed into history to become an instant American legend on Friday afternoon, November 22, 1963. Yet the tragic circumstances surrounding his death have since obscured an important fact: during the

Summer and Fall of 1963 J.F.K.'s political troubles had mounted steadily. In retrospect, New York Times editor Tom Wicker listed the President's problems: Congress refused to pass the Civil Rights Bill or the Administration's tax cut; Conservative Southern Democrats openly rebelled against the national Democratic party; the White Backlash surfaced in Northern cities; the T.F.X., Billy Sol Estes, and Bobby Baker scandals embarrassed the government; despite the heroics of the Cuban Missile Crisis, Fidel Castro remained firmly entrenched in Communist Cuba; and as the military and political situation in South Vietnam deteriorated, President Diem was deposed and murdered during a coup d'etat.21/

The New Right pointed out that President Kennedy's controversial measures had generated heated opposition during his last days in office. In the words of the National Review, "It is sobering to recall that there was great dissension, left and right, in respect to John Kennedy's policies, right up until the moment he died." Dan Smoot agreed: "Public opposition to the late President's policies had already reached the proportions of a major political revolt—and was growing fast."22/

Even the glittering Kennedy image had begun to tarnish badly. The awe-struck American people finally realized that the President's charismatic style simply disguised his meager results. As always, J.F.K. presented a marvelously handsome, witty appearance, "yet nothing, but nothing, important has been accomplished," complained William F. Buckley, Jr. Indeed an article written by Buckley a few months before the assassination titled, "The Decline of Mr. Kennedy?" suggested that "the grandiose rhetoric...is beginning to fall flat as the people discern the gruesome truth, that this efficient and likeable young man hasn't the least idea how to maneuver through the greatest crisis in world history." Furthermore, the week the President died, Victor Lasky's damaging biography J.F.K., The Man and the Myth topped the charts as America's best-selling, non-fiction book.23/

The public's growing disenchantment with the Kennedy Administration encouraged the New Right, already working hard to secure the next G.O.P. Presidential nomination for their own, favorite candidate, Arizona Senator Barry M. Goldwater. The New Right eagerly looked forward to the upcoming 1964 Election as a classic Liberal Democrat vs. Conservative Republican duel. Human Events described the 1964 Election as "The Battle of the Century: Kennedy vs. Goldwater." More-over, M. Stanton Evans, years later concluded that "in the autumn of 1963, John Kennedy looked like a very good prospect to lose the next presidential election—if his opponent were Barry Goldwater."24/

The political strength and self-confidence of the New Right reached its high point just prior to the murder of President Kennedy. According to Dan Smoot, "Before the assassination, there was a growing sense of optimism, almost of jubilation among American conservatives." With the benefit of hindsight, Barry Goldwater concurred: "the conservative revolution reached an astounding peak the week before the assassination of President John F. Kennedy."25/

Without question, the murder of J.F.K. took much of the steam out of the New Right. The memory of the slain President, the nation's deep yearning for unity, the sympathy for the new Chief Executive, coupled with the natural desire to give Lyndon Johnson "a fair chance" to show what he could do in office all helped the Liberal Democrats and hurt the New Right and Barry Goldwater.

The sudden accession of Lyndon Johnson to the Presidency upset the New Right's carefully laid plans to separate the more Conservative South from the rest of the Democratic party. The Kennedy years had produced a gradual estrangement between the Liberal Democratic Administration and the Southern wing of the party. Meanwhile, the Goldwater Republicans had made strong inroads down in Dixie, especially within the key state of Texas. Thus by the Fall of 1963 the South seemed ripe to reject Kennedy Liberalism and embrace Goldwaterism. As James J. Kilpatrick predicted, "Running against John Kennedy, Barry Goldwater could have swept the South." However, the murder of J.F.K. dramatically reversed the political situation in the South. As Kilpatrick observed, "politically, we are wiped out. We had built up three years of being against him. And now this capital investment in animosity has disappeared. No doubt we could work up a fresh loathing against Lyndon, given time and hard work, but there is not much time before the '64 convention..."26/

The Kennedy assassination on November 22, 1963 defused partisan politics quiet effectively for the next few months. The Economic Council Letter described the nation's quite tempo during early Spring, 1964: "The country is still in a lull. The short-run economic news is good. The turmoil in foreign affairs has momentarily subsided. Politics is muted. The Democrats are talking platitudes. What the Republicans are saying can hardly be heard." An uneasy calm descended upon the land, like the calm before the big storm. On April 11, 1964 the New Right paused briefly to bury its supreme hero General Douglas MacArthur. The Economic Council Letter commented, "The funeral of General MacArthur fitted the public mood exactly. An era had ended. No one could guess what would take its place."27/

The Racial Crisis in America

America's simmering racial crisis moved center stage during the Spring of 1964. The U.S. Congress, under prodding from the White House, finally ended a Southern filibuster and passed the landmark 1964 Civil Rights Act in June. Unfortunately, violence erupted in the backwoods of Mississippi. Three civil rights field workers from the

S.N.C.C. (Student Non-Violent Coordinating Committee) mysteriously vanished that same month. The trio included Andrew Goodman and Michael Schwerner, both White, and a Negro, James Chaney. After an extensive search through the rural countryside the F.B.I. located their savagely beaten bodies in August.

America's racial turmoil swept northward. The "Long Hot Summer" of 1964 became the first in a series of Black ghetto riots which annually visited major American cities for the remainder of the decade. The Summer months of 1964 featured disturbances in Bedford-Styvesant, Harlem, Philadelphia, and Rochester.

How did the New Right react to this nationwide racial crisis—a crisis which had become the key domestic issue in American life during the 1960's?

"Race, like sex, is a fundamental and
unalterable biological fact"

"Race, like sex," Revilo P. Oliver stressed, "is a fundamental and unalterable biological fact." The New Right firmly believed that the Black and White races differed significantly in basic intelligence, creativity, and talent. Thus the mentally inferior Black man could never function successfully within the intellectually demanding atmosphere of Western Civilization. The Citizen emphasized the Black man's "relatively poor record for enterprise and initiative in areas important to Western Civilization." Likewise, Rockwell wondered how anyone could "look at a pure, black, ape-like negro and imagine such an animal-like creature is the 'equal' of a cultured, sensitive gentleman of Western Civilization."[28]/

The White race, the New Right asserted, has contributed so much more to the advancement of civilization and culture than has the Black race. According to The Citizen, "The White man has demonstrated his superiority to the negro in capacity to create and maintain civilization of the types found in the modern Western World." In the same fashion, James J. Kilpatrick explained that "the Negro race, as a race, plainly is not equal to the White race, as a race, nor for that matter...has the Negro race, as a race, ever been the cultural or intellectual equal of the white race, as a race."[29]/

As a matter of record, Kilpatrick stated, the Negro race has never contributed anything worthwhile to the progress of human civilization; "What has man gained from the history of the Negro race? The answer, alas, is virtually nothing." Kilpatrick added, "From the dawn of civilization to the middle of the twentieth century, the Negro race, as a race, has contributed no more than a few grains to the enduring monuments of mankind."[30]/

156

The Perils of Race Mixing

To the New Right, the lessons of history clearly demonstrated the danger of introducing Negro blood into the great civilizations of the past. The White Sentinel pointed out that "Negro blood destroyed the civilization of Egypt, India, Phoenicia, Carthage, Greece and Rome." Thus widespread race-mixing between Blacks and Whites ultimately ruined even the most flourishing societies. As Marilyn R. Allen concluded, "A White race, or nation, once destroyed through race-mixing, is forever destroyed and its culture lost."31/

Therefore, all signs warned against the insanity of race-mixing. Gerald L. K. Smith decided that "nature as well as intelligence decrees that Negro blood should not be mixed with white man's blood" because "these people came out of barbarism and flesh-eating cannibalism less than 200 years ago." Smith denounced attempts "to mongrelize the race and destroy in one or two generations the sensitive qualities of civilization which required 5000 years to create." Destiny predicted that "Race mixing is bound to result in race suicide," while Dr. Medford Evans declared that "Race-mixing...is a form of race war, a war that the white man cannot possibly win." Thus "Nothing is more vital to our cause than to defeat the fashion-mongers of miscegenation."32/

The New Right rejected the Civil Rights Movement because racial integration inevitably led to racial mongrelization. As Carleton Putnam noted, "One cannot break down the social barriers among either sex without eventually breaking them down heterosexually."33/

The fear of Black-White sexual contact always heightened the South's opposition to integration. In the words of William D. Workman, Jr., "The white Southerner's concern over race relations is in substantial measure a concern over sex relations, for the sexual factor lies just beneath the surface of any discussion of integration."34/

Apart from race mongrelization the New Right listed some other deleterious effects of Black-White integration: "children and women are contaminated by vice, disease, dope, rapings, knifings, brawls..." Marilyn R. Allen further outlined how "All official statistics prove the uncleanness of the Negro race as a race, both as to contagious disease, sex lust, and criminal inclinations."35/

Despite the aforementioned drawbacks associated with Black-White race-mixing, "The vote-hungry politicians, the sappy clergymen and the unrealistic educators will continue to try to ram mongrelization down our throats." Indeed, the New Right saw Northern Liberals favoring race-mixing for several reasons: racial amalgamation brought "One-World" government closer; the Liberals felt guilty about their own

157

membership in the White race; and Northern big city Liberals sought political advantage by courting the rapidly swelling Black vote.36/

To begin with, the American Liberal connected race amalgamation with his utopian programs for "One-World". (See Chapter Six) As The Weekly Crusader observed, "You must understand that intermarriage of the races is a part of the liberal scheme for world government." Racial hatreds often divided the various peoples of the Earth. So the Liberals reasoned: Why not encourage Whites and non-Whites to marry and reproduce offspring? Within a few generations racial differences would disappear since everyone would belong to one gigantic, mongrelized, mulatto race.37/

Moreover, the American Liberals seemed rather guilty about their own membership in the White race. Dan Smoot maintained that "the liberal leaders of America have become quite insane about the question of race. They appear to have a sense of shame about being white people." In the same vein, Rockwell saw, "the White Race...being conquered by dark savages, mongrelized and taught to be ashamed of itself."38/

Lastly many Northern Liberal politicians loudly advocated race-mixing in order to woo the Black urban vote. Marilyn R. Allen noticed that "mongrelization of the races" is "being promoted by most of the politicians for the sake of votes." Similarly, the Manchester Union Leader censured, "this constant pandering to the negro vote...," while Storm Trooper complained that "almost every last one of our cowardly, demagogic politicians kisses black fannies for Black votes."39/

Ruthless Northern Liberal politicians or "Latter-Day Abolitionists," as William D. Workman, Jr. called them, singlehandedly manufactured the South's racial crisis. Black-White relations in Dixie had traditionally been excellent until the Northern agitators arrived. Workman explained how "white folks and colored folks have lived together in peaceful co-existence in the South for a long time, and can continue to do so to their mutual advantage if the pressures are removed." Likewise, Carleton Putnam stated, "The South, after generations of experience, had developed customs and a way of life with the Negro that took his limitations into consideration with a minimum of friction and a maximum of kindness."40/

"No Christian Southerner that I have
ever known hates the Negro"

The New Right frequently spoke out against racial hatred. The Whites must never hate the Black as individuals. As William Kullgren emphasized, "Never despise a man because of his race or color." Gerald

L. K. Smith concurred: "No Christian can hate another man because of his race, creed or color..."41/

However, the New Right saw absolutely no connection between blind racial hatred of Blacks and the White man's understandable personal preference not to associate with Blacks. William D. Workman, Jr. noted that "white people can prefer each other's company without hating persons who do not happen to be white." Another unnamed Southerner wrote:

> I have been in favor of negroes being treated fairly and have felt [that] many inequities should be erased. But I wouldn't want to associate with or live among white people who are as ignorant and dirty and smelly and with such low moral standards as a large portion of the negroes.42/

Thus while the New Right never despised the Black man as a person they did consider him vastly inferior to the Whites. Gerald L. K. Smith pointed out that "No Christian Southerner that I have ever known hates the Negro." Nevertheless, "He recognizes in the Negro a child race, fresh from the jungle, not sufficiently matured to take responsibility for running communities and determining the destiny of our nation." Carleton Putnam felt "only affection for the Negro" but deplored his low "levels of character and intelligence..." George Lincoln Rockwell also discussed the Negro's inferiority: "I don't hate niggers any more than I hate monkeys. But they don't belong out here on the streets with our women. They belong in Africa."43/

At this point a legitimate question arises: Did every single group composing the diverse coalition known as the New Right really consider the White race superior to the Black race? After all, the Movement contained more than just the traditionally racist Southern Rednecks. The New Right also contained groups such as reactionary businessmen, Catholic Isolationists, military leaders, and intellectuals all with very little direct personal interest in the preservation of the Jim Crow system, and, at first glance, no apparent reason to object to the Black man enjoying the same basic civil rights as other American citizens.

Nonetheless, all New Rightists held at least some racist attitudes towards Blacks. In fairness, the overwhelming majority of New Rightists never uttered the kind of crude, ugly racial slurs which came from boorish bigots like George Lincoln Rockwell or some of the worst, "Nigger-baiting," Dixie demagogues. Most New Rightists never made offensive, vicious statements about their fellow Black Americans in public. Yet even respectable members of the Movement (men and women who would never dream of openly labelling American Blacks as racially inferior) thought nothing of using highly revealing words like "animalistic" or "bestial" to describe Black Africans (see Chapter Six) or to denounce Black street criminals (see Chapter Three). Moreover, in the course of innumerable private conversations with New Rightists of all shades and varieties over the past fifteen years most, if not all, admitted to me during moments of candor that they thought the Black race, for whatever reason, simply did not measure up to the level of the White race.

"The law and the custom of generations"

With the exception of outspoken segregationists, most members of the New Right conceded that Southern Blacks had received unfair treatment under the Jim Crow system. Nevertheless, these New Rightists believed that the South must evolve its new system of race relations slowly and segregation must disappear gradually. William D. Workman, Jr. denounced any sudden attempt to "overthrow both the law and the custom of generations," while James J. Kilpatrick explained that "the ingrained attitudes of a lifetime cannot be jerked out like a pair of infected molars, and [some] new porcelain dentures put in their place. For this is what our Northern friends will not comprehend."44/

Furthermore, as the Jim Crow system faded away the South had to maintain strict law and order. Paul Sexson and Stephen Miles, Jr. suggested that "the South is not fighting for segregation, which almost all feel is a doomed institution. It is fighting for law and order." The New Right refused to sympathize with impatient Blacks who demanded instant results. Thus the New Right flatly rejected the disruptive civil disobedience tactics employed by Civil Rights demonstrators.45/

The entire Civil Rights Movement represented "a distinct threat to the very fundamentals of American constitutional government...," in the opinion of William D. Workman, Jr., since it threatened to overturn such time-honored, American political precepts as constitutionalism, states' rights, and respect for local customs. As Frank S. Meyer noted, "I know that the Negro people have suffered profound wrongs....But those wrongs cannot be righted by destroying the foundations of a free constitutional society, which is indeed the only basis upon which a joint and lasting solution of their problems is possible."46/

The New Right based its major objections to the Civil Rights Movement upon constitutional grounds. Occasionally, though, an extreme racist would criticize this legalistic approach. For example, Carleton Putnam lamented that Southern Whites "talk of states' rights when they should be talking anthropology..."47/

160

Civil Rights and Communism

The New Right maintained that the International Communist Conspiracy has traditionally exploited the racial issue in order to subvert the United States. J. Edgar Hoover pointed out that "since its inception, the Communist Party, U.S.A., has been alert to capitalize on every possible issue or event which could be used to exploit the American Negro in furtherance of party aims." News and Views observed that "Lenin and Stalin were astute enough to perceive forty-five years ago that the Negro question was America's Achilles Heel." Consequently, the Communists diligently sought to "Sovietize the American blackman."48/

The New Right asserted that the sanctimonious Communists have never really cared about extending the Negro's civil rights; they simply intended to stir up racial animosity within the United States. The Communists, in the estimation of Robert Welch, "don't care any more about actual Negro 'rights' than they do about growing mushrooms on the moon." J. Edgar Hoover concurred: "The party's objectives are not to aid the Negroes--but are designed to take advantage of all controversial issues on the race question so as to create unrest, dissention and confusion in the minds of the American people."49/*

The Communists also pushed for the passage of Civil Rights legislation as a means of enlarging the powers of the Federal Government in Washington en route to the ultimate creation of a totalitarian state. Report to America labelled Civil Rights legislation a "Blueprint for Dictatorship" and The Weekly Crusader called "Today's 'civil rights revolution'...a good excuse for another gigantic step towards establishment of total federal power over the lives of the American people." Likewise, Robert Welch outlined how the clever Communists "use the phony 'civil rights' slogan to stir up bitterness and civil disorder, leading gradually to police state rule by federal troops and armed resistance to that rule."50/

Civil Rights and Democracy

The Civil Rights bills, especially the 1965 Federal Voting Rights Act, served to lead the United States still further down the path toward democracy. (See Chapter Three) The New Right held that the sudden enfranchisement of millions upon millions of ignorant Southern Blacks

---

*Note--The New Right's racist leanings prevented them from adopting the easiest solution to the problem of Communist exploitation of Negro grievances--i.e. granting the Blacks full civil rights equality, thus removing the basic source of trouble.

would spell certain disaster. The New Right remembered with bitterness the ghastly Reconstruction experience (1865-1877) when the devastated Southern states first tasted the horrors of "Negro-Carpetbagger rule." Placing the ballot into the hands of the irresponsible Blacks would, once again, corrupt Southern politics and destroy constitutional government.

Finally, the New Right complained that the Civil Rights Movement established a bad precedent. In time, other groups would also take to the streets and break the law in order to achieve their political ends. The processes of government would degenerate as the people resort to mob tactics. Destiny examined the Voting Rights Bill of 1965 and commented, "We are now observing the evil outcome as the unreasonable spirit of the mob asserts itself, for their sic is no limit to the excesses to which a rabble-roused mob will go."51/

"The hottest political issue in the country"

America's racial crisis became a nationwide problem during the late Spring of 1964. A powerful White Backlash erupted in Northern cities fueled by street crime, open-housing, deteriorating neighborhoods, declining property values, soaring welfare payments, forced busing of school children and competition from Black workers for jobs. As the National Review Bulletin concluded, "They call it now The Backlash and its the hottest political issue in the country."52/

Expecting to capitalize upon the growing Northern White Backlash, Alabama Governor George C. Wallace, the very symbol of Southern resistance to integration, entered three Democratic party Presidential primaries during April and May of 1964. Wallace ran well in the state of Wisconsin (34%), Indiana (30%), and Maryland (43%) against favorite-son candidates pledged to deliver their convention delegates to President Lyndon Johnson.*

George Wallace conducted a curious, one-dimensional Presidential campaign. He simply refused to discuss the Vietnam War and frankly admitted that he knew little about foreign policy. In fact, Wallace boasted about his lack of expertise: "I have no experience...but you all know what the country is like now. It got that way through experience. What we need in Washington, now is a little inexperience." Instead Wallace hammered away at one basic theme: Civil Rights legislation

---

*Note--Governor George Wallace faced Wisconsin Governor John Reynolds in Wisconsin; Indiana Governor Matthew Welsh in Indiana; and Maryland Senator Daniel Brewster in Maryland.

In no 1964 Democratic Presidential primary did George Wallace confront President Lyndon Johnson directly.

threatened to expand the authority of the Federal Government over the private lives of the American citizens. He described the 1964 Civil Rights Act as "a political, not a moral issue. It is, in reality, a grab for federal power." Governor Wallace emphasized that sensitive racial subjects like open-housing and public school integration must be handled by local leaders or by private individuals and not by the national government in far-off Washington, D.C.53/

Wallace ran best in those traditional Democratic, ethnic, working-class districts most directly affected by the Black Revolution. Accordingly, the Governor's supporters predicted that the Wallace message would increase in popularity when the time came for other sections of the North to face the unpleasant realities of integration. Alabama Lieutenant Governor and future United States Senator James Allen noted, "In the next generation, ten large cities in the United States will have more than 50 per cent Negroes, and then Governor Wallace's views will be appreciated more."54/

Even members of the New Right who disliked Wallace's overt racism applauded the Governor's excellent showings in the Northern Presidential primaries. New Guard disagreed "strongly with Governor Wallace's adamant and unreasonable refusal to integrate Alabama's schools" but thought "the issue in Wisconsin was more clearly one of individualism vs. centralism." The National Review Bulletin, while describing, "a vote for Governor Wallace" as "a vote against an egalitarian blitzkrieg," suggested that...

> the massive white resentment that is taking shape in the urban centers of the Liberal Northeast, West and Midwest is not necessarily that atavistic racism the Negro leaders and the Liberal press say it is....The significance here is political, not racial. Wisconsinites had nothing to gain from favoring segregationist Wallace, except a clear warning to the Democratic Administration in Washington in re the civil rights bill: Feds Keep Off.55/

Lastly while most members of the New Right rejected Wallace's naked racism and obvious demagoguery, they advised the Republican party to exploit the White Backlash politically. The National Review Bulletin predicted that "the Democrats' nightmare will be fully reified when someone other than Wallace, someone without Wallace's racist leanings, comes out convincingly for civil rights temperance. There is no reason why such a man could not be a Republican."56/

"The chickens had come home to roost"

America experienced her worst "Long Hot Summer" of racial strife since 1919 during July and August of 1964. A wave of riots swept through Northern Black ghettos with major disturbances occurring in Bedford-Stuyvesant, Harlem, Rochester, and Philadelphia. The New Right sensed the seriousness of the situation. "Let's face it," one observer wrote, "in some sections of America we are at war in the streets..." Likewise, The Defender explained that "New York is in the throes of the greatest race war this nation has ever experienced--at least in our lifetime."57/

The New Right pointed out the irony of the race riots engulfing New York City. For Gotham had long been the financial benefactor of the Civil Rights activities down South. Now "The chickens had come home to roost," crowed the Cross and the Flag, since "New York City, which for years had been the base for organizing and encouraging black terror all over the United States, had finally become the Nation's first chief victim of black terror."58/

Furthermore, the New Right demanded flippantly that the United States Army enter Harlem to restore order. The Defender asked, "When is the Johnson Administration going to send federal troops into New York City?" After all, a minor incident at Little Rock, Arkansas back in 1957 had required the deployment of U.S. Army paratroopers. Surely a full-scale race war in Gotham should concern President Lyndon Johnson at least as much. But a sarcastic Mississippi Governor Ross Barnett wondered, "is he sending troops to Harlem? Of course not!"59/

Thus, under the shadow of a deepening racial crisis and spreading lawlessness, the Republican party met in San Francisco in July, 1964 to nominate for President an authentic member of the New Right, Arizona Senator Barry M. Goldwater.

164

CHAPTER SEVEN - Notes

1.   Dan Smoot Report, (November 4, 1963), p. 348;
Ibid., p. 349;
Rockwell Report, (December 1, 1963), p. 2.

2.   M. Stanton Evans, The Liberal Establishment (New York: The
Devin-Adair Company, 1965), p. 28;
Rockwell Report, (December 15, 1963), p. 3.

3.   National Review, (December 17, 1963), p. 528;
Cross and the Flag, (January, 1964), p. 2.

Jack Moffitt observed, "As though by prearrangement, the
commentators launched into a unanimous and unjustified accusation that
the public of the United States was actuated by fanatic hate, promoted
by patriotic Right-Wing groups." American Opinion, (September, 1964),
p. 75.

Finally, F. Clifton White lamented the fact that even the
"Voice of America" during its first broadcast announcing the President's
death described Dallas as "the center of the extreme right wing."   F.
Clifton White with William F. Gill, Suite 3505: The Story of the Draft
Goldwater Movement (New Rochelle, N.Y.: Arlington House, 1967), p.
246.

4.   The Weekly Crusader, (December 6, 1963), p. 2.

5.   Ibid.;
Ibid.;
(February 14, 1964), p. 6;
Dan Smoot Report, (December 23, 1963), p. 403;
According to Nazi leader Rockwell, "If Oswald had not been caught, the
assassination of President Kennedy would have led to the immediate
lynching of the whole anti-communist right-wing."   Rockwell Report,
(December 15, 1963), p. 11.

Likewise, Tocsin quoted another anti-Communist: "If the
President had been murdered by a right-winger one shutters [sic] to think
of the cries for blood that would have been shouted at the Attorney
General." Tocsin, (December 4, 1963), p. 1.

6.   The Weekly Crusader, (December 6, 1963), p. 4;
American Opinion, (January, 1964), p. 42.

7.   The Defender, (December, 1963), p. 11.

8.   American Opinion, (January, 1964), p. 39;
Rockwell Report, (December 15, 1963), p. 3.

In the words of Dan Smoot, "virtually all liberal spokesmen in the United States berate 'extreme rightists' for asserting that communism is dangerous in the United States." Smoot repeated "the liberal line" that "communists are not dangerous--that, indeed, 'right-wing extremists' are far more harmful than communists." Dan Smoot Report, (December 9, 1963), p. 391.

9.   Human Events, (December 7, 1963), p. 5.

10.   The Weekly Crusader, (December 6, 1963), p. 7;
Manion Forum Network broadcast (December 22, 1963);
Broyles, The John Birch Society, p. 154.

11.   Burnham, Suicide of the West, p. 220.

12.   Tocsin, (December 25, 1963), p. 1;
America's Future, (November 13, 1964), pp. 2-3;
"On the Right," October 1, 1964.

13.   Dan Smoot Report, (December 23, 1963), p. 402;
I.F. Stone's Weekly, (December 9, 1963), p. 8;
Senator Paul Douglas as quoted in the Chicago Tribune, December 7, 1963.

14.   Tocsin, (December 11, 1963), p. 2;
Dan Smoot Report, (December 9, 1963), p. 385.

National Review Editor William F. Buckley, Jr. brilliantly refuted this devious Liberal attempt to connect the New Right with the murder of President John F. Kennedy:

Moments after the assassination some of the most influential-- and self-righteous--opinion-makers in this country jumped to the conclusion that an Extreme Rightist did it. In a matter of hours a Communist was apprehended, and it transpired that it was he who had done the job. That disappointing reversal meant only a change of tactic. It could no longer be said that a rightist assassinated President Kennedy; but lynchers do not give up easily. The story then became that the Right had 1) created an 'atmosphere of hatred' which 2) generated the impulse which 3) galvanized the trigger-finger of 4) a Communist assassin.

Buckley then sarcastically related the following story: " 'Mommy,' the remark was made, 'is it true that John Wilkes Booth was member of the John Birch Society?' " National Review, (December 31, 1963), p. 559.

15.   Beacon-Light Herald, (March-April, 1964), p. 8.

In the same vein, Clarence Manion noticed that the Left decided "we all shared the terrible guilt of murdering the President; that the people of Dallas particularly were at fault, and that 'racists,' 'hate groups' and 'Right Wing Extremists' were primarily responsible for the assassination which, therefore and somehow, put the entire Nation to self-conscious shame." Manion Forum Network broadcast (December 8, 1963).

16.   Sacramento Bee as quoted in Dan Smoot Report, (December 23, 1963), p. 403.

17.   Human Events, (December 21, 1963), p. 4.

18.   American Opinion, (January 1964), p. 23; The Weekly Crusader, (December 6, 1963), p. 4.

Congressman John M. Ashbrook (Rep-Ohio) suggested, "that Oswald was a Soviet-oriented killer if not a Communist-trained one. His action was an alien action with no reference at all to the American scene." Manion Forum Network broadcast (January 12, 1964).

19.   Newsweek, (December 9, 1963), p. 22.

20.   Tocsin, (December 18, 1963), p. 3; Manion Forum Network broadcast (December 8, 1963); Tocsin, (December 11, 1963), p.2.

Congressman James B. Utt (Rep-California) emphasized that "the only teachers of hate and evil and violence are the communists." Beacon-Light Herald, (March-April, 1964), p. 9.

Finally, Senator John Tower (Rep-Texas) asked the American People to "remember that in talking about extremists, in talking about the purveyors of hate, the real purveyors of hate in this world, the real fomenters of class war and bigotry between and among people are the Communists." Human Events, (December 14, 1963), p. 5.

21.   Tom Wicker, "Lyndon Johnson vs. the Ghost of Jack Kennedy," Esquire, (November, 1965), p. 87.

22.   National Review, (December 17, 1963), p. 512; Dan Smoot Report (December 23, 1963), p. 407.

23. National Review, (August 13, 1963), p. 95;
Time (November 22, 1963), p. 6;
Victor Lasky, J.F.K., The Man and the Myth (New York: MacMillan, 1963).

24. Human Events, (August 3, 1963), p. 3;
Evans, The Future of Conservatism, p. 124.

25. Dan Smoot Report, (December 23, 1963), p. 402;
Barry M. Goldwater, The Conscience of a Majority (Englewood Cliffs, New Jersey: Prentice-Hall, Inc., 1970), p. 28.

26. National Review, (December 17, 1963), p. 524;
Recently, Goldwater himself revealed that he very nearly bowed out of the 1964 Presidential race, because, in the wake of the Kennedy assassination, he knew that he couldn't win. Barry M. Goldwater, With No Apologies (New York: William Morrow and Company, Inc., 1979), p. 160.

27. Economic Council Letter, (April 15, 1964), p. 1.

28. American Opinion, (January, 1963), p. 38;
The Citizen, (October, 1962), p. 8;
Rockwell Report, (April 15, 1963), p. 6.

29. The Citizen, (October, 1962), p. 8;
James J. Kilpatrick, The Southern Case For School Segregation (n.p.: Crowell-Collier Press, 1962), p. 26.

30. Kilpatrick, The Southern Case For School Segregation, p. 50.

31. The White Sentinel as quoted in the Beacon-Light Herald, (August-September, 1962), p. 30;
Marilyn R. Allen, Kingdom Digest, (August, 1960), as quoted in the Beacon-Light Herald, (March-April, 1961), p. 34.

32. Cross and the Flag, (April, 1962), p. 9;
Ibid., (January, 1963), p. 11;
Ibid., (October, 1963), p. 2;
Destiny, (September, 1961), p. 198;
The Citizen, (January, 1964), p. 12;
Ibid., p. 11.

Marilyn R. Allen insisted that the "mongrelization of the races...means the downfall of America as a great nation, and of the White Founding Race: which in turn means the downfall of Christianity and thereby the doom of Western Civilization." Beacon-Light Herald, (January, 1960), p. 39.

Likewise, Roy V. Harris, President of the White Citizens Councils of America emphasized, "We are fighting for the safety of our women and children....We are fighting to preserve the civilization of America. We are fighting to preserve the white race." The Citizen, (December, 1963), p. 8.

33.   Putnam, Race and Reason, p. 65.

34.   William D. Workman, Jr., The Case For the South (New York: The Devin-Adair Company, 1960), p. 211.

35.   Marilyn R. Allen, Kingdom Digest, (August, 1960) as quoted in the Beacon-Light Herald, (March-April, 1961), p. 32; Ibid., p. 33.

36.   Cross and the Flag, (February, 1963), p. 27.

37.   The Weekly Crusader, (May 24, 1963), p. 2.

38.   Dan Smoot Report, (April 8, 1963), p. 107; Rockwell Report, (December 15, 1962), p. 6.

39.   Beacon-Light Herald, (January, 1960), p. 39; Manchester Union Leader as quoted in Destiny, (December, 1962), p. 244; Storm Trooper, (September-October, 1964), p. 31.

Destiny added:

Politicians, for the sake of currying the negro vote, have lighted a fire that will become a holocaust of destruction before it can be extinguished. It will only be put out at the cost of many lives as the wild spirit of the jungle increasingly dominates the mind of the Negro under the provocation of unscrupulous leaders and political hacks. Destiny, (July, 1964), p. 127.

40.   Workman, The Case for the South, p. 121; Ibid., Foreword p. viii; Putnam, Race and Reason, p. 21.

41.   Beacon-Light Herald, (January-February, 1965), p. 3; Cross and the Flag, (April 1962), p. 10.

42.   Workman, The Case for the South, p. 112; Destiny, (October, 1963), p. 200.

43.   Cross and the Flag, (June, 1962), p. 6;
Putnam, Race and Reason, p. 7;
Danville, Virginia Register, November 20, 1963 as quoted in the
Rockwell Report, (December 1, 1963), p. 3.

44.   Workman, The Case for the South, p. 26;
Kilpatrick, The Southern Case For School Segregation, pp. 25-26.

      Paul Sexson and Stephen Miles, Jr. believed, "The South is
fighting liberal dictation that would pry up its whole moral and social
code." Sexson and Miles, The Challenge of Conservatism, p. 158.

45.   Sexson and Miles, The Challenge of Conservatism, p. 158.

46.   Workman, The Case for the South, p. 190;
National Review, (June 18, 1963), p. 496.

47.   Putnam, Race and Reason, p. 35.

48.   Human Events, (August 3, 1963), p. 11;
News and Views, (August, 1965), p. 14;
Ibid., p. 1.

      According to the John Birch Society Bulletin, "the Communists
had used the 'racial question' as grist for their mills for thirty years."
John Birch Society Bulletin, (January, 1961), p. 10.

49.   Welch, The Politician, p. 267;
Human Events, (August 3, 1963), p. 11.

50.   Report to America, (August, 1963), p. 3;
The Weekly Crusader, (July 26, 1963), p. 1;
Welch, The New Americanism, p. 39.

51.   Destiny, (April, 1965), p. 75.

52.   National Review Bulletin, (May 12, 1964), p. 5.

53.   Speech at Indiana University, April 23, 1964 as quoted in
George C. Wallace, Hear Me Out (Anderson, South Carolina: Droke
House Publishers, 1968), p. 58;
Ibid., p. 24.

54.   Marshall Frady, Wallace (New York: The World Publishing
Company, 1968), p. 167.

55. New Guard (May, 1964), p. 5;
National Review Bulletin, (May 12, 1964), p. 5;
Ibid., (April 28, 1964), p. 5.

56. National Review Bulletin, (May 12, 1964), p. 5.

57. Rex Karney in the Rockford, Illinois Star as quoted in
America's Future, (August 28, 1964), p. 7;
The Defender, (September, 1964), p. 7.

58. Cross and the Flag, (October, 1964), p. 32.

59. The Defender, (September, 1964), p. 7;
The Citizen, (July-August, 1964), p. 15.

171

CHAPTER EIGHT

BARRY GOLDWATER AND THE NEW RIGHT

Barry Morris Goldwater

The sun-baked territory of Arizona provided the birthplace in 1909 for Barry Morris Goldwater. The son of a wealthy merchant, young Barry Goldwater struggled through his freshman year at Phoenix Union High School and then transferred to the Staunton Military Academy located in Lexington, Virginia where he graduated in 1928. After a year at the University of Arizona he dropped out of college and went to work for the family-owned business. He distinguished himself in combat as a bomber pilot during the Second World War and then settled back into the comfortable routine of a prosperous Phoenix department store executive. Goldwater, a typical, small-town, civic-minded "booster," worked his way on to the Phoenix City Council and then rode General Dwight Eisenhower's coattails into the United States Senate in November, 1952. Goldwater's mediocre career in the U.S. Senate featured a dismal attendance record and few legislative accomplishments. The gregarious Arizona Solon spent more energy hitting the Republican Party banquet circuit. As a loyal Taft Republican, he passionately admired General Douglas MacArthur and staunchly defended Senator Joseph McCarthy. After serving an unimpressive term in Washington he emerged by default in November, 1958 as the leading Radical Right political figure in the United States.1/

Yet Barry Goldwater cannot simply be dismissed as just another run-of-the-mill political hack. In truth, this deeply principled, well-read man devoted himself to the study of history and philosophy. This warm, generous individual received respect and affection from both his Republican and Democratic colleagues in the U.S. Senate. The versatile Goldwater excelled as an aviator, gadgeteer, ham radio operator, and merchandiser of men's underwear. He won recognition for his knowledge of the Indian tribes of the American Southwest, kept active as a Major General in the Air Force Reserve despite his fifty-odd years and a bad leg, and possessing an extremely rare blood type had gallantly donated nearly 100 pints during the course of his lifetime.*

---

*Note--In Chapter One, I have classified Barry Goldwater as a Sunbelt Nouveau Riche type of New Rightist. However, Goldwater's education at the Staunton Military Academy, his heroic service during the Second World War, and his two decade association with the United States Air Force Reserve has also left a definite military imprint upon his thinking.

The Rise of Barry Goldwater

The mid-term elections of November, 1958 suddenly thrust Barry Goldwater into the national political spotlight. Goldwater easily won re-election to the United States Senate despite the huge Democratic party landslide that year. Furthermore, organized labor had targeted Goldwater as another reactionary dinosaur ripe for political extinction. Union funds poured into Arizona, reminiscent of organized labor's vigorous but unsuccessful 1950 campaign to oust Ohio's G.O.P. Senator Robert A. Taft. Thus Barry Goldwater in 1958, just like Robert Taft before him, had dramatically turned back labor's challenge and in so doing had captured the imagination of the Republican Party.

The Election of 1958 also resulted in the destruction of the promising, political career of California Republican William F. Knowland--the U.S. Senate Minority Leader and the Radical Right's best hope for the 1960 G.O.P. Presidential nomination. Senator Knowland had been facing stiff competition from his fellow Californian, Vice President Richard Nixon, for the right to represent the Golden State as its favorite-son candidate at the upcoming 1960 Republican National Convention. Knowland appraised the situation and concluded that he could gain control most effectively over the all-important California delegation by occupying the Governor's Mansion in Sacramento rather than by remaining in Washington. Accordingly, Knowland decided to seek the Governorship in 1958 instead of running for re-election to his U.S. Senate seat that year.

Unfortunately, Knowland's scheme to outflank Richard Nixon went awry when the Senator became hopelessly entangled in the Golden State's Byzantine-like politics. En route to Sacramento, Knowland had to elbow out of the way the incumbent Republican Governor Goodwin Knight who had wanted to stand for re-election. The powerful Knowland eventually forced the humiliated Knight to withdraw from the race. Governor Knight then attempted to save face by filing for Knowland's Senate seat! At any rate, this incredible game of musical chairs angered California voters who responded by sending both Knight and Knowland down to crushing defeats in November, 1958--the latter losing the gubernatorial contest to Democrat Edmund G. "Pat" Brown.

The Radical Right, which had expected to support Knowland for President in 1960, suddenly needed a new candidate. Hence Barry Goldwater filled that void. As Robert Welch remarked shortly after the G.O.P.'s 1958 Election debacle: "Now the one man who comes nearest to measuring up to all the needs and qualifications, whom we see on the political horizon at the present time, is Barry Goldwater....I'd love to see him President of the United States, and maybe some day we shall." Welch called Goldwater "a superb political organizer" and noted that he "inspires deep and lasting loyalty...is absolutely sound in his

Americanism, has the political and moral courage to stand by his Americanist principles, and...can be trusted to stand by them until hell freezes over."2/

A mild Goldwater-for-President boomlet developed during the Spring of 1960. Indeed Human Events enthusiastically described this growing interest in the Arizona Senator as "The Goldwater Phenomenon." Similarly, the National Review noted that while conservative sentiment has no organization or even personal vehicle around which to build....the phenomenon of Barry Goldwater may change that."3/

This support for Barry Goldwater reflected the lack of Radical Right confidence in President Eisenhower's successor Richard Nixon. At best, Vice President Nixon represented "a lesser of two evils" when compared with potential Democratic Party nominees such as Hubert Humphrey, Lyndon Johnson, John F. Kennedy, or Adlai Stevenson. However, unlike Nixon, Barry Goldwater truly spoke the language of the Radical Right. In the words of L. Brent Bozell, "Senator Goldwater is a different kettle of fish from Nixon. He is a principled conservative and gives every promise of remaining one down to the end of his political career."4/

The Radical Right promoted the Goldwater-for-President boomlet during the Spring and early Summer of 1960 for several reasons. First of all, the Radical Right used the Goldwater candidacy to present their ideas intact to the American public. As L. Brent Bozell pointed out, "Conservatives' most urgent task this election year--and there is no second job that remotely approaches it in importance--is to make sure their ideological position is preserved as a recognizable political alternative."5/

Secondly, some first-ballot convention votes for Goldwater would remind the Republican Party and the nation that the Radical Right still wielded some political clout. L. Brent Bozell saw "no better way for Republicans to serve the conservative cause than to give Senator Goldwater their complimentary votes on the first ballot." Such an effort "would have served notice on the political world that conservatism is still in business."6/

Next a strong Radical Right presence at the 1960 Republican National Convention would force Richard Nixon into making substantial concessions in order to secure his Right flank. Without such pressure from the Right, Nixon might take for granted his Right flank and then move closer towards the Center in search of votes in November. Thus the National Review disclosed that, "There are mounting within the Republican Party pressures against Mr. Nixon's attempts to Liberalize the party in time for the national election." Consequently, Senator

175

Barry Goldwater became a sharp thorn in Nixon's Right side during the pre-Convention maneuvering. L. Brent Bozell outlined this Goldwater strategy:

> Nixon, the Senator reasons, can be pushed Right if he is taught that he stands to lose more from the defection of his traditional conservative support than he ever might hope to gain by making himself more palatable to the Left....By beating the drums for conservative views and thrusting them into public prominence, he would try to reach Richard Nixon's hypersensitive political antennae and thus veer him to the right.7/

Moreover, Bozell observed that "A first ballot move for Goldwater-for-President would have the side effect of promoting his candidacy for Vice President." The Radical Right disagreed over the merits of a proposed Nixon-Goldwater ticket. The addition of the popular Barry Goldwater would certainly guarantee solid Radical Right support behind Richard Nixon in November. However, the Arizona Senator would lose much of his political independence as well as his ability to act as spokesman for the Radical Right philosophy. For as the Republican Party Vice-Presidential nominee Barry Goldwater would be required to stump the nation loyally on behalf of the moderate G.O.P Platform and would have to defend the unsatisfactory record of the Eisenhower-Nixon Administration. Of course, geography alone ruled out the idea of a Nixon-Goldwater team, since the need for a nationally balanced Republican Party ticket prevented the Californian Nixon from running with the Arizonan Goldwater.8/

Finally, the Radical Right looked beyond 1960. A strong showing by Goldwater at the G.O.P. Convention would place the Arizona Solon squarely in the national limelight as a promising Presidential prospect for the future. As L. Brent Bozell stated, "a serious Goldwater movement in the 1960 Convention--however small--would establish the Senator as a logical Presidential contender the next time around."9/

"Let's grow up, conservatives"

The G.O.P. National Convention of 1960 assembled in Chicago and nominated Richard Nixon as expected on the first ballot. Yet the Radical Right believed that Barry Goldwater remained the real favorite of the Republican delegates. Walter Trohan decided that "Goldwater was the darling of the delegates, but they gave their votes to Nixon." Likewise, Human Events added, "Although Nixon held all the cards, Barry Goldwater held all the hearts."10/

176

In addition, Goldwater had captured the imagination of the Republican youth. As William F. Buckley, Jr. suggested, "It was Goldwater, not Nixon or Eisenhower, who was the hero of the bright and dominant youth forces at the Chicago Convention." Indeed "Youth was everywhere at the Republican convention," as the National Review emphasized, and, "the ones who will be working hardest to guide the Republican Party in the future, were conservatives: and most of them Goldwater fans." The National Review predicted that the young, enthusiastic Goldwaterites "are going to be around for a long time to come."11/

Barry Goldwater provided the otherwise uneventful 1960 G.O.P. gathering with its only dramatic moment. After his friends had placed his name in nomination, the Arizona Senator made an electrifying personal appearance before the Convention. When Goldwater addressed the crowd he promptly withdrew his name from consideration, released his delegates, and urged his followers to support Richard Nixon in the interests of party harmony: "We've had our chance," Goldwater told his fellow Republicans, "and I think the conservatives have made a splendid showing at this convention....Now let's put our shoulders to the wheels of Dick Nixon and push him across the line. Let's not stand back." Goldwater then challenged the Radical Right to get busy and recapture the Republican Party at the grass roots level: "Let's grow up, conservatives. Let's, if we want to, take this party back--and I think we can someday. Let's get to work."12/

Barry Goldwater's speech to the Republican Convention created an indelible impression upon the minds of millions of Americans. L. Brent Bozell described "Goldwater's impact on Republicans who stayed home and watched him perform on TV." -- Among "people who had scarcely heard the name before, a Goldwater 'image' took shape: a plain-spoken man with Principles...and Courage...who is nonetheless worldly enough to avoid the pitfalls of intransigence." Indeed Goldwater left the Windy City as the single most dynamic force within the G.O.P. As Human Events wrote, "the firm-jawed Arizonan had emerged as the spiritual and intellectual leader of the Republican party." After the Convention adjourned "Conservative" or "Right-wing" members of the G.O.P. began calling themselves "Goldwater Republicans."13/

Furthermore, Barry Goldwater emerged from the 1960 G.O.P Convention as the political heir to the late Senator Robert A. Taft. As Walter Trohan remarked, Goldwater left Chicago "wearing the mantle of the late Senator Robert A. Taft of Ohio as the leader of the conservative wing of the party." In Barry Goldwater the American Right had suddenly found its most effective personal symbol since the death of Robert Taft back in 1953: "Not since Senator Robert Taft has a conservative been so adored, sought after and touted as the savior of his country and his party."14/

Goldwater loyally stumped the country on behalf of the Nixon-Lodge ticket during the Fall campaign of 1960. Indeed Human Events proudly boasted that "The Arizona conservative has turned out to be the star performer for the GOP, outshining Nixon, Rockefeller, Lodge and even Ike." In particular, Barry Goldwater excited youthful members of the Radical Right. As John Chamberlain noted, "The young who are taking Goldwater to their hearts seem to be enlisted in a war that will continue long past election day." 15/

Many Radical Rightists expected Republican Presidential nominee Richard Nixon to stumble against Democratic opponent John F. Kennedy. Thus Human Events speculated about Goldwater's future prospects: "If Nixon loses....the handsome jet pilot [Goldwater] would loom as a leading choice for the big prize in 1964." As a matter of fact, Goldwater himself prepared for a Nixon defeat in November. A month before the election the Arizona Senator disclosed that in the event of a Democratic victory he would be available for the 1964 G.O.P. Presidential sweepstakes.16/

"Only Four Years to 1964"

When John Kennedy narrowly squeaked past Richard Nixon the Goldwater machine shifted into high gear. For as Frank S. Meyer reminded his Radical Right brethren, they had "Only Four Years to 1964." Indeed by mid-November, 1960 Human Events magazine was already carrying advertisements for Goldwater campaign buttons; and by late November key supporters of the Arizona Senator were conducting secret strategy meetings to plan Goldwater's conquest of the 1964 G.O.P. Presidential nomination.17/

A nationwide "Goldwater in '64" boom during the Spring of 1961 coincided with the emergence of the New Right. Goldwater-for-President clubs sprang up and flooded the nation with "Goldwater in '64" automobile bumper stickers. Even Time magazine noticed the Goldwater phenomenon and called the Arizona Senator "the hottest political figure this side of Jack Kennedy."18/

The Goldwater forces systematically captured control of the Republican Party at the precinct level between 1961 and 1964. Author James T. Hunter explained how Goldwater's grass-roots strength had ultimately paved the way for his nomination in 1964: "Barry Goldwater had won the hearts of the majority of the active grass-roots Republicans who eventually elected the delegates to the national convention. It was as simple as that."19/

The clearest example of this New Right revolution at the grass-roots level occurred in the Deep South. Traditionally, the small, impotent Republican Party in Dixie resembled a collection of "rotten boroughs". Unable to win elections and composed mainly of Blacks and "Postmasters," the Southern G.O.P. depended totally upon Federal patronage dispensed by a national Republican administration in Washington. Consequently, the Southern Republicans supported the Eastern Liberal Establishment (which controlled the national G.O.P.) in exchange for financial assistance and spoils.

However, the growing interest in Barry Goldwater stimulated the creation of a strong, New Right, Southern Republican Party. Referring to the Arizona Senator, one South Carolinian remarked that "nobody has made such an impression on people here since Jefferson Davis and John C. Calhoun." No wonder a wave of "Resignation rallies" swept through the South, especially in Florida and Texas during 1961. In elaborate public ceremonies hundreds of Southern Democrats formally renounced their allegiance to the party of their forebears and joined the G.O.P. Goldwater's brand of Republicanism helped transform the previously weak Dixie G.O.P. into a powerful vehicle for the New Right.20/*

The New Right had seized control of the Republican Party in the South, the West, and in a good chunk of the Mid-Western Farmbelt by the Summer of 1964. Thus the 1964 G.O.P. National Convention which gathered in San Francisco awarded Arizona Senator Barry Goldwater its Presidential nomination on the first ballot.

In essence, Goldwater accomplished in 1964 what the great Ohio Senator Robert A. Taft had failed to achieve back in 1952. To start with, the New Right made sure to capture control of the Republican Party at the precinct level in order to send enough loyal Goldwater supporters to the San Francisco Convention as delegates. The New Right had since discovered the secrets of organization and the importance of paying close attention to every detail. As M. Stanton Evans explained, "The most notable difference between 1952 and 1964...was the careful homework on this score done by the Goldwater forces."21/

Secondly, the powerful Eastern Liberal Establishment had bribed a few of the weakest Taft delegates at Chicago with "Chase-Manhattan, Rockefeller family money" and had thoroughly demoralized the rest with clever slogans like "Taft can't win." However, while the same Eastern Liberal Establishment applied similar pressures at San Francisco in July,

---

*Note--Barry Goldwater understood that the creation of a New Right, "Lily-White," Southern Republican Party would surely drive the remaining Northern Blacks out of the G.O.P. Nevertheless, Goldwater told an Atlanta, Georgia press conference on November 18, 1961, "We're not going to get the Negro vote as a bloc in 1964 or 1968, so we ought to go hunting where the ducks are."

1964, the New Right stood firm for the Arizona Senator. M. Stanton Evans outlined how the Goldwater camp had taken the precaution to select "as delegates men and women who were deeply committed to the cause, and who could not be budged by slogans or the most insistent pounding of the media."22/

Next Barry Goldwater presented a much better public "image" than did the lackluster Robert Taft. Hence the Arizona Senator made a more attractive candidate. As an unidentified but prominent Eisenhower Republican stated, "Goldwater possesses a highly attractive and popular personality--appealing to the mass of voters--which Taft certainly didn't have." M. Stanton Evans concurred: "Goldwater won because he was able to capture the popular imagination in a way Taft could never do, and because his personality was more nearly fitted to the requirements of the age."23/

Finally, Taft had the enormously popular General Dwight D. Eisenhower as his major competition back in 1952. Luckily, Barry Goldwater faced a motley collection of mediocre opponents in 1964. New York Governor Nelson Rockefeller's untimely divorce and subsequent scandalous remarriage during the Spring of 1963 greatly damaged his political standing. Barry Goldwater himself administered the coup de grace when he defeated Rockefeller in California's winner-take-all Presidential Primary Election in June, 1964. Former Vice President Richard Nixon had conveniently eliminated himself from serious contention (at least temporarily) by bowing unexpectedly to Democrat Edmund G. "Pat" Brown in the 1962 California Gubernatorial race. (See Chapter Twelve) United States Ambassador in Saigon, Henry Cabot Lodge, Jr., the Boston Brahmin, finished a surprising first as a write-in candidate in the early New Hampshire Primary but then fizzled out. A last minute entry, the bumbling, Pennsylvania Governor William Scranton ineptly played the role of the final "stop-Goldwater" candidate. Michigan Governor George Romney simply never got off the ground.

"The midwife of contemporary conservatism"

The nomination of Barry Goldwater in July, 1964 gave the New Right a nationwide forum from which to preach its philosophy. Barry Goldwater proudly proclaimed his unswerving devotion to New Right principles and used his campaign as a vehicle to spread the message. Of course, as a practical politician the Arizona Solon questioned whether he could really hope to unseat incumbent President Lyndon Johnson in November, 1964. Nevertheless, Goldwater felt such an effort worthwhile if he could make a respectable showing. Moreover, Goldwater intended to plant the seeds of doubt concerning the current direction of American Liberalism thus beginning the long and arduous task of re-educating the American people towards the Right.

Yet Goldwater's critics wondered about the depths of his commitment to the philosophy of the New Right. According to this view, Barry Goldwater, an intellectually limited and perhaps mentally unbalanced individual, simply became the ideological captive of the New Right. As Mark Sherwin wrote, "Senator Barry Goldwater of Arizona is the knight in shining armor, the darling and the idol of the Right. He is also its prisoner..." Indeed, Richard Rovere has argued seriously that Goldwater became a hostage of the National Review crowd (L. Brent Bozell, William F. Buckley, Jr., and William A. Rusher). These New Right ideologues ghost-wrote most of Goldwater's books, magazine articles, syndicated newspaper columns (with assistance from Stephen Shadegg), and speeches. Thus these ghost-writers committed Goldwater in print and otherwise to a set of abstract political positions which the Arizona Senator never really understood.24/

Even the renowned observer, Professor Richard Hofstadter, suggested that Barry Goldwater's mind operated at two different levels: "A man like Goldwater...lives psychologically half in the world of our routine politics and half in the curious intellectual underworld of the pseudo-conservative..." In other words, Barry Goldwater possessed a split political personality. At times he would sound and act like a normal, healthy, Republican Party politician (granted, a little far to the Right); but at other times he would sink in the murky world of "paranoid," New Right extremism.25/

In truth, the Arizona Senator neither single-handedly founded the New Right nor simply played the role of the Movement's "front-man" who mindlessly parroted the philosophy of others. Instead both Barry Goldwater and the New Right emerged simultaneously around 1960. As James T. Hunter explained, "The rise of Barry Goldwater after the 1960 convention paralleled the growth of the anti-Communist movement....Each process complemented the other." National Review publisher William A. Rusher agreed: "The conservative movement found Senator Goldwater, Senator Goldwater found the movement; it was like the meeting of the Blue and the White Nile."26/

Edwin McDowell, an editorial writer for the Arizona Republic, characterized Goldwater's contribution to the New Right as that of its midwife:

> Time and again, just when it seemed that conservatism in the 1950's would die of political anemia--particularly after the death of Sen. Taft and after the disastrous elections of 1958--it was Goldwater who breathed new life into the conservative cause, who transformed it from an abstract theory into a viable political force. The Arizona senator, friend and foe alike agree, was the midwife of contemporary conservatism.

Furthermore, Goldwater represented, in the words of James T. Hunter, "the only political figure of significant stature in the early sixties who could inspire conservative anti-Communists to make the transition into American politics." Hence "Barry Goldwater became the symbol of modern conservatism." The New Right "appreciated his ideology and they respected him as a man."27/

Without question, the New Right deeply admired Barry Goldwater for his personal qualities. As Gerald Schomp, a one-time supporter of the Arizona Senator concluded, "Goldwater was everything that personifies 'goodness' to a Conservative--honest, ruggedly articulate, recklessly outspoken, uncompromising in his dealings and absolutely convinced that the American way is always and everywhere the divine way as well." Consequently, "Barry Goldwater's character," in James T. Hunter's opinion, "made him a fit champion of the conservative cause as much as did his philosophy." L. Brent Bozell agreed that the personality of Barry Goldwater excited the New Right as much as did his ideology: "His acceptance by the movement was due in part to what he said, and in part to the way he said it--to a personality and style that had elements of political magic." 28/

The Mind of Barry Goldwater: Domestic Policy

While Barry Goldwater possessed neither a particularly powerful nor a strikingly original mind his thought and rhetoric stamp him as an authentic New Rightist. The Arizona Lawmaker, for example, shared with the New Right a deep interest in ancient Roman history. Indeed as Fred Cook relates, "There is a Goldwater family legend that his mother tried to introduce him to Gibbons' Decline and Fall of the Roman Empire when he was only eight." No wonder Goldwater sprinkled references to "bread and circuses," "moral decay and ruin," "squabbling over the public dole," and "succumbing through internal weakness rather than fall before a foreign foe" throughout his books, magazine articles, newspaper columns, and campaign speeches. The New Right in turn sensed Goldwater's genuine concern that contemporary America might repeat the tragic fate of the Roman Empire. As Theodore Humes wrote, "Senator Goldwater knows history well. He knows what rotted Rome can rot the United States."29/ (See Chapter Three)

Along similar lines, the Arizona Senator frequently reminded the American people of their solemn "rights and duties" as "the guardians of Western Civilization." These obligations in Barry Goldwater's estimation included the protection of individualism against the encroachment of collectivism, the preservation of the free-enterprise system, and the upholding of traditional moral values."30/

First of all, Barry Goldwater outlined his personal philosophy of individual responsibility. He announced, "That each man is the best judge of his own well being....That each man is responsible for his own action....That each man has an individual conscience to serve and a moral code to uphold." Conversely, Goldwater lashed out against "the dead-end streets of collectivism" during his Acceptance Speech to the July, 1964 G.O.P. National Convention. He emphasized that "The good Lord raised up this mighty Republic to be a home for the brave and to flourish as the land of the free--not to stagnate in the swampland of collectivism..." A few months later the Republican Presidential Nominee demanded to know if "you want your children to live in a collectivized ant heap or in the open spaces of freedom?"31/

In his book The Conscience of a Conservative, the Arizona Senator considered the preservation of individualism to be one of the Right's most important roles: "Conservatism, throughout history, has regarded man neither as a potential pawn of other men, nor as a part of a general collectivity in which the sacredness and separate identity of individual human beings are ignored." Furthermore, the uniqueness of each person must be acknowledged. Goldwater believed that treating individuals like nameless, faceless drones invited tragic repercussions: "The Conservative knows that to regard man as part of an undifferentiated mass is to consign him to ultimate slavery."32/

Continuing in the same vein, Goldwater maintained that the commitment to the freedom and dignity of the individual stood as the cornerstone of the American way of life. This passionate devotion to individualism explained, in large measure, the extraordinary success of our republican experiment. For since its inception the United States has fostered a perfect climate in which each citizen has had the unparalleled opportunity to excel to the limits of his God-given abilities. And in Goldwater's view, these energetic and talented individuals have served America well: Our nation "grew great through the initiative and ambition of uncommon men."33/

Thus the world-wide decline in the value of individualism represented a tragedy of epic proportions. While campaigning for the Presidency in 1964 Barry Goldwater warned that "the individual, the private man, the whole man--you ! today stands in danger of becoming the forgotten man of our collectivized complex times."34/

Not surprisingly, Goldwater opposed the welfare state because he thought it destroyed individualism. He called the "programs of the welfare staters...an assault upon the dignity of the individual--designed to rob him of his independence, lessen his ability and his will to be self-sufficient, limit his opportunity, guide and determine his course in this world." While the welfare state eliminated individualism, it simultaneously fostered the growth of collectivism. Indeed Goldwater described the welfare state as a powerful tool in the hands of the collectivists: "The currently favored instrument of collectivism is the Welfare State." The Arizona Senator noticed the close connection between the two: "The collectivists have not abandoned their ultimate goal--to subordinate the individual to the State--but their strategy has changed. They have learned that Socialism can be achieved through Welfarism quite as well as through Nationalization."35/

Goldwater shared with the New Right a healthy distrust of big government. The Arizona Solon observed that "throughout history, government has proved to be the chief instrument for thwarting man's liberty." He quoted Lord Acton: "Power corrupts and absolute power corrupts absolutely."36/

No wonder the Arizona Senator told a Spartansburg, South Carolina political rally, "I fear Washington and centralized government more than I do Moscow." Goldwater also blamed a great part of America's alarming moral decay upon the ballooning size of government: "Government is the biggest enemy of moral values....Moral values decline as government grows." Goldwater promised if elected President to reverse this disturbing trend towards centralized government: The time will come, the Arizona Solon predicted,

> ...when Americans, in hundreds of communities throughout the nation, decide to put the man in office who is pledged to enforce the Constitution and restore the Republic. Who will proclaim in a campaign speech: 'I have little interest in streamlining government or in making it more efficient, for I mean to reduce its size. I do not undertake to promote welfare, for I propose to extend freedom. My aim is not to pass laws, but to repeal them. It is not to inaugurate new programs, but to cancel old ones that do violence to the Constitution, or that have failed in their purpose, or that impose on the people an unwarranted financial burden.'.

And, of course, Barry Goldwater intended to be exactly this kind of Presidential candidate.37/

Thus in keeping with this basic philosophy, 1964 G.O.P. Presidential Nominee Goldwater opened his Fall campaign with the ringing declaration that "this cancerous growth of the Federal Government must and shall be stopped" because the American citizens "face the grave danger of becoming servants of some Big Brother." Towards the close of the race he reiterated the same message: "Government must be cut down to size or we will surely lose our free society. We will go the age-old way of tyranny and oppression."38/

184

Moreover, Goldwater charged that the Johnson Administration sought to increase the powers of the Federal Government until it completely stifled the freedom of the individual American citizen: "Choose the way of this present Administration and you will have chosen the way of the regimented society, with a number for every man, woman, and child; a pigeonhole for every problem, and a bureaucrat for every decision."39/

As a counterweight to Washington's rapidly expanding authority over the lives of the American people Goldwater recommended a swift return to the strict principles of states' rights. The Arizona Solon noted that states' rights "is no mere slogan. It is the backbone of our Constitutional system." It remained "the cornerstone of the Republic, our chief bulwark against the encroachment of individual freedom by Big Government."40/

On the sensitive topic of civil rights, Goldwater personally sported an excellent record of genuine brotherhood towards people of all different races, ethnic groups, and creeds. Although raised as an Episcopalian, the Arizona Senator frequently boasted about his own half-Jewish ancestry: "I am proud of my Jewish father and grandfather. I've inherited some of the characteristics of the Jewish people and that has been a great advantage to me."* Goldwater denounced both racial discrimination and Southern Jim Crow segregation in the strongest terms. He told the United States Senate, "I am unalterably opposed to discrimination or segregation on the basis of race, color or creed, or on any other basis; not only my words, but more importantly my actions through the years have repeatedly demonstrated the sincerity of my feeling on this regard." Goldwater had even made a point of joining the National Association for the Advancement of Colored People, and as a Phoenix businessman during the late 1940's had led a successful fight to reduce discrimination against Mexican-Americans in his home state of Arizona. Finally, Goldwater loved and assisted the native Indian tribes throughout the Southwest.41/

---

*Note -- New Rightists like Barry Goldwater firmly believed that heredity plays a major role in determining an individual's basic personality traits. (New Right thought still retains unmistakable traces of late-nineteenth century Social Darwinist influence.) Thus when Goldwater speaks of having "inherited some of the characteristics of the Jewish people" he is using heredity to account for the apparent differences in behavior patterns, degrees of intelligence, or propensity for hard work which seem to exist among peoples of various racial and ethnic backgrounds. (For instance, see Chapters Six and Seven for an examination of the New Right's attitudes towards the Black race.)

185

Nevertheless, Goldwater's anti-centralized government philosophy affected his position on Civil Rights legislation. While utterly opposed to racial discrimination, the Arizona Senator blasted the Federal Civil Rights Bill of 1964 as a false remedy: "Like a three dollar bill--it's a phony." Goldwater lectured his Senate colleagues on the shortcomings of the measure: "Though the problem [of racial discrimination] is fundamentally one of the heart, some law can help--but not law that embodies features like these, provisions which fly in the face of the Constitution and which require for their effective execution the creation of a police state." Instead Goldwater suggested that "the key to racial and religious toleration lies not in laws alone, but ultimately, in the hearts of men. Individual action by every American, and this alone, will one day eliminate the stigma of discrimination from our society."42/

Finally, the Civil Rights Movement with its mass protests, and its civil disobedience tactics smacked of democracy and mob rule. Goldwater echoed the sentiments of the New Right when he stated that "we cannot resolve these great moral problems by recourse to demagogy, to violence, or to contempt for law and order." He added, "We have better and more lasting ways, within the framework of our constitutional system, to promote greater respect for the rights and liberties of all our people." For "any other course," he warned, "enthrones tyrants and dooms freedom."43/

The Arizona Senator made the preservation of the free enterprise system a central theme during his 1964 Presidential campaign. As the Republican Party standard-bearer reminded the nation, "Private property, free competition, hard work--these have been our greatest tools. Let us not discard them now !" He pledged to liberate the American economy from excessive government regulation. Goldwater intended "removing restrictions rather than imposing new ones--at every level of the economy."44/

Goldwater doubted the wisdom of Liberal, ivory-tower economists who tinkered with the American economy. As the Arizona Solon once lamented, "I don't believe we have a Democrat in the [Kennedy-Johnson] Administration who really understands the operation of the free enterprise system." Furthermore, Goldwater told N.B.C.'s "Meet the Press" that he "would be very happy if those government economists had ever earned a dollar out in the American enterprise system." Unfortunately, "they haven't."45/

Moreover, free enterprise was more than just an economic system for the production and distribution of material goods; it was also an outstanding way of life. The New Right deeply admired those personal character traits cultivated and rewarded under the free enterprise system. These included hard work, individual initiative, industriousness, and sobriety. Therefore, the demise of free enterprise would surely undermine the morale of the American people. Indeed historian Richard

186

Hofstadter correctly perceived that the Goldwater Movement feared "the decline of entrepreneurial competition will destroy our national character..."46/

Barry Goldwater favored an immediate return to traditional American moral standards. During his Acceptance Speech before the 1964 G.O.P. National Convention he complained that "our people have followed false prophets. We must and shall return to proven ways--not because they are old, but because they are true." Many citizens sensed this uncomfortable loss of direction. Goldwater detected "a stir in the land....a mood of uneasiness. We feel adrift in an uncharted and stormy sea. We feel that we have lost our way."47/

Goldwater outlined the shocking breakdown of American society during his 1964 Presidential race. He noted the "violence in our streets, corruption in our highest offices, aimlessness among our youth, anxiety among our elders." The serious problem of crime received special attention. Goldwater proclaimed that "Our wives, all women, feel unsafe on our streets."* He denounced, "gang rape in California," blasted the lenient U.S. Supreme Court for "pampering" vicious criminals and attacked "the apologists for collectivism" who "preach that society is to blame for crime not the criminal."48/

Goldwater censured the moral laxity of the Johnson Administration for contributing to the breakdown of American society: "Corruption, immorality and cynicism reach to our highest offices and touch our most cherished institutions. Scandal itself casts a shadow across the darkened White House. Bad example radiates downward..."** The Arizona Senator stressed that "where examples of morality should be set, the opposite is seen." Indeed "rather than moral leadership" the American people "have been given bread and circuses, spectacle and even scandal."49/

Sadly the once noble ideal of spirited public service had deteriorated into a selfish quest for personal wealth and glory. As

---

*Note--The tragic story of one New York City resident, Catherine Genovese, appalled the entire nation. In March, 1964 nearly a hundred citizens of Gotham stood by passively as a knife-wielding assailant carved up and slowly murdered this young woman as she screamed for help over the course of an incredible thirty-five minute span. Not a single bystander even bothered to telephone the police!

**Note--Goldwater's phrase "the darkened White House" refers to President Lyndon Johnson's much-ballyhooed effort to save taxpayer's money by turning out all unnecessary lights inside the Executive Mansion.

Goldwater noticed, "Public service, once selfless, has become for too many at its highest levels, selfish in motive and manner. Men who preach publicly of sacrifice, practice private indulgence." The Arizona Solon lamented that "Small men [i.e., Bobby Baker], seeking great wealth or power, have too often and too long turned even the highest levels of public service into a mere personal opportunity." Accordingly, Goldwater promised if elected President to return sound moral leadership to the White House. He looked "forward to the tomorrow in which high purpose and high morals will be restored to our high offices."50/

The Mind of Barry Goldwater: Foreign Policy

As a member of the New Right, Barry Goldwater took a hawkish, jingoistic stand on questions of foreign policy. To begin with, the Arizona Senator called for a complete victory over the International Communist Conspiracy: "We will never reconcile ourselves to the Communists' possession of power of any kind in any part of the World." Moreover, the United States should commence operations immediately by declaring "the world Communist movement an outlaw in the community of civilized nations....We should withdraw diplomatic recognition from all Communist governments including that of the Soviet Union, thereby serving notice on the world that we regard such governments as neither legitimate nor permanent."51/

Since Goldwater advocated nothing short of total victory over International Communism, he absolutely rejected any idea of negotiating a peaceful settlement of the outstanding disputes between the East and the West. He pointed out that "we'll never win our war against Communism by attempting to make adjustments and compromises with Communist governments." Indeed Goldwater flatly denied the existence of "such a thing as peaceful co-existence" because there could be "no co-existence with Communist power as long as they do not believe in God. It's as simple as that." Thus the Arizona Solon intended "to protect you against the soft-headed people who believe in co-existence with Communism."52/

Furthermore, Goldwater considered any diplomatic negotiations between the United States and the Communist nations utterly useless. These diplomatic overtures revolved around the mistaken notion "that peace can be kept by coming to terms with Communism rather than by overcoming Communism." Consequently, the Arizona Senator took a dim view of East-West summitry. "The only summit meeting that can succeed," he decided, "is one that does not take place."53/

Therefore, instead of recommending diplomatic contacts, Goldwater suggested a policy of direct confrontation with the Communist bloc. As mentioned previously, Goldwater demanded that

188

the United States sever all formal diplomatic ties with Communist nations: "If our objective is to win the Cold War, we will start now by denying our moral support to the very regimes we mean to defeat." According to the Arizona Senator, "Not only would withdrawal of recognition stiffen the American people's attitude toward Communism, it would also give heart to the enslaved peoples and help them to overthrow their captors."54/

In addition, Goldwater advocated, from time to time, some highly provocative measures (to say the least) designed to defeat the enemy. For instance, Goldwater insisted that the United States had missed a golden opportunity, in hindsight, to roll back Soviet power in Eastern Europe during the 1956 Hungarian uprising. For once the revolt had broken out, the American Army stationed in Western Europe should have rushed into Budapest ahead of the Russian troops and then issued the following ultimatum to the Soviets: Either remove the rest of the Red Army from Hungary or fight World War Three right there on the spot against the United States ! In the same fashion, the Arizona Solon favored knocking down the Berlin Wall which he assured could be safely accomplished "without the risk of war." Even after the celebrated downing of Francis Gary Powers' U-2 spy plane in May, 1960 had created an ugly international incident, Goldwater encouraged the resumption of U-2 espionage flights over Soviet territory. During the early stages of the Vietnam War, Goldwater wanted the U.S. Air Force to drop low yield atomic bombs on Red Chinese supply lines winding through North Vietnam. Finally, he considered the possibility of direct American military intervention to overthrow Communist nations. The U.S. must make the necessary preparations "to undertake military operations against vulnerable Communist regimes."55/

Goldwater conceded that an American strategy based upon provoking direct confrontations with the Communist bloc might lead to war. Nonetheless, the Arizona Lawmaker believed that "any foreign policy that this country adopts should not be afraid of war" because "If we are not willing to take risks in this world, we might as well give up." Goldwater denounced the "silly, sick, weak attitude" towards Communism "that permeates Washington." Unfortunately, "too many leaders today with shaking knees...fear taking risks." He scolded the "cry babies...who say [that] anything we do...will result in nuclear holocaust." Instead Goldwater favored returning "to the Eisenhower-Dulles doctrine of brinkmanship, where everybody knows we have the power and will use it."* He called brinkmanship "a great word."56/

---

*Note—Of course, the Radical Right had loudly criticized the Eisenhower Administration during the 1950's for failing to follow through with its avowed policy of "brinkmanship." (See Chapter Two)

Goldwater pointed out that the American people had always taken risks in order to defend freedom. He reminded his fellow citizens that the course of American history would have been quite different if great men like Douglas MacArthur, Paul Revere, or Daniel Boone had refused to take risks and "rock the boat." The Arizonan boasted that this traditional American courage still thrived in the Western parts of the country: "Out here in the West and Midwest, we're not constantly harassed by the fear of what might happen. Sure there are risks, but we've always taken risks." Goldwater then challenged the effete and decadent New Englanders to show the same kind of courage which had sparked the American Revolution two centuries ago: "Have the people of New England...changed in the last 200 years? Have we become a nation of cowards?" Is it really "any more dangerous today to risk war" than it was during colonial times? 57/

Moreover, Goldwater refused to consider the possibility of nuclear war "unthinkable." As the Arizona Lawmaker remarked, "If we are not prepared, under any circumstances....to fight a nuclear war, we might just as well do as the pacifists and the collaborationists propose - dump our entire arsenal into the ocean." Thus Goldwater parted company with those advocates of peace at any price who tried to appease the Communists just to avoid nuclear war: While "peace...is a proper goal of American policy...We do not want the peace of surrender."58/

On the other hand, Barry Goldwater had no intention of starting a nuclear war: "My opponents adroitly try to make it appear that I am in favor of nuclear war, that I would make war the prime instrument of our policy. I can't imagine what makes them think that. No one values life more than do I..."59/

Goldwater believed, in all sincerity, that the United States of America could achieve a complete and total victory over the enemy without at the same time touching off World War Three. As the Arizona Senator explained, "My critics have claimed, immediately on hearing the words 'victory' come from my lips, that I propose an all-out war. I am convinced, to the contrary, that we can win over Communism without ever firing a shot or dropping a bomb." For in Goldwater's estimation, whenever the United States applies sufficient pressure the Communists will automatically back down. The Russian retreat during the 1962 Cuban Missile Crisis proved this fact.60/*

---

*Note—The Cuban Missile Crisis, featuring an "eyeball to eyeball," Soviet-American confrontation, and ending abruptly with Nikita Khrushchev's humiliating capitulation, furnished additional proof for an idea already widely held by New Rightists that any convincing display of American strength and determination would ultimately break (Continued)

190

Interestingly enough, America's professed reluctance to use nuclear weapons actually increased the dangers of war ! As Goldwater noted:

> The surest path to nuclear war is for us to lull Russia into the misconception that we will never use the nuclear weapons. If and when so convinced, Russia will attack; and then, in defense of our freedom and our way of life, we will definitely strike back with all the power at our command. The bombs will fall.61/

Barry Goldwater, like the other members of the New Right, rejected the idea of disarmament. The Arizona Solon suggested, "that this whole argument for disarmament...is an extremely dangerous exercise in complete and total futility..." Instead, Goldwater pointed out the great virtue of nuclear weapons: "In the Old West, the six-gun was called the equalizer: it made all men the same height and the same strength. The atom bomb and its offspring, the nuclear bomb, have become the six-guns of today's world."62/

---

the Communists' "will". For the New Right, which still clings to old-fashioned, nineteenth century, highly romantic notions about warfare (i.e. "victory goes to the strongest nerve!"), drew an instant "lesson from history" after the Cuban Missile Crisis that if only the U.S. possessed the necessary "will to win" then a bloodless American triumph over Communism would follow in due course. (See Chapter Six)

Granted, the Soviet Union did, in fact, back down during this one particular incident. But this hardly guarantees that the Communists would always back down in every single instance, as the New Right suggests, whenever and wherever challenged by a strong-willed United States. Yet what else other than a firm belief in the classic dictum that "victory goes to the strongest nerve" could possibly account for Barry Goldwater's incredible assertion that the U.S. could charge right ahead and demolish the Berlin Wall "without the risk of war"? Apparently, the Arizona Senator did not expect the Soviets to lift a finger to stop us !

At the root, I detect a definite absence of respect for the Communist leaders as "men." As a typical New Rightist once told me, "Those sneaky Reds don't have enough guts to fight like real men right out in the open." Instead the cowardly Communist skulks around pursuing his policy of clandestine infiltration and subversion because, underneath all his brave rhetoric, the fact remains that the twin poisons of atheism and materialism have robbed the Communist of his manhood. And since the New Right viewed the Cold War as a giant, international game of "chicken" (or "brinkmanship") the United States would always win if we possessed the stronger will and the firmer nerve.

Goldwater assumed that the atomic weapons were the products and not the cause of international frictions. As he told the United States Senate, "nuclear weapons are not the cause of tensions in this world," consequently, "if all were to disappear magically overnight, the tension would remain so long as world Communism remains dedicated to aggression..." Therefore, the Arizona Solon cast his vote against the 1963 Nuclear Test Ban Treaty negotiated between the United States and the Soviet Union. Goldwater announced that "if it means political suicide to vote for my country and against this treaty, then I commit it gladly." Goldwater added, "I do not vote against the hope of peace, but only against the illusion of it. I do not vote for war, but for strength to prevent it."63/

Unfortunately, Goldwater held a cavalier attitude toward the serious environmental problems posed by the discharge of radioactive materials from atmospheric nuclear explosions. He flippantly called nuclear fallout "less a present threat than smog and fumes of everyday life." He declared that "Communist-induced hysteria on the subject of radio-active fallout" had frightened the United States into originally suspending its nuclear testing program. He responded to the Soviet decision to resume atmospheric testing in 1961 by boasting, "Let them do it. We'll just test a bigger one."64/

As expected, Barry Goldwater favored a strong United States military establishment. He insisted that "We must strive to achieve and maintain military superiority. Mere parity will not do." Surely as a fiscal Conservative the Arizona Senator regretted the costly expenditure of tax dollars for defense. Nevertheless, Goldwater was "not in favor of 'economizing' on the nation's safety." As the Arizonan explained, "I deplore the huge tax levy that is needed to finance the world's number one military establishment." However, "even more do I deplore the prospect of a foreign conquest, which the absence of that establishment would quickly accomplish."65/

Barry Goldwater deeply admired the U.S. armed services (where he once served with distinction) and respected military judgment. Indeed during a moment of candor the former-bomber pilot admitted that "perhaps I have been too close to the military and perhaps lean too heavily on that direction." At any rate, Goldwater paid the highest compliment to America's military leaders: "In this day and age when military power is the greatest deterrent to war that we have, it is accurate to say that our generals and admirals are, in fact, strategists of peace as well as experts on war."66/

Moreover, Goldwater supported Right-wing foreign military dictatorships especially when they prevented a nation from turning Communist. As the Arizona Senator told A.B.C.'s "Issues and Answers", "I don't object to a dictatorship as violently as some people do because I realize that not all people in this world are ready for democratic

192

processes. If they have to have a dictator in order to keep Communism out, then I don't think we can object to that." Consequently, "I don't look upon military juntas as the great evil that the [Johnson] White House does."67/

Finally, Goldwater, a graduate of Staunton Military Academy and a lifelong student of military history, heaped lavish praise upon the German army. Accordingly, the Arizona Senator favored the complete rearmament of West Germany. While American Liberals no doubt gagged at such a prospect, Goldwater "wouldn't be afraid of an armed Germany again" because "the only country in this world that Russia really fears is Germany-armed." Thus while the rearming of West Germany "might cause trouble...I think it's worth the risk."68/

Barry Goldwater's strong support for the United States armed services played a central role in his 1964 Presidential race against Lyndon Johnson. Goldwater charged that "in simplest terms, the defense policies of this Administration add up to unilateral disarmament." As mentioned earlier, Goldwater opposed the 1963 Nuclear Test Ban Treaty with the Soviet Union. He condemned Defense Secretary Robert McNamara's reorganization of the Pentagon which increased the influence of civilian "Whiz Kids" while ignoring career military officers. The G.O.P. Presidential Nominee also bemoaned the decision to abandon plans to produce the Air Force's costly, pet, B-70 bomber project.69/

However, Goldwater's greatest controversy surrounded his statements that certain high-ranking American military officers should be allowed to make the awesome decision whether or not to employ nuclear weapons in time of war. Thus Goldwater emphasized that while "I would not use atomic weapons when conventional weapons will do the job....I would leave it up to the commanders." Once installed in the Oval Office as President, in the event of war Goldwater intended to "turn to my Joint Chiefs of Staff and say 'Fellows, we made the decision to win, now it's your problem.' "70/

Lastly a virulent strain of national chauvinism infected Barry Goldwater's political philosophy. As he told his fellow Senators, "I don't give a tinker's dam what the rest of the world thinks about the United States as long as we keep strong militarily." Goldwater resented tiny, third-rate countries tweaking Uncle Sam's nose in forums such as the United Nations: "The United States should begin acting like a world power and quit groveling on its knees to inferior people who...come to New York."71/

An obscure Phoenix, Arizona department store executive named Barry Morris Goldwater quietly entered the United States Senate in January, 1953. By the end of the decade he had emerged as the spiritual leader of a crusade destined to become the most powerful radical Right-wing movement in American history. The culmination occurred at San Francisco in July, 1964 as the New Right, now in full control of the Republican Party, dutifully nominated the Arizona Senator to be the G.O.P. standard-bearer.

Obviously, Goldwater played an instrumental role in the rise of the New Right. For the Arizona Solon possessed a charismatic personality around which the New Right could easily rally, thus becoming the living symbol of the growing Movement. Barry Goldwater also succeeded in bridging the gap between an abstract Rightist philosophy and the turbulent world of partisan politics.

However, the Arizona Senator appeared upon the national scene at a most opportune moment. Consequently, he benefited from a pair of political trends which, of course, would have occurred irrespective of Goldwater. The Arizona Lawmaker rode the growing wave of anti-Communist sentiment during the early 1960's, propelled by a frustrating sense of "cold war battle fatigue." (See Chapter Two) Goldwater also capitalized upon the rift developing between the Northern and Southern wings of the Democratic Party over the issue of civil rights. This enabled a strong, New Right Republican Party to surface in the South by attracting thousands of disgruntled Democrats.

CHAPTER EIGHT - Notes

1.   Interesting biographies of Barry Goldwater include: Jack Bell, Mr. Conservative: Barry Goldwater (Garden City, New York: Doubleday & Company, Inc., 1962);
Fred J. Cook, Barry Goldwater: Extremist of the Right (New York: Grove Press, Inc., 1964);
Frank R. Donovan, The Americanism of Barry Goldwater (New York: MacFadden-Bartell Corporation, 1964);
Edwin McDowell, Barry Goldwater: Portrait of an Arizonan (Chicago: Henry Regnery Company, 1964);
Stephen Shadegg, Barry Goldwater: Freedom is His Flight Plan (New York: Fleet Publishing Corporation, 1962);
Rob Wood and Dean Smith, Barry Goldwater (New York: Avon Book Division, 1961).

2.   Welch, The Blue Book of the John Birch Society, p. 95;
Ibid;
Ibid.

3.   Human Events, (April 7, 1960), p. 1;
National Review, (April 9, 1960), p. 221.

4.   L. Brent Bozell, National Review, (June 18, 1960), p. 388.

5.   Ibid.

6.   Ibid.

7.   National Review, (April 9, 1960), p. 221;
Ibid., (June 18, 1960), p. 388;
Ibid., (August 13, 1960), p. 74.

8.   Ibid., (June 18, 1960), p.388.

9.   Ibid.

10.   Human Events, (August 11, 1960), p. 1;
Ibid., (August 4, 1960), p. 3.;

L. Brent Bozell concluded that the Arizona Solon...

emerged as the sentimental favorite of the party rank-and-file. Considering the delegates themselves, it was universally conceded that in an open convention Barry Goldwater would have won their nomination for Vice President. And some observers said that if the delegates had

195

been free to vote their preferences, he would have been nominated for President. National Review, (August 13, 1960), p. 74.

11.   National Review, (September 24, 1960), p. 172; Ibid., (August 13, 1960), p. 68.

12.   McDowell, Barry Goldwater: Portrait of an Arizonan, p. 27.

13.   National Review, (August 13, 1960), p. 74; Human Events, August 4, 1960), p.3.

Even Theodore H. White, the chronicler of modern Presidential elections, dates the start of the Goldwater Movement back to the 1960 Republican National Convention. Theodore H. White, The Making of the President 1964 (New York: Atheneum Publishers, 1965), p. 93.

14.   Human Events, (August 11, 1960), p. 1; Sherwin, The Extremists, p. 26.

Likewise, Rob Wood and Dean Smith pointed out that at the 1960 G.O.P. Convention the Arizona Solon "now wore the mantle which had slipped from the shoulders of the dying Senator Robert A. Taft seven years before." Wood and Smith, Barry Goldwater, p. 7.

Immediately after the 1960 G.O.P. Convention L. Brent Bozell announced that Goldwater "had become the undisputed leader of the conservative movement. Not since Taft had there been such a leader." National Review, (August 13, 1960), p. 74.

Human Events revealed that "conservatives now have a leader in Goldwater, a real successor to Taft, who may well dominate the party four or eight years hence." Human Events, (August 4, 1960), p. 2.

Somewhat later Theodore Humes suggested that "Goldwater has supplied his party with most of the moral and intellectual leadership that it has enjoyed since the passing of Robert Taft." Human Events, (April 27, 1963), p. 54.

15.   Human Events, (October 13, 1960), p. 482; John Chamberlain in the Wall Street Journal as quoted in Human Events, (November 17, 1960), p. 576.

16.   Human Events, (August 4, 1960), p.3; Cook, Barry Goldwater: Extremist of the Right, p. 129.

17. National Review, (December 3, 1960), p. 344;
Human Events, (November 17, 1960);
Stephen Shadegg, What Happened to Goldwater (New York: Holt,
Rinehart and Winston, 1965), p. 38.

18. Cook, Barry Goldwater: Extremist of the Right, p. 141;
Time, (June 23, 1961), p. 12.

19. White and Gill, Suite 3505: The Story of the Draft Goldwater
Movement describes the careful planning which went into the campaign
for Goldwater's 1964 G.O.P. Presidential nomination;
Hunter, Our Second Revolution, p. 48.

20. Time, (June 23, 1961), p. 12;
Human Events, (October 6, 1961), p. 657;
Statement by Barry Goldwater at a press conference in Atlanta, Georgia
on November 18, 1961 as quoted in Thomas Morgan, ed. Goldwater
Either/Or, p. 22.

21. Evans, The Future of Conservatism, p. 262.

22. Ibid., p. 263.

23. Human Events (December 22, 1963), p. 971;
Evans, The Future of Conservatism, p. 262.

24. Sherwin, The Extremists, p. 26;
Richard Rovere, The Goldwater Caper (New York: Harcourt, Brace &
World, Inc., 1965), p. 118.

25. Hofstadter, The Paranoid Style in American Politics and Other
Essays, p. 100.

26. Hunter, Our Second Revolution, p. 44;
Partisan Review, (Fall, 1964), p. 593.

27. Human Events, (September 14, 1963), p. 4;
Hunter, Our Second Revolution, p. 10.

28. Gerald Schomp, Birchism Was My Business (Toronto, Canada:
The MacMillan Company, 1970), p. 15;
Hunter, Our Second Revolution, pp. 43-44;
National Review, (August 13, 1960), p. 74.

29. Cook, Barry Goldwater: Extremist of the Right, p. 31;
Human Events, (April 27, 1963), p. 54.

30. Goldwater, Why Not Victory?, p. 88.

31.   New York Times, September 4, 1964;
Goldwater,Where I Stand, p. 14;
Ibid., p. 9;
New York Times, September 11, 1964.

32.   Goldwater, The Conscience of a Conservative, pp. 12-13.

33.   Ibid., p. 12.

34.   New York Times, September 4, 1964.

35.   Human Events, (February 18, 1960), p. 2;
Goldwater, The Conscience of a Conservative, p. 71.

36.   Goldwater, The Conscience of a Conservative, pp. 16-17.

37.   Speech by Barry Goldwater on September 15, 1960 as quoted in
Look, (April 21, 1964), p. 86;
Look, (September 24, 1963), p. 77;
Goldwater, The Conscience of a Conservative, p. 23.

38.   New York Times, September 4, 1964;
New York Times Magazine, (November 1, 1964), p. 102.

39.   New York Times, September 4, 1964.

40.   Goldwater, Where I Stand, p. 38;
Goldwater, The Conscience of a Conservative, pp. 25-26.

41.   Bell, Mr. Conservative: Barry Goldwater, p. 42;
U.S. Congress, Senate, Congressional Record, 88th Cong., 2nd Sess.,
June 18, 1964, vol. 110, Part II, pp. 14318-14319.

42.   Time, (July 12, 1964), p. 35;
U.S. Congress, Senate, Congressional Record, 88th Cong., 2nd Sess.,
June 18, 1964, vol. 110, Part II, p. 14319;
Goldwater, Where I Stand, p. 39.

43.   Goldwater, Where I Stand, p. 40;
Goldwater, The Conscience of a Conservative, p. 38.

44.   New York Times, September 4, 1964;
Goldwater, Where I Stand, p. 115.

45.   Washington Star, January 18, 1964 as quoted in Morgan, ed.,
Goldwater Either/Or, p. 38;
"Meet the Press", N.B.C. Television Network broadcast, January 5, 1964.

46. Hofstadter, The Paranoid Style in American Politics and Other Essays, Introduction, p. xii.

47. Goldwater, Where I Stand, p. 9; New York Times, September 4, 1964.

48. Goldwater, Where I Stand, p. 10; New York Times, September 4, 1964; Ibid., September 11, 1964; Ibid., September 16, 1964; New York Times Magazine, (November 1, 1964), p. 23.

49. New York Times Magazine, (November 1, 1964), p. 23; Goldwater, Where I Stand, p. 10.

50. New York Times, September 4, 1964; Goldwater, Where I Stand, p. 10; Speech before the Platform Committee of the Republican National Convention, San Francisco, California, July 10, 1964.

51. Goldwater, Why Not Victory?, p. 118; Goldwater, The Conscience of a Conservative, p. 123.

52. Manion Forum Network broadcast (January 21, 1962); New York Times Magazine, (September 17, 1961), p. 17; New York Times, January 18, 1964; Ibid., March 21, 1964.

53. Goldwater, Where I Stand, p. 68; Goldwater, Why Not Victory?, p. 65.

Goldwater summed up his feelings on East-West diplomacy with the following observation:

The next time we are urged to rush to the conference table in order to 'relax world tensions,' let our reaction be determined by this simple fact: the only 'tensions' that exist between East and West have been created, and deliberately so, by the Communists. They can therefore be 'relaxed' by the Kremlin's unilateral act. The moment we decide to relax tensions by a 'negotiated compromise' we have decided to yield something of value. Goldwater, The Conscience of a Conservative, p. 106.

54. Goldwater, The Conscience of a Conservative, p. 110; Ibid., p. 109.

55. Goldwater, The Conscience of a Conservative, p. 125; Los Angeles Times, November 3, 1963; Ibid., September 6, 1962;

Newsweek, (May 20, 1963), p. 29;
Goldwater, The Conscience of a Conservative, p. 124.

56.   Cook, Barry Goldwater: Extremist of the Right, p. 180;
Los Angeles Times, April 26, 1963;
New York Times, October 10, 1964;
Ibid., March 6, 1964;
"Issues and Answers", A.B.C. Television Network broadcast, April 7, 1963;
Hartford, Connecticut Press Conference, October 24, 1963 as quoted in Look, (April 21, 1964), p. 84;
New York Times, March 6, 1964.

57.   California Press Conference, May 25, 1964 as quoted in Mattar, Barry Goldwater: A Political Indictment, p. 145;
Saturday Evening Post, (August 24-31, 1963), p. 23;
New York Times, March 3, 1964.

58.   Goldwater, Why Not Victory?, p. 156;
Goldwater, The Conscience of a Conservative, p. 92.

59.   Goldwater, Why Not Victory?, p. 155.

60.   Manion Forum Network broadcast (January 21, 1962).

61.   Goldwater, Why Not Victory?, p. 181.

62.   Speech delivered in New York City, November 12, 1962 as quoted in The Weekly Crusader, (June 28, 1963), p. 6;
Goldwater, Why Not Victory?, p. 22.

63.   U.S. Congress, Senate, Congressional Record, 88th Cong., 1st Sess., September 19, 1963, vol. 109, Part 13, pp. 17557-17558.

64.   New York Times, September 30, 1963;
Goldwater, The Conscience of a Conservative, p. 113;
Phoenix Gazette, April 26, 1962 as quoted in Morgan, ed., Goldwater Either/Or, p. 54.

65.   Goldwater, The Conscience of a Conservative, p. 122;
Ibid., pp. 113-114.

66.   U.S. Congress, Senate, Congressional Record, 88th Cong., 1st Sess., September 23, 1963, vol. 109, Part 13, p. 17719;
Goldwater, Why Not Victory?, p. 180.

67. "Issues and Answers", A.B.C. Television Network broadcast, April 7, 1963;
New York Post, June 16, 1964.

68. Los Angeles Times, April 29, 1963.

69. Goldwater, Where I Stand, p. 67.

70. San Diego, California Press Conference, May 26, 1964 as quoted in the New Republic, (July 25, 1964), p. 14;
New York Times, July 11, 1964.

71. U.S. Congress, Senate, Congressional Record, 88th Cong., 1st Sess., September 23, 1963, vol. 109, Part 13, p. 17718;
New York Times, December 9, 1960.

CHAPTER NINE

THE ELECTION OF 1964

"A choice, not an echo"

Nearly every member of the New Right loved and admired Barry Goldwater. As William F. Buckley, Jr. wrote, "it isn't just youthful enthusiasts who like Goldwater—it is just about every American conservative...." Buckley paid tribute to Goldwater as "one of the few genuine radicals in American public life. A radical conservative..." Thus when the Arizona Senator ran for President in 1964, expressions of support poured in from New Rightists everywhere. For instance, Gerald L. K. Smith announced proudly that "for the first time in my mature life a major political party has nominated a candidate for president worthy of respect." Former Texas Congressman Martin Dies came out of political retirement to appear personally with Goldwater at a campaign rally in the Lone Star State, while Dean Clarence Manion lauded the Arizona Senator for catching "the imagination of millions of Americans in all sections of the country, not as a Republican, but as the out-spoken adversary of atheistic Communism and the unapologetic proponent of American strength, national independence and constitutional government.1/

The New Right certainly expected great deeds from Barry Goldwater. Author Ralph de Toledano labelled the Arizona Solon "the answer to the vast wasteland of American Liberalism." The Defender backed Goldwater because he offered "Americanism against one-worldism, independence against interdependence, outspoken policy against secretive pussy-footing, civic morality against liberal promiscuity, religious freedom against the fear of State Churchism, the chance to remain American against the threat of being mongrelized."*

---

*Note—This curious phrase, "religious freedom against the fear of State Churchism," was one of the few anti-Catholic remarks I encountered during my reading of New Right literature. In point of fact, anti-Catholicism, once a mainstay of the American Radical Right as late as the 1920's (see Chapter One), had all but disappeared by the Sixties. The nomination and election of John F. Kennedy, a Roman Catholic as President of the United States in 1960, definitely evoked bitter hostility from Radical Rightists; but the brunt of their attacks upon Kennedy centered around his Liberalism rather than this Catholicism.

New Right Evangelical Protestants actually welcomed the Roman Catholic Church as powerful ally in the struggle against International Communism while reactionary wealthy Catholics (surely a sign of their assimilation into the maintream of American life) joined the fight against social reform at home.

Likewise, Phyllis Schlafly described Goldwater as the ideal Republican Presidential Nominee since "He can be counted on to face the issues squarely. He will make the kind of forthright hard-hitting campaign that American voters admire." Instead of political double-talk the Arizona Senator spoke the plain truth. Instead of stale rhetoric he presented the electorate with a bold, fresh, new vision of America. Thus Goldwater "will truly offer the voters," in the opinion of Phyllis Schlafly, "a choice, not an echo."2/

New Right Criticism of Barry Goldwater

However, isolated criticism of Senator Goldwater did surface occasionally from within the ranks of the New Right. First of all, Barry Goldwater's half-Jewish ancestry earned him the enmity of the American Nazi Party. As George Lincoln Rockwell lamented, "It is discouraging and depressing to see so many good right-wingers, particularly knowledgeable anti-Semites, falling for the Jew faker, Goldwater." On the other hand, the anti-Semitic Reverend Gerald L. K. Smith and the Ku Klux Klan endorsed Goldwater. As Reverend Smith remarked, "True enough, he has Jewish blood in his veins, but he is a devout Christian and a lifetime member of a Christian church."3/

A more substantial complaint against Goldwater concerned the dangers of linking the fortunes of the New Right with a single personality, no matter how attractive. As Dan Smoot warned, "Conservatives should continue to support Goldwater if they think this a good means of building conservative strength in the Republican Party; but, for the sake of our Republic, they should not devote all of their political effort to Goldwater." For the New Right as a movement must always remain more than just a personal vehicle for the political ambitions of any one man, even the beloved Barry Goldwater. As Frank S. Meyer commented, "it would be utopian to believe that any political victory, even the election of Barry Goldwater to the Presidency, could by itself fulfill the conservative vision."4/

Consequently, the Presidential nomination of Barry Goldwater in July, 1964, while representing an important step in the political maturation of the New Right, did not, by any means, signify the end of the battle. In the words of Willmore Kendall, "American Conservatism was not born or even re-born, with the Goldwater nomination...American Conservatism does enter a phase with the Goldwater nomination and the Goldwater acceptance speech." The New Right always understood that partisan political activity alone represented only a portion of the overall solution to America's many problems. As Frank S. Meyer pointed out...

The conservative movement...is not limited in its perspectives to the arena of the purely political. It looks towards nothing less than a deep-going renewal of American life in the spirit of the Western and American tradition--a renewal at every level of existence: social, intellectual, philosophical, spiritual, as well as political. Its ends cannot be attained by a political victory alone, important though such a victory is.5/

Nevertheless, the major criticism leveled at the Arizona Solon centered around his dual allegiance: Goldwater emerged as the premier national political spokesman for the New Right while at the same time remaining a loyal member of the Republican Party. This situation created an obvious conflict since the best interests of the New Right did not always coincide with the best interests of the Republican Party. When the two collided, as happened often, Barry Goldwater invariably placed the welfare of the G.O.P. foremost. Indeed nobody could ever question his total dedication to his party. As William F. Buckley, Jr. wrote, "Goldwater is, and always will be, a member of the Republican team."6/

Barry Goldwater instinctively knew that the rough and tumble world of partisan politics required compromises and sacrifices of principle for the sake of party harmony. Of course, as a consummate team player, Goldwater drew fire from a few members of the New Right who stood on the sidelines and hence could afford the luxury of retaining their ideological purity. However, most New Rightists understood that Goldwater had no alternative--he simply had to keep his good standing within the Republican Party if he ever expected to receive its Presidential nomination. Thus the New Right forgave the Arizona Senator's occasional transgressions secure in the knowledge that only the intense pressures of Republican Party politics had forced Goldwater to retreat on matters of conscience.

Goldwater's leadership role within the Republican Party greatly reduced the bargaining position of the New Right. Since the party loyalist Goldwater had promised in advance to support any G.O.P. Presidential nominee, he could never then walk out leading a Right-wing defection. Thus the Arizona Senator had unwittingly dissipated most of his leverage by laying his cards on the table before the bidding actually started. As L. Brent Bozell explained, "Without a believable threat-- whether it is to stay home, or not to work, or to bolt--the minority (the Radical Right) has no leverage, and thus has no power." Bozell reminded his readers that "this does not mean the threat must be carried out; only that it be made." Likewise, Frank S. Meyer discussed the restraints placed upon the New Right when it worked within the confines of the Republican Party:

So long as conservatives cannot see beyond loyalty to the Republican party..., they are foredoomed to defeat....If they make it clear in advance that whatever the Republican Party does it will have their support, the logic of politics dictates that the Republican Party will remain a Liberal party. Under such circumstances, the conservative vote is locked in as a Republican vote—which predetermines that the Liberal argument will prevail: "The conservatives have nowhere else to go; so, to win, the Republicans must nominate a Liberal candidate and write a Liberal platform."7/

Moreover, Barry Goldwater's total dedication to Republicanism caused him to turn his back upon the New Right at various crucial times for the sake of party unity. As early as 1960 this tendency came to light when Goldwater refused to actively challenge Richard Nixon for the G.O.P. Presidential nomination. As Dan Smoot later complained, "Senator Goldwater's greatest disservice to the conservative movement occurred in 1960....Goldwater gave the conservatives no leadership whatever....At a critical moment, he folded and gave his support to Nixon." Desperately eager for a G.O.P. victory at all costs in 1968 he pragmatically backed the moderate Richard Nixon again over an authentic New Rightist, California Governor Ronald Reagan. (See Chapter Twelve.) Goldwater's position in 1968, that nearly any Republican nominee represented a vast improvement after eight bitter years of Liberal Democratic rule, earned him the charge of "selling 'Republicanism'—good, bad, or indifferent." Similarly, Goldwater supported President Gerald Ford over Ronald Reagan at the 1976 G.O.P. National Convention held in Kansas City. Indeed the Arizona Senator's crucial endorsement of President Ford provided the narrow margin of victory over Reagan, especially among several key Southern delegations.8/ (See Chapter Thirteen)

In retrospect, the New Right hardly needed deadly enemies with good friends like Barry Goldwater. The New Right eventually came to understand this during the years of reflection after the Arizona Senator's 1964 Presidential Campaign debacle. While the New Right still loved and respected the man from Phoenix, they realized sadly that he had been, on balance, a total disaster for their movement.

Barry Goldwater and George Wallace

Barry Goldwater failed to cement a working alliance with Alabama Governor George C. Wallace in time for the November, 1964 Presidential Election. In fact, the Arizona Senator made no particular effort to secure Governor Wallace's blessings and the lack of a political understanding between the two men never bothered the Goldwater camp at the time. However, in hindsight, this dealt a significant blow to

Goldwater's already rather slim Presidential prospects, for the G.O.P. desperately needed Wallace's sizeable Democratic constituency in the General Election against Lyndon Johnson. This entire episode deserves a thorough explanation.

Surely, Barry Goldwater had good reasons for avoiding George Wallace. The Alabama Governor had recently emerged as America's premier defender of Jim Crow segregation with his defiant stand inside the school house door at the University of Alabama the year before. Meanwhile, Goldwater had drawn great criticism for his so-called "Right-wing extremism" and was frantically attempting to moderate his image as the November General Election approached. Thus he hardly needed close identification with George Wallace's demagogic racism. Consequently, the G.O.P. Presidential Nominee saw no advantage to be gained by reaching an accord with the flamboyant Alabama Governor.

Furthermore, the Alabama Governor's noisy political style deeply offended the gentlemanly Arizona Senator. For George Wallace took Goldwater's calm, reasoned, New Right philosophy, added a dose of Southern Redneck Populism, and transformed the message into a blatant appeal to human emotions. This smacked a demagoguery and Barry Goldwater had no use whatsoever for rabble-rousers. (See Chapter Three)

Finally, George Wallace loomed as a distinct threat to Goldwater's position as undisputed leader of the New Right. Perhaps, the popular, exciting Alabama Governor might someday outshine the rather low-key Arizona Senator. Certainly, from Wallace's standpoint it made little sense to challenge Goldwater's hegemony in 1964. The Arizona Senator, after all, had just captured control over the G.O.P. while Wallace remained just a promising Democratic newcomer. The year 1964 rightfully belonged to Barry Goldwater; George Wallace looked towards 1968 and beyond.

On the other hand, Barry Goldwater viewed George Wallace as a dangerous rival. True enough, the two men avoided any direct confrontations during the Spring of 1964 since the Republican Goldwater and the Democrat Wallace had entered different Presidential primaries. Nevertheless, the Arizona Senator, who always considered Wallace a pariah, saw no need to enhance the status of his unscrupulous opponent by concluding a political alliance. For every alliance implies recognition and, at least, a certain degree of approval and Goldwater never wanted to recognize the demagogic Alabama Governor as a legitimate national political entity. Instead Goldwater chose to ignore the existence of George Wallace.

The George Wallace phenomenon surprised everyone in the Goldwater camp. As a matter of fact, the Goldwater strategists had decided to piece together an electoral majority composed of the farm states plus the Sunbelt, and had written off completely the large Northern and Eastern cities. Yet the Alabama Governor's excellent showing in the Wisconsin, Indiana, and Maryland Presidential Primaries during the Spring of 1964 revealed a growing working-class disenchantment with American Liberalism. For George Wallace drew substantial support from urban, ethnic, blue-collar voters who had once cast ballots for Franklin D. Roosevelt and John F. Kennedy. Indeed the Alabama Governor had broken fresh ground as he successfully preached the gospel of the New Right (albeit Southern Redneck style) to Northern Democrats who had traditionally turned a deaf ear to men such as Robert Taft or Barry Goldwater.

George Wallace eventually dropped out of the race shortly after the 1964 Presidential primary season ended, but not before he had firmly established himself as a credible national candidate for the future with both a large Northern and Southern following. Of course, George Wallace never did endorse his party's Presidential nominee Lyndon Johnson; but the Alabama Governor also failed to throw his support behind Barry Goldwater. The astute Wallace, sensing Goldwater's various shortcomings which made his resounding defeat in November all but inevitable, chose to remain independent and avoid any association with the upcoming G.O.P. disaster.

For Wallace realized that Barry Goldwater's dry constitutionalism coupled with his intellectual pretensions could never excite the masses; that Goldwater's small-town Waspishness prevented him from building a genuine rapport with urban America; and that his longstanding antipathy towards organized labor had alienated the working classes. In contrast, George Wallace adopted an anti-intellectual, plain-talking, "Populist," oratorical style, scrupulously paid deference to the various nationality groups in the cities, and sang warm words of praise for labor unions--all time-honored customs of the Democratic Party. For the fact remains that the Republican Barry Goldwater and the Democrat George Wallace spoke to vastly different constituencies.

In essence, the free-wheeling, Alabama Redneck George Wallace and the respectable, nouveau riche, Arizona businessman Barry Goldwater represented quite distinct (and in some ways incompatible) American political traditions. As mentioned in Chapter One, Southern Rednecks, usually rather Liberal on bread and butter issues, have not been permanent members of the Radical Right throughout the entire twentieth century. Thus while the extraordinary racial and cultural tensions of the 1960's drove the pro-welfare state Southern Rednecks into the same camp with economic reactionaries like Barry Goldwater, this obvious marriage of convenience, in a political sense, was never completely consummated.

Republican Presidential Nominee Barry Goldwater actually carried George Wallace's Deep Southern constituency in the November

1964 General Election against Democrat Lyndon B. Johnson. The Arizona Senator won Alabama, Georgia, Louisiana, Mississippi, and South Carolina. All of these Southern states except South Carolina went for George Wallace four years later when the Alabaman campaigned as a third party candidate on the American Independent ticket. (See Chapter Twelve.) However, the Arizona Senator failed to bring Wallace's Northern Democratic following into the Republican fold in November, 1964. As the Alabama Governor himself noted in retrospect: "In the last election, Mr. Goldwater was running as a Conservative, but he did not have the support and confidence of the working people in our country. For some reason they feared that he was not in their (best) interest."9/

During the Fall of 1964 Barry Goldwater refused to exploit the Northern, urban, White Backlash as George Wallace had done so effectively the previous Spring. Indeed well before the Fall campaign began the Arizona Solon had privately reassured his Democratic opponent President Lyndon Johnson that he, Goldwater, would never link the constitutional issue of civil rights legislation, on the one hand, with racially explosive subjects such as violent Black street crime, on the other. Of course, by stubbornly ignoring the potential White Backlash vote, Goldwater certainly knew that he was throwing away his only real chance to woo the Wallace Democrats. But the Arizona Solon remained too much of an idealist and a gentleman to stoop to racial demagoguery. As the National Review Bulletin commented, "his incorruptible sense of decency prevents him from capitalizing on the backlash and encouraging...anti-Negroism..."10/

Finally, the tension between Barry Goldwater and George Wallace in 1964 highlighted a major crisis of leadership facing the New Right: How to find an electable Presidential candidate with the perfect blend of political chemistry; someone who combined the respectability of a Goldwater with the oratorical flair of a Wallace; someone to exploit the White Backlash—but in a nice way; someone with broad popular appeal which cut across party lines, to unite Goldwater Republicans with Wallace Democrats. Such a man appeared upon the national political scene quite by accident in late October, 1964. His name was Ronald Reagan. (See Chapter Eleven)

"They are the kind we need in politics"

Barry Goldwater frequently defended his New Right supporters against charges of extremism. For example, the Arizona Senator praised the members of the notorious John Birch Society: "A lot of people in my home town (Phoenix) have been attracted to the society and I am impressed by the type of people in it. They are the kind we need in politics." He added, "They are the finest people in my community." Furthermore, the John Birch Society stood for the highest American ideals: "They believe in the Constitution, they believe in God, they

209

believe in Freedom." Consequently, Goldwater did not "consider the John Birch Society as a group to be extremist." Thus "The Birch Society...constitutes no danger," and actually represented "a far less menace to the United States than the Americans for Democratic Action or the United Auto Workers."11/

On the other side of the coin, Barry Goldwater realized that certain strident New Rightists gave the entire Movement a bad reputation. The Arizona Senator pointed out that "one of the things that make conservatism hard to sell is that its exponents make such violent, damn fool statements."12/

Yet Barry Goldwater violated his own dictum, on occasion, by edging "into the language of the fringe," in the words of Jack Bell, a friend and supporter. Similarly, even the sympathetic Richmond News-Leader called Goldwater "the most impolitic politician of our acquaintance" because of his rhetorical faux pas.13/

Goldwater's classic oratorical blunder occurred during his Acceptance Speech delivered in front of the 1964 G.O.P. National Convention in San Francisco. In that memorable address the newly selected Republican Party standard-bearer clearly endorsed the merits of "extremism." For as Goldwater told the gathering, "Extremism in the defense of liberty is no vice. Moderation in the pursuit of justice is no virtue." These two phrases simply destroyed whatever remained of Goldwater's election prospects. As F. Clifton White acknowledged ruefully, "with those fateful words...Senator Goldwater had seemed to identify himself with the very groups that the public had been led to believe would drive us into nuclear war with world Communism."14

Indeed the conflict between Barry Goldwater, the New Right ideologue and Barry Goldwater, the aspiring G.O.P. Presidential candidate, ultimately crippled his campaign. For as Liberal critic Richard Rovere has pointed out, the Arizona Senator had become a prisoner of his earlier, reckless, and in some cases, ghost-written statements on all sorts of issues. Rovere noted that Goldwater "has said, or allowed others to say for him, things that no politician in his senses would dream of saying." No wonder, author Robert J. Donovan joked that "Barry Goldwater entered the campaign with certain built-in handicaps, and he made the most of them."15/

"This is still a free country, ladies and gentlemen"

Furthermore, the boorish behavior of the Goldwater supporters at the 1964 G.O.P. National Convention discredited the whole New Right Movement. Unreconstructed Southerners waved Confederate flags, uttered ugly racial slurs at the handful of Blacks unlucky enough to attend this Convention, and even set the coat of a Black delegate from

Pennsylvania on fire during a howling, pro-Goldwater floor demonstration. It came as no surprise that Pennsylvania Senator Hugh Scott, the leader of the stop-Goldwater forces at San Francisco, saw fit to denounce "the barbarism of the lunatic fringe in the Goldwater ranks." Senator Scott stressed that "at no time did the Goldwater leaders either apologize for the uncivilized behavior of some of their followers or publicly urge their zealots to temper their actions." Senator Scott suggested, "Perhaps it would have been too much for the original followers of Barry Goldwater to repudiate the infiltrators of the hard-line right, since many of these fanatics were the Senator's most articulate and active missionaries."16/

Thus the relationship between the Goldwaterites and the so-called "extremist hate groups" became the major issue at the 1964 G.O.P. Convention. The proposed Republican Platform contained a plank condemning the American Communist Party for its extremism. However, the Eastern Liberal Establishment wing of the G.O.P. wanted the delegates to go on record against extremism from both the Left and the Right. Oregon Republican Governor Mark Hatfield presented the Liberal case during his Keynote Address: "There are bigots in this nation who spew forth the venom of hate. They must be overcome, and this applies to the Ku Klux Klan, the John Birch Society, the Communist party and the hundreds of others like them." Of course, it goes without saying that the New Rightists had no intention of lumping the Ku Klux Klan and the John Birch Society into the same category with the Communist Party. Accordingly, the Goldwater delegates voted down decisively the substitute Platform plank.17/

The Convention debate itself over the question of "extremist hate groups" gave the Goldwater supporters yet another opportunity to discredit their own cause. For when New York Governor Nelson Rockefeller rose to denounce "Right-wing extremism" the Goldwaterites seated up in the Cow Palace galleries showed themselves at their worst by shouting down the speaker. At one point the New York Governor, unable to compete with the jeering crowd, reminded the gathering, "This is still a free country, ladies and gentlemen." Once again the Goldwaterites had disgraced their own Movement with their uncontrolled behavior. As Presidential chronicler Theodore H. White wrote, "as the TV cameras translated their wrath and fury to the national audience, they pressed on the viewers that indelible impression of savagery which no Goldwater leader or wordsmith could later erase."18/

In hindsight, the hostile reception accorded to Nelson Rockefeller, so disturbing back in 1964, had become quite commonplace in American public life by decade's end. Indeed the whole incident looks rather mild when compared with the 1968 Democratic Party fiasco at Chicago, for instance. Nevertheless, the New Right deserves censure for casting the first stone back in 1964 thereby breaking the well-accepted, sportsmanlike code of American political conduct.

211

Finally, the Goldwaterites expressed their intense displeasure with the news media. The New Right has always looked upon the large metropolitan dailies, the national circulation news magazines like Time and Newsweek, and the three major television networks as the tools of the Eastern Liberal Establishment. For, in truth, the national news media distrusted Barry Goldwater and his Movement and fully intended to use every available weapon (from slander and vilification to outright distortion of his positions on the issues) in order to sabotage his candidacy. Consequently, any mention of the news media would instantly send the Goldwater delegates into a rage. As Fred Cook observed, "many of the Goldwater cohorts stood and jeered and shook their fists at newspaper and television reporters....One got the indelible impression that some of Goldwater's [partisans] would like to lynch newsmen."19/

"We just want to make them mad, make their stomachs
turn"

Moreover, some of the Arizona Senator's over-zealous followers committed impolitic excesses during the 1964 General Election. For example, fanatics removed the portraits of Presidents Abraham Lincoln and Dwight Eisenhower from the offices of the Republican National Committee in Washington in a bizarre attempt to purge all traces of moderate influence from G.O.P. history. Local Republican headquarters served as distribution centers for all kinds of outrageous New Right literature. Volunteers sold an estimated 17 million books and pamphlets including such classics as J. Evetts Haley's A Texan Looks at Lyndon, Phyllis Schlafly's A Choice, Not An Echo, and John Stormer's None Dare Call it Treason. Throughout the South the most rabid segregationists jumped aboard the Goldwater bandwagon and in a few states actually took over the day-to-day management of the campaign. Finally, authors Benjamin Epstein and Arnold Forster have pointed out that the John Birch Society "misused the campaign as a vehicle to spread their own political propaganda and to recruit new members." No wonder Republican Party historian George H. Mayer has labelled the 1964 Goldwater fiasco "The Amateur Hour."20/

However, the controversy surrounding the presentation of the film "Choice" demonstrated most clearly the extraordinary tensions within the Goldwater camp between the burning enthusiasm of the New Right partisans, on the one hand, and the restrictions placed upon Presidential candidates by the age-old requirements of practical politics, on the other. The "Mothers for a Moral America," a group loosely associated with the Citizens for Goldwater-Miller organization, had produced "Choice", a short motion picture narrated by actor Raymond Massay dealing with the decaying state of contemporary American society. The "Mothers For a Moral America" intended to broadcast the film "Choice" as a half-hour, prime-time, television special during the closing weeks of the campaign.

The film "Choice," while hardly a documentary masterpiece, unquestionably touched a sore nerve with New Rightists. As Russell Walton, Public-Relations Director for the Citizens for Goldwater-Miller organization admitted, "We just want to make them mad, make their stomachs turn." "Choice" featured busty girls wearing topless bathing suits (the fashion innovation of the 1964 season), sleazy strip tease joints packed with wide-eyed patrons, pornographic books and magazines displayed at street-corner newsstand racks, young couples dancing the "twist" with reckless abandon at wild night clubs, Black ghetto rioters and looters, and the likes of Bobby Baker and Billy Sol Estes, both corrupt former cohorts of President Lyndon B. Johnson.21/

The film "Choice" never implicates the President directly. Nonetheless, one particular sequence strongly hints that L.B.J.'s personal decadence had something to do with the decline of traditional American morality. For the President had raised some eyebrows when he loaded several reporters and a few six-packs of cold beer into his limousine, and then personally chauffeured the gang for a short spin around the vicinity of the L.B.J. Ranch at extremely high speeds. Consequently, this utterly tasteless film "Choice" depicts a big, black Lincoln Continental roaring down a Texas highway while the unseen driver (obviously L.B.J.) nonchalantly tosses empty beer cans out the front window.22/

Although excerpts from "Choice" did appear on evening news broadcasts, responsible G.O.P. campaign officials intervened in time to prevent the entire film from reaching the nation's air waves. So the "Mothers For a Moral America" reluctantly cancelled their program, much to the disappointment of the rabid Goldwater supporters. The Arizona Senator himself repudiated the documentary as offensive, racist, and an encouragement to rioters and looters. Yet Goldwater objected to its style rather than to its contents. Nearly every contemporary vice presented in this film had already been mentioned by Goldwater at least a dozen times during the course of his Presidential campaign. But "Choice" smacked of demagoguery with its blatant appeals to prejudice and emotion.23/

The cancellation of "Choice" signified that responsible officials had finally regained the upper hand within the Goldwater camp over the Senator's more reckless followers. In addition, the G.O.P. National Committee, just prior to the November Election, disavowed Haley's A Texan Looks at Lyndon, Schlafly's A Choice Not an Echo, and Stormer's None Dare Call it Treason and ordered all local Republican Party headquarters across the country to halt the distribution of these books immediately. Of course, most of the G.O.P. district offices, now controlled by zealous New Rightists, simply ignored the National Committee's request and continued selling the materials.24/

213

Moreover, soon after the July, 1964 G.O.P. National Convention Presidential Nominee Goldwater retreated from some of his more outlandish positions. He scrapped his proposals to eliminate the graduated income tax, Social Security, and the Tennessee Valley Authority. He labelled suggestions that he "would have overrun Cuba and used atomic weapons in Vietnam" as "outright and utter lies." The Arizona Solon had frightened many Americans during his Acceptance Speech before the G.O.P. National Convention when he proclaimed that "Extremism in the defense of liberty is no vice." By early August Goldwater had clarified his thoughts on the subject of "extremism." The Senator declared that "Extremism is not Americanism; it is totalitarianism. Extremism is not valor; it is cowardice. Extremism does not serve justice; it promotes anarchy." He concluded, "Extremism has no place in America."25/

Finally, a hastily convened G.O.P. Summit Meeting held at Hershey, Pennsylvania on August 12, 1964 found a conciliatory Goldwater reaffirming his devotion to traditional Republican Party principles and rejecting "extremism." After conferring with former President Dwight Eisenhower, former Vice-President Richard Nixon, New York Governor Nelson Rockefeller, Pennsylvania Governor William Scranton, and a dozen other G.O.P. governors Goldwater announced, "I seek the support of no extremist--of the left or right....We repudiate character assassins, vigilantes, Communists and any group such as the Ku Klux Klan that seeks to impose its views through terror and violence."26/

Yet despite the harmful antics of his followers, Barry Goldwater, in the last analysis, bears the ultimate responsibility for the magnitude of the Republican Party defeat in November, 1964. For the Arizona Senator had alarmed countless millions of voters with "his truculent, vague, flippant, and frequent references to nuclear weapons." (Chapter Eight examines Goldwater's various controversial statements on the subjects of brinkmanship, nuclear bombs, radioactive fallout, World War Three, etc.) Thus many Leftists dubbed Goldwater "Doctor Strangelove," and a Liberal Republican critic chided the Arizona Senator for speaking "in terms of low-yield nuclear weapons as though one would use them to kill crabgrass." Consequently, many Americans saw Goldwater as a trigger-happy maniac just itching to push the nuclear button launching World War Three. As Minister W.O.H. Garman of Wilkinsburg, Pennsylvania pointed out, "Millions were actually led to fear Barry as a maniac who would blow up the world with hydrogen bombs."27/

Thus Theodore H. White concluded that "War and peace were to be the dominant issue of the campaign of 1964," and, "Barry Goldwater was to be destroyed by this issue." The Arizona Senator himself evidently realized this fact since quite soon after the election he emphasized that "The whole campaign against me was run on [a] fear of me." Years later the 1964 G.O.P. Presidential Nominee admitted that his opponents had created "a caricature of Goldwater which was so grotesque that, had I personally believed all the allegations, I would have voted against my own candidacy."28/

The Treachery of the Eastern Liberal Establishment

The nomination of Barry Goldwater represented a triumph for the Sunbelt over the Eastern Liberal Establishment wing of the Republican Party. In the words of National Review Publisher William A. Rusher, the year "1964 marked an historic turning-point—the moment long-range control of the GOP passed from the East to a new and more conservative coalition of the Midwest, the West and the South." Likewise, Destiny magazine agreed: "The Goldwater nomination and the appointment of Arizonians to high positions in the Republican party organization is a major shift of control of the party from eastern big interests, Moderates and Liberals to southwestern interests and Conservatives."29/

The Goldwaterites had eagerly awaited the end of Eastern Liberal Establishment hegemony over the Republican Party. William F. Buckley, Jr. remarked that "almost literally Goldwater was forced to run by Americans who seemed, some of them, to be asking primarily for their own emancipation from the decadent East." The Arizona Senator himself looked forward to the termination of Eastern domination (or any other connections with the East): "Sometimes I think this country would be better off if we could just saw off the Eastern Seaboard and let it float out to sea."30/

From the perspective of the Eastern Liberal Establishment, the infidels now controlled the Temple of the Republican Party. Barry Goldwater and his New Right supporters had unceremoniously dislodged the Eastern Liberal Establishment from its traditional position of leadership atop the G.O.P. Thus reclaiming the White House in November, 1964 played a secondary role to their recapturing control over the Republican Party; for the Eastern Liberal Establishment could tolerate another Presidential term for Liberal Democrat Lyndon Johnson much easier than spending the next four years with Barry Goldwater as the nation's Chief Executive. As Dan Smoot noted, "liberal Republicans (Lodge, Scranton, Rockefeller, Nixon, Eisenhower, et al.) would rather see Republicans lose the presidential contest than see Barry Goldwater win it."31/

Liberal Republicans refusing to campaign on behalf of the 1964 Goldwater-Miller ticket included New York Governor Nelson Rockefeller, New York Senators Jacob Javits and Kenneth Keating, New York Congressman John Lindsay (soon to be Gotham's next Mayor), Massachusetts Senator-to-be Edward Brooke, and Michigan Governor George Romney. Goldwater's major convention opponent, Pennsylvania

Governor William Scranton coughed up a lukewarm endorsement. Furthermore, the Eastern Liberal Establishment heaped scorn upon the Arizona Senator. In Governor Rockefeller's judgment, for Goldwater "To extol extremism whether 'in defense of liberty' or 'in pursuit of justice' is dangerous, irresponsible and frightening." Governor Scranton wrote an open letter to Goldwater complaining, "You have too often casually prescribed nuclear war as a solution to a troubled world." The Pennsylvania Governor warned that "Goldwaterism has come to stand for a whole crazy-quilt collection of absurd and dangerous positions that would be soundly repudiated by the American people in November."32/

The entire unedifying Presidential campaign came to a merciful conclusion on November 3, 1964 when Lyndon Johnson overwhelmed Barry Goldwater at the polls. Having violated every sensible rule of American electoral politics Barry Goldwater paid the high price for his stubborness and his convictions. The Arizona Senator's grotesque blunders, coupled with the vulgar excesses committed by some of his devoted followers, had obscured the important issues of 1964. In truth, the country desperately needed a thorough discussion of its growing problems, and the Election of 1964 represented the last opportunity for the nation to chart a rational future course before the turmoil of the later 1960's made an intelligent debate all but impossible.

Finally, the New Right had come quite aways by 1964—but not yet far enough. At least, Senator Goldwater had captured the G.O.P. Presidential nomination which had barely eluded Senator Robert Taft back in 1952. Goldwater had fallen far short of the ultimate goal--the White House—in 1964. The New Right realized that a very long journey still lay ahead.

CHAPTER NINE - Notes

1.   William F. Buckley, Jr., Rumbles Left and Right (New York: G.P. Putnam's Sons, 1963), p. 40;
Ibid., p. 31;
Cross and the Flag, (September, 1964), p. 5;
Rovere, The Goldwater Caper, pp. 145-146;
Manion Forum Network broadcast (June 14, 1964).

2.   Ralph de Toledano, The Winning Side: The Case For Goldwater Republicanism (New York: G.P. Putnam's Sons, 1963), p. 165;
The Defender, (June, 1964), p. 22;
Phyllis Schlafly, A Choice Not An Echo, 3rd ed. (Alton, Illinois: Pere Marquette Press, 1964), p. 78.

3.   Rockwell Report, (March 1, 1964), p. 2;
Cross and the Flag, (June, 1963), p. 23.

4.   Dan Smoot Report, (June 17, 1963), p. 190;
National Review, (November 5, 1963), p. 386.

5.   New Guard, (October, 1964), p. 8;
National Review, (November 5, 1963), p. 386.

6.   Buckley, Rumbles Left and Right, p. 34.

7.   National Review, (August 13, 1960), pp. 74-75;
Ibid., (December 3, 1960), p. 344.

8.   Dan Smoot Report, (June 17, 1963), p. 190;
John J. Synon, The Citizen, (March, 1968), p. 13;
Regarding Goldwater's activities in later years, 1972 A.I.P. Presidential Candidate John Schmitz recently confided to me: "I used to wonder if Goldwater had actually written The Conscience of a Conservative. Nowadays I wonder if he had actually ever read it!"

9.   John J. Synon, ed., George Wallace: Profile of a Presidential Candidate (Kilmarnock, Virginia: Ms, Inc., 1968), p. 82.

10.   Barry Goldwater interview with the Arizona Republic as quoted in the National Review, (January 16, 1968), p. 27;
National Review Bulletin, (August 4, 1964), p. 5.

11.   Time (April 7, 1961), p. 19;
Ibid., (June 23, 1961), p. 16;
New York Times, July 18, 1964;

"Meet the Press", N.B.C. Television Network broadcast, November 19, 1961;
Mattar, Barry Goldwater (A Political Indictment), p. 87.

12. Bell, Mr. Conservative: Barry Goldwater, p. 114.

13. Ibid.;
Richmond News-Leader as quoted in Report to America, (January, 1964), p. 5.

14. Goldwater, Where I Stand, p. 16;
White and Gill, Suite 3505, The Story of the Draft Goldwater Movement, p. 15.

15. Rovere, The Goldwater Caper, p. 48;
Robert J. Donovan, The Future of the Republican Party (New York: The New American Library, 1964), p. 45.

16. Hugh Scott, Come to the Party (Englewood Cliffs, New Jersey: Prentice-Hall, Inc., 1968), pp. 5-6.

17. New York Times, July 14, 1964;
For an excellent account of the 1964 G.O.P. National Convention see:
Fred J. Cook, Barry Goldwater: Extremist of the Right (New York: Grove Press, Inc., 1964);
Hugh Scott, Come to the Party (Englewood Cliffs, New Jersey: Prentice-Hall, Inc., 1968);
Theodore H. White, The Making of the President 1964 (New York: Atheneum Publishers, 1965).

18. White, The Making of the President 1964, p. 211;
Ibid., p. 212.

19. Cook, Barry Goldwater: Extremist of the Right, p. 178.

20. Edward Brooke, The Challenge of Change (Boston: Little, Brown and Company, 1966), p. 17;
David Danzig, "Conservatism After Goldwater," Commentary, (March, 1965), p. 34;
J. Evetts Haley, A Texan Looks at Lyndon (A Study in Illegitimate Power) (Canyon, Texas: Palo Duro Press, 1964);
Phyllis Schlafly, A Choice Not An Echo 3rd ed. (Alton, Illinois: Pere Marquette Press, 1964);
John Stormer, None Dare Call It Treason (Florissant, Missouri: Liberty Bell Press, 1964);
Epstein and Forster, Report on the John Birch Society 1966, p. 4;
George H. Mayer, The Republican Party 1854-1966, 2nd ed. (New York: Oxford University Press, 1967), p. 528.

21. New York Times, October 21, 1964.

22. Ibid.

23. Ibid., October 24, 1964;
Shadegg, What Happened to Goldwater, pp. 254-255.

24. Bryan W. Stevens, The John Birch Society in California Politics (West Covina, California: The Publius Society, 1966), p. 1.

25. Goldwater, Where I Stand, pp. 40-46;
Open Letter to Edgar C. Bundy, August 13, 1964 published in News and Views, (November, 1964), p. 10;
Matter, Barry Goldwater (A Political Indictment), p. 92;

By the way, the phrase "Extremism in the defense of liberty is no vice, moderation in the pursuit of justice is no virtue," was inserted into Goldwater's Acceptance Speech at the behest of Political Science Professor Harry Jaffa, who had in mind an old statement of Cicero's: "I must remind you, Lords, Senators, that extreme patriotism in the defense of freedom is no crime and let me respectfully remind you that pusillanimity in the pursuit of justice is no virtue in a Roman." Goldwater, With No Apolgies, p. 190.

26. Charles McDowell, Jr., Campaign Fever (New York: William Morrow and Company, 1965), p. 142.

27. Mattar, Barry Goldwater (A Political Indictment), pp. 177-178;
Maxwell Geismar, Ramparts Magazine, (November, 1964), p. 12;
Herbert Aptheker, Political Affairs, (September, 1964), p. 759;
Mattar, Barry Goldwater (A Political Indictment), pp. 177-178;
The Weekly Crusader, (November 27, 1964), p. 5;
An interesting account of the smear campaign against Barry Goldwater is Lionel Lokos, Hysteria 1964 (New Rochelle, N.Y.: Arlington House, 1967).

28. White, The Making of the President 1964, p. 24;
U.S. News and World Report, (December 21, 1964), p. 47.;
Goldwater, The Conscience of a Majority, p. 40.

29. National Review, (October 17, 1967), p. 117;
Destiny, (September, 1964), p. 184.

30. National Review Bulletin, (January 21, 1964), p. 1;
Chicago Tribune, September 30, 1961.

31. Dan Smoot Report, (July 20, 1964), p. 225.

32. New York Times, July 18, 1964; Shadegg, What Happened to Goldwater, p. 153.

CHAPTER TEN

THE NEW RIGHT AND VIETNAM

"This is the Korean impasse all over again"

In the eyes of the New Right, the Vietnamese conflict of the 1960's resembled, in so many ways, the Korean conflict of the early 1950's. Both small, Asian nations contained a Communist Northern half and a free Southern half divided along a demilitarized line (38th Parallel in Korea--17th Parallel in Vietnam). Both the North Korean and North Vietnamese Communist regimes were puppets of the Soviet Union and Red China while the free governments of South Korea and South Vietnam owed their continued existence to support furnished by the United States. And in both cases, the Communist North sought to conquer the non-Communist South.

Moreover, the United States responded to both Communist challenges by sending American soldiers into combat while, at the same time, avoiding a real military victory. First of all, Democratic President Harry S. Truman had refused to win the Korean War and the next Democratic Chief Executive, John F. Kennedy also decided to pursue the same, fruitless, no-win course in Vietnam. As Human Events predicted in March, 1962, "The United States may find itself in a quicksand operation in South Vietnam if the Kennedy Administration doesn't reverse its present policy there." Thus "despite the stepped-up US operations...the Korean 'stalemate' philosophy still prevails in the Kennedy Administration..." Human Events concluded that "Kennedy is choosing to fight another Korean-type war." Likewise, the National States' Rights Party complained that in Vietnam "Kennedy intends to use American troops...under the same no-win policy that was used in Korea."1/

Then too, the New Right maintained that the United States (prior to 1965) repeated the identical mistake as in Korea by steadfastly refusing to carry the war to the enemy. Indeed "it is time," in the words of Professor Anthony Bouscaren, that "we penetrated the Communist side of the fifty yard line." Barry Goldwater, in the same vein, insisted that "we must not again -- as we did in Korea -- tolerate a so-called 'privileged sanctuary' from which Communism feeds its military aggression in Vietnam." Similarly, Human Events deplored the fact that Kennedy, "following Truman's cue in the Korean War,...has permitted the enemy to regroup and supply itself in unharassed 'privileged sanctuaries' in North Vietnam, Red China, Cambodia and Laos."2/

The New Right feared yet another useless expenditure of young American lives, this time in Vietnam. For as Barry Goldwater announced, "America cannot again afford the tragedy of sending our boys into a war we will not permit them to win." So unless the United

States made a major effort for victory in Indochina then the whole war seemed hardly worth the bother. In the opinion of Goldwater's 1964 Vice Presidential running-mate William E. Miller, "we either should win or get out, one or the other."3/

Finally, the New Right anticipated a defeat in Vietnam, just like they felt we had suffered in Korea. As early as 1964 Destiny reported that "we lost the Korean War," and now, "we are losing the conflict in Vietnam," while the Economic Council Letter called the Indochina War "the Korean impasse all over again."4/

"Neutralism...is repugnant to freedom"

The New Right rejected a neutralist type solution for Southeast Asia. Destiny warned that "non-alignment, or neutralism, is no deterrent to aggression" and Barry Goldwater echoed the same sentiments: "Neutralism -- an attitude of indifference in this struggle between Communism and free societies -- is repugnant to freedom. Free men will not support it. Communism, as an aggressive factor, will ultimately not permit it."5/

Indeed the New Right believed that neutralism functioned as a potent weapon in the arsenal of the International Communist Conspiracy. For as The Weekly Crusader explained, "what are generally considered to be neutral nations are actually neutral on the communist side." Likewise, Senator Goldwater called neutralist and coalition governments which included Communist members "merely way stations on the road to Communist domination." He pointed out that "coalition government in today's world is a tactic of the enemy." Thus "when the Communists join any kind of a coalition government, it is always with the intention of dominating and taking over that government." Therefore, "every time we insist on a coalition government with a Communist and a neutral we automatically set up a two-to-one situation against freedom."6/

The New Right reacted with anger to what it saw as the Kennedy Administration's sell out of Laos in 1962 through the negotiation of an agreement with the Soviet Union at Geneva which established a Communist-dominated Neutralist government. For instead of confronting the Red menace head-on "we retreated behind the skirts of neutralism," complained William F. Buckley, Jr. No wonder a somewhat melodramatic Ronald Reagan observed that America was "preparing to drink the bitter cup of capitulation in Laos only partly diluted by face-saving devices."7/

Worst of all, the New Right thought that the Kennedy Administration ignored the lessons of history: After gobbling up Laos the Communists would continue to threaten the rest of Southeast Asia. A naive John Kennedy during the last year of his life discovered that the enemy had no intention of halting his advances. As <u>Destiny</u> noted, "Having stupidly accepted a Red-tinged 'neutral' government in Laos, the Kennedys looked on in dismay while the Communists flouted the 1962 Geneva agreement and continued to make aggressive inroads in Southeast Asia."<u>8</u>/

"Failures infest the jungles of Vietnam"

By the Summer months of 1964 America's military and political position throughout Indochina had deteriorated drastically. As <u>Destiny</u> reported, "The Southeast Asian situation goes from bad to worse....Not only is the military situation serious in both Laos and South Vietnam but we are very close to a crisis of confidence throughout East Asia. Likewise, Phyllis Schlafly warned that "Vietnam, slipping fast into Communist clutches, is now embroiled in a bloody war in which American boys are fighting and dying with little hope, under the policies of the present Administration, of winning." She demanded to know, "How long will the Communists continue to kill Americans and humiliate us before the world? The Johnson Administration has no answer."<u>9</u>/

The Republican National Convention meeting in San Francisco in July, 1964 adopted a Platform charging that L.B.J.'s Administration "has encouraged an increase of aggression in South Vietnam by appearing to set limits on America's willingness to act -- and then, in the deepening struggle, it has sacrificed the lives of American and allied fighting men by denial of modern equipment." In contrast, the 1964 G.O.P. Platform pledged to "move decisively to assure victory in South Vietnam. While confining the conflict as closely as possible, America must move to end the fighting in a reasonable time and provide guarantees against further aggression." Moreover, "We must make it clear to the Communist world that, when conflict is forced with America, it will end only in victory for freedom."<u>10</u>/

Barry Goldwater's Acceptance Speech at the July, 1964 Republican National Convention also denounced the Democrats for the declining situation in Southeast Asia. The new G.O.P. Presidential Nominee emphasized that "Failures mark the slow death of freedom in Laos. Failures infest the jungles of Vietnam." Goldwater reminded his party that "Yesterday it was Korea; tonight it is Vietnam. Make no bones of this. Don't try to sweep this under the rug. We are at war in Vietnam." On another occasion, Goldwater labelled the conflict "no minor skirmish" but rather "a major battlefield of the free-world struggle against the Communist threat to engulf all of free Asia." Consequently, the American government must strive for a total victory in Vietnam: "The basic requirement for an effective U.S. policy in Southeast Asia is the decision -- and the will to back it up -- that victory is our goal."<u>11</u>/

223

Unfortunately, the Johnson Administration shrank from the challenge of Communism in Southeast Asia: "We are at war in Vietnam -- yet the President who is the Commander-in-Chief of our forces refuses to say whether or not the objective is victory." Candidate Goldwater listed the various shortcomings of the Democrats' Vietnam policy: "timidly refusing to draw our own lines against aggression -- deceitfully refusing to tell even our own people our full participation -- and tragically letting our finest men die on battlefields unmarked by purpose, pride, or the prospect of victory."12/

Despite the criticisms directed against the American involvement in the Vietnam War, Barry Goldwater had no intention of removing the U.S. presence from the area: "No responsible world leader suggests that we should withdraw our support from Vietnam." Therefore, the Arizona Senator wished to "make it abundantly clear...that we aren't going to pull out of Southeast Asia. But that we are going to win in fact."13/

Finally, Barry Goldwater advocated vigorous tactics against the Communists in order to achieve victory in Southeast Asia. For instance, "The supplies of the Communist invader have got to be cut off. This means threatening or actually interdicting the supply routes from Red China, Laos, and Cambodia." Or, "I'd drop a low-yield atomic bomb on Chinese supply lines in North Vietnam, or maybe shell 'em with the Seventh Fleet." Goldwater also mentioned the problem of locating the elusive enemy hidden along jungle trails and suggested that "defoliation of the forests by low yield atomic weapons could well be done," because "When you remove the foliage, you remove the cover."14/

J.F.K. and the Cuban Missile Crisis

The controversy surrounding America's Vietnam policy inevitably reached center stage during the 1964 Presidential contest. As America's Future remarked, "In Washington in this presidential election year every issue gets turned into a political question, including all international crises in our crisis-ridden era. The one in Vietnam was no exception." Thus G.O.P. Nominee Barry Goldwater prepared to blast away at Democratic incumbent Lyndon Johnson.15/

Nevertheless, sitting Presidents have often turned international incidents to their own political advantage. Indeed the New Right always suspected that Democratic President John F. Kennedy had deliberately contrived the Cuban Missile Crisis during late October, 1962 in order to influence the mid-term elections scheduled for early November. As the National Review Bulletin observed, "There is general agreement that President Kennedy timed his Cuban blockade perfectly" to coincide with the Fall elections. After the Missile Crisis with the Soviet Union suddenly subsided the National Review wondered, "Was it, then only an election gimmick all along?....the timing is hard to explain on any other account."16/

Having been badly burned by J.F.K.'s Cuban Missile Crisis stunt during the Fall of 1962, the New Right approached the 1964 Presidential campaign year with caution, fully expecting Kennedy to spring yet another one of his convenient "crises" on the voters in time for Election Day. Not surprisingly, during J.F.K.'s last month in office before his November 22, 1963 assassination Human Events cynically asked, "What's the big crisis Kennedy's planned for 1964?"17/

L.B.J. and the Gulf of Tonkin Incident

After the assassination of John Kennedy on November 22, 1963 the Presidency passed to Lyndon B. Johnson. The New Right had little respect for L.B.J.'s honesty or integrity. Consequently, the New Right expected L.B.J. to follow in John Kennedy's footsteps and manufacture another dubious international incident in time to sway the upcoming 1964 General Election. As one L.B.J. foe wondered, "How will Lyndon Baines Johnson, master politician, beguile the American voters into thinking that he must be returned to the White House?" Journalist Kent Courtney told I. F. Stone during the G.O.P. National Convention in July, 1964 that Barry Goldwater would capture the Presidency unless" we run into a contrived international crisis." Finally, Dan Smoot disclosed that "Many who have studied the record of Lyndon B. Johnson believe he would do anything to help his election this fall -- even contrive a war if necessary."18/

Considering the wretched Democratic record in Southeast Asia, coupled with the savage assaults coming from Goldwater, the New Right predicted that L.B.J.'s dramatic international "crisis" for the purpose of insuring his reelection would center around Vietnam. As the National Review Bulletin noted on June 9, 1964...

> Everyone now agrees that Lyndon Johnson is going to have to do something, and that that something will probably have to pack considerable firepower....The timing will be difficult. Johnson must act late enough not to appear to be taking a lead from Goldwater, but soon enough to make certain that any unexpected detonations don't take place in the immediate pre-election period. Best guess: a new military approach to begin in July or August.19/

Thus the events surrounding the Gulf of Tonkin Incident during the first week in August, 1964 hardly surprised the New Right. When North Vietnamese P.T. boats fired upon two American warships (U.S.S.

225

Maddox and U.S.S. Turner Joy) stationed off the coast of Indochina, New Rightists maintained that President Lyndon Johnson was using the skirmish as a convenient pretext to drop a few bombs on North Vietnam in retaliation. Nazi leader George Lincoln Rockwell charged that the traitorous "Lyndon Benedict Johnson asked for the attack." Similarly, Dan Smoot referred to the Gulf of Tonkin episode as the "1964 Rerun" of the 1962 Cuban Missile Crisis, while a prominent G.O.P. Congressman lamented that L.B.J. "has done it to us again."20/

The New Right understood that the pressures of domestic politics (applied primarily by themselves) had forced L.B.J. to take action against North Vietnam. As Phyllis Schlafly and Admiral Chester Ward pointed out, "Some response had to be made, or the Administration would go into the campaign branded as 'soft' on Communism and weak in the face of Red military strength." Likewise, Counterattack suggested that North Vietnam "made a mistake it would not have made had it realized that this is an election year in the United States. The Red regime ordered attacks on American warships off Vietnam. The very first attack brought on a crisis."21/

Many Liberal observers at the time also interpreted L.B.J.'s strong reaction at the Gulf of Tonkin as a political stunt designed to silence Goldwater. For example, I. F. Stone wondered, "Who was Johnson trying to impress? Ho Chi Minh? Or Barry Goldwater?" In the same fashion, Richard Rovere commented "that the rise of Gold-water....determined the timing and magnitude of the military responses which L.B.J. ordered in the Gulf of Tonkin...."22/

This display of American firepower directed against North Vietnam apparently refuted Barry Goldwater's allegations that L.B.J. lacked the courage to stand up to the Communists in Southeast Asia. For immediately after the retaliatory raids the President's conduct of the Vietnam War registered a sharp rise in approval in the public opinion polls. Therefore, America's Future reported that the Democrats were gloating "that the President's decisive action...had taken the Vietnam issue out of the campaign."23/

The Gulf of Tonkin episode certainly presented L.B.J. with "a heaven-sent opportunity," in the words of Tom Wicker, to react to Communist agression while giving "credibility both to his restraint and to his strength." For as the friendly Dallas Morning News explained, President Johnson appeared "firm but not rash, rough but not belligerent, courageous but not impulsive." Lyndon Johnson had momentarily silenced his Hawkish critics on his Right flank, while the Doves on his

Left side were thankful that "trigger happy" Barry Goldwater wasn't their Commander-in-Chief.24/*

Lastly, the Gulf of Tonkin escapade enabled President Johnson to disarm his Liberal detractors, especially Senate Doves J. William Fulbright of Arkansas, Ernest Gruening of Alaska, George McGovern of South Dakota, Wayne Morse of Oregon, and Gaylord Nelson of Wisconsin. L.B.J. used the crisis to ram through Congress his Gulf of Tonkin Resolution purporting to demonstrate national, bipartisan support behind the Chief Executive. After a personal meeting with the

---

*Note--The sudden escalation of the Vietnam War during the Spring of 1965 has helped create the popular myth that Democrat Lyndon Johnson ran as the "peace candidate" throughout the 1964 Presidential Campaign only to reverse his position treacherously after the November Election. As Liberal Professor Seymour Melman complained bitterly during an early anti-Vietnam War teach-in, "The man in the White House isn't behaving as the man we elected." New Guard, (June, 1965), p. 6.

Thus in the years after 1965 the American Left felt betrayed by President Johnson. Indeed the final proof of L.B.J.'s perfidy came in June, 1971 with the shocking disclosure of the Pentagon Papers.

Nevertheless, the fact remains that President Lyndon Johnson had campaigned against Barry Goldwater as the "peace candidate" only in a nuclear war. The President clearly rejected any use of nuclear weapons in Vietnam whereas Goldwater had advocated atomic defoliation of the Southeast Asian rain forests as well as nuclear strikes upon enemy supply routes. However, aside from his pledge to abstain from using nuclear weapons L.B.J. never guaranteed any sort of permanent peace in Vietnam. Rather he promised that if the Communist aggression continued he would then respond by cautiously stepping-up American participation in the war using only conventional forces as opposed to Goldwater's irresponsible, reckless program of nuclear escalation.

President Johnson sincerely hoped and prayed that American soldiers would not have to enter the conflict: "We don't want our American boys to do the fighting for Asian boys." Yet during the last month of the campaign, as South Vietnam trembled upon the brink of total collapse, James Reston of the New York Times disclosed that "some prominent officials" were talking "openly about expanding the war..." Thus, in spite of L.B.J.'s calming public assurances, Reston correctly observed that the President did not rule out a wider war in the future. New York Times, October 2, 1964.

In defense of Lyndon Johnson, and for the sake of historical accuracy, the American voters went to the polls on November 3, 1964 to choose between the super-Hawk Goldwater, or the moderate-Hawk Johnson. The notion that L.B.J. ran as the "peace candidate" in 1964 remains an illusion in the minds of the American Left.

President the highly skeptical J. William Fulbright agreed to become the Senate Floor Manager for the Resolution. The President assured Fulbright, who in turn quietly notified the other reluctant Senate Doves, that the major purpose of the Gulf of Tonkin Resolution was to force Barry Goldwater to endorse the Administration's policy in Vietnam, thereby removing this delicate issue from the upcoming Fall campaign. So in the end, all but two Senators, Alaska Republican Ernest Gruening and Oregon Democrat Wayne Morse, finally voted for the measure. Years later, a bitter J. William Fulbright remarked, "Imagine we spent all of an hour and forty minutes on that resolution. A disaster; a tragic mistake. We should have held hearings. The resolution would have passed anyway, but not in its present form. At the time, I was not in a suspicious frame of mind. I was afraid of Goldwater."25/

The New Right and the Gulf of Tonkin Incident

The Gulf of Tonkin episode created real political problems for G.O.P. Presidential Nominee Barry Goldwater. On the one hand, he supported the retaliatory air strikes against North Vietnam because "We cannot allow the American flag to be shot at anywhere on earth if we are to retain our respect and prestige." Goldwater welcomed L.B.J.'s new found courage and hinted to the press that the recent barrage of criticism coming from the G.O.P. had stiffened the Administration's policy.26/

On the other hand, Barry Goldwater pointed out that this one-time demonstration of American air power did not signify any great change of strategy. For L.B.J. still refused to extend the bombing raids into North Vietnam on a regular basis. Thus Communist supply routes leading into South Vietnam remained unmolested.27/

Under normal circumstances, therefore, Barry Goldwater would have blasted L.B.J.'s handling of the crisis as a complete sham, and a response far too weak to halt Communist aggression in Southeast Asia. However, for once the Arizona Senator controlled his tongue. So while the President used the Gulf of Tonkin episode to harden his public image, Goldwater used the same crisis to show some welcome restraint. Accordingly, the G.O.P. Nominee kept a low profile during the incident and stood patriotically behind the President.

Yet the New Right renewed its harsh criticism of L.B.J. soon after the initial flurry of activity surrounding the Gulf of Tonkin Crisis died down. Barry Goldwater, returning to the offensive, demanded that President Johnson now "prosecute the war in Vietnam with the intention of ending it." The G.O.P. Nominee added that the "taking of strong action simply to return to the status quo is not worthy of our sacrifices." New Guard agreed:

Almost all Americans supported the President's action in response to the PT boat attacks off the coast of Vietnam. But it must be strongly pointed out and emphasized that it was just that, a response -- an incident, not a program or a new policy; a tactical reaction, not a new winning strategy. America cannot let this one action (defense against the PT boat attacks) obscure a multitude of other needed actions.28/

Furthermore, as the political and military situation in Southeast Asia rapidly disintegrated during the Fall of 1964 President Johnson desperately stalled for time. As Barry Goldwater told a Madison Square Garden campaign rally in late October, "Americans are dying in Vietnam. He sits tight and silent until after the election." The New Right suspected that soon after the November balloting had safely passed L.B.J. would negotiate another Laotian-style agreement imposing a Communist-dominated Neutralist regime on South Vietnam. One observer explained that "strong rumors persist throughout Washington of an Administration trial balloon on a 'settlement' in Vietnam with some sort of...coalition-neutralist government."29/

Thus the future American strategy in Southeast Asia hung in limbo as the Presidential campaign ended on an ominous note. Two days before the election a sudden, Vietcong mortar attack upon the Bien Hoa Air Base in South Vietnam, destroying six B-57 bombers and killing five Americans, forewarned of a deepening United States involvement on the opposite side of the world. Millions of nervous voters, somewhat wary of L.B.J., but more afraid of Barry Goldwater, decided to cast their ballots for the incumbent President on Tuesday, November 3, 1964 while praying for the best.30/

"Prepare to Scuttle!"

President Lyndon Johnson's Vietnam policy continued drifting aimlessly in the weeks and months immediately following his overwhelming reelection triumph in November, 1964. L.B.J. simply refused to move in one direction or the other. As the National Review asked, "does American and Western power stay in the Southeast Asian region, or get out? And...it is apparent that no decision has been taken in Washington." New Guard suggested that "Time is running out for us to find out what is going on in Vietnam and in President Johnson's mind," while another observer insisted that, "Only the United States can straighten out the mess. Vietnam awaits the Johnson solution." Likewise, the recently defeated Republican Presidential Nominee Barry Goldwater held that, "The Johnson Administration's moment of truth in South Viet Nam is rapidly approaching." In fact, "We are facing disaster in South Viet Nam." Unfortunately, "The Administration has yet to confide to us the true nature of the conflict and our long-range plans, if any."31/

President Johnson could not continue his vacillation indefinitely; for without a firm U.S. commitment to victory coupled with substantial American military intervention, South Vietnam would have soon collapsed. As American Opinion explained, "If we do not elect to win this war—and there is no indication that the Johnson Administration is permitting our men to fight it to win -- we must be prepared for a Vietnamese Dunkirk." Similarly, Washington Report emphasized that "President Johnson...finds himself unable to do much more than try a little bluffing while sitting tight with the present policy and hoping for a miracle. While possible, miracles seldom happen, so the outlook must be for the loss of Vietnam."32/

The New Right anticipated a humiliating American withdrawal from Vietnam disguised as a face-saving neutralist settlement. As South Carolina Senator J. Strom Thurmond disclosed, "We are losing that war, and despite official assurances, it is no secret in Washington that the U.S. instead of trying to save Southeast Asia, is looking for a way to pull out and save face." Consequently, Thurmond predicted that "a deal will be made to neutralize Viet Nam and all of Southeast Asia will go Communist." The National Review believed that "On South Vietnam, it begins to look as if the order has gone out: 'Prepare to Scuttle!'" If true, the National Review demanded an American withdrawal at once instead of prolonging the agony of defeat: "If we are to get out, then let's get out fast. It's not worth much more of our soldiers' blood to get a face-saving formula to cover a capitulation."33/

L.B.J. Escalates the Vietnam War

Thus President Johnson's decision to bomb North Vietnam on a daily basis beginning on February 7, 1965 came as a pleasant surprise to the New Right. The intense pressure applied from the Right had apparently borne fruit by preventing L.B.J. from abandoning South Vietnam. President Johnson surely did not wish to "lose Vietnam" to the Communists thus providing the New Right with the ammunition for another round of "McCarthyism." In L.B.J.'s own words:

> I knew our people well enough to realize that if we walked away from Vietnam and let Southeast Asia fall, there would follow a divisive and destructive debate in our country....A divisive debate about 'who lost Vietnam' would be, in my judgment, even more destructive to our national life than the argument over China had been.34/

Nonetheless, the American bombing raids against North Vietnam failed to satisfy the New Right. As New Guard noted, "the decision to fight it out was good and necessary, but now we should be stepping up the attack." Sadly, "the appeasement crowd in the State Department and the Executive branch continue to advise and influence the President, and his long range policies undermine the good effect of his initial decisions." In the same fashion, Human Events complained that, "At one point LBJ plays the hawk; the next moment the dove." In short, while the President bombed the enemy he still pressed for a negotiated settlement rather than a military victory.35/

Indeed, many New Rightists viewed the air strikes against North Vietnam as a last ditch attempt to save face before negotiating a complete American withdrawal from Southeast Asia coupled with the establishment of a Communist-dominated Neutralist regime in Saigon. In the estimation of James Burnham, President Johnson was "conducting a rearguard skirmish to cover a withdrawal. He will settle for almost any formula that will save American face." M. Stanton Evans reported that Administration officials "see the current outburst of retaliatory action against North Vietnam as a necessary prelude to negotiations for final settlement. Such a settlement, in all likelihood, would result in a 'neutralization' agreement for Vietnam similar to that achieved in 1962 for Laos."36/

"really swat the Communists"

The New Right advocated a full-scale bombing campaign directed against North Vietnam. As retired Air Force General Curtis Le May outlined it, "The military task confronting us is to make it so expensive for the North Vietnamese that they will stop their aggression against South Vietnam and Laos." Therefore, "If we make it too expensive for them, they will stop. They don't want to lose everything they have." "You won't get anywhere," Le May concluded, "until you do go in there and really swat the Communists."37/

The New Right felt that President Johnson placed too many important North Vietnamese targets off limits during the bombing campaign. As Dan Smoot stated, "before ordering the bombing, President Johnson had sacrificed the effectiveness of that decision by announcing that we would not bomb major cities, harbors, and vital industrial installations." Likewise, Eric Butler highlighted the weakness of L.B.J.'s air assault against the enemy:

> Thus, far from the bombing of North Vietnam improving the situation in South Vietnam, the end result has been a further lowering of morale as it became obvious that the Johnson Administration was really still adhering to its no-win policy. The news, that President Johnson had notified Moscow that the bombing raids were

not designed to widen the conflict in South Vietnam did
not improve Asian morale.38/

Finally, the air sorties directed against North Vietnam
represented only a partial solution to the problem of Communist
aggression throughout Southeast Asia. For the New Right believed that
Red China and not North Vietnam remained the real instigator. Dan
Smoot advised President Johnson to "hit the center of communist power
in Asia. That is not in the jungles south of Hanoi: it is in Peiping, the
capital of Communist China!" Anthony Harrigan warned that "we have
hardly begun to fight in Asia. But fight we must or, in the fullness of
time, Chinese-led guerrillas will be in Mexico's Yucatan Peninsula or
across the Rio Grande." Since "the Viet Cong is but an advanced guard
of a resurgent Chinese Empire," Anthony Harrigan called the Vietnam
War "a key military campaign in the containment of Communist China
and the reduction of its power."39/

"The President is not seeking to regain
the global strategic initiative"

The New Right realized that L.B.J.'s limited bombing of North
Vietnam did not signal any great change in America's global policy
against Communism. As James Burnham concluded:

> The President is not seeking to regain the global
> strategic initiative. He has not embarked on...what he
> intends to be an advance. Nor has he decided to draw a
> basic defensive line in South Vietnam....He has not
> indicated any hostile intent toward North Vietnam or
> Communist China. He has not demanded the defeat or
> liquidation of the National Liberation Front or the
> Vietcong, nor excluded a South Vietnamese government
> including or even dominated by the Communists; only
> that 'external aggression' shall cease. He has not
> declared a general U.S. objective of blocking the advance
> of Communism into Southeast Asia....40/

The New Right found evidence for this conclusion in the fact that
the American escalation in Vietnam during the first months of 1965
coincided with the expansion of business and cultural ties with the Soviet
Union. As California G.O.P. Congressman Glenard Lipscomb complained, "The widespread efforts to expand trade with Communist bloc
nations point to one of the most glaring inconsistencies in the area of
our national policy today." In theory, "At the present time we are
engaged in stopping a relentless Communist drive to take over South
Vietnam." Yet in practice, "unbelievable as it may seem, while all this
is going on the drive to open the gates to increased trading with
Communist nations apparently is continuing to gain momentum." M.

Stanton Evans observed that "the Vietnam commitment was precariously out of phase with the rest of the administration's foreign policy...."41/

Moreover, an infuriated Robert Welch demanded to know why the United States continued sending foreign aid to Communist Eastern European nations which in turn transferred these supplies to North Vietnam. In Welch's opinion, "this borders on insanity." And since North Vietnamese soldiers were killing American boys, how could the United States permit her Free World allies to conduct normal business with Hanoi? As M. Stanton Evans remarked, "even as American men were being sent into Vietnam in increasing numbers, U.S. allies were doing a flourishing trade with Hanoi."42/

Then too, the widening of the war against distant North Vietnam seemed to make little sense so long as the Communists still controlled Cuba only ninety miles away. In the words of Frank S. Meyer, "from the point of view of essential national interest and...of tactical and logistical advantage...Cuba, not Vietnam, should have been the scene for a serious rollback of Communist aggression." Likewise, James Burnham emphasized that "Cuba is not on the opposite side of the world...but ninety miles from our own continental coast...." Burnham found it "strange that we are doing so much -- however short of enough -- in relation to Cuba." He offered this piece of advice: "the best move we could make in the Vietnamese war would be to oust Castro."43/

The Failure of American Liberalism in Vietnam

Nevertheless, since the United States Government had selected Southeast Asia as the place to stop Communist aggression by force of arms, the New Right patriotically accepted this decision. New Rightists called for a quick, efficient, military victory in Vietnam and expected very little difficulty. After all, as Anthony Harrigan stressed, "We have the ships. We have the planes. We have the weapons." Therefore, "The United States, with its vast technological and military resources, cannot be defeated by weak Asian powers -- not on the battlefield."44/

The final ingredients for an American victory in Vietnam consisted of wise, courageous leadership and loyal, sturdy citizens. As Anthony Harrigan announced, "All that is required for victory is firm leadership, historical understanding and a resolute people." Harrigan defined the issue succinctly: "If we possess the will to win, victory will follow on the battlefields and on the high seas."45/ (See Chapter Six and Eight)

But the New Right warned that timid civilian leadership could always nullify a nation's military superiority. Indeed, the New Right sensed President Lyndon Johnson's reluctance to unleash American fire-power in Vietnam, complaining that the Liberal philosophy infecting the

Johnson Administration severely hampered successful prosecution of the war. James Burnham predicted a disaster for L.B.J.'s program in Vietnam "unless he brings himself to a conscious rejection of Liberalism."46/

The Liberal Johnson Administration, the New Right said, treated Vietnam as a political rather than a purely military problem. In the estimation of Anthony Harrigan, "The United States needs to recognize...that the problems in Southeast Asia are essentially military, not political." Thus the New Right blasted President Johnson for failing to concentrate American attention upon a swift military solution. As one observer grumbled, "Here is the U.S. -- the world's greatest military power -- and we cannot defeat one hundred thousand Asiatic guerillas ! Isn't that rediculous [sic]."47/

Furthermore, New Rightists held that in the best spirit of American Liberalism, the President proposed a billion dollars in foreign economic aid to finance a Southeast Asian Development Program as an inducement to the Reds to reach a peaceful accord. As Walter Trohan noted, "President Johnson is offering American dollars and know-how to Communists in Southeast Asia as a way of buying an end to the war in Viet Nam." It goes without saying that the New Right found two major faults with L.B.J.'s generous "Great Society" plan for Indochina. First of all, "How can President Johnson end poverty in Southeast Asia," the Economic Council Letter wondered, "when he does not yet have a correct diagnosis of the poverty in Harlem or Appalachia?" (See Chapter Eleven.) Second, the enemy had no intention of joining Lyndon Johnson's Indochinese "War on Poverty". As Dan Smoot remarked, L.B.J. "virtually offered the communists a billion-dollar bribe if they would quit fighting to negotiate. The communists sneered."48/

In conclusion, despite the rhetoric from President Johnson, the daily bombing raids over North Vietnam, and the introduction of American ground forces, the Vietnam War had become a second Korea. Once again the United States had entered upon a limited war in Asia. Nevertheless, most New Rightists stood firmly behind the President while, simultaneously, urging a drastic escalation in the level of fighting: "It is now our duty to back LBJ's present policy, and even more so to advocate its strengthening and of course its continuation. We are moving in the right direction, and we conservatives must make certain that this trend is continued."49/

In time, the New Right ironically became the staunchest supporter of a Liberal Democratic President whose major opposition now came from the vocal, anti-war faction within his own party. Surely only the most extraordinary set of circumstances could have ever brought the members of the New Right to President Johnson's defense. However,

L.B.J.'s old-style Liberalism suddenly looked mild by the Spring of 1965, as the "New Left" erupted on to the American political scene.

The New Right and the New Left

The New Left which emerged into national prominence during the mid-1960's offered an interesting parallel to the New Right. Both of these movements challenged the reigning creed of American Liberalism and both heartily disliked the Eastern Liberal Establishment; both stressed grass roots political action; and both pictured themselves as youthful movements destined to ride the wave of the future.

However, common ground quickly disappeared. The New Left condemned the New Rightists as bluenoses, prudes, religious fanatics, trigger-happy militarists, racists, and anti-Semites. In the eyes of the New Left, the New Right represented an American Fascist Movement. Conversely, the New Right denounced the New Leftists as sexual deviates, drug addicts, atheists, effeminate cowards, and race mongrelizers. From the outset, the New Right viewed the New Left as Communist-inspired, -financed, and -directed.

The rise of the New Left during the mid-1960's hardly surprised the New Right. As a matter of fact, both sides had fought a kind of running battle with one another since the beginning of the decade. The initial clash occurred in San Francisco during May, 1960 as a wild melee erupted between police and New Left demonstrators who were picketing sessions of the notorious House Un-American Activities Committee demanding its abolition.50/ (Through the years the H.U.A.C. has been the Radical Right's favorite Congressional committee.)

At any rate, the House Un-American Activities Committee produced a forty-five minute documentary film "Operation Abolition" about this incident. Pieced together from local television news footage shot during the disturbance, and narrated by Committee staff member Fulton Lewis III, "Operation Abolition" linked prominent Bay Area Communists and their friends with this violent attempt to disrupt the Committee's hearings. The New Right praised the film for its accuracy and courage and gladly distributed "Operation Abolition" to meetings of patriotic organizations all across the country. For this incident, in the words of Robert Welch, furnished an instructive example of "Communist riot and terror tactics...."51/

By the Spring of 1964 the San Francisco Bay Area bustled with increasing New Left agitation (closely monitored by an alarmed New Right). New Left Civil Rights sympathizers staged "sit-ins" at local hotels and automobile dealerships to protest discriminatory hiring practices against Negroes. In the midst of this turmoil the Republican Party held its quadrennial National Convention at the Cow Palace in the

City by the Golden Gate Bridge during July, 1964. The New Right gave an unintentional boost to the New Left -- for the events surrounding the G.O.P. Convention helped transform a small, hard-core, group into a mass student movement.

On the eve of the G.O.P. gathering opponents of the front-running Barry Goldwater journeyed across the Bay to the campus of the University of California at Berkeley. These political organizers recruited students to picket the Cow Palace against the Arizona Senator and to build friendly crowds for the stop-Goldwater candidate Pennsylvania Governor William Scranton. Some Berkeley students, who were already firmly convinced that Barry Goldwater was a racist, reactionary, trigger-happy maniac, hardly needed any outside encouragement to get them to demonstrate against the Arizona Senator.

These events angered former California Senator William F. Knowland, publisher of the powerful Oakland Tribune and the Chairman of the California Goldwater campaign. For University of California regulations specifically prohibited the recruitment of students on campus property for outside political activities. Knowland, a crusty, old New Rightist, had other complaints, too. Berkeley Civil Rights protesters had been picketing his newspaper, the Oakland Tribune, demanding that Publisher Knowland hire more Negro workers. Thus Knowland, a man with considerable influence, placed a few discreet telephone calls to University officials who then cracked down on the students' unlawful political activities. When school resumed in September, 1964 the students' forceful resistance to this sudden restriction of their political freedom produced the crucial spark which ignited the "Free Speech Movement."

Interestingly enough, the campus groups supporting Senator Goldwater also bitterly resented the University Administration curbing their political freedom. Although opposed to any unlawful or violent actions, the Young Republicans and the California Students for Goldwater joined with their New Left classmates in opposition to University policy during the early days of the "Free Speech Move-ment."52/

The Nature of the New Left

The New Right charged that hard-core Communists had directed the Berkeley "Free Speech" protest. As the Washington Report warned, "the key role played by the Communist Party and several of its splinter groups has somehow become obscured." Dan Smoot agreed: "Communists incited and led the 1964 student riots at the University of California in Berkeley. The riots had no specific, localized objective. They were part of a prolonged testing operation." For the Communists, as Dan Smoot concluded, "after years of testing, are finding a way to

236

promote civil disobedience which is a key to communist conquest of our nation, from within."53/

Moreover, the Washington Report outlined the seriousness of the Berkeley situation: "a campus revolution....could spread throughout the Nation unless college and university authorities act with determination to curtail the activities of professional agitators." Likewise alarmed, America's Future compared the University of California, Berkeley demonstrations with "the dangerous revolutionary activity generally associated with some European and Latin American campus activity in which immature and hot-headed youth is manipulated by smart, devious and dedicated outside influences."54/

Finally, the New Right viewed the brazen New Left rebels as the epitome of degeneracy. Descriptions included "sleazy," "smelly," "unkempt," "strangely-attired," and "questionable gender." Shocked by their constant use of "four-letter-words" and other vulgar obscenities the New Right renamed the "Free Speech Movement" the "Filthy Speech Movement." No wonder, News and Views called the New Left a "revolutionary overthrow of proven standards of decency, morality, [and] righteousness,...which made...the United States a great nation envied by the rest of the world."55/

The Anti-Vietnam War Movement

The swiftly growing Anti-Vietnam War Movement joined the already established Civil Rights and Free Speech Movements early in 1965 as the major focal points of New Left concern. As South Carolina Senator J. Strom Thurmond explained, "the so-called civil rights movement" cannot "be separated from the total insurrection with which we are faced; which includes the campaigns and activities of the professed pacifists protesting our Viet Nam policies and those loosely referred to as 'students' who are engaged in the so-called 'campus revolt.' "56/

The New Right denounced the prime tactic of the early Anti-Vietnam War Movement--the "teach-ins." First organized at the University of Michigan on March 24, 1965 these all-night "teach-ins" soon swept college campuses across the United States. The National Review defined the "teach-ins" as a student-faculty gathering where...

> professors of Michigan, Harvard, Columbia, Pennsylvania, Chicago, California and the other great centers of our intellectual life harangue their students about the evils of anti-Communism, the hopelessness of resistance to the wave of the future and the necessity for immediate American retreat from Vietnam.57/

The New Right believed that the Anti-Vietnam War Movement posed certain dangers. For Southeast Asia might fall — not because of any Communist military superiority — but rather, because the American people might lose their zest for fighting and then pressure the United States Government into withdrawing our troops. In the words of Anthony Harrigan, "If we are defeated in Vietnam...We will have allowed the Communists to break our will to win." Consequently, the struggle to influence American public opinion overshadowed the struggle upon the battlefields of Indochina itself. As the National Review observed, "The main engagements of the Southeast Asian war continue to be fought along a line stretching from the Berkeley campus of the University of California to the White House driveway." James Burnham concurred: "In the present Vietnam conflict the decisive front is in the U.S., not in Southeast Asia; and on the U.S. front the war is going badly."58/

In the end, the New Right, after some soul searching, reluctantly endorsed L.B.J.'s limited escalation in Vietnam. At least President Johnson had rejected the demands of the New Left to pull out of Southeast Asia altogether. In short, a combination of patriotism and gratitude to L.B.J. for small favors moved the New Right to back the beleaguered President. This explains why, for instance, members of the Young Americans for Freedom (Y.A.F.) demonstrated in front of the White House on February 20, 1965 in support of the President in order to counter New Left, Anti-War protesters representing the Students for a Democratic Society (S.D.S.).59/

Unfortunately, this loyalty to L.B.J. proved unproductive in the long run, for the New Right became linked in the American public's mind with the President's increasingly unpopular Vietnam War policy — a policy which, incidentally, the New Right never really favored.

In summation, the New Right primarily wanted the United States to fight a war to liberate Cuba, not save South Vietnam. Besides, Communist China, rather than tiny North Vietnam, remained the true enemy in Asia. The New Right blasted L.B.J.'s limited war strategy and sought to replace it with a positive program for a military victory. Ironically, the New Right wound up supporting American military intervention in the wrong part of the world against the wrong opponent, by means of a limited war strategy it never endorsed, under the leadership of a Liberal Democratic President it thoroughly detested, in order to help L.B.J. refute the New Right's own charges that the President was soft on Communism !

CHAPTER TEN - Notes

1. Human Events, (March 10, 1962), p. 160;
Ibid., (January 26, 1963), p. 68;
Beacon-Light Herald, (June–July, 1962), p. 79.

2. News and Views, (February, 1963), p. 3;
Goldwater, Where I Stand, p. 29;
Human Events, (January 26, 1963), p. 68.

3. Goldwater, Where I Stand, p. 29;
"Meet the Press", N.B.C. Television Network broadcast, July 19, 1964.

The Reverend Kenneth Goff complained that "we are playing chess with the lives of our American boys." Beacon-Light Herald, (October-November-December, 1965), p. 10.

4. Destiny, (April, 1964), p. 76;
Economic Council Letter, (June 1, 1964), p. 3.

5. Destiny , (January, 1963), p. 5;
Goldwater, Where I Stand, p. 59.

6. The Weekly Crusader, (June 14, 1963), p. 5;
National Review, (January 30, 1962), p. 50;
Goldwater, Why Not Victory?, p. 173;
Ibid., p. 169.

7. William F. Buckley, Jr., Dialogues in Americanism (Chicago: Henry Regnery Co., 1964), p. 20;
Human Events, (July 21, 1961), p. 457.

Barry Goldwater also criticized the neutralization of Laos: "The decision in Laos to conclude a worthless truce and accept a coalition including Communists laid open that country's long boundaries to Communist infiltration." Goldwater, Where I Stand, p. 54.

8. Destiny, (September, 1963), p. 187.

9. Ibid., (August, 1964), p. 153;
Schlafly, A Choice Not An Echo, p. 8;
Ibid., p. 16.

10. 1964 Republican Party Platform reproduced in Kirk H. Porter and Donald Bruce Johnson, National Party Platforms, 1840-1960, Supplement 1964 (Urbana, Illinois: The University of Illinois Press, 1965), p. 39;
Ibid., p. 48.

11.   Goldwater, Where I Stand, p. 10;
Ibid., p. 13;
Ibid., p. 28.

12.   Ibid., p. 13;
Ibid., p. 12.

13.   Ibid., p. 28;
Interview with Der Spiegel, (June 30, 1964) as quoted in the New York Times, July 11, 1964.

14.   Time, (June 12, 1964), p. 34;
Newsweek, (May 20, 1963), p. 29;
"Issues and Answers", A.B.C. Television Network broadcast, May 24, 1964.

15.   America's Future, (August 21, 1964), p. 1.

16.   National Review Bulletin (November 27, 1962), p. 4;
National Review, (December 4, 1962), p. 420.

17.   Human Events, (November 16, 1963), p. 5.

18.   Donald J. Lambro in New Guard, (July, 1964), p. 13;
I.F. Stone's Weekly, (July 27, 1964), p. 3;
Dan Smoot Report, (August 17, 1964), p. 261.

19.   National Review Bulletin, (June 9, 1964), p. 4.

20.   Rockwell Report, (August 15, 1964), p. 5;
Dan Smoot Report, (August 17, 1964), p. 258;
Ibid., p. 261.

21.   Schlafly and Ward, Strike From Space, p. 30;
Counterattack, (August 14, 1964), p. 134.

Likewise, Dan Smoot drew the connection between L.B.J.'s dramatic, forceful air-strike against North Vietnam and the vigorous domestic political criticism emanating from Barry Goldwater:

On July 15, 1964, Senator Barry Goldwater of Arizona was nominated Republican candidate for President. One of the many reasons for Goldwater's massive public support is that millions of Americans are sick of the policy (initiated by Truman in Korea, and continued by Eisenhower, Kennedy and Johnson) which involves our best sons in foreign wars, prohibits them from using the best tactics and weapons to win the wars, and, when they are captured, abandons them to humiliation, torture, and death. It was obvious that defeatist policies in

Vietnam would become a damaging campaign issue against President Johnson in the elections this year. Something had to be done. <u>Dan Smoot Report</u>, (August 17, 1964), p. 260.

22.   I.F. Stone's Weekly, (August 24, 1964), p. 2;
Rovere, <u>The Goldwater Caper</u>, p. 123.

23.   Joseph C. Goulden, <u>Truth is the First Casualty</u> (Chicago: Rand McNally & Co., 1969), p. 77;
<u>America's Future</u>, (August 21, 1964), p. 1.

Additional authors in agreement with this interpretation include:

Roland Evans and Robert Novak, <u>Lyndon B. Johnson and the Exercise of Power</u> (New York: The New American Library, 1966);
John Galloway, <u>The Gulf of Tonkin Resolution</u> (Cranbury, New Jersey: Fairleigh Dickinson University Press, 1970);
George F. Gilder and Bruce K. Chapman, <u>The Party That Lost Its Head</u> (New York: Alfred A. Knopf, 1966), p. 35;
David Halberstam, <u>The Best and the Brightest</u> (New York: Random House, 1972);
Marvin Kalb and Elie Abel, <u>Roots of Involvement</u> (New York: W.W. Norton & Company, Inc., 1971);
Tom Wicker, <u>J.F.K. and L.B.J.</u> (New York: William Morrow & Company, Inc., 1968).

24.   Wicker, <u>J.F.K. and L.B.J.</u> p. 226;
<u>Dallas Morning News</u>, August 6, 1964 as quoted in <u>Dan Smoot Report</u>, (August 17, 1964), p. 262.

25.   Halberstam, <u>The Best and the Brightest</u>, pp. 418-419;
Galloway, <u>The Gulf of Tonkin Resolution</u>, p. 75.

26.   Edward V. Windchy, <u>Tonkin Gulf</u> (Garden City, New York: Doubleday & Company, Inc., 1971), p. 12.

27.   Ibid., p. 5.

28.   Jack Bell, <u>The Johnson Treatment</u> (New York: Harper & Row, 1965), p. 198;
<u>New Guard</u>, (September, 1964), p. 16.

29.   <u>New York Times</u>, October 27, 1946;
Donald J. Lambro in <u>New Guard</u>, (September, 1964), p. 15.

30.   Wicker, <u>J.F.K. and L.B.J.</u>, p. 238.

31.   National Review, (February 23, 1965), p. 137;
New Guard, (March, 1965), p. 4;
Captain Guild in Report to America, (January, 1965), p. 3;
Human Events, (January 16, 1965), p. 3.

32.   American Opinion, (February, 1965), p. 32;
Washington Report, (January 11, 1965), p. 3;
Similarly, Allan Ryskind wrote, "Now...the United States must develop a
'win' policy...or lose all of Southeast Asia." New Guard, (March, 1965),
p. 10.

33.   Common Sense, (January 15, 1965), p. 1;
Report to America, (February, 1965), p. 8;
National Review, (January 12, 1965), p. 8;
Ibid., (February 23, 1965), p. 137.

34.   Lyndon B. Johnson, The Vantage Point (New York: Holt,
Rinehart and Winston, 1971), pp. 151-152.

35.   New Guard, (June, 1965), p. 3;
Human Events, (May 8, 1965), p. 5.

36.   National Review, (May 18, 1965), p. 412;
National Review Bulletin, (March 16, 1965), p. 5.

37.   Curtis E. Le May with Mac Kinlay Kantor, Mission With Le
May: My Story (Garden City, New York: Doubleday & Company, Inc.,
1965), p. 564;
Ibid., pp. 464-465.

38.   Dan Smoot Report, (June 21, 1965), p. 198;
American Opinion, (April, 1965), p. 40.

39.   Dan Smoot Report, (June 21, 1965), p. 198;
National Review, (March 9, 1965), p. 187.

40.   National Review, (May 18, 1965), p. 412.

41.   Human Events, (March 20, 1965), p. 15;
Evans, The Future of Conservatism, p. 99.

42.   Welch, The New Americanism, p. 154;
Evans, The Politics of Surrender, p. 373.

43.   National Review, (February 22, 1966), p. 162;
Ibid., (March 9, 1965), p. 186.

44.   Ibid., (March 9, 1965), p. 187;
Ibid., p. 207.

45.   Ibid., p. 187;
Ibid., p. 207.

46.   Ibid., (June 1, 1965), p. 456.

47.   Ibid., (March 9, 1965), p. 187;
H.S. Riecke, Jr., as quoted in Common Sense, (April 15, 1965), p. 4.

48.   Human Events, (April 17, 1965), p. 11;
Economic Council Letter, (April 15, 1965), p. 2;
Dan Smoot Report, (June 21, 1965), p. 198.

49.   Ed Wermers, Dixon, Illinois letter to the editor published in
New Guard, (May, 1965), p. 26.

50.   A good example of the New Right's assessment of the 1960
H.U.A.C. Riot can be found in William F. Buckley, Jr., The Committee
and Its Critics (New York: G.P. Putnam's Sons, 1962).

51.   William L. O'Neill, Coming Apart (Chicago: Quadrangle Books,
1971), p. 277;
Welch, The New Americanism, p. 58;
An excellent account of the New Left can be found in Edward J.
Bacciocco, Jr., The New Left in America (Stanford, California: Hoover
Institution Press, 1974).

52.   Dan Smoot Report, (February 8, 1965), p. 45;
Hal Draper, Berkeley: The New Student Revolt (New York: Grove Press,
Inc., 1965), p. 51.

53.   Washington Report, (February 8, 1965), p. 1;
Dan Smoot Report, (February 8, 1965), p. 41.

54.   Washington Report, (February 8, 1965), p. 4;
America's Future, (March 16, 1965), p. 1.

55.   News and Views, (May, 1965), p. 2;
E. Merrill Root in American Opinion, (June, 1965), p. 65;
America's Future, (March 26, 1965), p. 3;
News and Views, (May, 1965), p. 2.

56.   Economic Council Letter, (May 15, 1965), p. 1.

57.   National Review, (May 4, 1965), p. 356.

58.   Ibid., (March 9, 1965), p. 207;
Ibid., (May 4, 1965), pp. 355-356;
Ibid., (June 15, 1965), p. 499.

59.   New Guard, (April, 1965), p. 22.

CHAPTER ELEVEN

THE GREAT SOCIETY AND THE RISE OF RONALD REAGAN

"This is probably Lyndon Johnson's year..."

The New Right took a long, hard look at the American political situation in the months and years after Barry Goldwater's Presidential defeat on November 3, 1964. The New Right desperately searched for a satisfactory answer to explain the unprecedented size of their debacle. In addition, New Right post-mortem speculations centered around the probable impact of Goldwater's huge election loss upon the future of their Movement.

To begin with, the astute observer William F. Buckley, Jr. nearly four months before Election Day summed up candidate Barry Goldwater's basic predicament: "This is probably Lyndon Johnson's year, and the Archangel Gabriel running on the Republican ticket probably could not win." After all, L.B.J. remained an extremely popular incumbent President throughout 1964. The Vietnam War and America's urban racial crisis had not yet boiled over. In addition, the U.S. economy surged ahead during 1964 with employment and wages rather high coupled with a low rate of inflation. Finally, Lyndon Johnson had entered the White House on November 22, 1963 amidst the tragedy of the Kennedy assassination with a large reservoir of sympathy and good will from the American people which lingered on for the next year or two.1/

Perhaps even Barry Goldwater had not expected to capture the White House in 1964. The Arizona Senator had originally sought the nation's highest office, at least in part, to prove a point. He had hoped to make a respectable showing (around 45-48% of the popular vote) against President Johnson, and intended to use the Republican Party nomination to proselytize for the New Right and plant the seeds of doubt in the country concerning the current direction of Liberal America.2/

What Happened to Barry Goldwater in 1964?

After some thought and reflection the New Right came to the inevitable (and somewhat consoling) conclusion that Barry Goldwater never had the slightest chance in 1964 against President Lyndon Johnson. In words of James T. Hunter, "Even if the President had not been a superb politician he probably would have been unbeatable in 1964." Barry Goldwater himself suggested that "any Republican would have lost. Defeating Johnson in 1964 just wasn't in the cards."3/

Of course, the assassination of Democratic President John F. Kennedy had cast a cloud over the entire 1964 Election. As Dan Smoot noted, "The gigantic emotional backwash of the assassination was a major force in shaping President Johnson's victory and Senator Goldwater's defeat in 1964."4/

Then too, "Goldwater lost because he waged a miserable campaign," according to the Arizona Senator's long-time friend and admirer Stephen Shadegg. Moreover, the G.O.P. Presidential Nominee "appeared to be unable to articulate any significant philosophical concepts, and between July and November [1964] he failed to advance effectively a single new positive proposal." Dan Smoot called Goldwater "never a willing or strong leader of the constitutional conservatives, nor even an articulate spokesman for their philosophy." Immediately after the November Election a poll conducted among the men and women who had attended the July, 1964 G.O.P. National Convention in San Francisco as delegates revealed some interesting opinions. Sixty-nine percent of this basically pro-Goldwater group censured the Republican Nominee for his failure to discuss the issues in depth while eighty-two percent disliked the Arizona Senator's conduct of his 1964 Presidential Campaign.5/

Goldwater's advocacy of the use of tactical nuclear weapons in Vietnam as well as his so-called "Right-wing extremism" had also harmed his chances. Report to America board member Theodore S. Watson stated that L.B.J. beat Goldwater "because of fear from propaganda that Senator Goldwater was 'trigger happy' and could get us into war, social security would be discontinued and he was an 'extremist.' " Phyllis Schlafly and Admiral Chester Ward concurred: "All hands agree that the decisive issue of the 1964 presidential election was nuclear war. The majority did not vote for Lyndon Johnson because he is photogenic, but because they were convinced by campaign oratory and television spots that LBJ would keep the peace better than Barry Goldwater."6/

Thus in the New Right's judgment, the devastating results of the 1964 Election did not constitute an outright rejection of their political philosophy. As Ronald Reagan emphasized, "All of the landslide majority did not vote against the conservative philosophy, they voted against a false image our Liberal opponents successfully mounted." Along the same path, New Guard discovered, "After reflection about the campaign...conservatism has not been defeated...many fine conservative Congressmen and Senators ran far ahead of Sen. Goldwater and...there was actually no debate of conservatism vs. liberalism between the two Presidential candidates."7/

Finally, the New Right felt that the treachery of the Eastern Liberal Establishment wing of the Republican Party contributed to Goldwater's fiasco at the polls. The Weekly Crusader labelled "The Lodges, the Scrantons and the Rockefellers" as "veritable Trojan Horses within the Republican camp." For Messrs. Henry Cabot Lodge, Jr.,

William Scranton, and Nelson Rockefeller among others "began the undermining of Goldwater by harping on the Big Lie of 'trigger happiness,' 'his irresponsibility' and other falsehoods of a similar ilk coined for the sole and only purpose of destroying the Arizona Senator even before convention time in San Francisco." No wonder, William F. Buckley, Jr. complained that "Senator Goldwater is being blamed for a defeat that was largely the result of the lurid transcription of his views by his fellow Republicans."8/

As expected, the Democrats took full advantage of the squabbling within the G.O.P. ranks. New Guard remarked that "Every major issue used by the Democrats had first been used by Republican opponents of Barry Goldwater in the bitter primary contests." The Weekly Crusader emphasized that "The Lodges, the Scrantons and the Rockefellers... prepared the ammunition that was later to be used by the Democratic Party to good purpose in obtaining its impressive plurality of votes against the Republican Party." In the same fashion, Dan Smoot reported how...

> Liberal and 'moderate' Republicans at the San Francisco convention provided the weapons of slander and villification which Democrats used during the campaign to frighten millions into believing that Goldwater was a maniac who wanted to incinerate the world with nuclear weapons and that he was a monster who wanted to see old people starve.9/

Along these lines, former Vice President Richard Nixon furnished the one pleasant surprise of the 1964 Presidential Campaign to the New Right. Richard Nixon had refused to join the members of the Eastern Liberal Establishment who had pinned the "Right-wing extremist" tag upon Barry Goldwater. Instead the loyal trooper Nixon stumped the nation enthusiastically on behalf of Goldwater and the entire G.O.P. slate during the Fall of 1964. Nixon's performance earned him the grudging respect of the New Rightists and represented an important step forward in his political comeback. (See Chapter Twelve)

The Great Society

The day after Barry Goldwater's electoral defeat the American Liberal Community officially pronounced the New Right "politically dead." As James Reston of the New York Times observed, "Barry Goldwater not only lost the presidential election yesterday but the conservative cause as well." Indeed, the Left demanded a formal surrender from the New Right followed by a complete disbandment of their Movement coupled with a sincere apology for being so grossly out of political and philosophical synchronism with the rest of modern, progressive America. In the words of William F. Buckley, Jr., the

247

Liberals "supposed that the electorate had once and for all spoken on the subject, and that therefore the only realistic thing a conservative could do was to fold up his tent, and hitch-hike along with history."10/

Without question, the American Liberal Community enjoyed trouncing Senator Goldwater and his Movement. As Rita Gormley wrote, "Armed with righteousness and a general aura of being a minnow in the mainstream, our liberal friends now gloat over our 'come uppance.' " America's Future added: "In the continuing election post-mortems, the liberal-left has been proclaiming happily the death of the conservative philosophy in America."11/

Of course, the November, 1964 Election did not permanently destroy the New Right. However, Barry Goldwater's defeat did cost the G.O.P. a net total of thirty-eight seats in the United States House of Representatives. Coupled with the diminished Republican strength in the U.S. Senate the New Right now stood by helplessly as a new wave of Democratic Liberalism swept through Congress. As Richard Rovere noted ironically, Barry Goldwater's huge loss "has cleared the ground for a rampant liberalism."12/

The New Right tried to batten down the hatches and ride out the Liberal storm. The National Review described the New Right's strategy as "fall back and regroup." New Rightists fully expected another Liberal Democratic Administration's "hundred days" (a la Franklin D. Roosevelt in 1933) ramming through Congress "just about every screwball, crackpot, left-wing, socialist idea that has been mentioned in this century, and which has not already been legislated."13/

Indeed, the landmark 89th Congress (1965-1966), under intense prodding from President Lyndon Johnson, passed a dazzling social reform package known as the "Great Society" over the bitter but fruitless objections of the badly outnumbered New Rightists. Some of the highlights of Lyndon Johnson's "Great Society" included the Voting Rights Act (1965), Model Cities Program (1966), Anti-Proverty Programs (1965), Federal Aid to Education (1965), Medicare (1965), reform of the Immigration Laws (1965), plus significant Consumer Protection and Environmental legislation.14/

The New Right blasted L.B.J.'s Great Society as the wrong prescription for America's many ills. Economist Hans Sennholz lamented that "At one of the most critical moments of American history, when Communism is besieging Western Civilization on all continents...Lyndon B. Johnson, our landslide President, ushers in the 'Great Society'." Hans Sennholz charged that the "Great Society...dulls public awareness of our critical problems with Communism...and the racial turmoil in our cities." Moreover, in the same tradition as Franklin D. Roosevelt's hated "New Deal", Sennholz called L.B.J.'s Great Society "a Calamity Deal on the eve of the greatest debacle in our history."15/

The Great Society, New Rightists maintained, intended to finance its ambitious programs to eliminate poverty in America by taxing the prosperous and the industrious. Thus the egalitarian goals of the Great Society threatened to redistribute the wealth. (See Chapter Three) As Don Bell Reports explained, "The Great Society requires the elimination of poverty which, in simpler terms means the redistribution of wealth." In the same vein, Dr. George S. Benson wondered, "Can this Great Society that the President talks about really eliminate poverty...or does he have in mind just another Marxian way to redistribute the wealth?"16/

The New Right characterized L.B.J.'s Great Society as "utopian." In the opinion of Don Bell Reports, "The Great Society, then, is the same old dream of Utopia; the same old kingdom of heaven that is to be created by man..." The National Review decided that "President Johnson's Great Society doesn't exist and never will, first because he has no clear idea about what it is, and second because his vague gropings are Utopian and therefore impossible." The New Right utterly rejected the concept of Utopia believing instead that the truly great society exists only in God's Heaven not on man's Earth.17/

Consequently, the grandiose, utopian schemes designed by President Johnson and his Great Society engineers will inevitably bring failure and disillusionment. As the National Review warned, "a great deal of positive harm is done when political leaders raise hopes that are, and they know it, doomed." Similarly, Don Bell Reports noted that "a dream that always begins with the hope of bringing heaven to earth...always ends with the establishment of hell on earth."18/

Furthermore, government welfare programs cannot solve the chronic problems of poverty. The answer lies deep within each individual citizen. As Don Bell Reports announced, "Just as man must -- personally -- seek his own salvation with fear and trembling, so also must he personally overcome poverty...."19/

Finally, the United States of the 1960's suffered from an acute moral and spiritual sickness which billions of Federal dollars could never cure. The National Program Letter predicted that "we shall have no great society until there are good people to comprise it as well as build it." Destiny outlined the need for "a great spiritual renaissance" since "there is no point in welcoming 'a new world coming' if the corrosive rot eating away at the vitals of the present order is allowed to continue its destructive action." Destiny summed up the sentiments of the New Right concerning America's moral crisis:

No great society can ever materialize where criminals, plying their trade, are pampered and coddled by judicial rulings; when violence stalks the streets of our cities; when robbery and murder become everyday occurrences and criminals, when apprehended, are soon turned loose again to repeat former acts of violence or commit new offenses.

Until it becomes safe for law-abiding citizens to walk our streets and stroll in our parks unafraid, for children to play in their yards and in playgrounds without being molested, and banking institutions and business concerns may serve the public without being harassed by holdup men and burglars, there will be no great society....

Chaos, not greatness, threatens the American way of life today and until, as a people, we become willing to set our national house in order according to the Divine pattern for the establishment of righteousness, it is utter folly to prate about building a "great society."20/

As L.B.J.'s Great Society became unravelled by the late 1960's James T. Hunter perceived that "Americans are beginning to see that it is going to take more than the expenditure of billions of Federal dollars to solve the problems of the cities." The American people "sense that what is wrong with the Great Society cannot be cured with money."21/

"there are 26 million of us"

The New Right remained very much alive even after Barry Goldwater's shellacking in the November, 1964 Presidential contest. America's Future discounted Liberal reports of the Movement's demise by calling such misleading rumors "greatly exaggerated" (like the erroneous news of Mark Twain's death). Indeed the immediate Post-Election Period found New Rightists like Minister W.O.H. Garman of Wilkinsburg, Pennsylvania in a fighting mood: "Shall we toss in the sponge and quit? No! A thousand times no! The battle has just begun." 22/

Nevertheless, the New Right understood that any future, full-scale assault upon American Liberalism required more troops. As Ronald Reagan explained, "There are no plans for retreating from our present positions, but we can't advance without reinforcements." The Weekly Crusader spoke about "the enormous task yet facing informed patriots--that is the tough job of awakening many more Americans to the truth about our steady national decline into disaster." William F. Buckley, Jr. stressed that "unless conservatives realize that massive public education must precede any hope of a Presidential victory, they will never have a President they can call their own."23/

The Republican Party with Barry Goldwater as its standard-bearer in 1964 did receive some twenty-six million votes even in defeat; and "a party that polls over twenty-five million votes," as former California Senator William F. Knowland reasoned, "is neither bankrupt nor on its deathbed." Meanwhile, Dan Smoot sarcastically remarked that Barry Goldwater ran rather well for an "extremist" candidate supposedly far outside the mainstream of American political life "supported only by bigots and racists...."24/

Many New Rightists chose to interpret the results of the 1964 Presidential Election quite optimistically. Ronald Reagan reminded his fellow member of the Movement that "there were 26 million of us and we can't be explained away as die-hard party faithfuls." Martin Dies considered the sizeable Goldwater vote "the most encouraging sign of our times," while Dr. Frederick Curtis Fowler, a Presbyterian Minister from Duluth, Minnesota pointed with pride to the "over 26 million fellow Americans voting conservative...," and declared that "November 3rd is not more than a temporary setback. Rome was not built in a day....The political philosophy of Liberalism will be defeated."25/

More importantly, today's political minority might easily become tomorrow's political majority. William F. Buckley, Jr. suggested that "one year's landslide loss is not necessarily a permanent thing in a dynamic society, and there is no reason for American conservatives to believe...that the time will never come again when the American people can correct our public policies." Frank S. Meyer boldly proclaimed that "Conservatives stand today nearer to victory than they ever have since Franklin Roosevelt. A shift in the vote of 12 per cent of the electorate is the goal of the next four years."26/

The New Right stressed the other positive accomplishments of the Goldwater nomination and Presidential race. New Guard noted that "Conservatives have proved their strength and can no longer be regarded lightly by their adversaries, the liberals." Interestingly enough, the Liberal critic Professor Richard Hofstadter agreed with the New Right's conclusions: "The right-wing enthusiasts were justified...in the elation they expressed, even in defeat, over the Goldwater campaign....They have demonstrated that the right wing is a formidable force in our politics and have given us reason to think that it is a permanent force."27/

The Goldwater Campaign established a solid nucleus of dedicated, youthful, New Right political activists. As Dan Smoot observed, "A great number of Goldwater's supporters were young people, not worn by years of defeat. Youth, zealous in a noble cause, will not quit." No wonder, one excited New Rightist gloated, "Conservatism is now back and young, tough, and aggressive....It means to hold every advantage gained, and go on to final victory."28/

The Goldwater Movement, New Rightists held, had transformed the G.O.P. from a helpless pawn of the Eastern Liberal Establishment into an effective tool of the Conservatives. Thus according to Frank S. Meyer, "1964 represented, despite the electoral defeat, a potential massive victory for conservatism through the rehabilitation of the Republican Party as an available institutional vehicle for conservatism." Similarly, M. Stanton Evans called "the Goldwater candidacy -- the mere fact of his nomination...an enduring victory for conservatism."29/

Barry Goldwater and the Deep South

With Barry Goldwater heading the Republican ticket the G.O.P. carried five Deep Southern states (Alabama, Georgia, Louisiana, Mississippi, and South Carolina) for the first time since Reconstruction days. So Goldwater's "Southern Strategy" succeeded, at least in part. (See Chapters Eight and Twelve.) White voters throughout the Deep South deserted the Johnson-Humphrey ticket in droves while some of these lifelong Democrats subsequently abandoned "the party of their fathers" forever.30/

The G.O.P. received a tremendous boost during the Fall of 1964 when South Carolina's Democratic Senator J. Strom Thurmond officially switched his allegiance to the Republican Party. Senator Thurmond, the first major Deep Southern officeholder to defect to the G.O.P., aired his various dissatisfactions with the national Democratic Party:

> It is leading the evolution of our nation to a socialistic dictatorship...has encouraged lawlessness, civil unrest, and mob actions...has established and pursued for our government a no win foreign policy of weakness, indecision, accommodation, and appeasement....
> The Democratic Party, as custodian of government, has sent our youth into combat in Vietnam, refusing to call it war, and demanding of our youth the risk of their lives without providing either adequate equipment or a goal of victory.31/

The New Right sensed the significance of Senator Thurmond's conversion to Republicanism. The National Review Bulletin labelled Thurmond's switch "one of those by-products of the Goldwater candidacy that will ripple through the political history of this country for many years to come," while in the estimation of New Guard, the South Carolinian's move "opens up a whole new trend in party realignment that is long overdue in national and local politics."32/

The "White Backlash" and the G.O.P. Future

Finally, in the wake of Goldwater's Presidential defeat the New Right decided to focus more attention upon the "White Backlash," hoping to exploit America's growing racial troubles for political gains. These "White Backlash" issues included street crime, open housing, deteri-

252

orating neighborhoods, declining property values, soaring welfare payments, forced busing of school children, competition from Black workers for jobs, and preferential treatment for minority citizens. (See Chapter Seven.) Thus the American Mercury asserted that the "exploitation of the 'White backlash' is not only political horsesense to the Republicans, it is the only way for the GOP to ever establish itself as the majority party in America." 33/

The results of the November, 1964 Election in California clearly demonstrated the strength of the "White Backlash." This traditionally progressive, far-Western state gave President Lyndon Johnson a 1.3 million vote plurality over Barry Goldwater. Yet Californians easily passed a statewide referendum (Proposition 14) repealing an open housing law (Rumford Fair Housing Act) recently enacted by the California State Legislature in Sacramento. California voters also surprised everyone by sending motion picture actor George Murphy to the United States Senate. George Murphy, a member of the New Right, narrowly defeated Liberal Democrat Pierre Salinger in a spirited contest revolving around Salinger's outspoken support for open housing.

The New Right noted the importance of the open housing controversy in California. In the opinion of the Cross and the Flag, the November, 1964 Election "proved that the voters of California were more interested in preserving their racial integrity than who was to be President of the United States." The Citizen pointed out that "whenever voter attention was focused on the question of race, America is still a white man's country !" Nazi leader Rockwell, responding to campaign slogans circulated by California's open housing advocates to reject the referendum (Proposition 14) and thus not vote to "legalize hate," announced with glee that "Millions of Californians did vote to 'legalize hate' for Communist Race-mixing." 34/

The Post-Election Purge

New Rightists refused to relinquish control of the G.O.P. to the Liberals and Moderates even after the Goldwater debacle. As Ronald Reagan declared, "I don't think we should turn the high command over to leaders who were traitors during the battle just ended." Yet the logic of the situation called for a gentle purging of the New Right elements from control of the Republican Party machinery. Historically, a badly beaten party dumps its unpopular political cargo and moves towards the Center in order to reenter the political mainstream. And as Richard Nixon observed, the G.O.P. under Barry Goldwater had drifted "too far to the right." 35/

Therefore, the G.O.P. National Committee quickly removed Dean Burch, the principle architect of the Goldwater fiasco, from his powerful position as Republican National Chairman on January 21, 1965.* With Barry Goldwater's tacit approval Ray Bliss, a G.O.P. Moderate, replaced Dean Burch as National Chairman. William A. Rusher commented, "It is, after all, a hoary tradition that our political parties atone for their national defeats by sacking the incumbent chairman of the party's national committee." In a similar action, Republicans in the U. S. House of Representatives dumped their crusty, old Minority Leader Charles Halleck of Indiana in favor of Michigan Moderate Gerald Ford. 36/

After the downfall of Dean Burch, the new G.O.P. Chairman Ray Bliss efficiently liquidated the remaining New Rightists from the highest councils of the Republican National Party. As "Cato" lamented, "Hand it to Ray Bliss: he has discreetly purged every living, breathing Goldwaterite from Republican National Headquarters." Likewise, Phyllis Schlafly complained that "The election of Bliss was the signal to start a purge of conservatives at every level of Republican politics. Loyal Goldwater supporters were systematically eliminated from the Washington headquarters of the Republican National Committee." 37/

"What do we do now?"

The New Right drifted aimlessly during the vital rebuilding years 1965-1966 without strong national leadership at the helm. Barry Goldwater had lost not only the 1964 Presidential Election but his own U.S. Senate seat as well, which had inconveniently come up for reelection that same November. Moreover, the Arizonan had lost much of his zest for battle. And with "Barry gone," as Garry Wills explained, "there was no national figure with any political sex-appeal." 38/

Indeed the New Right now paid the price for the Movement's longstanding, exclusive infatuation with Barry Goldwater and its failure to develop alternative national political figures. Dan Smoot had foreseen this problem as early as June, 1963 when he begged, "for the sake of our Republic" Conservatives "should not devote all of their political effort to Goldwater." 39/ (See Chapter Nine)

Political observer Robert J. Donovan outlined the New Right's dilemma in the aftermath of Goldwater's demise: "There is no second level of national leaders on the right, no obvious successor to the

---

*Note--Nothing seemed to go right for the snakebitten Goldwaterites during the 1964 General Election. Barry Goldwater selected a new G.O.P. National Chairman Dean Burch, whose name soon became mistakenly identified with the notorious John Birch Society in the American public's mind. Thus some voters actually thought that the John Birch Society was directing the Goldwater campaign !

254

Goldwater mantle." Accordingly, Goldwater's 1964 Vice Presidential running-mate William Miller faded into obscurity. Newly elected California Senator George Murphy, an intellectual lightweight, remained little more than a tired, old political hack. An uninspiring personality handicapped Texas Senator John Tower, while South Carolina Solon J. Strom Thurmond, a recent convert to the G.O.P., lacked firm party ties. William F. Buckley, Jr. had lots of fun running for Mayor of New York City in 1965 but captured only thirteen percent of the vote. Besides belonging to the wrong party (the Democrats), George C. Wallace never received support from the "respectable" members of the New Right. In addition, the Alabama Governor, ineligible for reelection in the Fall of 1966, watched his home state power-base erode slowly away. (Wallace then surprised everyone by running his wife Lurleen for Governor of Alabama and winning.)40/

The New Right sensed this loss of direction and momentum with their Movement as well as the painful absence of dynamic national leadership. In the words of Phyllis Schlafly, "Grassroots Republicans...felt isolated, alone, and leaderless. There was no national political organization in which they could coalesce and maintain esprit de corps." Similarly, James T. Hunter insisted that "the conservative movement was still alive in the hearts and minds of its resting warriors, even if they had no central rallying point." However, "With no campaign to stir them, with no candidate champion about whom to rally, they faced the burning question: 'What do we do now?' "41/

The Rise of Ronald Reagan

Ronald Reagan's electrifying entrance upon the national political stage during the closing days of the 1964 Presidential race provided the New Right with its only real excitement in an otherwise dreary Fall campaign. On the night of October 27, 1964 Ronald Reagan delivered a brilliant television speech on behalf of the floundering Goldwater-Miller ticket. This masterful, nationwide broadcast entitled "A Time for Choosing"* instantly transformed Reagan into a New Right political

---

*Note--The idea that the United States stood at the crossroads in the year 1964 and that the voters faced a definite "choice" as to the nation's future course dominated the Goldwater campaign strategy. Barry Goldwater himself often began his speeches with the words, "Choose the way of this present Administration...." (See, for instance, the New York Times, September 4, 1964.) Author Phyllis Schlafly published a best-selling book describing how candidate Goldwater offered, "A Choice, Not An Echo." (See Chapter Nine) The group "Mothers For a Moral America" titled their film about the unsavory state of contemporary American morality, "Choice". (See Chapter (Continued)

superstar, propelled him into the California Governorship two years later, and established the handsome, ex-Hollywood "B" movie actor as a solid G.O.P. Presidential contender for 1968.

Ronald Reagan, a former Left-wing Democrat, symbolized the millions of middle-aged citizens who had once enthusiastically supported the party of Franklin D. Roosevelt but had become thoroughly disenchanted with the direction of American Liberalism by the early 1960's. Furthermore, as a relatively recent convert to the Radical Right's brand of Republicanism, Ronald Reagan proved the old adage that the newest member of the church choir sings the loudest. At any rate, the clever, ambitious entertainer carved out a new political career for himself at a time of life when most men contemplate a comfortable retirement.42/

During the early 1960's, Ronald Reagan constructed a strong political base within the Golden State. He frequently spoke at California Republican Party fund-raising events and along the G.O.P. banquet circuit. Obviously impressed by Reagan's philosophy and style, the New Right mentioned his name, on occasion, as a possible opponent against California's hated Liberal Republican U.S. Senator Thomas Kuchel in the June, 1962 G.O.P. Primary Election. Reagan also served during the Fall of 1964 as California Co-Chairman of the Citizens for Goldwater-Miller organization.43/

However, Ronald Reagan's big break came on the night of October 27, 1964 when he delivered his forceful address "A Time For Choosing" before a nationwide television audience. Political analysts Stephen Hess and David Broder called Reagan's election eve appeal "the most successful national political debut since William Jennings Bryan electrified the 1896 Democratic convention with his 'Cross of Gold' speech...and it made Reagan a political star overnight."44/

Ronald Reagan's speech "A Time For Choosing" represented a classic exposition of New Right principles. Reagan attacked the usual list of sins including appeasement, big wasteful government, bureaucracy, foreign aid, the United Nations, and, of course, "the soup kitchen of the welfare state." He contrasted "the maximum of individual freedom consistent with law and order" on the one hand with "the ant heap of totalitarianism" on the other. Reagan pronounced International Communism "the most evil enemy mankind has know in his long climb from the swamp to the stars." 45/

Unfriendly critics described Reagan's television performance as "corny." In the words of author Joseph Lewis:

Nine) Ronald Reagan called his national television broadcast, "A Time for Choosing."

Part pedagogue, part pitchman, Reagan salted the talk with enough information, culled from The Reader's Digest and Congressional Record, to gloss over his sweeping accusations with a mantle of factuality. Paragraph by paragraph, he soared to a bravura finale that sounded like Jimmy Stewart's oration in Mr. Smith Goes to Washington.46/

Nevertheless, Ronald Reagan's speech struck a responsive chord with New Rightists. The National Review Bulletin judged the telecast "fabulously effective" while James T. Hunter deemed the address "perhaps the most effective effort of the campaign." The New Right agreed that Ronald Reagan had outlined clearly the Movement's basic philosophy and objectives in simple, logical terms which the average American citizen could easily comprehend. M. Stanton Evans decided that "Reagan stated the case for the conservative position with force and eloquence...," while Frank S. Meyer noted that "the dramatic success of Ronald Reagan's broadcast is both evidence that it is possible to make conservative principles understandable and an example of a way of doing it."47/

Thus Ronald Reagan represented a vast improvement over Barry Goldwater. The magnetic Californian, as Theodore H. White observed, "seemed to possess all the Goldwater virtues with none of his flaws." For Reagan's pleasing personality outshone Goldwater's gruff abrasiveness; Reagan could articulate concepts while the Arizona Senator fumbled for words; and Reagan's slick rhetoric stood in marked contrast with Goldwater's blunt indiscretions. Indeed Bruce Weinrod, a Reagan support in 1968, discussed these stylistic differences between both men: "Where Goldwater deliberately shocked people, and this was what was needed, Reagan has the ability to present the conservative view in an extremely smooth manner." Likewise, Joseph Lewis classified "Reaganism" as "a refinement of Goldwaterism" only much more "palatable...friendly and engaging, devoid of the bitterness that often crept into conservative speeches...sophisticated and urbane...." Thus, "in the dying days of the Goldwater campaign, the American public got a preview of post-Goldwater conservatism" in the person of Ronald Reagan who blended Senator Robert Taft's political beliefs with President Dwight Eisenhower's charm.48/

Ronald Reagan and the California Governorship

After Reagan's television broadcast "A Time For Choosing," the New Right made plans to run the photogenic, ex-movie star for the California Governorship in 1966 against incumbent Democrat Edmund G. "Pat" Brown. Plagued by student unrest at the University of California, Berkeley,the August, 1965 Watts Riot, and a state financial crisis, Pat

Brown looked ripe for defeat. Moreover, George Murphy's victory over Pierre Salinger in the U.S. Senate race in November, 1964 paved the way for Ronald Reagan by demonstrating that a Hollywood celebrity could win election to public office in the Golden State.49/

Accordingly, Ronald Reagan breezed through the G.O.P. Primary held in June, 1966 against token opposition led by former San Francisco Mayor George Christopher. Reagan then scored a stunning one million vote triumph over Pat Brown in the November, 1966 General Election. Thus Reagan attracted additional national attention by soundly trouncing Democratic giant-killer Pat Brown, who had once beaten G.O.P. heavyweights William F. Knowland back in 1958 and Richard Nixon back in 1962 for the California Governor's chair.

Finally, Reagan surprised the experts by forging a broad based coalition in a major urban state. James T. Hunter boasted that Reagan's election "has knocked into a cocked hat the 'liberal' myth that...a conservative cannot win in a large industrial state." In the same vein, the National Review Bulletin commented that "In the nation's most populous state, it was Ronald Reagan all the way. The million-vote size of his victory -- in California, with its top-heavy Democratic majority in party registration -- proved that Reagan has successfully broken out of the single-faction straitjacket."50/

Ronald Reagan Looks Towards 1968

The moment Ronald Reagan announced his candidacy for the Governorship of the Golden State early in 1966 he instantly became a potential G.O.P. Presidential contender for 1968 and beyond. Lee Edwards, a young New Rightist, predicted that "if Ronald Reagan wins" the California Governorship, "he will be an obvious candidate for the Republican nomination for President -- if not in 1968, then certainly in 1972...."51/

The smashing election victory over California's incumbent Governor Pat Brown in November, 1966 formally legitimized Ronald Reagan's position as authentic Presidential timber. The National Review Bulletin declared, "This month's election served as trial heats for the GOP's 1968 Nomination Derby....No matter what pro forma disavowals he now makes, Reagan takes his place among the favorites." Similarly, James T. Hunter foresaw Reagan as "a significant force -- possibly a nominee -- in the 1968 G.O.P. convention."52/

Governor-elect Ronald Reagan wasted little time before cranking up his Presidential campaign machinery. In fact, by mid-November, 1966 (a scant ten days after his triumph) Reagan instructed his staff to draw up detailed plans for a conquest of the 1968 G.O.P. Nomination. Soon F. Clifton White, the brilliant New Yorker who had mapped out

258

Barry Goldwater's 1964 pre-convention strategy, joined the growing Reagan camp. As the next logical step Governor Reagan disclosed in February, 1967 his intentions of controlling the large California delegation to the 1968 G.O.P. Convention as a favorite-son candidate. Finally, the "Godfather" of the New Right, Barry Goldwater himself told a press conference on May 3, 1967 that "If Ronald Reagan decides he wants to run, he will be the Republican nominee in 1968."53/

Nonetheless, Ronald Reagan's path towards the G.O.P. Presidential Nomination contained a whole string of obstacles. First, although his political philosophy had shifted starboard during the early 1950's, he had never actually switched his party affiliation from Democrat to Republican until 1962. Therefore, old wheelhorses such as Richard Nixon or Nelson Rockefeller far outranked Reagan in the number of years of loyal party service.

Secondly, Ronald Reagan lacked sufficient political experience. Indeed, Barry Goldwater warned Reagan that the Democrats would destroy him on this very issue. For Reagan held no public office until his inauguration as Governor of California in January, 1967, and his Hollywood motion picture career hardly qualified him for the White House (not withstanding the cynics who maintain that every President must know about acting). At any rate, James J. Kilpatrick observed that "Ronald Reagan has a long list of attractive assets, offset by inexperience and by an actor's background." Garry Wills concurred: "Reagan...had all the sex-appeal in the world, but no political base or record or experience." Clearly, any realistic appraisal of Ronald Reagan's Presidential prospects in 1968 had to include his utter lack of political seasoning.54/

In the meantime, perceptive California Democrats, sensing a potential superstar in the making, hounded the politically naive Ronald Reagan unmercifully until totally exasperated, he foolishly bowed to their pressures and gave his pledge to serve a full, four year term (1967-1971) if elected Governor. Thus Reagan promised not to seek the 1968 Republican Presidential Nomination as an active candidate. No doubt, Reagan soon regretted his thoughtless (and unnecessary) declaration of non-candidacy, since it severely restricted his political flexibility. Henceforth, Reagan campaigned for the nation's highest office very discreetly, almost surreptitiously, while at the same time reaffirming his solemn vow to the people of California to remain in Sacramento. However, the increasing discrepancy between his firm commitment not to run, on the one hand, and the glaring fact of his growing national campaign effort, on the other, cost him both credibility and support. For as Dan Smoot complained, Reagan's "status as a non-candidate candidate made him look ludicrous..."55/*

---

*Note—Just suppose for the moment that Ronald Reagan instead (Continued)

259

Then too, the painful memories of Barry Goldwater's November, 1964 fiasco against Lyndon Johnson damaged Ronald Reagan's

---

*Note (Continued)
of George Murphy had run for the U. S. Senate from California against Democrat Pierre Salinger back in 1964. It seems safe to assume that California voters would have then sent Ronald Reagan to Washington (like they did for George Murphy). As Joseph R. Cerrell, Salinger's 1964 Campaign Manager recently told me, "There is no reason to believe that Ronald Reagan couldn't have won just as easily as George Murphy did in 1964."

Ronald Reagan, of course, encountered several major obstacles as he campaigned for the 1968 G.O.P. Presidential Nomination. (Once again, these problems included his relative lack of service to the Republican Party, his absence of previous political experience, his Hollywood film background which raised doubts about his qualifications for the nation's highest office, and his ringing declaration during the 1966 Gubernatorial race that he would not run for President in 1968.) Consequently, had Reagan been elected U.S. Senator from California in 1964 rather than Governor two years later, these political liabilities which plagued his Presidential candidacy right from the very start might well have been overcome.

Had Ronald Reagan been elected U. S. Senator in November, 1964, a) he would have been able to amass by 1968 a four-year record of public service in Washington instead of only a two-year record as Governor in Sacramento; b) he would have acquired greater expertise in the areas of national affairs and foreign policy in Washington rather than in Sacramento; c) he would have emerged as the Republican Party's big winner in 1964 in the midst of a Democratic landslide (Reagan's 1966 triumph, while quite impressive, occurred during a strong G.O.P. year and thus he only shared the spotlight with many other victorious Republicans); d) the embarrassing questions surrounding Reagan's 1968 Presidential plans which surfaced during his 1966 Gubernatorial race might never have arisen at all back in 1964.

On the negative side, had Ronald Reagan been elected to the U.S. Senate in November, 1964, the Governorship of the Golden State would have fallen into G.O.P. hands anyway in 1966. The new California Republican Governor might have entertained Presidential aspirations of his own and thus might have challenged Reagan for control of the California delegation sent to the 1968 G.O.P. National Convention in Miami Beach. Or perhaps a Liberal Republican Governor might have attempted to derail Reagan's Presidential candidacy by undermining his home state political base. From Washington Reagan would have missed the entire University of California, Berkeley Student Revolt of 1967-1968, an event which focused favorable attention upon California's New Right Governor as he boldly stood up to campus militants. However, as a United States Senator, the enterprising Reagan might have made national headlines on some other issue.

Presidential prospects in 1968. For American political parties, traumatized by defeat and torn by dissension, traditionally swing back towards the Center and nominate a moderate "unity" candidate at the next national convention. The New Right detected such pressures emanating from G.O.P. Liberals and Moderates. According to M. Stanton Evans, "Republicans are told to turn their backs on conservatism," and Phyllis Schlafly agreed: "We are told that Republicans must win at any price, and that the price of victory in 1968 is 'unity' under a 'moderate'...." Worst of all, as Frank S. Meyer lamented, a few discouraged New Rightists had unfortunately succumbed to the seductive argument that half a loaf is better than none: "some conservatives...talk as though the victory of any Republican would be a victory for conservatism."56/

Finally, after his inauguration in Sacramento on January 1, 1967 Ronald Reagan's Presidential bandwagon steadily picked up momentum until suddenly, during the early Summer of 1967, a bizarre, homosexual scandal surfaced within the highest echelon of the Governor's newly assembled California State Administration. Needless to say, these revelations of misconduct threw Reagan's national campaign badly off stride. Unbeknownst to Reagan, one of the Governor's trusted lieutenants was a homosexual, and used his influence to recruit other homosexuals for key positions on the Governor's staff. Ronald Reagan, obviously shaken by these embarrassing disclosures, quickly fired the homosexuals and then, somewhat disillusioned with politics in general, retreated into virtual seclusion for several months. Meanwhile, without the Governor's full attention, his California State Administration drifted aimlessly. In the words of one Reaganite, "The Governorship went into receivership."57/

Nevertheless, Ronald Reagan continued accumulating strong support throughout the remainder of 1967. The National Convention of Young Republicans officially endorsed the California Governor for the upcoming 1968 G.O.P. Presidential Nomination. Moreover, Reagan, following in Barry Goldwater's footsteps, captured the hearts of grassroots Republicans all across the Sunbelt. Indeed M. Stanton Evans remarked that "the surge toward Reagan in the fall of '67 resembled, in its basic configurations, the surge toward Goldwater in the fall of '63."58/

The Return of the New Right

The shock of the Goldwater debacle on November 3, 1964 had stunned the New Right temporarily. Yet within a year or two the Movement had regained much of its momentum and vigor. As William F. Buckley, Jr. observed, "the conservative movement was not terminated on the day that Lyndon Johnson beat Barry Goldwater so decisively at the polls." Likewise, Liberal opponents Benjamin Epstein and Arnold Forster came to the same conclusion:

Many Americans believed that the stern rebuke the national electorate administered to Barry Goldwater... spelled the death knell once more of Right-Wing extremism in our country. Unfortunately, they were wrong. In truth, the 1964 campaign period served as the Radical Right's great opportunity to organize its following more effectively and to unify itself more solidly. They used it well. 59/

The results of the Fall Elections of 1966 restored the New Right's poise and confidence. Voters across the United States revolted against the excesses of the Democrats' "Great Society" programs, expressed impatience with L.B.J.'s reluctance to prosecute the Vietnam War to a victorious conclusion, and watched with alarm the rapid spread of the New Left. As James T. Hunter pointed out, the New Right "is growing stronger as the weaknesses of liberalism are becoming more apparent daily. There is nothing to indicate that the revelation of liberalism's decay will not continue." 60/

Ironically, the American public by 1966 complained bitterly about those same problems which candidate Barry Goldwater had raised unsuccessfully during his 1964 Presidential Campaign. Indeed M. Stanton Evans suggested that "Barry Goldwater was two years before his time." Furthermore, without Goldwater's rhetorical faux pas to obscure the real issues in 1966 the embarrassed Liberals now had to explain the spreading confusion and breakdowns in American society. As James T. Hunter remarked, "With no conservative candidate to label as a trigger-happy warmonger, liberals will have to do battle with many of the conservative ideas which continue to appeal to multitudes of voters." 61/

In conclusion, President Lyndon Johnson had defeated Senator Barry Goldwater at the polls on November 3, 1964. Yet despite this crushing setback, the zealous members of the New Right refused to acknowledge defeat gracefully and slip quietly out of sight into the pages of the history books, remembered only as a curious footnote to the 1960's. Instead, they painstakingly rebuilt their Movement around a dynamic, attractive, new political personality—Ronald Reagan—a much more electable Presidential candidate than either Robert Taft or Barry Goldwater.

Therefore, the New Right faced the immediate future with confidence. They believed that the American people, increasingly disenchanted with the direction of American society, seemed ready, at long last, to embrace Ronald Reagan's brand of New Right Republicanism in 1968.

262

CHAPTER ELEVEN - Notes

1. "On the Right", June 16, 1964.

2. Newsweek, (May 20, 1963), p. 28.

3. Hunter, Our Second Revolution, p. 96;
Barry Goldwater interview with the Arizona Republic as quoted in the National Review, (January 16, 1968), p. 28.

4. Dan Smoot Report, (November 9, 1964), p. 353.

Likewise, William F. Buckley, Jr. pointed out that...

> overlying the whole business was the long and tragic shadow of the corpse of John F. Kennedy. A traumatized people cried out for a period of serenity; a good long rest period in the political sanitarium....Three Presidents in twelve months is the kind of thing they go for in the banana republics, or the Balkans; not in America. National Review, (October 20, 1964), p. 902.

5. Stephen Shadegg, "Conservatism and Political Action," in Robert A. Goldwin, ed., Left, Right and Center (Chicago: Rand McNally & Company, 1965), p. 123;
Dan Smoot Report, (November 16, 1964), p. 364;
Shadegg, "Conservatism and Political Action," in Goldwin, ed., Left, Right and Center, p. 123.

6. Report to America, (January, 1965), p.7;
Schlafly and Ward, Strike From Space, p. 92.

7. National Review, (December 1, 1964), p. 1055;
New Guard, (December, 1964), p. 5.

8. The Weekly Crusader, (November 13, 1964), p. 4;
National Review Bulletin, (November 24, 1964), p. 7.

9. New Guard, (December, 1964), p. 8;
The Weekly Crusader, (November 13, 1964), p. 4;
Dan Smoot Report, (November 16, 1964), pp. 363-364.

10. New York Times, November 4, 1964;
"On the Right", January 25, 1966.

11. New Guard, (February, 1965), p. 15;
America's Future, (November 20, 1964), p. 1.

12. Rovere, The Goldwater Caper, p. 173.

13.   National Review, (February 23, 1965), p. 137;
Economic Council Letter, (November 15, 1964), p.3.

14.   A complete list of L.B.J.'s legislative accomplishments can be found in Walt W. Rostow, The Diffusion of Power (New York: The Macmillan Company, 1972), pp. 330-332.

15.   American Opinion, (February, 1965), p. 28;
Ibid., p. 31.

16.   Don Bell Reports, (June 12, 1964) as quoted in the Beacon-Light Herald, (September-October, 1964), p. 81;
National Program Letter, (August, 1964), p. 2.

17.   Destiny, (December, 1964), p. 243;
Don Bell Reports (June 12, 1964) as quoted in the Beacon-Light Herald, (September-October, 1964), p. 80;
National Review, (January 26, 1965), p. 50

18.   National Review, (January 26, 1965), p. 50;
Don Bell Reports, (June 12, 1964) as quoted in the Beacon-Light Herald, (September-October, 1964), p. 81.

19.   Don Bell Reports (June 12, 1964) as quoted in the Beacon-Light Herald, (September-October, 1964), p. 81.

20.   National Program Letter (March, 1965) p. 1;
Destiny, (February, 1965), p. 28;
Ibid., (September, 1965), p. 188;
Ibid., p. 189.

21.   Hunter, Our Second Revolution, p. 137.

22.   America's Future, (November 20, 1964), p. 1;
The Weekly Crusader, (November 27, 1964), p. 8.

23.   National Review, (December 1, 1964), p. 1055;
The Weekly Crusader, (November 13, 1964), p. 2;
National Review, (January 12, 1965), p. 16.

24.   William F. Knowland as quoted in Donovan, The Future of the Republican Party, p. 69;
Dan Smoot Report, (November 9, 1964), p. 358.

25.   National Review, (December 1, 1964), p. 1055;
American Opinion, (January, 1965), p. 69;
The Weekly Crusader, (November 20, 1964), p. 8

26. Donovan, The Future of the Republican Party, p. 69;
National Review, (December 1, 1964), p. 1057.
        As Christian Economics Editor Howard Kershner also
explained, "Our country belongs to the minority as well as the majority
and....a minority of two to three....may easily become the majority in
the next election." Christian Economics, (January 12, 1965), p. 1.

27. New Guard, (December, 1964), p. 5;
Hofstadter, "Goldwater and Pseudo-Conservative Politics," The Paranoid
Style in American Politics and Other Essays, p. 137.

28. Dan Smoot Report, (November 9, 1964), p. 359;
Dr. Frederick Curtis Fowler as quoted in The Weekly Crusader,
(November 20, 1964), p. 8.

29. National Review, (June 13, 1967), p. 640;
Ibid., (May 30, 1967), p. 596.

30. See Bernard Cosman, Five States For Goldwater (University,
Alabama: University of Alabama Press, 1966);
Mark Michaels, New Guard, (October, 1964), p. 15.

31. Lachicotte, Rebel Senator, p. 236;
Ibid., p. 238;
Ibid., p. 239.

32. National Review Bulletin, (September 29, 1964), p. 1;
New Guard, (November, 1964), p. 4.

33. American Mercury, (Winter, 1966), p. 4.

34. Cross and the Flag, (February, 1965), p. 4;
The Citizen, (November, 1964), p. 23;
Rockwell Report, (November, 1964), p.2.

35. National Review, (December 1, 1964), p. 1055;
Donovan, The Future of the Republican Party, p. 68.

36. National Review, (July 12, 1966), p. 668.

37. Ibid., (June 1, 1965), p. 449;
Phyllis Schlafly, Safe-Not Sorry (Alton, Illinois: Pere Marquette Press,
1967), p. 149.

38. National Review, (August 27, 1968), p. 848.

39. Dan Smoot Report, (June, 17, 1963), p. 190.

40. Donovan, The Future of the Republican Party, p. 73.

41.   Schlafly, Safe-Not Sorry, p. 149;
Hunter, Our Second Revolution, p. 121;
Ibid., p. 119.

42.   For background on Ronald Reagan see:
Bill Boyarsky, The Rise of Ronald Reagan (New York: Random House, 1968);
Lou Cannon, Ronnie and Jesse (Garden City, New York: Doubleday & Company, Inc., 1969);
Lee Edwards, Reagan; a political biography (San Diego, California: Viewpoint Books, 1968);
Stephen Hess and David S. Broder, The Republican Establishment (New York: Harper & Row Publishers, 1967);
L. Edmond Leipold, Ronald Reagan: Governor and Statesman (Minneapolis, Minnesota: T. S. Denison & Company, Inc., 1968);
Joseph Lewis, What Makes Reagan Run? (New York: McGraw-Hill Book Company, 1968);
Ronald Reagan with Richard G. Hubler, Where's the Rest of Me (New York: Duell, Sloan and Pearce, 1965);
George Henry Smith, Who is Ronald Reagan?
(New York: Pyramid Books, 1968).

43.   Human Events, (July 28, 1961), p. 469.

44.   Hess and Broder, The Republican Establishment, pp. 253-254.

45.   Lewis, What Makes Reagan Run?, p. 3;
Ibid., p. 6;
Ibid., p. 3;
Ibid., p. 6.

46.   Ibid., p. 7;
Ibid., p. 5.

47.   National Review Bulletin, (January 18, 1966), pp. 4-5;
Hunter, Our Second Revolution, p. 113;
Bruce Weinrod, New Guard, (Summer, 1968), p. 8;
Evans, The Future of Conservatism, p. 272;
National Review, (December 29, 1964), p. 1145.

48.   Theodore H. White, The Making of the President 1968 (New York: Atheneum Publishers, 1969), p. 35;
New Guard, (Summer, 1968), p. 8;
Lewis, What Makes Reagan Run?, p. xi;
Ibid., p. 7.

49.   Boyarsky, The Rise of Ronald Reagan, p. 105.

50.   Hunter, Our Second Revolution, preface, p. 7;
National Review Bulletin, (November 22, 1966), p. 4.

51.   Human Events, (February 19, 1966), p. 119.

52.   National Review Bulletin, (November 22, 1966), p. 4;
Hunter, Our Second Revolution, p. 114.

53.   White, The Making of the President 1968, p. 35;
Barry Goldwater, May 3, 1967 Press Conference in St. Louis as quoted in
Lewis, What Makes Reagan Run?, p. 185.

54.   Richard J. Whalen, Catch the Falling Flag (Boston: Houghlin,
Mifflin Company, 1972), p. 12;
National Review, (November 14, 1967), p. 1263;
Ibid., (August 27, 1968), p. 848;

55.   Dan Smoot Report, (August 26, 1968), p. 138.

56.   Evans, The Future of Conservatism, p. 13;
Schlafly, Safe-Not Sorry, p. 173;
National Review, (December 12, 1967), p. 1385.

57.   As related in Lou Cannon, Ronnie and Jesse, p. 184;
For details of the scandal see Lou Cannon, Ronnie and Jesse;

       During a private conversation on August 23, 1976 California
political expert Bill Boyarsky told me how much political and
psychological damage the homosexual scandal did to Ronald Reagan's
Presidential prospects: "The damage was great."

58.   Evans, The Future of Conservatism, p. 288.

59.   "On the Right", (January 25, 1966), p. 45;
Epstein and Forster, Report on the John Birch Society 1966, p. ix.

60.   Hunter, Our Second Revolution, p. 135.

61.   National Review, (November 1, 1966), p. 1091;
Hunter, Our Second Revolution, p. 141.

CHAPTER TWELVE

THE NEW RIGHT AND 1968

"We witness a spineless surrender to violence"

In the eyes of the New Right, the United States of America teetered upon the brink of a collective nervous breakdown by the year 1968. Phyllis Schlafly along with Admiral Chester Ward asserted that "Our cities have become more dangerous than the jungles infested by Viet Cong guerrillas. Serious crime has gone up 88% in eight years." Schlafly and Ward described our city parks as "wilder than the frontier towns of 150 years ago and, for women, far more fearful." Worst of all, "we witness a spineless surrender to violence—to rioters, looters, arsonists, murderers, rapists, street mobs, university students carrying obscene signs, 'peace' demonstrators, pornographers, revolutionaries, and blackmailers." In fact, "The President's own commission admitted that the domestic crisis in our land is the most alarming since the Civil War." Likewise, William F. Buckley, Jr. diagnosed the appalling sickness infecting American life by 1968:

> Five years with Mr. Lyndon Johnson working away at the achievement of a Great Society sees young men fearful of having to die in Vietnam, other young men and women fearful of attending colleges and universities without being embroiled in riots, men, women and children fearful of murderers, robbers, and muggers, old people fearful of the decline in the value of their savings, parents fearful of the decreasing quality of education, Negroes terrorized by Negro revolutionists, whites terrorized by white revolutionists, the entire community wracked by the impotence of our foreign policy and the utter failure...to help the wretched people of Czechoslovakia.1/

Indeed the racial, social, and moral problems which the New Right had repeatedly warned about since the beginning of the decade now boiled over and threatened to tear the country apart. When the New Right had raised these difficult issues back in 1961 they remained a lonely voice in the wilderness. When Barry Goldwater had dared to discuss these questions during his campaign for the Presidency back in 1964 the smug electorate largely ignored his message. However, by 1968 the New Right saw its prophecies fulfilled and, to a great extent, its political philosophy vindicated.

As a mass movement the New Right reached its peak of influence upon American life in 1968; and the members of the New Right, feeling this surge of power and momentum, considered 1968 to be their year of destiny. In the words of William F. Buckley, Jr., "There is in the air a sense of great excitement among conservatives who have reason to believe that their time is coming." 2/

Having briefly set the stage, let us now turn to the specific events of 1968--a year replete with surprises--indeed, quite possibly the most incredible, topsy-turvy year in all of American history.

"War drags on and on and on in Vietnam"

American policy in Southeast Asia had thoroughly exasperated the New Right by 1968. The "war drags on and on and on in Vietnam," Phyllis Schlafly complained, "killing American boys by the thousands-- with no hope of victory." Furthermore, the bewildered U.S. public could not understand why President Lyndon Johnson steadfastly refused to bring this conflict to a swift, triumphant conclusion: "Everywhere Americans ask, 'Why don't we go ahead and win it? ' "3/

Accordingly, the confused American people witnessed the curious spectacle of a small military power--North Vietnam--matching the mighty United States of American blow for blow. The National Program Letter called the Vietnamese conflict a "hot war which pits a pigmy half-nation against a world colossus--with the pigmy in the role of the aggressor, and the colossus taking severe and unrelenting punishment." Similarly, Phyllis Schlafly emphasized that "Our nation...should surely be able to defeat the poor little half-country of North Vietnam in a three-year war."4/

New Rightists maintained that America's half-hearted efforts in Southeast Asia reflected President Lyndon Johnson's "no-win," appeasement-oriented philosophy. As Christian Economics Editor Howard Kershner noted, "The impasse in Vietnam with all its concomitants arises from...the soft and inadequate policy of preferring to appease the enemy, rather than to defeat him." Dr. Medford Evans stressed that L.B.J. sought to "reassure the sophisticated that there is no intention of carrying things in Vietnam to the point of military victory." Evans characterized "the fighting in Vietnam" as "a sort of therapeutic bloodletting, which may actually prevent the Americans from becoming involved in any more serious military venture" against World Communism. 5/

"The white flag of surrender in Vietnam"

President Johnson's sudden decision on March 31, 1968 to de-escalate the Vietnam War and open peace talks infuriated the New Right. In the opinion of Frank S. Meyer, "President Johnson ran up the white flag of surrender in Vietnam...," when he unexpectedly agreed to

270

halt America's bombing of North Vietnam and scamper towards the conference table in Paris. For the New Right remembered bitterly the Communist obstinacy during the long, torturous negotiations held at Panmunjon between July, 1951 and July, 1953 while American boys continued dying on the battlefields of Korea. Ronald Reagan, who claimed that "De-escalation has usually resulted in the deaths of more Americans," favored instead "a step-up in the war." 6/

To the New Right, L.B.J.'s decision to scale down the Vietnam War on March 31, 1968 smelled like a typical, cowardly sellout of a friendly anti-Communist regime through the guise of forming a neutral, coalition government a la Laos in 1962. (See Chapter Ten) As James T. Hunter warned:

> The greatest danger in the present almost pleading drive of the United States toward negotiations is that the beleaguered President will cave in under the relentless pressure from dove candidates and settle for the Communist dream—a coalition government in the South, embracing the savage Viet Cong as equal partners. This would be tantamount to handing the Communist North a sanctioned victory—a victory it could not achieve militarily. 7/

"The worst humiliation our nation has ever suffered"

In the midst of the Vietnam fiasco the Communist regime of nearby North Korea attacked an American intelligence ship, the U.S.S. Pueblo, stationed in the international waters off the Korean coast on the morning of January 23, 1968. After a brief battle the vessel surrendered. Thus the U.S.S. Pueblo loaded with ultra-secret, electronic surveillance gadgetry plus a crew of eighty-three American sailors fell into North Korean hands.

The New Right exploded with predicable anger as the news of the Pueblo's capture flashed across the wires. Dr. Medford Evans called the seizure an "unparalleled insult to the American flag" while Phyllis Schlafly and Admiral Chester Ward labelled the incident "the worst humiliation our nation has ever suffered." The United States, in the eyes of the New Right, had stood by helplessly as yet another puny, two-bit, Asian nation had tweaked Uncle Sam's nose. Senator J. Strom Thurmond of South Carolina pointed out that the Pueblo Affair "revealed to the world that the United States would suffer unbelievable insult before using force for retaliation." 8/

Instead, the New Right demanded a swift response against North Korea for its arrogant seizure of the Pueblo. Dr. Medford Evans announced that "Americans wanted a Teddy Roosevelt Perdicais-alive-

271

or-Raisuli-dead ultimatum from the White House." Yet as J. Strom Thurmond noted, "The people of the United States and the world waited breathlessly for the awful retribution that the United States would visit upon North Korea for its irresponsible act." However, "They waited, and waited, and waited." 9/

Worst of all, the New Right said, the Pueblo's crew had failed, for some inexcusable reason, to scuttle their vessel and thus prevent the North Koreans from capturing the priceless espionage equipment on board. William F. Buckley, Jr. advocated, "A bombing raid...with orders to sink our own ship," and in the event that "the marksmanship of our pilots is a little rusty and it turns out that we also sank the North Korean boats that brought in the Pueblo, why, you can't win them all." 10/

"Psychotic Black Nationalists and revolutionary delinquents"

America's racial crisis intensified during the Spring of 1968. The tragic murder of the Reverend Dr. Martin Luther King, Jr. on April 4, 1968 in Memphis, Tennessee ignited Black ghettos all across the nation. All told, 168 American cities experienced riots, including Washington, D.C. where fires raged a scant two blocks from the White House itself and where U.S. Army troops patrolled the steps of the Capitol Building armed with machine guns. In this atmosphere, author Gary Allen summed up the sentiments of the New Right: "Americans are sick of... the looting and burning of our cities by psychotic Black Nationalists and revolutionary delinquents." 11/

As expected, the New Right entertained no sympathy for the "Poor Peoples' March" which descended upon Washington, D.C. with much fanfare during the early Summer of 1968 demanding jobs, welfare reform, and a basic redistribution of America's wealth. Thus the National Review contemptuously dismissed the "Poor Peoples' March" as another "Coxey's Army"--that motley crew of unemployed workers and students who journeyed to the nation's capital on a similar mission way back in 1894. Moreover, Frank S. Meyer reminded his fellow New Rightists that "it was with just such tactics that the Jacobins led the mob of Paris to overawe the Assembly and usher in the terrorist stage of the French Revolution."12/

"Demagogic moralizing on a theme of collective guilt"

On July 29, 1967 in the midst of America's fourth consecutive "Long Hot Summer" of racial turmoil in her cities President Lyndon Johnson appointed a special National Advisory Commission on Civil

Disorder to investigate the causes of these riots. The Commission, headed by Illinois Democratic Governor Otto Kerner, issued its eagerly awaited report on March 1, 1968. Attempting to arouse the public's conscience, the Kerner Commission blamed the violence on "white racism" and condemned the White majority's reluctance to allow Blacks the opportunity to enter the mainstream of American life. As a result, the report warned that "Our nation is moving toward two societies, one black, one white—separate and unequal." 13/

The New Right utterly rejected the Kerner Commission's findings. According to the National Review Bulletin, "The Commission hastily explains away all the urban riots, crimes and troubles by demagogic moralizing on a theme of collective guilt: 'white racism is essentially responsible.' " Therefore, the report represents "A general absolution, in short, for all the arson, looting, vandalism, rape, mayhem and murder that strikes a non-white fancy." Philosopher Ernest Van Den Haag noted that "the Commission clearly suggests that the riots have come as a pusishment for our sins.... Undoubtedly a religiously orthodox explanation, but not a scientific one."14/

In addition, New Rightists held that this one-sided report refused to censure the real culprits—the Blacks who actually started the riots and the irresponsible White Liberals who encouraged them. As Frank S. Meyer complained, "the Commission has put the blame everywhere but where it belongs, everywhere, that is, except upon the rioters and upon the liberals who, with their abstract ideology, prepared the way for the riots by their contempt for social order and their utopian egalitarian enticements and incitements." 15/

The Unholy Trio: Robert Kennedy, Eugene McCarthy, and Hubert Humphrey

When Lyndon Johnson ordered a de-escalation of the Vietnam War on the evening of March 31, 1968, he also disclosed his decision not to seek another term as President. Suddenly, the race for the Democratic Party Nomination burst wide open as New York Senator Robert Kennedy, Minnesota Senator Eugene McCarthy, and L.B.J.'s Vice President Hubert Humphrey jockeyed for position. While rejoicing at the President's political downfall, the New Right feared the trio of Kennedy, McCarthy, and Humphrey much more than L.B.J.

The New Right simply despised Robert Kennedy. While serving as United States Attorney General during the John F. Kennedy Administration, Robert Kennedy had coaxed his brother, the President, into integrating the University of Mississippi in 1962 and the University of Alabama the following year. After J.F.K.'s death Robert Kennedy, now turned "carpetbagger," entered the U.S. Senate from New York State in November, 1964.

Now as a recognized leader of the young, New Left wing of the Democratic Party, Robert Kennedy, in the eyes of the New Right, had become by the Spring of 1968 "a symbol for nihilistic forces from the Haight-Ashbury District of San Francisco...," in the words of Dr. Medford Evans. Garry Wills called Kennedy "Bob Dylan on the stump" while William F. Buckley, Jr. lamented that "tens of thousands of college students moo over Bobby Kennedy who has delusions of being Ringo Starr." Buckley blasted Bobby's campaign "technique to egg on hysterical adulation."16/

The next contender for the 1968 Democratic Presidential Nomination, Minnesota Senator Eugene McCarthy, attracted relatively little attention from the New Right, which focused instead upon the stronger candidates (Senator Robert Kennedy and Vice President Hubert Humphrey). The New Right dismissed Eugene McCarthy, the darling of the A.D.A. crowd (the Americans for Democratic Action), as a political lightweight--a sort of modern day Don Quixote. Indeed the National Review labelled McCarthy the "Man From La Mancha."17/

The final candidate for the Democratic Presidential Nomination, Vice President Hubert Humphrey, represented, in the view of the New Right, the epitome of a big-labor, big-government, free-spending, share-the-wealth politician. Consequently, the New Right described Hubert Humphrey as "The evangelist of the Welfare State." Furthermore, Humphrey infuriated the New Right by seeming to encourage the Blacks trapped inside America's ghettos to riot. For Humphrey had once declared in New Orleans in July, 1966 that if he, personally, had the misfortune to live in a slum, "I think you'd have more trouble than you have already, because I've got enough spark in me to lead a mighty good revolt."18/

George Wallace Forms the American Independent Party

Some members of the New Right did not expect the G.O.P. to nominate another New Right candidate for President in 1968. The American Mercury cautioned that "The Republican Party, today, is solidly in the hands of the Eastern Liberal Establishment." Likewise, John J. Synon pointed out that "The Conservative Republicans, in 1964, took their best shot with Barry Goldwater and the result was tragic." Therefore, the G.O.P. in 1968 would not repeat the same disastrous experience of 1964 by running another New Rightist. Instead the G.O.P. would select a more attractive, Moderate Presidential candidate.19/

Fully anticipating the nomination of a G.O.P. Moderate in 1968, the supporters of George Wallace quickly assembled a third political party, the A.I.P. (American Independent Party) in order to run the former Alabama Governor for the Presidency. As a general observation, the least respectable elements within the New Right Movement

(Southern Rednecks, Forgotten Rightists, and para-military groups) played the major role in organizing the American Independent Party.20/

A distinctly Southern flavor pervaded George Wallace's American Independent Party of 1968, much like J. Strom Thurmond's Dixiecrat Party of 1948. George Wallace, of course, ran as a national candidate in 1968, while J. Strom Thurmond back in 1948 had restricted his campaign activities to below the Mason-Dixon line. Yet both Wallace and Thurmond before him attempted to siphon off enough electoral votes from the two major parties to throw the Presidential Election into the U.S. House of Representatives for a decision. In this manner, Wallace and Thurmond had hoped to hold the balance of power between the Democrats and Republicans and then wheel-and-deal from an enviable position of strength.

"He appeals to the lowest instincts of the demos"

The more restrained members of the New Right wanted nothing, whatsoever, to do with the rabble rouser George Wallace. For instance, the National Review Bulletin blasted, "Wallace's ruthless demagogy," while Frank S. Meyer deplored the fact that Wallace "translates the frustrations, the legitimate fears, of the solid Americans to whom he appeals, into hatreds. Not content with castigating the errors of our recent leadership, he appeals to the lowest instincts of the demos."21/

Moreover, George Wallace's third-party threatened to undermine the American constitutional system. Ohio Congressman John M. Ashbrook charged that "Wallace's candidacy amply demonstrates a frivolous attitude toward our two-party system, a system which has been a principal foundation of our national political stability." Likewise, Barry Goldwater characterized "Wallace's candidacy" as "a danger to the two party system that has served us well," because, "If Wallace gets enough votes to encourage other dissidents of either the Right or Left to form their own parties, we might well end up with a multi-party system," which, "given our present Constitution...could mean disaster for America."22/

Then too, as the National Review pointed out, the American Independent Party unwisely distracts "conservative energy from the difficult, but eminently possible, task of defeating Liberalism, in the Republican Party..." Instead, the New Right, in the opinion of James T. Hunter, "must concentrate on strengthening the most conservative party [the Republicans] and attempting to make it more conservative." Therefore, the New Right "must renounce the temptation to form a third party, thus weakening the G.O.P. and insuring the continued success of the liberal wing of the Democratic party at the presidential level."23/

Richard Nixon--"the pro"

On the Republican side, the astonishing political comeback of Richard Nixon represented, without question, the central event of this incredible year 1968. Once labelled "the two-time loser" by Frank S. Meyer back in 1964, the seemingly washed-up Richard Nixon had somehow rebounded to capture the G.O.P. Presidential Nomination by August, 1968. Three months later the American people narrowly elected Richard M. Nixon President of the United States. 24/

Yet Richard Nixon's political resurrection did not really surprise the members of the New Right. Having battled Nixon continually since 1952, the New Rightists respected their old adversary as a crafty, ruthless, yet superbly talented politician. Barry Goldwater described Nixon as "one of the cleverest political strategists in our nation's history." The National Review Bulletin considered Nixon "a competent, intelligent, experienced professional politician...," while James J. Kilpatrick simply called Nixon "the pro."25/

Richard Nixon had lost the 1960 Presidential Election to Democrat John F. Kennedy by a scant one-hundred-thousand votes. Consequently, Nixon remained a strong G.O.P. Presidential contender even after his slim defeat. Nixon surveyed the situation and decided to skip a possible rematch against J.F.K. in 1964; instead Nixon chose to bide his time until 1968. Meanwhile, Nixon returned home to his native California in order to reestablish his political base.

Nixon entered the 1962 Golden State Gubernatorial contest. But the growing New Right-wing of the California G.O.P., now on the verge of seizing control of the state party, had backed their own candidate Joe Shell. Nixon ultimately vanquished Joe Shell in June, 1962 after a bruising Republican Primary fight. In the process, Nixon declared war upon one of Joe Shell's principal allies--the John Birch Society. The former Vice President, in a move designed to discredit Joe Shell, denounced the John Birchers as "kooks and nuts" and attempted unsuccessfully to purge them from the California G.O.P. As the National Review noted, "Mr. Nixon set out...to oust every man-jack Bircher from the Republican Party in California ."26/

The New Right evened the score against Richard Nixon during the November, 1962 General Election. Incumbent Democratic Governor Edmund G. "Pat" Brown nosed out Nixon for the Governorship, in large part, because many angry New Right Republicans failed to vote for Nixon. As William F. Buckley, Jr. stated, "the conservatives...beat him. And he knows that." As a matter of fact, Richard Nixon himself told James J. Kilpatrick the same thing: "We had done better than anyone ever imagined we would do with the Democrats and independents. It was our own Republicans who let their party down in that election. 27/

Richard Nixon might well have slipped quietly into political oblivion following his California defeat. However, on the evening of November 11, 1962 the A.B.C. Television Network aired an extraordinary documentary entitled "The Political Obituary of Richard Nixon" hosted by veteran newscaster Howard K. Smith.* Several guests discussed the various phases of Richard Nixon's career including Alger Hiss, of all people, the convicted perjurer and alleged Communist spy whom Nixon had hounded from public life during the late 1940's. Now the spectacle of Alger Hiss self-righteously sitting in judgment of even a scoundrel like Richard Nixon made the New Right boiling mad. Nixon received a tremendous outpouring of sympathy, prompting the National Review Bulletin to observe prophetically that "The Political Obituary of Richard Nixon" may have inadvertently saved Nixon from oblivion. 28/

After his November, 1962 defeat, Nixon abandoned California, relocated in New York City, and officially joined the Eastern Liberal Establishment. The former Vice President became a senior partner commanding a six-figure salary in a prestigeous Wall Street law firm and moved his family into the same Fifth Avenue apartment building as Nelson Rockefeller!

When John F. Kennedy died from an assassin's bullet on November 22, 1963, Richard Nixon reappraised his own political position. He now wanted the 1964 Republican Presidential Nomination against Democrat Lyndon Johnson. Nevertheless, with Barry Goldwater solidly entrenched as the G.O.P. front-runner Nixon could only pray for a deadlocked convention when the Party might then turn to him as a Moderate, compromise candidate. Therefore, Nixon participated in the Eastern Liberal Establishment's stop-Goldwater drive, but always from behind the scenes. Of course, Nixon also made sure to remain on excellent terms with the Goldwaterites. When the Arizona Senator received the G.O.P. Presidential Nomination in July, 1964 Richard Nixon graciously led the calls for Republican Party harmony.

Nixon vigorously supported Barry Goldwater during the 1964 Fall Campaign while the Eastern Liberal Establishment wing of the G.O.P. avoided their own Party's Presidential Nominee like the plague. Nixon

---

*Note—The day after his California loss Richard Nixon had announced his political retirement at the conclusion of a stormy, post-election press conference: "You won't have Nixon to kick around anymore, because, gentlemen, this is my last press conference!" Nixon's statement coupled with his Gubernatorial defeat led A.B.C. Television to produce "The Political Obituary of Richard Nixon" assuming that indeed his long career in public life had finally come to an end. See Theodore H. White, The Making of the President 1968 (New York: Atheneum Publishers, 1969), p. 42.

performed yeoman's service travelling 25,000 miles, visiting thirty-six different states, speaking on behalf of 150 Republican candidates. The Goldwaterites deeply appreciated Nixon's loyalty to both Barry Goldwater and to the G.O.P. Nixon's efforts clearly raised his standing among the members of the New Right. 29/*

Yet immediately after Goldwater's election defeat, Richard Nixon, declaring that the Republican Party had wandered "too far to the right," quietly played a leading role in the removal of Dean Burch as G.O.P. National Chairman and the liquidation of the remaining Goldwaterites from the Republican National Committee. 30/ (See Chapter Eleven)

Furthermore, Richard Nixon emerged from the November 1964 Goldwater debacle as the leading national spokesman for the Republican Party, almost by default. G.O.P. Liberals like Henry Cabot Lodge, Jr., Nelson Rockefeller, George Romney, and William Scranton had deserted the Goldwater-Miller ticket and thus had forfeited their right to lay claim to Republican Party leadership. After his loss, Barry Goldwater remained a virtual pariah, and former President Dwight D. Eisenhower's health soon began to fail—and that left only Richard Nixon at the G.O.P. helm. In addition, as the Vietnam War escalated Nixon's reputation as an expert on foreign affairs made him the ideal Republican counterweight to Democratic President Lyndon Johnson.

Richard Nixon's reconciliation with the New Right continued strongly after the November, 1964 Presidential Election. Barry Goldwater himself, in January, 1965, offered warm words of praise for Nixon:

> I want to express my heartfelt thanks and gratitude to Dick Nixon who worked harder than any one person for the ticket this year. Dick, I will never forget it! I know that you did it in the interests of the Republican party and not for any selfish reasons. But if there ever comes a time I can turn those into selfish reasons, I am going to do all I can to see that it comes about.

Goldwater's favorable remarks obviously constituted an open invitation to Richard Nixon to go ahead and seek the 1968 G.O.P. Presidential Nomination. Years later William A. Rusher observed, "In retrospect, it seems clear that Barry Goldwater's own ringing

---

*Note—Had Barry Goldwater somehow been elected President in November, 1964 I believe Richard Nixon would have been appointed Secretary of State.

endorsement of Nixon, 'way back in early 1965, was one of the most important boosts that Nixon's candidacy was to receive." 31/

Nixon effectively exploited his position as the Republican Party's premier national spokesman during the Fall Campaign of 1966. On the stump Nixon played up traditional New Right themes, sounding at times virtually indistinguishable from the Barry Goldwater of 1964. Indeed, the National Review, noting Nixon's shift "toward the Right" and his Goldwateresque rhetoric, asked, "Sound like anyone you used to know back in 1964?" 32/

Richard Nixon's "Southern Strategy"

Despite Barry Goldwater's Presidential defeat, the G.O.P. still remained after November, 1964 a Conservative political party dominated by the New Right, Sunbelt-Farmbelt coalition. As M. Stanton Evans pointed out early in 1968, "The 1964 GOP...nationwide alliance of Midwestern, Southern, and Western states...has grown stronger in the intervening years." Evans predicted that "The conservatives who nominated Goldwater can effectively control the choice of Republican presidential candidates for the foreseeable future—if they become aware of their own strength. 33/

The ascendancy of the New Right within the Republican Party reflected, more than anything else, the long awaited revolution in Southern G.O.P. politics. Released, at last, from its perpetual bondage to the Eastern Liberal Establishment, the Dixie Republicans now assumed their natural position on the extreme starboard side of the political spectrum. (See Chapter Eight.) The South also received a bonus of extra delegates at the 1968 G.O.P. National Convention as a reward for supporting the Goldwater-Miller ticket in the November, 1964 Presidential Election. Thus the Southern states, which had furnished only 19% of the total delegates at the 1952 G.O.P. Convention in Chicago, sent a hefty 27% to Miami Beach in 1968. 34/

The South, obviously, played a crucial role in Richard Nixon's campaign for the 1968 Republican Presidential Nomination. Consequently, in keeping with his so-called "Southern Strategy" Nixon courted key Southern G.O.P. leaders such as Senators J. Strom Thurmond of South Carolina and John Tower of Texas. Moreover, Nixon's hawkish pronouncements on Vietnam coupled with his tough stance on law and order at home found a receptive audience throughout Dixie. Beyond that, Nixon's "Southern Strategy," looked ahead to the November, 1968 Presidential Election. Nixon expected to capture a large share of the South's electoral votes even if Alabama's George Wallace ran as a third-party candidate. Finally, by means of his "Southern Strategy," Richard Nixon hoped someday to forge a new majority coalition in American politics by bringing the formerly Democratic "Solid South" into the Republican camp on a permanent basis.

Nixon's "Southern Strategy" bore fruit during an historic meeting held at the Marriott Motor Hotel in Atlanta, Georgia on May 31, 1968. Nixon reached an understanding with G.O.P. leaders J. Strom Thurmond, John Tower, and thirteen Southern and Border State Republican Party chairmen. In exchange for their support on the first ballot at the upcoming G.O.P. National Convention in Miami Beach, Florida Nixon gave his assurances on a whole range of subjects. He promised not to select a Liberal for his Vice Presidential running-mate; extensive patronage for Southern Republicans; a slow down on public school desegregation; continued large expenditures for national defense; and Conservative United States Supreme Court appointments. 35/

How Richard Nixon Defeated Ronald Reagan

Yet in spite of Richard Nixon's clever "Southern Strategy," it seems remarkable, in retrospect, that the Southern states voted for the former Vice President at the 1968 G.O.P. National Convention rather than for Ronald Reagan, an authentic New Rightist. The same Southerners who had enthusiastically supported Barry Goldwater back in 1964 wound up endorsing Richard Nixon in 1968. Why after a full decade of struggle did the New Right, now on the verge of recapturing control over the Republican Party in Miami Beach and then electing the next President of the United States in November, choose to rebuff their own Ronald Reagan, and cast their lot with their old enemy Richard Nixon? This surprising turn of events requires a deeper explanation for it represents the great political mystery of 1968. 36/

To begin with, Richard Nixon obtained a solid, two-year headstart over Ronald Reagan during the period from November, 1964 until November, 1966 when the badly bruised New Right looked upon Richard Nixon as the only possible Republican counterweight to the Presidential ambitions of the hated G.O.P. Liberals, Nelson Rockefeller and George Romney. Accordingly, many members of the New Right, out of sheer desperation, jumped aboard the Nixon bandwagon before November, 1966—when Ronald Reagan remained a promising but as yet politically unproven newcomer. Moreover, even after Reagan's smashing Gubernatorial victory in November, 1966 the former actor's thoughtless and completely unnecessary declaration of non-candidacy severely hampered his 1968 Presidential Campaign. (See Chapter Eleven)

Secondly, Ronald Reagan avoided challenging Richard Nixon directly. For if Nixon stumbled before Reagan had firmly consolidated his position, the Eastern Liberal Establishment would then step into the leadership vacuum and nominate Nelson Rockefeller or George Romney. Indeed at a private meeting held in July, 1967 Reagan agreed to give the more experienced Nixon the first crack at the 1968 G.O.P. Nomination and pledged to enter the race as an active candidate only if Nixon should falter. The New Right, obsessed with the Liberals Rockefeller and Romney, used Nixon as their stalking-horse for Reagan only to discover much too late that the wily Nixon had meanwhile sewn-up a first ballot victory. 37/

Next the former Vice President simply out-maneuvered the California Governor for New Right support. By employing vastly superior tactics, Nixon secured endorsements from many of the old Goldwaterites (principally in the South) ahead of the poorly organized, and at times downright inept Ronald Reagan. Thus Los Angeles Times political writer Bill Boyarsky concluded that Nixon beat Reagan in 1968 because "Nixon always knew how to play the game of Republican Party politics. 38/

Lastly, Nixon swept several G.O.P. Presidential primaries held during the Spring of 1968. Unfortunately for Reagan, the major contested primaries all took place in Liberal Republican states (New Hampshire, Wisconsin, and Oregon) and Nixon crushed Reagan in their only real head-to-head duel in Liberal Oregon 73% to 23% (with 4% write-in vote for Nelson Rockefeller). Of course, Barry Goldwater had also done quite badly throughout most of the 1964 G.O.P. primary season. However, Goldwater then finally beat his chief competitor Nelson Rockefeller in California's dramatic winner-take-all Primary in early June, 1964 to wrap up the nomination. Yet the citizens of the Golden State could not give Ronald Reagan an equally significant victory in June, 1968 over his strongest opposition Richard Nixon because this time the California Governor ran unopposed as the favorite son candidate. 39/

The New Right at Miami Beach

Even though Nixon captured the primaries, the plain fact remains that the New Right sent more than enough delegates to the 1968 G.O.P. National Convention in Miami Beach to bestow the Presidential Nomination upon Ronald Reagan. Nevertheless, the New Right passed up this golden opportunity to select Reagan and chose instead to award Richard Nixon with a first ballot triumph. In the words of William A. Rusher, "Richard Nixon was nominated...because, and only because, a majority of the conservatives present had decided to support him. 40/

Evidently, the former Vice President's patient courtship of the Southern states paid off handsomely in the end, since the New Right delegates from Dixie provided the margin of victory as they voted overwhelmingly for Richard Nixon rather than for their ideological comrade-in-arms Ronald Reagan.

Still Nixon's air-tight "Southern Strategy" nearly collapsed at the last moment. The Dixie delegates almost stampeded the Convention for the dynamic California Governor. As Human Events reported, "Reagan came very close to unravelling Nixon's majority strength in the South." Three extraordinarily powerful and persuasive men—John Tower, J. Strom Thurmond, and Barry Goldwater—barely held the New Right Southern delegates in line for Nixon. The National Review Bulletin noted, "the major role in the Nixon campaign of Thurmond, Goldwater, and Tower," who begged, cajoled, and browbeat the Southerners into voting against their beloved Ronald Reagan. Indeed the diligent efforts of Tower, Thurmond, and Goldwater on behalf of Richard Nixon proved decisive since "Southern delegates were hard put to believe these leaders were not making the best decision for the conservative cause. 41/

Texas Senator John Tower delivered his Lone Star State's delegation (the largest single bloc of Southern votes at the 1968 Convention) forty-one to fifteen in favor of Richard Nixon over Ronald Reagan; a remarkable feat because Texas is Reagan country. (Just witness Reagan's clean sweep over President Gerald Ford in the 1976 G.O.P. Presidential Primary Election in Texas.) 42/

With regards to Senator J. Strom Thurmond of South Carolina, political writer Jules Witcover suggested that "on the past-performance charts, if ever there was a Ronald Reagan man, it would be Thurmond...." Yet the South Carolina Solon wound up squarely in Richard Nixon's corner in 1968—an event which prompted William A. Rusher to observe that "many conservatives who preferred Reagan have wondered what on earth can have persuaded Strom Thurmond to make his... declaration for Richard Nixon."* At any rate, J. Strom Thurmond single-handedly tamed his pro-Reagan South Carolina delegation on the brink of revolt, and cast all twenty-two Convention votes for Richard Nixon. 43/

Another central influence on the New Right in 1968 was Barry Goldwater, who personally visited each wavering Southern delegation on the Convention floor to shore up Richard Nixon's sagging support. To convince the New Right Southerners to vote for Nixon, Goldwater spread

---

*Note—South Carolina Senator J. Strom Thurmond's devotion to the philosophy of the New Right had certainly not diminished one bit. Thurmond published a book, The Faith We Have Not Kept, in June, 1968, dealing with classical New Right themes such as Communism, crime, moral decay, and the fall of the ancient Roman Empire. See J. Strom Thurmond, The Faith We Have Not Kept (San Diego, California: Viewpoint Books, 1968).

the false rumor that Ronald Reagan would gladly become Nixon's Vice Presidential running-mate: "I know Ron and he'll take the second spot," when, in fact, Reagan had repeatedly refused to consider such an offer. 44/

Richard Nixon and the Specter of Nelson Rockefeller

Nonetheless, the crucial question still remains unanswered: with Ronald Reagan readily available for the 1968 Republican Presidential Nomination, why did the great majority of New Right Convention delegates cast their ballots for their old enemy Richard Nixon? Indeed even William F. Buckley, Jr. has described the New Right's astonishing loyalty to the former Vice President as "spooky" since Ronald Reagan, and not Richard Nixon embodied the very heart and soul of their Movement. 45/

First of all, Nixon looked like a sure winner in November and the bulk of the New Rightists, as faithful Republicans, desperately yearned for both party unity and victory at the polls. David A. Keene wrote in New Guard that "Richard Nixon is a pro; he won't make the mistakes that the media will be looking for; he has demonstrated in the primaries that he can hold the party together and...can win in November." Similarly, Dan Smoot insisted that...

> The consuming passion of the Republican convention was the desire to get a Republican into the White House, regardless of what he stands for. The convention was obsessed with winning. One comment, heard so often it became a refrain during those four days in August, was that this year Republicans were being pragmatic, avoiding ideology. 46/

While Richard Nixon hardly represented the perfect G.O.P. Presidential Nominee, the New Right did consider him infinitely preferable to a Liberal Democrat such as Lyndon Johnson or Hubert Humphrey. As David A. Keene pointed out, "Richard Nixon may not be the conservative candidate in the sense that Senator Goldwater was, but he is certainly a conservative candidate that we can and should support." Human Events concurred: "To be sure, the philosophy of Richard Nixon... is not vintage Goldwater." Yet Nixon stands "clearly to the right of center and should be acceptable to most conservatives...." Phyllis Schlafly and Admiral Chester Ward asked, "Does this mean that Richard Nixon is the answer to all our problems and will change our country overnight?" Schlafly and Ward responded, "Of course not," but at the very least, the election of Nixon would remove the hated Liberal

Democrats from the White House. 47/

In addition, many New Rightists observed welcome signs of personal growth and political maturity in Richard Nixon. Accordingly, the National Review praised Nixon for belonging "to that rare species able and willing to learn from errors of the past." Likewise, William F. Buckley, Jr. remarked that "Mr. Nixon...during the past few years...has shared some of the disillusions with liberalism which are the waystations to political maturity." 48/

In fact, it seemed as though Richard Nixon had finally made his peace with the New Right. As Human Events noted, "Conservatism is an idea whose time has come and Richard Nixon appears to have no intention of resisting it." Nixon even acknowledged the existence of a kind of symbiotic relationship between himself and the New Right when he confided to William F. Buckley, Jr. that "Barry Goldwater found out you can't win an important election with only the Right Wing behind you. But I found out in 1962 that you can't win an election without the Right Wing." 49/*

Furthermore, Human Events advised the members of the New Right to support Richard Nixon vigorously because "Nixon...if elected, will owe his victory to conservatives." (In short, climb aboard the Nixon bandwagon and then receive the spoils of office.) The prospect of patronage, no doubt, seduced some New Rightists to vote for a winner in Richard Nixon. Indeed as M. Stanton Evans observed, the Nixon camp at the 1968 G.O.P. National Convention in Miami Beach "used the hope of patronage as a powerful persuader." 50/

Therefore, the New Right found several perfectly satisfactory ways to rationalize its decision to vote for Richard Nixon at the 1968 Republican National Convention. Of course, the New Right could live with Richard Nixon heading the G.O.P. ticket. After all, the Radical Right had supported him, albeit unenthusiastically, back in 1960 against Democrat John F. Kennedy. Nevertheless, the New Right certainly did not work day and night for eight long, frustrating years between 1960 and 1968 in order to award Richard Nixon the G.O.P. Presidential Nomination once more. Granted, the New Right could always tolerate Nixon, but the former Vice President looked quite pale besides the electrifying Ronald Reagan who embodied their Movement par

---

*Note—A reference to the 1962 Governor's race in California where the former Vice President barely lost to Democratic incumbent Edmund G. "Pat" Brown in part because many angry New Rightists in the Republican Party refused to vote for Nixon. (See the full account of the 1962 California Gubernatorial Election previously mentioned in this chapter.)

excellence. What then really prevented the New Right from simply mobilizing its majority strength at Miami Beach and selecting the charismatic California Governor as the 1968 Republican Party Nominee?

The true explanation for the New Right's action at Miami Beach involves the complicated political situation existing between the rival ideological factions at the 1968 Republican National Convention. To set the stage, Ronald Reagan commanded the G.O.P. Right, Richard Nixon held the G.O.P. Middle, while New York Governor Nelson Rockefeller occupied the G.O.P. Left.

The front-runner Richard Nixon's shaky base of support consisted, in large part, of restless New Rightists who threatened to stampede to Ronald Reagan at a moment's notice. Such a sudden shift towards the California Governor would simultaneously destroy Richard Nixon's position in the Center, thus creating a temporary power vacuum in the G.O.P. Middle. Nelson Rockefeller might then quickly slip into the vacant Center and take the Presidential Nomination. Thus the political collapse of Richard Nixon might produce a Rockefeller, rather than a Reagan victory.

Consequently, the alarming prospect of the hated kingpin of the Eastern Liberal Establishment, Nelson Rockefeller, winning the Grand Prize itself, frightened the New Right. As National Review Publisher William A. Rusher pointed out, the Nixon camp skillfully exploited this fear to prop up Nixon's faltering candidacy: "Nixon's own lieutenants were busy strumming this same tune to susceptible conservatives: Rockefeller will get you if you don't watch out !" In a similar fashion, author Gary Allen outlined how the specter of Nelson Rockefeller played a key role in the Nixon strategy: "Nixon had to have an enemy on the Left to make him a salable commodity to the conservatives.... [for] if Nelson Rockefeller came out against Hell, many conservatives would begin to find redeeming qualities in Satan."51/

Objectively, New York Governor Nelson Rockefeller never possessed sufficient delegate strength at the 1968 Miami Beach Convention to capture the G.O.P. Presidential Nomination; but then neither did General Dwight D. Eisenhower, for that matter, appear to have enough votes back in 1952 in Chicago. Yet the Eastern Liberal Establishment somehow took the prize from Ohio Senator Robert Taft anyway. (See Chapter Two.) So prominent New Rightists, including J. Strom Thurmond, feared another such Eastern Liberal Establishment victory at Miami Beach in 1968.52/

Basically, the New Right's momentous decision to vote for Nixon boiled down to one central point: in order to nominate Ronald Reagan, the New Right had to take a dangerous gamble. For Ronald Reagan could gain delegate support only at the expense of Richard Nixon and such a strategy might backfire, thus paving the way for Nelson

Rockefeller. In the end, the New Right, once-burned-twice-shy, chose to play safe and stick with Nixon. The devoted members of the New Right had not abandoned their political convictions, but with the traumatic memories of Chicago-1952 embedded deep within their minds it is small wonder that the New Rightists at Miami Beach in 1968 simply lost their nerve?

Richard Nixon vs. George Wallace

The New Right heartily applauded Richard Nixon's performance at the 1968 Miami Beach Convention. The newly crowned G.O.P. Presidential Nominee picked Maryland Governor Spiro T. Agnew, an outspoken (though relatively recent) advocate of domestic "law and order" as his Vice Presidential running-mate. In the process of selecting Spiro Agnew, Nixon passed over the Eastern Liberal Establishment's "glamour boys," New York Mayor John Lindsay and Illinois Senator Charles Percy. Furthermore, Nixon pleased the New Right with his tough acceptance speech at the Convention. Human Events described Nixon's address as "masterful..., hard hitting and inspirational," while dealing "with almost all the issues that concern conservatives." Thus "Whatever his past failings, former Vice President Nixon has gotten the Republican party off to a sound start." Likewise, Frank S. Meyer characterized Nixon's Address as "firm in content and a fitting challenge to Liberalism in tone." Meyer happily observed "a very different Nixon from the always cautious often trimming, Nixon of 1960." Therefore, "if the rest of the campaign is conducted on this level, conservatives can support the Republican ticket with confidence."53/

Without question, Republican Presidential Nominee Richard Nixon felt considerable pressure on his Right flank from American Independent Party Candidate George Wallace. Both politicians competed for the New Right votes, especially in the Southern states. Indeed by the end of the campaign Nixon's rhetoric sounded virtually indistinguishable from George Wallace. As Gary Allen noted, "There was hardly a dime's worth of difference between a Nixon campaign speech and a Wallace campaign speech, except for Wallace's more colorful colloquialisms." Dan Smoot echoed the same thoughts: "Perceiving the enormous popular appeal of Wallace's stand on law and order, on local control of local institutions, on the bussing of school children, on the Supreme Court--Richard Nixon, during the last two weeks before election, sounded almost exactly like George Wallace."54/

Meanwhile, Richard Nixon received an unexpected boost early in October, 1968 when George Wallace's third-party candidacy conveniently self-destructed. Retired Air Force General Curtis Le May, the Vice Presidential running-mate on Wallace's A.I.P. ticket, committed the same disastrous blunder which had ruined Barry Goldwater back in 1964 by talking fast and loose about nuclear weapons.55/ (See Chapter Nine)

The selection of Hubert Humphrey by the Democratic National Convention in August, 1968 also hurt George Wallace's Presidential prospects throughout the South. For the Nixon camp cleverly spread the message that any support for George Wallace, by siphoning off strength from Richard Nixon, would ultimately help the Liberal Democrat Hubert Humphrey capture the White House. In the words of Barry Goldwater, "a vote for Wallace that otherwise would have gone to Dick Nixon profits only one person—our old friend Hubert Horatio Humphrey. Is that what you really want?"56/

Moreover, a vote for George Wallace represented a futile, unconstructive protest, since the flamboyant Alabama Governor could not possibly win. J. Strom Thurmond described to his fellow South Carolinians how "your ultimate choice will be between Republican Richard Nixon and Democrat Hubert Humphrey because a Third Party candidate cannot be elected." Along the same lines, Barry Goldwater wrote "that Governor Wallace has absolutely no chance to be elected President of the United States." Goldwater lamented that "some conservatives are thinking of...voting for George Wallace." The Arizonan pleaded with the New Right not to "make the mistake of thinking that such a vote is going anywhere but right down a rathole."57/

In the end, the vast majority of New Rightists outside the Deep South decided to endorse the once-hated, but now-respected, Richard M. Nixon for the Presidency of the United States over George C. Wallace. As Human Events announced, "We are under no delusion that Nixon is a perfect conservative. Nor do we believe that a Nixon Administration will be a flawless model of constitutional government....Nevertheless, Nixon appears to us to be the best conservative candidate on the horizon." And after urging the members of the New Right to cast their ballots for Richard Nixon, William F. Buckley, Jr. added, "So then, let us hope. For the best."58/

"Nixon was the One"

Republican Richard Nixon captured the White House on November 5, 1968 with a narrow half-million vote plurality over Democrat Hubert Humphrey. (Nixon received 43.4% while Humphrey received 42.7%. The American Independent Candidate George Wallace polled 13.5% of the nation's vote.) So despite Richard Nixon's slender margin of victory over Hubert Humphrey the American public, in the eyes of the New Right, had loudly voiced its displeasure with the direction of Democratic Party Liberalism. M. Stanton Evans pointed out that 57% of the country's electorate supported the "two candidates, President-elect Nixon and former Governor George Wallace, who represented a repudiation of the Liberal position from different perspectives." Thus the Manion Forum Network called the results a "Landslide Against Liberalism." Similarly, the Economic Council Letter gloated that the election "was a colossal vote of repudiation" against Democratic Party Liberalism.59/

The New Right seemed quite satisfied with Richard Nixon's victory, although the members of the Movement realized that Nixon's personal triumph did not mean a complete triumph for their political philosophy. As the National Review observed, "Richard Nixon has, thus, a clear mandate from the nation. And it is a conservative mandate. Not 'extreme right wing', or even clearcut unmixed conservative perhaps, but undeniably from the conservative side of the spectrum."60/

Nonetheless, the hopeful New Right saw the election of Richard Nixon in November, 1968, as, possibly, the start of an exciting, new era of Conservatism in America. Accordingly, Human Events predicted that "the Nixon victory still could turn into a major triumph for conservatism." M. Stanton Evans struck the same note of optimism: "with the Nixon victory and the big Wallace vote there is a very large opening to the Right in our politics, with a chance for Nixon to change the direction and the momentum of American politics.... So, in the Presidential arena I think that this was, indeed, a victory for Conservatism."61/

Furthermore, the New Right definitely intended to keep a close watch upon the Nixon Administration. The Movement expected newly-elected President Richard Nixon to remember his obligations to his New Right supporters and to fulfill his campaign pledges. As Human Events announced, "this is no time for conservatives to relax or become complacent." Instead, "now is the time for us to increase our vigilance and make sure that campaign promises do not evaporate into campaign oratory."62/

Finally, many New Rightists felt a trifle uneasy since, as the National Review Bulletin remarked, "we do not have, in advance, a very clear idea of what a Nixon Administration is going to be like." However, Nixon owed his nomination and election to the New Right. Consequently, the new President had to steer a firm starboard course, or did he? A disturbing thought flashed through minds of New Rightists everywhere: would Richard Nixon actually betray the New Right and conduct a Moderate, Internationalist Administration once safely installed at 1600 Pennsylvania Avenue? The Liberty Letter examined the possibility but incredulously dismissed such a swindle:

> we can't believe that Nixon would pull such a double-cross on his Conservative supporters. Surely, the Conservatives who supported Nixon must have some solid reasons for doing so. We've taken the Conservatives who supported Nixon at their word that Nixon was the One.63/

CHAPTER TWELVE - Notes

1. Phyllis Schlafly and Admiral Chester Ward, The Betrayers (Alton, Illinois: Pere Marquette Press, 1968), p. 5;
National Review, (September 24, 1968), p. 977.

2. "On the Right", January 13, 1968.

3. Schlafly, Safe-Not Sorry, p. 6.

4. National Program Letter, (July, 1968), p. 2;
Schlafly, Safe-Not Sorry, p. 6.

5. Christian Economics, (February 20, 1968), pp. 1-2;
Medford Evans, The Usurpers (Boston: Western Islands Publishers, 1968), p. 7.

6. National Review (May 7, 1968), p. 453;
National Review Bulletin, (April 16, 1968), p. B59.

7. Hunter, Our Second Revolution, p. 142.

8. Medford Evans, The Usurpers, p. 1;
Schlafly and Ward, The Betrayers, p. 6;
J. Strom Thurmond, The Faith We Have Not Kept (San Diego, California: Viewpoint Books, 1968), p. 54.

9. Medford Evans, The Usurpers, p. 6;
Thurmond, The Faith We Have Not Kept, p. 54.

10. "On the Right," January 30, 1968.

11. American Opinion, (October, 1968), p. 68.

12. National Review, (May 21, 1968), p. 480;
Ibid., (March 26, 1968), p. 283.

13. Report of the National Advisory Commission on Civil Disorders commissioned by the U.S. National Advisory Commission on Civil Disorders (New York: Bantam Books, 1968);
Ibid., p. 2;
Ibid., p. 1.

14. National Review Bulletin (March 19, 1968), p. B41; National Review, (March 26, 1968), p. 284.

15. National Review (March 26, 1968), p. 283.
16. American Opinion, (February, 1968), p. 40;
National Review, (August 27, 1968), p. 848;
Ibid., (April 23, 1968), p. 414.

17. National Review, (April 9, 1968), p. 337.

18. Ibid., (August 13, 1968), p. 771;
Ibid., (April 23, 1968), p. 379.

19. American Mercury, (Summer, 1968), p. 3;
Synon, ed., George Wallace: Profile of a Presidential Candidate, p. 133.

20. Fiery Cross, (November, 1968), p. 39;
Human Events, (October 19, 1968), p. 9;
American Mercury, (Summer, 1968), p. 3;
Common Sense, (September 15, 1968), p. 3;
Cross and the Flag, (June, 1968), p. 7;
American Opinion, (September, 1968), p. 70;
Dan Smoot Report, (November 4, 1968), p. 180.

21. National Review Bulletin (June 11, 1968), p. B89;
National Review, (November 19, 1968), p. 1170.

22. National Review, (October 22, 1968), p. 1048;
Ibid., p. 1060.

23. Ibid., (May 16, 1967), p. 527;
Hunter, Our Second Revolution, p. 147.

24. National Review, (April 21, 1964), p. 319.

25. Goldwater, The Conscience of a Majority, p. 44;
National Review Bulletin, (August 20, 1968), p. B129;
National Review, (November 14, 1967), p. 1267.

26. Personal recollection from the 1962 Campaign;
National Review, (July 31, 1962), p. 49.

27. William F. Buckley, Jr., The Governor Listeth (New York: G.P.
Putnam's Sons, 1970), p. 28;
National Review, (November 14, 1967), p. 1273.

28. See Edwin McDowell, National Review (December 31, 1962),
p. 511;
National Review Bulletin, (November 27, 1962), p. 2.

29. Nick Thimmesch, The Condition of Republicanism (New York:
W.W. Norton & Company, Inc., 1968), pp. 86-87.

30. Donovan, The Future of the Republican Party, p. 68.

31. Hess and Broder, The Republican Establishment, p. 172;
National Review, (December 3, 1968), p. 1206.

32. National Review, (September 6, 1966), p. 867.

33. Evans, The Future of Conservatism, p. 165;
Ibid., p. 162.

34. Ibid., p. 165.

35. Jules Witcover, The Resurrection of Richard Nixon (New York: G.P. Putnam's Sons, 1970), p. 311.

36. Three excellent accounts of how and why Richard Nixon defeated Ronald Reagan for the 1968 G.O.P. Presidential Nomination are: William A. Rusher, "What Happened at Miami Beach?," National Review, (December 3, 1968), p. 1206; Jules Witcover, The Resurrection of Richard Nixon (New York: G.P. Putnam's Sons, 1970); Garry Wills, Nixon Agonistes (Boston: Houghton, Mifflin Company, 1970).

37. Wills, Nixon Agonistes, p.256.

38. Conversation with Bill Boyarsky, August 23, 1976.

39. White, The Making of the President 1968, p. 136.

40. National Review, (December 3, 1968), p. 1206.

41. Human Events, (August 17, 1968), p. 3; National Review Bulletin, (September 3, 1968), p. B142.

42. White, The Making of the President 1968, Appendix B, p. 440.

43. Witcover, The Resurrection of Richard Nixon, p. 309; National Review, (December 3, 1968), p. 1209; Human Events, (August 17, 1968), p. 3.

44. Wills, Nixon Agonistes, p. 256; Goldwater disclosed that he spoke personally with a number of the delegates at the request of Nixon. The impact was considerable: "A survey of those who attended as delegates to the Republican Convention in 1968 made by an independent research group after the convention revealed that 20.7 percent of the delegates said they were influenced to vote for Nixon as a result of their meetings with me those two days." Goldwater, With No Apologies, p. 207.

45. William F. Buckley, Jr. as quoted in Cannon, Ronnie and Jesse, p. 275.

46. New Guard, (Summer, 1968), p. 11; Dan Smoot Report, (August 26, 1968), p. 138.

47. New Guard, (Summer, 1968), p. 11;

Human Events, (August 17, 1968), p. 1;
Schlafly and Ward, The Betrayers, p. 120.

48. National Review, (August 27, 1968), p. 838;
Ibid., (November 5, 1968), p. 1097.

49. Human Events, (October 19, 1968), p. 7;
Charles Lam Markham, The Buckleys (New York: William Morrow & Company, Inc., 1973) p. 331.

50. Human Events, (October 19, 1968), p. 7;
Dan Smoot Report, (August 26, 1968), p. 138.

51. National Review, (December 3, 1968), p. 1208;
American Opinion, (October, 1968), p. 67.

52. National Review, (December 3, 1968), p. 1209.

53. Human Events, (August 17, 1968), p. 1;
Ibid., p. 4;
National Review, (August 27, 1968), p. 859.

54. Gary Allen, Richard Nixon: The Man Behind the Mask (Boston: Western Islands, 1971), p. 45;
Dan Smoot Report, (November 18, 1968), p. 187.

55. See Witcover, The Resurrection of Richard Nixon, pp. 412-413 for a complete account of General Le May's impolitic statements.

56. National Review, (October 22, 1968), p. 1061.

57. Human Events, (October 5, 1968), p. 5;
National Review, (October 22, 1968), p. 1061;
Ibid., p. 1060.

58. Human Events, (October 19, 1968), p. 7;
National Review, (November 5, 1968), p. 1098.

59. Manion Forum Network broadcast, (November 17, 1968);
Economic Council Letter, (November 15, 1968), p. 1.

60. National Review, (November 19, 1968), p. 1150.

61. Human Events, (November 16, 1968), p. 1;
Manion Forum Network broadcast, (November 17, 1968).

62. Human Events, (November 16, 1968), p. 4.

63. National Review Bulletin, (December 24, 1968), p. B201;
Liberty Letter, (December, 1968), p. 2.

EPILOGUE, 1969–1980

CHAPTER THIRTEEN

THE LEAN YEARS, 1969-1977

The Frustration of the Nixon Era

Richard M. Nixon took the Presidential Oath of Office on January 20, 1969 after having pulled off one of the most remarkable political swindles of the twentieth century—a swindle which, to this very day, few New Rightists will acknowledge openly. For to admit that they had been royally duped by their old nemesis Richard Nixon would raise serious doubts regarding the soundness of the New Right's political judgments, and, incidentally, of their perception of people's character. But deep in their hearts most New Rightists eventually came to the sad realization that back in 1968 they had let slip a golden opportunity to turn the country in a truly starboard direction.

At any rate, the fear of completely alienating Nixon (and thus losing what little influence they still possessed) kept most New Rightists squarely in line behind the new G.O.P. President. Nevertheless, there can be no question that Nixon's entire tenure in office (1969-1974) greatly disappointed the New Right since his middle-of-the-road, Internationalist Administration resembled, in its basic contours, the frustrating Eisenhower Administration of the 1950's. (See Chapter Two.) Indeed the well-publicized marriage of Nixon's youngest daughter Julie with Dwight Eisenhower's grandson David merely served to underscore the striking parallel between both Republican Administrations.

In domestic affairs, despite frequent flourishes of lofty, New Rightist rhetoric (often furnished by Nixon's mouthpiece, Vice President Spiro T. Agnew) the Nixon Administration quietly permitted the "Great Society" legislation of the Kennedy–Johnson Era to remain essentially intact. Moreover, much to the New Right's distress, the American welfare state continued its expansion under the Nixon Regime. Federal spending for social programs increased dramatically, as did the size of the Government's budgetary deficits, and ultimately the inflation rate. Moreover, the President asked Congress to establish a National Health Care System in January, 1971, imposed wage and price controls in the summer of that same year, and, concurrently, devalued the United States dollar. In retrospect, a disgruntled Barry Goldwater observed that "Richard Nixon ran [in 1968] as the conservative, oppposed to increased federal spending and deficit financing. Then he embraced the policy of Lord Keynes and increased both the spending and the deficit."1/

In foreign affairs, a protege of none other than the hated Nelson Rockefeller, Dr. Henry Kissinger, quickly out-maneuvered Richard Allen, a New Rightists who had served on Nixon's 1968 Presidential

Campaign Staff, to become the Administration's dominant personality. (Richard Allen would resurface once again in 1980, first as then-Presidential candidate Ronald Reagan's Foreign Policy Advisor, and subsequently as President Reagan's National Security Advisor.) In any event, the ascendancy of Kissinger after 1969 clearly indicated to the New Right that in the realm of foreign affairs Nixon had decided to cast his lot with the Eastern Liberal Establishment.2/

Three years later Nixon infuriated New Rightists everywhere by journeying first to Red China in February, 1972 and then to the Soviet Union in May. The mere presence of an American President in Peking signified to the world that the United States was prepared, at long last, to recognized the legitimacy of the Chinese Communist Revolution. And if such a prospect by itself wasn't bad enough, the New Right foresaw the day when America's new friendship with Red China would require the severing of U.S. diplomatic relations with Taiwan, or perhaps even the outright liquidation of the New Right's beloved, anti-Communist regime on Formosa. No wonder the appalling spectacle of Richard Nixon toasting to Chairman Mao's health provoked a caustic comment from California G.O.P. Congressman John Schmitz (soon to become the American Independent Party's 1972 Presidential Nominee): "I have no objection whatsoever to Nixon going to Red China. I'm just sorry that he's ever coming back!"3/

Moreover, three months later the Moscow Summit Meeting witnessed the signing of an historic Strategic Arms Limitation Treaty (S.A.L.T. I) wherein the United States, to the distress of the New Right, officially abandoned any further quest for clearcut military "superiority" vis-a-vis the Soviet Union. Henceforth, the U.S. would be content to maintain mere "parity" or "rough equivalency." In the New Right's eyes, the S.A.L.T. I Agreement represented yet another tragic step in America's three-decade-long "retreat from victory." (See Chapter Five)

The Nixon Administration's continuing conduct of a limited, no-win war in Southeast Asia also greatly frustrated the New Right. By the Spring of 1972 the President had managed to withdraw the bulk of American combat forces, and although the actual conclusion of a peace agreement with North Vietnam was delayed until January, 1973, as far as the New Right was concerned the handwriting was already on the wall. For Nixon's avowed goal of "Peace with honor" amounted to little more than a face-saving gesture designed to allow the United States to extricate herself completely before her client state, South Vietnam, eventually collapsed. Thus the New Right was distraught, but hardly surprised when, two years later under Nixon's successor Gerald Ford (after what author Frank Snepp has cynically described as a "Decent Interval"), Saigon fell before the final Communist onslaught.4/

In order to dramatize the New Right's growing disenchantment with the overall thrust of the Nixon Administration, Ohio G.O.P.

Congressman John M. Ashbrook entered several Republican Presidential primaries against Nixon during the spring of 1972. Ashbrook, who as a young attorney back in 1961 had played an instrumental role in the early stages of the "Draft Goldwater" Movement (See Chapter Eight) and who had later served as National Chairman of the American Conservative Union, took issue with Nixon's foreign and domestic policies in a low-keyed, almost scholarly way. Yet Ashbrook's candidacy represented a purely symbolic challenge to the President's renomination since New Rightists had no real intention of deserting either the President or the G.O.P. in 1972, especially in light of the fact that the Democratic Party had seemingly fallen into the hands of the dreaded New Left Activists. (See Chapter Ten) Thus after defending his earlier support for John Ashbrook, columnist William F. Buckley, Jr. announced his intention to vote for Richard Nixon in November against New Left Democrat George McGovern because, compared with the incumbent President, "McGovern is a thousand times worse."5/

The Attempted Assassination of George Wallace

Alabama Governor George Wallace, after having run as the American Independent Party's Presidential candidate in 1968, had meanwhile returned to the Democratic fold by 1972 in order to make a second run for the White House under the Democratic banner. (Wallace had initially sought the Democratic Nomination back in 1964--See Chapter Seven.) This time around, Wallace hardly mentioned the Republican incumbent Richard Nixon, choosing instead to concentrate his fire upon his fellow Democrats Hubert Humphrey, George McGovern, Edmund Muskie, et al. Wallace did pull off a stunning victory in the March, 1972 Florida Primary where his strong stance against mandatory, court-ordered, school busing struck a receptive nerve among angry Democratic voters. However, two months later Wallace was seriously wounded and partially paralyzed by an assassin's bullet in Laurel, Maryland on the eve of that state's Presidential Primary contest. In the wake of the shooting, the outraged voters of both Maryland as well as Michigan (which held its Primary the same day) presented the Alabama Governor with his greatest national political triumph. Yet despite his victories in both Maryland and Michigan, Wallace ultimately proved incapable of stopping the New Left's candidate, George McGovern, from capturing the Democratic Presidential Nomination.

Wallace recovered sufficiently in time to attend the 1972 Democratic National Convention held in Miami Beach in July. Predictably, the Alabama Governor refused to endorse his party's standard bearer George McGovern. Yet Wallace also turned his back upon Republican Richard Nixon as well as upon American Independent Party Candidate John Schmitz, who had received the A.I.P. Nomination only after Wallace had declined the honor. Despite Wallace's refusal to support Nixon, the Alabama Governor's New Right Southern Redneck consitituency voted overwhelmingly for the President the November General Election. Thus Richard Nixon in 1972 carried the Wallace vote without the Governor's explicit blessing, just as Barry Goldwater had done back in 1964.

In retrospect, the shooting of George Wallace became the single, most significant event of the 1972 Presidential Campaign from the New Right's standpoint. For the Alabama Governor's crippling injury effectively served to eliminate him as a vigorous force in national politics. True enough, four years later Wallace made one last bid for the Democratic Presidential Nomination during the spring of 1976. But the once formidable campaigner was now but a shadow of his former self, and, accordingly, was clobbered in the primaries by Jimmy Carter. Afterwards, the Alabama Governor, in a desperate attempt to salvage what remained of his Southern political base, endorsed Carter for President, thereby forfeiting any further claim to the leadership of the New Right Movement.

In the long run, Ronald Reagan turned out to be the chief beneficiary of George Wallace's political demise. For without the fiery Alabama Governor siphoning off a good portion of the New Right's time, energy, money, and votes (as he had done in 1964, 1968, and again in 1972) Reagan could now mobilize the entire Movement behind himself. Indeed Reagan's near upset of incumbent Republican President Gerald Ford in 1976 was due, in large measure, to the fact that Reagan had by this time already inherited most of the ailing Alabama Governor's sizeable New Right constituency. Four years later, with Wallace removed completely from the picture, Reagan easily defeated his major rivals Howard Baker, George Bush, and John Connally for the 1980 G.O.P. Presidential Nomination, and then went on to score a smashing victory in November over Democrat Jimmy Carter.

The New Right and Watergate

The New Right reached its absolute nadir during the celebrated Watergate Scandal (1973-1974). In yet another fit of monumental political stupidity, most members of the New Right wound up staunchly defending Richard Nixon's innocence, and strenuously resisted any and all attempts to proceed with the impeachment of the obviously corrupt Chief Executive. Thus instead of expediently abandoning Nixon's sinking ship, like other smart politicians, New Rightists foolishly remained steadfastly loyal to the President until the bitter end. Once again for their misplaced devotion to Richard Nixon (of all people) New Rightists succeeded only in disgracing their own movement. (Perhaps, at times, the New Right has a secret death wish—what else could explain their incomprehensible conduct?)

300

Arizona Senator Barry Goldwater himself typified the New Right's masochistic attitude towards Richard Nixon. A strong defender of the President until the final hours, the Arizona Republican reluctantly came to the conclusion that Nixon must resign his office only after the White House Tapes disclosure of Monday, August 5, 1974 had proved beyond a shadow of a doubt that the President had been lying about his involvement in the Watergate Cover-up right from the beginning. When such truth was made public, an angry Goldwater informed the President's Chief of Staff General Alexander Haig that "I have been deceived by Richard Nixon for the last time." Goldwater added that "A majority of the Republicans in the Senate share my feelings."6/

That Goldwater should have come to such a realization at so late a point in time is a clear indication of his inability or unwillingness to protect his own personal interests, the interests of the G.O.P., or the interests of the New Right itself when dealing with the likes of Richard Nixon. This becomes especially difficult to understand when we learn from Goldwater (and I have no reason to doubt his confession) that he himself had never trusted Nixon all along ! As the outspoken Arizona lawmaker explained in his recently published memoirs:

> Throughout my years in public life I have always had reservations about Richard Nixon. Despite our long association, I never felt that I truly knew him. In the moments of tension and stress we shared, he always seemed to be too well programmed, to be carefully calculating the ultimate effect of everything he did or said.7/

In similar fashion, California Governor Ronald Reagan remained another last ditch supporter of the beleaguered President, although, by that late date, he too should have known better. Like Goldwater, Reagan stuck by Nixon up until the final hours when the incriminating disclosures on the White House Tapes made it well-nigh impossible for the President to continue in office. One wonders what thoughts must have been going through Ronald Reagan's mind a short while later as he watched Vice President Gerald Ford take the oath as the nation's new Chief Executive. For had the California Governor really been interested in running as Nixon's Vice President back in August, 1968, Reagan would surely have been selected instead of Spiro T. Agnew. (See Chapter Twelve.) The haunting knowledge that he, Reagan, could have been the one to succeed Nixon on Friday, August 9, 1974 (if only he had made a different choice back in 1968) probably played a signficant role in the aging California Governor's surprising decision to make yet another run for the White House, first in 1976, and then again in 1980.

Gerald Ford Assumes the Presidency

Gerald R. Ford, the United States' only non-elected President, assumed the nation's highest office on Friday, August 9, 1974. Basically, the New Right had nothing against the new Chief Executive, either politically or personally. Indeed, if anything, the New Right expected a Ford Administration to be a bit more Conservative than Richard Nixon's Administration had been. Of course, Ford was not a New Rightist by any stretch of the imagination. But as the G.O.P. House Minority Leader between 1965 and 1973, Ford had demonstrated an ability to work together harmoniously with the New Rightists on Capitol Hill. Clearly, as was the case with his predecessor Richard Nixon, the New Right could live quite comfortably with a man like Gerald Ford occupying the White House.

Yet within the span of a few short months the new President took a number of steps which drastically lowered his standing among New Rightists. First of all, Ford chose New York Governor Nelson Rockefeller to serve as his Vice President—and the reader can gather by now exactly how New Rightists felt towards their old, arch-enemy Nelson Rockefeller. (Just witness the New Right's suspicion regarding the Rockefeller-inspired Trilateral Commission which had been established in 1973.)

Moreover, the selection of Rockefeller, coupled with the increased influence of the Governor's protege, Secretary of State Henry Kissinger, signified to the New Right that the hated Eastern Liberal Establishment had gained the upper hand in the new Ford Administration, especially in the crucial realm of foreign policy. Indeed the new President appeared to need the services of a Kissinger to a far greater extent than had Richard Nixon since, in the New Right's opinion, the bumbling, inarticulate Gerald Ford seemed utterly incapable of fathoming the complexities of foreign affairs, let alone managing them all by himself.

Second, Ford quickly granted former-President Richard Nixon a full, unconditional pardon for any and all Watergate related crimes which he may have committed while in office. Of course, the New Right endorsed the Nixon pardon in principle. As California Governor Ronald Reagan explained, the former-Chief Executive had already "suffered enough" by virtue of the mere fact of having to resign from the world's most powerful position in disgrace. Yet while New Rightists were reluctant, as always, to criticize publicly anything associated with Nixon, they privately felt that Ford's timing of the pardon was "unfortunate," to say the very least. Two months later in the November, 1974 General Election the American voters, furious over Watergate, inflation, energy shortages, unemployment, recession, and now the Nixon pardon, handed the G.O.P. (and New Rightists in particular) a huge defeat—the worst suffered by the G.O.P. since the Goldwater debacle of

1964. (Republicans lost forty-nine House seats and five in the Senate.) Thus in the aftermath of the November, 1974 Election, the nation's various state legislatures, governors' mansions, and to an increasing degree the United States Congress itself, would soon be completely dominated by Democrats, many of them newly elected Liberals, who threatened to initiate another round of social reform legislation and welfare state expansion. Unwilling as usual to shoulder any part of the blame themselves for the election fiasco, New Rightists instead focused blame upon Gerald Ford, the man who, as President, was at least nominally responsible for the G.O.P. disaster.8/

Third, Ford (who had promised during his confirmation hearings as Vice President back in 1973 that should he somehow succeed to the Presidency, he would definitely not be a candidate for re-election in 1976) promptly changed his mind once installed in the White House, and decided to seek a second term after all. However, the unsatisfactory results of the November, 1974 General Election created the impression among New Rightists that the politically inept Gerald Ford would surely lose the upcoming 1976 Presidential Contest to any one of a number of Democrats, thereby removing the final obstacle from the path of a resurgent American Liberalism. On this ground alone, New Rightists opposed a Ford candidacy in 1976, even if California Governor Ronald Reagan had not intended to run. (And, as we all know, Reagan did, in fact, decide to run.)

The Challenges of the 1970's

Someone once remarked that as far as each particular American family was concerned, the decade of the 1950's really began whenever they purchased their first television set. If so, then the decade of the 1970's really began the moment when they could no longer find any gasoline for their family car. Such are the little incidents which, to the average citizen, herald the dawn of a new era.

The America of the early 1970's had been, more or less, an appendage to the turbulent, but prosperous 1960's. Thus the 1972 Nixon-McGovern Presidential Election was still fought within the old framework of 1960's politics, with the issues of Vietnam and the satisfaction of pent-up minority group grievances dominating the campaign. True enough, the United States had slipped into a mild recession in 1970-71. But 1960's style prosperity had apparently returned in full force by 1972. However, the year 1973 ushered in a whole new set of economic problems which, henceforth, would occupy the nation's attention for the remainder of the decade. Indeed these new economic issues would finally serve to give the 1970's its own distinctive flavor.

These economic shocks of 1973-74 (which included the Beef Shortage, the Energy Crisis, the Arab Oil Embargo, and Double-Digit Inflation, followed by the worst business slump since the Great Depression) reawakened the New Right from the complacency of the Nixon Years. The New Right realized that post-Vietnam America had suddenly found herself in very deep economic trouble.

The Beef Shortage

The initial shock to jolt the nation, for want of a better name, was called the "Beef Shortage." During the Summer months of 1973, New Rightists, along with other Americans, noticed that beef had begun disappearing from supermarket freezer cases all across the nation. This annoying development provided the public, in the opinion of the New Right, with a dramatic lesson in the workings of the free market economy. In fact, the Beef Shortage would simply serve as a preview to the Energy Crisis later that year. For our purposes, both events deserve a closer examination since they went a long ways towards restoring the American people's confidence in the free market which eventually proved to be a great boon for the New Right's political fortunes.

By way of brief background to the Beef Shortage, G.O.P. President Richard Nixon had imposed a ninety-day wage and price freeze during August, 1971 to be followed by an indefinite period of active government wage and price "restraint." Although New Rightists deferred as usual to Nixon on the issue, they hardly hid their displeasure with the freeze since philosophically they opposed the government tampering with the free marketplace. In their eyes, the laws of supply and demand, not Presidential fiat, should determine the level of wages and prices. However, New Rightists also realized that the President had come under tremendous political pressure to "do something" about inflation. And unless the inflation rate subsided somewhat and the nation's economy began moving again, the American voters might well remove the Nixon Administration from power in the upcoming November, 1972 Presidential Election. Such an alarming prospect genuinely frightened New Rightists, who still viewed a Republican like Nixon (with all his faults) as infinitely better than a Democrat like, say, Hubert Humphrey, Edmund Muskie, or George McGovern. The deleterious effects of a wage-price freeze would no doubt eventually surface, but hopefully only after the November, 1972 Presidential Contest had safely passed.

This was precisely what happened. After Nixon's November, 1972 re-election had safely passed, the deleterious effects of the wage-price guidelines began to appear. For instance, the nation's cattlemen, unable to pass along spiraling feed costs on to the consumer in the form of higher wholesale beef prices, simply refused to bring their livestock to slaughter. Thus by the Summer of 1973 sirloin steak had become as

304

scarce as gasoline was to become six months later. By their actions the nation's cattlemen (many of whom, incidentally, were New Rightists themselves) taught the American public a powerful lesson—a lesson which the country had nearly forgotten during the prosperous 1960's— that in a free enterprise system economic activity (whether it be livestock raising, oil exploration, or whatever) will not take place without adequate financial incentives. Indeed a lifetime's worth of New Right pamphlets and sermons warning about the terrible consequences of government interference in the marketplace could never have made the same impact upon the American people as did a single month without beef on their dinnertables.

The Energy Crisis

The American public learned yet another bitter lesson the following Winter of 1973-74 when the Energy Crisis finally shattered the economic optimism inherited from the comfortable 1960's. Now at last the grim realities of the 1970's began to sink in. For even without the temporary Arab Oil Embargo (a direct result of the October, 1973 Arab-Israeli War) a severe Energy Crisis was in the offing. America's own domestic production of oil, natural gas, coal, and nuclear power had long been hampered by numerous government imposed restrictions. New Rightists were keenly sensitive to this problem since energy producers were among the New Right's strongest political supporters, especially in the Southern and Western states. For instance, New Rightists were well aware that in an attempt to please consumers (particularly those in the energy-poor Northeastern states) the Federal Government had long controlled oil and natural gas prices at an artificially low level, which removed the financial incentives to develop new fields. Moreover, the Federal and State Governments, responding to pressures from Liberal Environmentalists, had imposed various restrictions which, combined with the government's usual penchant for red tape, had delayed important construction projects such as the Alaska Oil Pipeline, had shackled the American coal industry, and had impeded the building of nuclear power plants—a source of energy greatly favored by New Rightists.

At any rate, America's smoldering Energy Crisis was brought to a head as a result of the October, 1973 Arab Oil Embargo. The major oil producing nations operating through O.P.E.C. (Organization of Petro-leum Exporting Countries) took advantage of the situation to raise the world's oil prices enormously, thereby altering permanently the tradi-tional economic relationship between the advanced nations and the underdeveloped states. For by boosting oil prices, the Third World Nations gave notice that they would no longer continue subsidizing, in effect, the industrialized nations such as the United States with cheap raw materials. Henceforth, America's prosperity at home would never again be purchased at the expense of the underdeveloped world. This transformation amounted to a virtual "International Economic Revolution"—an historic event which had a profound effect upon the American people's attitudes towards their country's future economic policy.

The International Economic Revolution 1973-74

The International Economic Revolution of 1973-74 did serve to weaken substantially the American public's long-standing commitment to an Internationalist economic policy. Indeed, since the Second World War, the United States (under the leadership of the Eastern Liberal Establishment wings of both major political parties) had operated under the assumption that the country's prosperity was dependent upon prosperity abroad. This line of thinking led to the 1944 Bretton Woods Agreement, which established the International Monetary Fund and the World Bank; the 1947 Marshall Plan to rebuild war-ravaged Europe; Truman's 1949 "Point Four" Program, Kennedy's 1961 Alliance for Progress, and the various other U.S. foreign aid programs; the 1962 Trade Expansion Act, which led to the productive "Kennedy Round" of negotiations designed to lower tariffs; as well as sporadic efforts to establish closer commercial ties with even our Communist adversaries.

As late as August, 1971, at a time when the American people's attachment to an Internationalist economic policy had begun to waver, President Richard Nixon had still felt compelled to reaffirm his dedication to the principle of economic internationalism. Thus while in the process of suspending the convertibility of U.S. dollars into gold (leading to the dollar's subsequent devaluation), Nixon pledged to seek a new, more workable international monetary arrangement to replace the obsolete Bretton Woods system. And while slapping a temporary, 10-percent surcharge on imported manufactured products (directed mainly against Japan) the President made a point of extolling the virtues of "free trade."

However, it seems safe to say that the New Right has never enthusiastically supported America's internationalist economic policy. For as old-fashioned Economic Nationalists at heart, New Rightists strongly believe that America's prosperity begins and ends at home. In short, the nation must always rely upon her own economic strength. As a matter of fact, the New Right's economic philosophy resembles William McKinley's 1896 Republican Party Platform, favoring as it does a high protective tariff for American industry, as well as a sound U.S. dollar fully convertible into gold both domestically and internationally.*

---

*Note—Back in Chapter Five, I mentioned that the New Right's economic philosophy reflects pure nineteenth century "Laissez-Faire"— but a distinctly American version, not to be confused with the British (Continued)

Furthermore, in keeping with their philosophy of Economic Nationalism, the New Right opposed the U.S. Foreign Aid Program since (in addition to their numerous other objections outlined in Chapter Six) a much more efficient way of promoting domestic prosperity would be simply to cut taxes, which would otherwise have gone for Foreign Aid, thereby furnishing U.S. business with extra capital to invest at home. Under this arrangement, economic benefits would first accrue to the business class, and from there would then "trickle down" to the rest of American society, thus creating a broadly based prosperity.

Finally, while New Rightists certainly had nothing against foreign trade per se, they strenuously objected to any government policy predicated upon the idea that America's prosperity should be dependent upon it. For as Economic Nationalists the member of the New Right understood that governments might properly employ tariffs and import quotas as effective weapons when dealing with other nations. And despite the economic benefits which would surely accrue to the United States as a result of "free trade" with the Communist Bloc, New Rightists long favored a complete embargo on all commerce with Communist nations, even though such a policy would wind up denying U.S. businessmen access to a full third of the Earth's population!

At any rate, the International Economic Revolution of 1973-74 served to legitimize the New Right's Economic Nationalism as a plausible alternative to the Eastern Liberal Establishment's three-decade-old policy of Internationalism. And as we shall see in the following chapter, the American people's renewed interest in Economic Nationalism and self-sufficiency played a key role in the New Right's resurgence during the late 1970's, culminating in the election of Ronald Reagan to the White House in November, 1980.

Double-Digit Inflation

Meanwhile, the fiscal situation in Washington, D.C. went from bad to worse. After 1973 the Federal Government, in essence, gave up any pretense of trying to run a tight ship. The Federal Budget now became permanently unbalanced. And the unhealthy combination of huge Government deficits and the sudden O.P.E.C. oil price increases touched off double-digit inflation by 1974. The New Right watched with anger as the Federal Government refused to scale down spending to match tax revenues in order to achieve a balanced budget. Rather, the Government simply borrowed ever increasing sums of money to cover

---

variety. The New Right's idea of "free enterprise" is strongly nationalistic, and jingoistic, in direct contrast with the internationalism, pacifism, and anti-imperialism of the so-called "Manchester School" of Free Trade economics.

current expenses, thereby adding to the already astronomical National Debt, while, in effect, raising taxes by permitting unchecked inflation to push citizens into higher tax brackets with no relief forthcoming.

The American Economy of the 1970's found itself caught in the grip of a vicious cycle. The basic underlying inflation would sooner or later evoke a tight-money response from the Federal Reserve Board, which, in turn, would slow business activity bringing on a recession, which would then be alleviated by a new round of government spending, and so forth. This was the pattern for the Recessions of 1970-71, 1974-75, and 1980-81. And instead of peaks of prosperity sandwiched in between the valleys of recession, the U.S. Economy was saddled with a curious affliction which came to be known as "stagflation"—that is, chronic inflation coupled with high unemployment and little or no real economic growth. Moreover, with taxes too high, government red tape and regulations too burdensome, and the business climate too uncertain, speculation and inflation hedging became much more profitable than good old-fashioned work or honest, job producing investment.

Ironically, back in 1964 G.O.P. Presidential Nominee Barry Goldwater had warned against the evil consequences of inflation. But it had seemed curiously out of place for the Arizona Senator to have discussed such a "quaint" topic at a time when America was enjoying what appeared to have been permanent, non-inflationary prosperity. If fact, when Goldwater had mentioned inflation most young Americans barely knew what he was referring to, since to them inflation was something they had read about in high school history textbooks which described how the citizens of Weimar Germany had carted around stacks of worthless paper money in wheelbarrows just to buy a loaf of bread. And even the great majority of their elders (bolstered by the experience of World War Two and Korea) had assumed that American-style inflation could only be the result of consumer product shortages on the home front during wartime and immediately afterwards. The relatively mild inflation of the Vietnam War Era (1965-73) merely served to reinforce this belief.

Furthermore, the majority of the American people had come to believe that, if worse came to worse, the Federal Government could simply "prohibit" inflation. The effective World War Two Wage and Price Freeze seemed to furnish a case in point. Yet New Rightists thought otherwise. The nation's World War Two Wage and Price Controls had proved effective, not necessarily because such action constituted sound economics, but rather because the American people, recognizing the gravity of the situation, had patriotically agreed to work for less money than they might have ordinarily commanded. In short, economic activity had continued to take place, despite the burden of controls, because the American people were more than willing to help subsidize the War effort. But as I discussed earlier, under the normal economic conditions of the 1970's, America's cattlemen, for instance, saw no compelling reason (patriotic or otherwise) to help subsidize the American consumer by producing beef at an artificially low price.

The persistent post-Vietnam War inflation came as an unpleasant surprise to many Americans who had hitherto more or less assumed that the problem would eventually subside once the nation's participation in the conflict had finally ended. Now however, by 1973 America's role in Vietnam was over, yet inflation began increasing. Worst of all, the Beef Shortage clearly indicated that the usual, last ditch remedy for inflation—i.e., wage and price controls—simply no longer worked. The American people arrived at the realization after 1973 that inflation could not be solved merely by government edict.

Consequently, after 1973 the American public began rethinking the entire question of inflation, while the main culprit in this mess, the Federal Government itself, attempted to obfuscate the matter as always. Thus there followed the predictable search for the "causes" of inflation. In due course, the O.P.E.C. oil producers, the "excessive" union wage settlements in basic industries, the poor productivity rate among U.S. workers, even the bad weather (which led to crop failures) were singled out as possible scapegoats, both by the Federal Government as well as by its allies in the Eastern Liberal Establishment-oriented National News Media.

Ultimately though, the American public began discovering the best kept secret in Washington — that the dubious financial practices of the Federal Government constituted the true, underlying "cause" of inflation. For Uncle Sam had long been flooding the country with fiat money so as to give the nation's economy the appearance of growth when, in fact, little or no growth was occurring, so as to enable the politicians to satisfy the numerous powerful special interest constituencies demanding increased levels of government spending for their own pet projects, and so as to permit the politicians to avoid an unpopular (but necessary) "official" tax increase by simply allowing inflation to push citizens into higher tax brackets.

New York City's Bankruptcy

The heretofore virtually unthinkable suggestion that Uncle Sam might well be engaging in unsound, perhaps even highly dubious financial practices, gained credence in 1975 when New York City went "bankrupt." The American people learned the truth that the citadel of the Eastern Liberal Establishment had borrowed and spent itself into insolvency, all the while hiding its shady financial dealings from the public as well as from investors, and then when the City's neat little pyramid scheme finally collapsed had tried to lay the blame elsewhere. And if the Eastern Liberal Establishment had done that to New York City (with the connivance, of course, of its political allies, the Democratic Party

309

Machine and the public employee unions) then Washington D.C. was hardly safe as long as it remained firmly within its clutches.9/

Oddly enough, once again it had been an outspoken New Rightist, this time William F. Buckley, Jr., who, when he ran unsuccessfully for Mayor of New York back in 1965, had predicted that the City's unsavory financial practices would one day lead to disaster. However, Buckley, like Goldwater, had been little more than a Cassandra—a prophet whose warnings repeatedly went unheeded. As a matter of fact, a decade later when New York City tottered on the verge of financial collapse, author Ken Auletta, writing in New York magazine, reflected back upon Buckley's earlier warnings and the negative responses to them at the time. Auletta remarked that "judging by the reaction, one would have though Buckley had proposed to drop the atom bomb on Israel."10/

Yet the combination of unstopable peacetime inflation coupled with the financial plight of New York, Cleveland, and a host of other American cities, gradually convinced a majority of the American people that the government itself remained the real source of the nation's economic malaise. As we shall see in the next chapter, by November of 1980 the American voters were willing to elevate to the White House New Right Republican Ronald Reagan, who had categorically stated that government, and government alone, was the true cause of inflation.

Troubles Abroad: Southeast Asia

Meanwhile, the United States' post-1973 economic turmoil found itself reflected in the realm of foreign affairs. Momentarily, at least, the bulk of the American people seemed to have lost the confidence (not to mention the desire) to play a leading role abroad. Neo-Isolationism became the watchword of the day.

The nation's prestige and influence throughout the world community plummeted in a decline reminiscent of the years 1960-61 which, as described back in Chapter Two, had helped prod the New Right into action in the first place. Therefore, it was not surprising that after 1973 America's malaise abroad helped the New Right snap out of its Nixon-induced stupor.

In far off Southeast Asia the final act of America's frustrating, two-decade-old drama was played out as Saigon fell to the Communist onslaught in the Spring of 1975. Virtually alone among Americans, New Rightists from all walks of life clamored for one last, eleventh hour effort to turn back the surging red tide and thus save the anti-Communist Thieu Regime in South Vietnam. However, by this late date the majority of the American people wanted nothing more to do with this dreadful little war. And so, despite the expected, pro forma, face-saving protests from President Gerald Ford and Secretary of State Henry

Kissinger, the Democratic-controlled Congress (reflecting the true sentiments of the American public in this matter) prevented the President from taking any last minute military action. After having sacrificed 57,000 American lives in vain, the United States Government, to the utter dismay of the New Right, was washing its hands of the whole stinking mess.

Then, to rub salt into the wound, the U.S. Government began the process of acknowledging that the Vietnam War had been a tragic mistake all along. This process started when President Gerald Ford unveiled in September, 1974 his conditional amnesty plan for draft dodgers and military deserters. By January, 1977 this transformation was completed as the newly inaugurated Chief Executive, Jimmy Carter (who had campaigned the previous year denouncing the "ugliness of Vietnam" while characterizing the conflict as "racist" and "immoral"), issued virtually a blanket pardon for all Vietnam War resistors.11/

Nevertheless, as much as the New Right publicly mourned the fall of South Vietnam, in hindsight the Movement benefited enormously by the removal of this vexing issue from the American political scene. As I noted back in Chapter Ten, the New Right had unwittingly found itself saddled with the onus for the Vietnam disaster. For even though the Movement had opposed from the beginning L.B.J.'s original limited war strategy, New Rightists wound up supporting a limited war as the lesser of two evils (the alternative evil being a complete American pullout) and thus took the blame accordingly. At any rate, once Saigon had finally fallen to the Communists, the American public could now focus its full attention upon the problems of the 1970's--a development which, ultimately, was destined to rebound to the New Right's advantage.

Other Troubles Abroad: Africa, Europe, Latin America

The New Right viewed the fall of South Vietnam in May, 1975 as simply part of a worldwide Communist (primarily Soviet) offensive designed to capitalize upon the United States' temporary mood of Isolationism in light of the American people's preoccupation with domestic problems and their loss of interest in foreign affairs generally. Consequently, along with the usual Soviet intrigues in the Middle East, the Communists took the initiative in Africa, Western Europe, and Latin America while the befuddled United States reacted inappropriately, or not at all.

For openers, in what New Rightists saw as a deliberate attempt to outflank the United States in the Middle East from the Southern direction (via Black Africa), the ever-mischievous Soviets backed an insurgent movement in Angola. Unfortunately, after the truth became public knowledge that the Ford Administration was secretly aiding the Pro-Western Angolese faction, the Democratic controlled U.S. Senate

311

quickly passed a resolution forbidding any further American assistance. Then too, the United States apparently reacted sluggishly as the Soviets extended their influence into Mozambique, Ethiopia, and Somali. And to make matters worse, strong, behind-the-scenes arm-twisting applied by the Ford Administration (primarily by Secretary of State Kissinger) helped persuade Rhodesian Prime Minister Ian Smith (himself a long-time New Right favorite) to begin dismantling his White Supremacy regime and to facilitate the transition to Black majority rule--an eventuality which New Rightists looked upon with open disgust. (See Chapter Six)

Next, in Western Europe, the years 1974-75 witnessed the demise of the New Right's two favorite authoritarian regimes--Salazar's in Portugal and Franco's in Spain. New Rightists (Catholic Isolationists in particular) lamented the developments in the Iberian Peninsula. For not only did local Communists resurface in both Portugal and Spain (indeed for a time it appeared possible that Portugal might fall under Communist control), but in a larger sense, the events in Spain, to the distress of New Rightists, represented a symbolic reversal of the results of the Spanish Civil War (1936-39).

In addition, the European Security Conference of 1975 (which produced the so-called Helsinki Agreement) wound up legitimizing the Soviet Union's World War Two territorial acquisitions in Eastern Europe. In exchange the Soviets "promised" to respect "human rights" -- whatever that was worth. New Rightists predictably lambasted the Ford Administration for ever signing such an accord which, in their opinion, sealed the fate of millions trapped behind the Iron Curtain, all for the sake of a worthless guarantee from the Soviets regarding "human rights."

Finally, not only did the Soviet Union increase its already menacing presence in Cuba (shades of the early 1960's--See Chapter Two) but the Soviets began recruiting Cuban mercenaries to fight along-side Black Liberation forces in Africa. In the meantime, the Ford Administration continued with negotiations designed to hammer out a new treaty with Panama dealing with the ultimate disposition of the Canal. New Rightists suspected that the United States Government was preparing (after yet another "decent interval") to surrender American sovereignty over the Canal Zone. Indeed, when the American public began to get wind of the shape these negotiations were taking, the Panama Canal issue became a major bone of contention between Ford and Reagan during the 1976 G.O.P. Presidential Primary season.

Continued Decadence at Home

Alongside economic and foreign troubles, the seemingly relentless assault upon the traditional American family helped mobilize the New Right into action during the post-Vietnam period. For the very bedrock of the New Right's beloved "American Way of Life"—the institution of the family itself—received a number of traumatic shocks which included the passage of the Equal Rights Amendment, the Supreme Court's decision legalizing abortion on demand, as well as the apparent unchecked spread of both pornography and sexual promiscuity. Of course, these so-called family issues had aroused the New Right's concern back during the 1960's. (See, for instance, Chapter Three) But the 1970's witnessed an alarmingly successful effort to give a measure of legal sanction (if not outright government encouragement) to these heretofore deeply disturbing social trends.

To begin with, in 1972 Congress passed the Equal Rights Amendment to the U.S. Constitution. Initially, at least, New Rightists voiced only token opposition to the Amendment, in part because then-President Richard Nixon had given the measure his blessing (New Rightists as usual were loath to challenge Nixon directly), and in part because they had not yet come to see the E.R.A. as a threat to the entire American social order. After all, the E.R.A. had originally been passed by Congress in 1972 ostensibly as a purely legal measure designed to eradicate the last vestiges of discrimination against women. The New Right considered the E.R.A. more of a nuisance than anything else. Only later when the New Right discovered to its chagrin that aggressive judges and government bureaucrats were eagerly looking forward to using the E.R.A. as a means of making social policy, did the New Right's opposition to the measure stiffen. By 1976 New Rightists (under the skillful leadership of arch anti-Feminist Phyllis Schlafly) had been able to persuade at least thirteen states from ratifying the Amendment -- enough to prevent its final adoption.

A major factor in hardening the New Right's resistance to the E.R.A. was the January, 1973 U.S. Supreme Court Abortion Ruling, which demonstrated quite clearly to the New Right that even with four, supposedly Conservative Nixon appointees sitting on the bench, the High Court was still capable of handing down monstrous opinions--on a par with, say, the infamous 1954 Public School Desegregation Decision or the hated 1962 School Prayer Ruling. (See Chapter Five). Consequently, should the E.R.A. become the law of the land, the High Court might very well use the statute to mandate far-reaching social changes at the behest of Radical Feminists. Moreover, since the 1973 Abortion Decision was seen as a victory for the Women's Movement (which had earlier lobbied successfully for Congressional passage of the E.R.A.), New Rightists, as opponents of abortion, automatically stepped up their fight against the recently approved E.R.A. as a tactic in their crusade to halt abortion on demand. In other words, the Women's Movement, because of its pro-Abortion stance, had suddenly become a prime enemy to the New Right in the wake of the Supreme Court's incredible ruling.

Then too, post-Vietnam America witnessed the coming of age, so to speak, of the country's pornography industry. Of course, New

Rightists like F.B.I. Director J. Edgar Hoover had waged a running battle against "smut" all through the 1960's when lewd books, magazines, and films had still been a more or less illicit, "underground" business. (See Chapter Three). However, to the New Right's disgust, pornography suddenly acquired a measure of respectability after 1973, especially among "liberated" circles. Indeed, movies like "Deep Throat" helped make pornography a "chic," socially acceptable phenomenon. And aided by numerous favorable judicial rulings, the pornography fad quickly spread across the nation.

To add insult to injury, by 1976, at a time when the American public had shown signs of becoming bored with ordinary, run-of-the-mill, sex acts, more deviant themes featuring sado-masochism and child abuse moved center stage. As expected, New Rightists led the fight against this second generation of open, easily accessible "smut." In fact, largely as a result of their prodding, the U.S. Congress in 1977 went so far as to outlaw all, so-called "Kiddie Porn." Interestingly enough, the New Right's vigorous campaign directed against "Kiddie Porn" was reminiscent of the earlier "WASP Inquisition's" campaign against the White Slavery traffic (i.e., organized prostitution rings) back during the days just prior to the First World War. (See Chapter One).

The American public's growing acceptance of pornography coincided with its acceptance of a new code of personal sexual conduct. To the New Right's horror, pre-marital sex became the norm in many sections of the nation, while extra-marital sex (including "Open Marriage", "Swinging", and "Wife Swapping") received an enormous amount of favorable media attention. But perhaps most alarming of all, homosexuals and lesbians both "came out of the closet" (i.e., went public) demanding civil rights as well as public legitimation of their deviant life style.

Furthermore, to the New Right's dismay, the government itself aided and abetted the spreading Sexual Revolution. Some "Progressive" states, like California, enacted so-called "Consenting Adult" bills which removed criminal penalties for everything from sodomy to homosexuality. Taxpayer supported public health clinics managed, at least for a time, to bring all the major strains of venereal disease under control--thus removing one of the chief drawbacks associated with promiscuous sexual conduct. Minors received the right to obtain contraceptive devices, often without parental permission. And as I alluded to earlier, the Supreme Court's decision to allow abortion-on-demand overnight transformed this once back-alley medical procedure into a clean, safe, effective, birth control method of last resort, so to speak. Thus the combination of freedom from police harassment, the ready availability of contraceptive devices, the lessened fear of veneral disease, as well as the advent of legal (indeed oftentimes taxpayer-subsidized) abortion, all served to remove the traditional "evil consequences" associated with having sexual relations outside the confines of marriage.12/

Interestingly enough, if New Rightists had been guided strictly by practical considerations, they could have very easily endorsed all of the aforementioned changes. After all, the removal of criminal penalties for private sexual acts between consenting adults would free the police to concentrate upon the more serious violent crimes which directly threatened the personal safety of New Rightists themselves. The elimination of venereal disease would upgrade the public's general health, which, among other benefits, would result in increased productivity for American workers and higher profits for American business accordingly. And the ability of unmarried men and women to obtain both contraceptive devices as well as abortions would help reduce illegitimacy, particularly among the country's poor, non-White population—a development which racist New Rightists could not help but look upon with great satisfaction. (See Chapter Three)

Nevertheless, New Rightists rejected practical considerations and vigorously opposed the Sexual Revolution. For when push came to shove, New Rightists (no doubt reflecting their own stern religious upbringing) were much more interested in punishing vice than in really eradicating it. Sad to say, New Rightists frequently took perverse delight when promiscuous citizens were arrested by police on morals charges (and thus held up to public ridicule), contracted venereal disease, experienced the shame of having a child out of wedlock, or died while undergoing an abortion.

Now as far as New Rightists were concerned, if in the process of punishing vice it just so happened that vice was also eradicated, then well and good. But New Rightists always insisted that punishment should take top priority—even if such punishment should, in fact, redound to their own discomfort. Surely, by any stretch of the imagination, it was in the New Right's own self-interest to allow, say, unmarried Black teenage girls to obtain contraceptive devices, rather than pay heavy taxes to support their illegitimate children. However, stubborn New Rightists would not be swayed by such "practical" arguments. (See Chapter Three)*

---

*Note—Incidentally, the New Right's overwhelming compulsion to punish sinners rather than making a serious effort to solve social problems can be seen clearly in their response to the blight of heroin addiction. New Rightists positively enjoyed watching heroin addicts fall into police custody and forced to undergo the agony resulting from the immediate withdrawal of the drug ("cold turkey"). Of course, for years New Rightists were well aware that addicts could be weaned off the drug gradually and painlessly under proper medical supervision. Yet they (Continued)

The New Right Awakens

It had become quite apparent by 1975 that the supposed bulwarks designed to protect the United States both at home and abroad, which New Rightists had come to rely upon to hold back the raging waters, could no longer be trusted anymore. Richard Nixon (for whatever he was worth) had departed the scene the year before courtesy of Watergate. And, as I pointed out earlier, Nixon's successor, the affable Gerald Ford, was proving nearly useless in stemming the tide. Additionally, Ford looked like a sure loser in the upcoming 1976 Presidential race against the Democrats. The G.O.P. itself remained in shambles after Watergate and the November, 1974 Election debacle. And the U.S. Supreme Court turned out to be a grave disappointment even though four of the nine Justices had been handpicked by Nixon himself. Indeed the Burger Court's Decisions were seen by many New Rightists as no better, and, in some ways, far worse than the Warren Court's Decisions of the 1950's and 60's. (See Chapter Five)

All in all, New Rightists saw no alternative but to roll up their sleeves and become politically involved once again. Therefore, as the New Right reemerged from out of the shadows of the Nixon Years, the

---

strenuously resisted attempts to spend taxpayer funds for drug rehabilitation facilities, since such "Progressive" clinics would deprive New Rightists of the immense pleasure of teaching heroin addicts (and society at large) a lesson about the dangers of drug abuse. So a number of addicts, who no doubt desperately wanted to get off heroin, wound up committing crimes in order to support their expensive heroin habit because they saw the horrors of "cold turkey" as their only alternative to continued drug use.

Moreover, the New Right's longstanding tacit approval of what became known during the 1960's as "police brutality" simply served to hinder the nation's efforts to combat violent street crime. For nothing alienated civil libertarians from the otherwise completely legitimate war on crime as did the New Right's condoning of extra-legal police practices designed to "punish" suspected offenders. Not content with mere incarceration, New Rightists wanted police to inflict sound thrashings on culprits too. Thus New Rightists traditionally looked the other way as law enforcement personnel dispensed informal "street justice" with routine police beatings. Meanwhile, New Right groups (such as the John Birch Society) sponsored a "Support Your Local Police" campaign and vehemently opposed efforts to establish civilian review boards designed to allow citizens and their elected officials the opportunity to monitor police activities more closely. And finally, not satisfied with seeing social outcasts like homosexuals, for instance, simply ostracized, New Rightists quietly encouraged police officers (as well as self-appointed vigilantes) to keep these "deviates" in line with periodic physical abuse.13/

militant activism of the early 1960's (the Goldwater Era) also resurfaced. And to preside over the New Right's return to national political prominence there stood none other than the old trooper, Ronald Reagan.

The Reappearance of Ronald Reagan

After losing the 1968 G.O.P. Presidential Nomination to Richard Nixon, Ronald Reagan resumed his day-to-day activities as California's Governor and seemed content to maintain a relatively low profile until 1974. True enough, the Governor of the nation's most populous state can hardly slip out of sight altogether, especially since the occupant is usually considered Presidential timber. Yet between August, 1968 (when he lost the G.O.P. Nomination at Miami Beach) and August, 1974 (when Nixon resigned the Presidency) Reagan seemed content to run an efficient, scandal-free administration in Sacramento, and utter an occasional, off-the-cuff, hawkish pronouncement on foreign affairs. In the midst of his quiescent period, Reagan managed to win an easy reelection victory to the California Governorship in November, 1970 over his Democratic opponent Jesse Unruh.

By 1974 as his second term as California Governor was drawing to a close, Reagan paused to evaluate his political future. He still retained a high degree of popularity among California voters. Thus, conceivably, Reagan could have won reelection to a third term in Sacramento, despite the fact that 1974, on the whole, was shaping up as (and ultimately proved to be) a very bad year for Republican candidates across the country. Nevertheless, after some thought Reagan decided not to seek a third term. He had probably grown slightly bored with the Governorship after eight years. Besides, even if he had been reelected in November, 1974 he would still have had to face an increasingly heavy Democratic majority in the California State Legislature--an opposition majority which would have effectively thwarted any of the Governor's new initiatives. Perhaps too, Reagan reflected back upon the fate of then two-term incumbent Governor Pat Brown whom Reagan had defeated back in 1966, although, it's fair to add that a previous Republican Governor, Earl Warren, had been elected three times.

Reagan also toyed briefly with the idea of running for the United States Senate seat from California. However, even the position of California Senator represented a significant step down for someone like Reagan who had held the Governorship. In truth, the only other job which Reagan coveted was the Presidency itself. Besides, Reagan realized that popular, Democratic incumbent Senator Alan Cranston would be a difficult, if not impossible, figure to beat, especially during a strong Democratic year such as 1974. Indeed when Reagan failed to challenge Cranston, the assignment fell to California State Senator H. L.

317

"Bill" Richardson (a former John Birch Society member) who went down to a crushing defeat.

In the end, Reagan decided against seeking either a third term as Governor or contesting Alan Cranston's U.S. Senate seat. So in January, 1975 Reagan said goodbye to Sacramento and left public service after eight years. He subsequently accepted an invitation to join the ABC Radio Network as a daily political commentator—a position which enabled him to keep his name in the public's eye for the time being. Meanwhile, he toured the country building a base of support in case he decided to challenge G.O.P. incumbent President Gerald Ford in 1976.

In addition, just to keep his full range of options open, Reagan privately allowed his name to be bandied about as a possible Right-wing, third party Presidential candidate for 1976. (Reagan's highly publicized meeting with Alabama Governor George Wallace during this period served to fuel speculation that indeed a Reagan-Wallace ticket, or vice versa was in the works.) In the meantime, New York attorney John Sears, a former-1968 Nixon Campaign staffer, assumed overall command of Reagan's burgeoning campaign team, and soon began waging what amounted to a virtual "Cold War" against Gerald Ford. After nearly a year of frantic jockeying for position in the Presidential derby, Reagan made his intentions official by formally announcing his candidacy for the nation's highest office (as a Republican, of course) on November 20, 1975.14/

Ford vs. Reagan

Under normal circumstances one would have automatically assumed that an incumbent Republican President like Gerald Ford (regardless of his political leanings) would have been immune from any serious challenge mounted by a Right-wing member of his own party— particularly in light of the fact that Ford deliberately made an effort to appease the Reaganites by forcing his Vice President Nelson Rockefeller to rule himself out of consideration for another term. Nonetheless, by the time the 1976 Presidential Primary season finally rolled around, the voters found themselves witnessing a curious battle between Ronald Reagan and Gerald Ford starting in frigid New Hampshire.

In retrospect, 1976 turned out to be Ronald Reagan's poorest campaign for public office. Perhaps, as some have suggested, his heart really wasn't in the race. Whatever the reason, Reagan failed to come out swinging at the bell against Gerald Ford. Rightly or wrongly, the former-California Governor may have feared that G.O.P. voters would resent any strong, personal attacks upon a sitting Republican President. Besides, Reagan had always taken the high road in all his previous campaigns back in California. Up until this time he had scrupulously adhered to the so-called Republican "Eleventh Commandment"—which

318

read, "Thou shalt not speak ill of any fellow Republican"—a timely piece of wisdom concocted after the 1964 Goldwater fiasco when Republicans had butchered one another to the delight of Democrats. (See Chapter Nine)

Worse yet, Reagan unwittingly allowed himself to be placed on the defensive right from the outset of the campaign. True enough, the Liberal-biased National News Media dredged up some of his old, Right-wing pronouncements, many dating all the way back to 1964. But Reagan (as did Goldwater himself) foolishly supplied his enemies with plenty of fresh ammunition. For example, the former-California Governor lost the first primary, New Hampshire, to President Ford by a mere 1,300 votes, after having unveiled a fuzzy plan to "transfer" ninety-billion dollars worth of Federal programs to the states and local communities--a suggestion which, among other things, would have sharply raised local taxes in a lightly taxed state like New Hampshire. In another early primary, Florida (home of many senior citizens), which Reagan lost by only 53% to 47%, the press as well as the Ford Campaign had a field day attacking the former-Governor's ambiguous position on Social Security. And later on in the primary season, Reagan's Goldwateresque statements concerning T.V.A. probably cost him a sure victory in otherwise friendly Tennessee.

Indeed it now appears that Reagan squandered a Heaven-sent opportunity to knock Ford completely out of the race by winning a few, key, early primaries such as New Hampshire and Florida. After all, prior to his razor-thin New Hampshire victory in late February, 1976 former-Grand Rapids Congressman Gerald R. Ford had never even won so much as a statewide contest in his entire political life. America's one and only non-elected Chief Executive entered the 1976 Presidential Primary season as a basically untested electoral commodity, to say the very least. And a few quick primary defeats at the hands of Ronald Reagan would undoubtedly have earmarked the President as a big "loser," whereupon the rank and file G.O.P. members (especially the Party activists who bother to vote in the primaries) would have followed their natural ideological inclinations and cast their ballots for the former-California Governor. Therefore, since Reagan, not Ford, represented the true heart and soul of the post-1964 Republican Party, without the powerful incumbency factor helping Ford, Reagan would have won the G.O.P. Nomination hands down (as he was to do very easily four years later).

By the time the Southern and Western state primaries came around, Reagan had recovered his stride, scoring a number of impressive victories to offset President Ford's strength in the Northeastern Industrial Belt. Along the way, Reagan managed a clean sweep of the delegates in Texas by hammering away at the Administration's negotiations to "giveaway" the Panama Canal. And Reagan routed the President in the biggest prize of all, California's Winner-Take-All

Primary. When the dust settled, Reagan wound up garnering more total popular votes during the 1976 Presidential Primary season than did Gerald Ford. However, as a result of his bad start, his inexplicable failure to battle the President for every last delegate (particularly in important primary states such as Wisconsin and New Jersey), and his own supporters' organizational mistakes in some of the non-primary states, Reagan came to the August, G.O.P. National Convention in Kansas City approximately fifty-odd delegate votes short of securing the Presidential Nomination.

Shootout in Kansas City

Former movie actor Ronald Reagan must have approached the 1976 G.O.P. National Convention in Kansas City with the haunting feeling that he'd already seen this picture once before—back in 1968 at Miami Beach, to be precise. For at both Republican gatherings Reagan was the popular choice of the majority of the delegates. But in both cases a G.O.P. Moderate (Nixon in 1968, Ford in 1976) walked away with the Grand Prize. As I noted back in Chapter Twelve, New Rightists chose Nixon at Miami Beach in order to prevent Nelson Rockefeller from gaining the Nomination. By 1976 the threat of a Rockefeller coup had subsided to the point where such a possibility no longer occupied the delegates' mind. However, this time around a number of technically uncommitted New Right delegates threw their support to Ford in the end after having been contacted personally by the President, indeed in some instances after having been invited to the White House for a friendly chat in the Oval Office! Such is the enormous advantage of an incumbent President, which Ford utilized to an unprecedented degree in his search for G.O.P. Convention delegates.

Furthermore, the antics of Barry Goldwater must have also evoked a strong sense of deja vu for Reagan. At the outset of the 1976 Presidential Campaign Goldwater had given Gerald Ford a tremendous boost (as he had likewise once done for Richard Nixon back in 1965—See Chapter Twelve) by announcing that the differences between Ford and Reagan were not significant enough to warrant denying renomination to a sitting Republican President. However, by Convention time, for reasons known only to himself, Goldwater was actively engaged in heaping verbal abuse upon Reagan—in some cases for Reagan's current positions, many of which could have easily passed for 1964-vintage Goldwater! In fact, the Arizona Senator's shabby performance so disgusted New Rightists everywhere that it came as no surprise when Goldwater's own son, Barry Jr., a Congressman from suburban Los Angeles, wound up as a loyal member of Reagan's California Delegation.

In any event, as the Kansas City Convention date drew near it became increasingly apparent to the Reagan camp that Gerald Ford had just enough votes (both among committed as well as uncommitted delegates) to win a narrow first ballot victory. So Reagan Campaign

320

Strategist John Sears dreamed up an imaginative last minute ploy, which probably deserved a better fate. Sears convinced Reagan to arrange a deal to give the Vice Presidential Nomination to Pennsylvania's heretofore Liberal G.O.P. Senator Richard Schweiker, of all people, who would suddenly discover his lifelong devotion to Conservative principles. The announcement of this deal was made prior to the Convention itself in the hopes of (1) regaining the initiative from the President by a dramatic stroke; (2) forcing the President likewise to disclose his own personal choice for Vice President, which might serve to anger some of his own supporters; and (3) picking up additional strength for Reagan among the uncommitted delegates of the Northeast, particularly in Schweiker's home state of Pennsylvania. None of these results, however, came to pass. And coupled with the fact that a number of the uncommitted New Right delegates from Mississippi and South Carolina tearfully cast their first ballot votes for Gerald Ford despite being Reaganites at heart (shades of 1968!), the President ultimately prevailed 1187 to 1070, thus earning the dubious right to run against and lose to Democrat Jimmy Carter in November.

The New Right in Defeat - 1976

Despite Reagan's bitter defeat at Kansas City, both he and the New Right had managed to accomplish a great deal during 1975-76. The former-California Governor's excellent showing in the later stages of the Republican Presidential Primary season clearly helped restore the Movement's spirit and confidence. And the mere fact that Reagan nearly unseated an incumbent President served to remind the nation, in no uncertain terms, that the New Right was still very much alive and kicking. Indeed, Reagan's achievements of 1975-76 foreshadowed a New Right resurgence in the years immediately ahead. Strangely enough, all things considered, Reagan and the New Right were probably quite fortunate that they wound up losing to Ford, since 1976 turned out to be a Democratic year anyway—more precisely, a Jimmy Carter year. As events transpired in November, 1976, Gerald Ford suffered a narrow defeat at the hands of the Democratic Party Nominee Carter. Ronald Reagan would have been utterly routed by Carter this time around.

Finally, during 1975-76 Reagan himself laid important ideological groundwork for the future. More than any other prominent American politician, Reagan became firmly identified in the public's mind with a policy of sharply reducing inflation even at the painful cost of a temporary recession. We now know with the benefit of hindsight that the majority of the country had not yet come around to Reagan's point of view back in 1975-76. But, as I remarked earlier, Reagan's insistence that inflation was the underlying cause of the nation's economic woes (and that the woes of inflation were directly traceable to government) eventually gained acceptance among not only Republicans, but also among many Democrats and Independents, who helped elect him to the

Presidency in November, 1980. Consequently, the ideological seeds which Reagan planted back during the years 1975-76 ultimately bore fruit. And with regards to Reagan himself, the only question was going to be, would he personally still be around in time to reap the benefits, or was 1976 to be the then, sixty-five year old, former-California Governor's last political hurrah?

1. Barry M. Goldwater, With No Apologies (New York: William Morrow and Company, Inc., 1979), p. 293.

2. Interestingly enough, New Right author Gary Allen personally told me that "the appointment of a Rockefeller man like Kissinger in the first place should have been a clear indication that Nixon was hooked-up with the Eastern Liberal Establishment." Conversation with Gary Allen, Los Angeles, March, 1979.

3. Related to me personally during a conversation with John Schmitz, Los Angeles, June, 1979.

4. Frank Snepp, Decent Interval (New York: Random House, 1977).

5. Personal recollection, June, 1972.

6. Goldwater, With No Apologies, p. 265.

7. Ibid., p. 268.

8. Personal recollection, September, 1974.

9. For an excellent account of the New York Financial Crisis see former-Treasury Secretary William E. Simon's, A Time For Truth (New York: McGraw-Hill Book Company, 1978), Chapter Five.

10. New York (October 27, 1975), p. 29.

11. Personal recollection from the 1976 Presidential Campaign.

12. During this same period, the California State Legislature also infuriated New Rightists by enacting a statute decriminalizing the private possession of small amounts of marijuana.

13. Author Alan Crawford, in his superlative book, Thunder on the Right: The "New Right" and the Politics of Resentment (New York: Pantheon Books, 1980), examines quite well the New Right's "macho", vigilante character.

14. For an excellent account of Reagan's role in the 1976 Presidential Campaign, the reader should consult Jules Witcover's, Marathon: The Pursuit of the Presidency, 1972-1976 (New York: Viking Press, 1977).

CHAPTER FOURTEEN

THE COLLAPSE OF AMERICAN LIBERALISM, 1977-1980

The "Myth of F.D.R.'s Unfinished Agenda"

Ever since the 1930's American Liberalism has been living off the momentum generated by Franklin D. Roosevelt and the New Deal. In the process, American Liberalism invented what I call the "Myth of F.D.R.'s Unfinished Agenda"--that is, the idea that during the Great Depression the New Deal set forth a magnificent public philosophy which could serve as a virtual blueprint for an American Utopia, and that for the past half-century various sinister Reactionary elements or unforeseen circumstances have repeatedly intervened to thwart the clear will of the American people, thus preventing the United States from realizing the New Dealers' original dreams. The Myth of F.D.R.'s Unfinished Agenda has been used by American Liberals to justify every new reform impulse (both at home and abroad), as well as to explain away any adverse side-effects which may have resulted from their social experimentation. And it was precisely this myth--the Myth of F.D.R.'s Unfinished Agenda--which the American people finally came to grips with during the period 1977-80, and wound up rejecting decisively.

In a nutshell, the Myth (complete with its colorful cast of heroes and villains) goes something like this: During his first term as President (1933-37), F.D.R., with broad popular support behind him, laid the foundations for a national welfare state. However, after the New Deal had accomplished its initial goal of restoring the American Middle Class to health, F.D.R.'s Conservative opponents in Congress blocked the New Deal's more ambitious attempts to assist the chronically disadvantaged-that "one-third of a nation," in Roosevelt's own words, which, after the Great Depression had run its course, would still remain "ill-housed, ill-clad, ill-nourished." The advent of World War Two, of necessity, put further domestic reform on the back burner. But, unfortunately, F.D.R. then died in April, 1945 just as he was preparing to lead a glorious, new post-War crusade to fulfill the New Dealer's fondest dreams by completing the task of building a just and prosperous society for all Americans. In addition, F.D.R. died at a critical moment in history when his carefully laid plans for a bright, peaceful, new world order, based upon international cooperation sponsored by the newly established United Nations, was about to come to fruition. Thus F.D.R.'s bold, exciting, imaginative, but, of course, unrealized visions of 1945 became, in subsequent years, the basis for American Liberalism's "Myth of F.D.R.'s Unfinished Agenda."1/

When F.D.R. died suddenly in April, 1945, into the Presidency stepped Harry S. Truman, a man who lacked Roosevelt's personal magnetism, political acumen, and ideological commitment to lead a major revival of American Liberalism. Worse yet, Truman and his

325

advisors started the Cold War by picking a needless fight with the peace-loving Soviet Union, thereby shattering the years of trust, cooperation, and goodwill meticulously cultivated by F.D.R. himself during the Second World War. Thus an unhappy combination of frustrated social reform at home and dangerously mounting tensions abroad was the net result of Truman's untimely accession to power.

In fact, by 1948 many American Liberals had become so thoroughly disenchanted with both President Truman and the Democrats that they flirted briefly with the Progressive Party's Presidential Nominee Henry A. Wallace--a man who had kept the New Deal's pristine idealism alive. A living link with the now-departed demi-god Roosevelt (he had once served as F.D.R.'s Vice President from 1941-45), Henry A. Wallace had the political courage to challenge head-on the twin demons of reaction at home and mindless anti-Sovietism abroad. Nevertheless, once it had become apparent that Wallace could not possible win the 1948 Presidential Election, American Liberals threw their support back to Truman, who, the Myth notes approvingly, emerged during the Campaign as good old "Give 'em hell, Harry," and who then went on to strike a blow for Liberalism (and for the nation's common people) by upsetting Republican Thomas E. Dewey.

But alas, no sooner had President Truman's "Fair Deal" program been unveiled than disaster struck again--a new war, this time in distant Korea, and the rise of an unscrupulous demagogue at home, in the person of the unspeakable Senator Joseph McCarthy. Thus Truman's "Fair Deal" sputtered as the American public's attention became fixated on the battle against Communism in both far-away Korea and in our nation's own State Department (among other places). Then along came the soothing, grinning Dwight Eisenhower, who won the 1952 Presidential Election over Democrat Adlai Stevenson--a man raised to sainthood by the Myth because, in addition to his eloquence, Stevenson had campaigned for the White House promising to "talk sense to the American people." But Ike won, partly because he had announced that if elected he would "go to Korea," and partly because the voters had not yet discovered what a crook G.O.P. Vice Presidential Nominee Richard Nixon really was (despite Nixon's unconvincing performance during his infamous "Checkers Speech").

The United States was finally rescued from the eight year somnambulence of the Eisenhower Era by the handsome, young, Irish Prince, John F. Kennedy, who as the nation's new President in 1961, pledged to get the country "moving again" (with "vigor") in a definite Liberal direction, but who was tragically assassinated before his ambitious "New Frontier" legislation could be enacted. Upon Kennedy's death in November, 1963 a usurper, the uncouth Lyndon B. Johnson, assumed command of the Federal Government. Thus for the second time in as many decades, the course of history had been altered for the worse, the American peoples' will had been thwarted, and the U.S. Presidency had fallen into illegitimate hands, all as the result of the passing of the two great, popularly-elected, Liberal leaders, F.D.R. and J.F.K. After November 22, 1963 the Myth now became "The Unfinished Agenda of F.D.R. and J.F.K."

Nonetheless, by some artful persuasion (as well as by some not so subtle arm-twisting) L.B.J. managed to guide his remarkable "Great Society" program through Congress between 1964-66, thereby taking a giant step towards realizing the New Dealers' earlier dreams. Best of all, the American people overwhelmingly approved the "Great Society" in November, 1964 by reelecting L.B.J. to another term while, in the process, utterly rejecting the arch-Reactionary Barry Goldwater. But then disaster struck again. For although the American people had voted for L.B.J. as the "Peace Candidate" in November, 1964, the treacherous usurper in the White House soon unleashed an aggressive war in Vietnam. And so the good intentions of L.B.J.'s "Great Society" were dissipated by yet another foreign conflict.

By 1968, American Liberalism had produced a new pair of courageous leaders, each campaigning for the Democratic Presidential Nomination as the personal incarnation of the "Unfinished Agenda." The two, Senators Eugene J. McCarthy (the political heir to Adlai Stevenson) and the late President Kennedy's brother Robert, successfully mobilized the nation's latent Liberal spirit against both the seemingly interminable War in Vietnam and the racism, poverty, and despair at home. Sadly though, Robert Kennedy himself was assassinated just as he was about to capture the Democratic Presidential Nomination, and from there march triumphantly on to the White House in November. With Robert Kennedy removed from further consideration, Eugene McCarthy (who had earlier single-handedly knocked L.B.J. himself out of the Presidential race) now picked up the Liberal banner only to have the Nomination stolen from him at the August, 1968 Chicago Convention by L.B.J.'s Vice President, Hubert H. Humphrey, with the help of Mayor Richard Daley and his Chicago Police Department goon squads.

Yet the Myth suddenly transforms Hubert Humphrey, the villain of the Chicago Convention, into Hubert Humphrey, the defender of American Liberalism against both the slimy Richard Nixon and the Fascistic George Wallace in the November, 1968 General Election. The Myth laments Humphrey's narrow defeat at the hands of Nixon and suggests that if Wallace had not run as an independent, or if a few hundred thousand more disgruntled Liberals had bothered to cast their votes for the Democratic Nominee, then American Liberalism would have still been able to prevent the Presidency from falling into the clutches of that arch-rogue, Richard Nixon.*

Once installed in the Oval Office, Nixon made sure that the nation never got the opportunity to complete the work of building the "Great Society." And when a new champion of the Cause emerged in 1972 -- Senator George McGovern (a political heir to both Henry Wallace and Robert Kennedy)--Nixon and his band of political thugs employed every illegal, immoral weapon at their disposal to sabotage the Democrats. Therefore, although Nixon obtained a whopping 60% of the popular vote against McGovern, the November, 1972 Presidential Election could not be construed as an actual repudiation of Liberalism, since Nixon's dirty tricks coupled with McGovern's inability to project the right "public relations image" had grossly distorted the final results. Besides, within two years the Watergate Scandal had exposed Nixon and his entourage as corrupt Reactionaries, completely out of step with the true Progressive sentiments held by the overwhelming majority of the American people.

Regrettably, by 1976, just when it appeared certain that American Liberalism was on the verge of coming into power once again (to complete, at long last, the "Unfinished Agenda") a new obstacle suddenly appeared in the person of Democrat Jimmy Carter. Indeed, the election of Carter to the Presidency in November, 1976 proved especially galling for American Liberals since Senator Ted Kennedy (the peoples' first choice, and the rightful heir to the office once occupied by F.D.R. and J.F.K.) would have easily beaten Carter, if only the doubts surrounding Kennedy's personal character (the incident at Chappaquiddick) had not made it impossible for the Senator to run this time around.

Nevertheless, despite the political albatross of Chappaquiddick hanging around his neck, Ted Kennedy decided to contest the 1980 Democratic Presidential Nomination against the now-incumbent Chief Executive Jimmy Carter. However, Kennedy came up short, and once again it was a foreign crisis--this time in Iran--which sent voters rallying behind the President (at least initially) in a demonstration of support for the fifty-two American hostages. Moreover, even though the popularity of Liberalism was already in serious eclipse by the summer of 1980, Ted Kennedy still managed to bring tears to the eyes of Democrats everywhere when he stood before his Party's National Convention in New

---

*Note--Incidentally, American Liberals have always considered Richard Nixon's rise to power as somewhat "illegitimate" since he had won election to public office at the beginning of his career by allegedly conducting vicious smear campaigns against Jerry Vorhees in 1946, and Helen Gahagan Douglas in 1950. (See Chapter Two)

York City and reiterated both his and American Liberalism's unflagging commitment to the "Unfinished Agenda": "For all those whose cares have been our concern, the work goes on, the cause endures, the hope still lives and the dream shall never die."2/

Finally, during the closing days of the 1980 Fall Campaign a desperate Jimmy Carter also felt compelled to invoke the Myth on his own behalf. Finding himself trailing G.O.P. Presidential Nominee Ronald Reagan by a sizeable margin in the public opinion polls, the Democratic Standard-Bearer frequently made reference to the obvious contrast between the party of F.D.R. and J.F.K., on the one hand, and the party of Herbert Hoover and Richard Nixon, on the other. Then too, Carter often brought up the name of his Vice President Walter Mondale, as if to underscore the Carter Administration's link with Mondale's political mentor, the late Hubert Humphrey, one of the Myth's favorite leaders (only at times, of course!).

The Myth is Finally Tested, 1977-1980

Now it goes without saying that the "Myth of F.D.R.'s and J.F.K.'s Unfinished Agenda" contains so many obvious contradictions, loose ends, and gross distortions of history, as to render it totally absurd. Yet this simple, moralistic recitation of events constitutes the single, most powerful myth in modern American politics. In fact, the Second Coming of American Liberalism has been one of the most eagerly awaited happenings of recent times.

However, up until January, 1977, when Jimmy Carter and the Democrats regained power, the Myth had never really been put to the acid test, so to speak. Consequently, Liberalism's precipitous decline occurred only after Carter's Inauguration, when it became readily apparent that it could no longer offer viable solutions to America's pressing foreign and domestic problems. (Although, of course, Ted Kennedy would argue during his unsuccessful 1980 Presidential bid that the country's troubles required an even greater dose of Liberalism!)

First of all, on the domestic front ever since the 1930's Liberalism had been sold to the American people as a pragmatic public philosophy geared for action and designed for the solution of problems. Therefore, it should have come as no surprise that when Liberal solutions failed to correct the country's ills after 1977, the American people began looking elsewhere for alternatives--and the major alternative just so happened to be furnished by the New Right. True, there were other possible alternatives such as a less dogmatic brand of Liberalism, or perhaps a genuinely Moderate approach. But the American public proved quite unwilling to accept "business as usual." The New Right thus became the chief beneficiary of the collapse of American Liberalism because it promised action--drastic action--based upon a radically

329

different approach to problem solving. Indeed by 1980 the New Right's philosophy can be described as an idea whose time, as they say, had come.

Second, in the realm of foreign affairs, the events of the period 1977-80 helped shatter that portion of the Myth which held out hope for a peaceful world under the auspices of the United Nations. The dreadful experience of the fifty-two American hostages in Iran demonstrated quite convincingly that the world at large was not yet ready for the rule of International Law as envisioned by the U.N.'s founders back in 1945. And the brutal, 1979 Soviet invasion of neighboring Afganistan destroyed the idea that a genuine accommodation with the Kremlin was a relatively easy matter to arrange. Indeed, in the aftermath of the brazen Soviet move, President Jimmy Carter took pains to disassociate himself from the Myth by making the startling public admission that only now, in the wake of the Afganistan Episode, did he fully comprehend the true nature of the Soviet menace. Yet when the smoke finally cleared, it was the Myth itself, rather than Jimmy Carter personally, which wound up suffering the greatest damage as the result of the President's incredibly frank revelation.

Jimmy Carter

Jimmy Carter, the man chosen by fate to preside over the collapse of American Liberalism, appeared, at first glance, to be a rather unlikely looking candidate for such a dubious distinction. After all, Jimmy Carter's early political rise in Georgia (up to the Governorship in 1970) could be attributed, in large measure, to the strong support which he received from George Wallace's Southern Redneck constituency. Indeed during his successful 1970 Campaign for the Georgia Statehouse, Carter, on more than one occasion, went so far as to proclaim himself an authentic "Redneck." And even after he had become the 1976 Democratic Presidential Nominee, the National News Media still enjoyed describing Carter's home town of Plains as someplace straight out of Erskine Caldwell's Tobacco Road.

But, of course, there was another, more important side to Jimmy Carter--the graduate of Annapolis, the U.S. Naval Officer, the world traveler, the thoughtful, well-read man--who came to share many of the basic assumptions of American Liberalism by the time he became President, if not well before. Thus the "real" Jimmy Carter, in a historical sense, can be seen as a product of the South's small, but influential, non-racist, Democratic political tradition, in the mold of, say, an Estes Kefauver. Interestingly enough, Tennessee Senator Estes Kefauver had swept a number of Democratic Presidential Primaries back in 1952 by running against the corruption in Washington, which, at that time, meant essentially running against his own party. Nevertheless, despite his string of primary victories, Kefauver failed to receive the

Democratic Presidential Nomination back in 1952 because the primary system had not yet become the decisive factor in selecting party nominees, as it has become today. However, a quarter of a century later another Southern "outsider," Jimmy Carter, managed to capture the Democratic Presidential Nomination by adopting Kefauver's tactic of running against the Washington, D.C. Establishment (this time consisting of a Republican Chief Executive and a Democratic Congress), and by capitalizing upon the American public's distrust of "professional politicians" in the wake of Watergate.

Carter's curious duality (half suave urbanite, half hillbilly Redneck) accounted for the secret of his political success in 1976. For Carter somehow achieved the impossible--to unite McGovern and Wallace Democrats behind his candidacy. The Liberals, by and large, applauded his platform, while Conservatives appreciated his personal qualities as an unpretentious, homespun, Fundamentalist Baptist. As a matter of fact, many perceptive Democrats (including some 1972 McGovernites) had spotted Carter well before 1976, and, tired of their endless feuding with the Wallaceites, decided to back a "good old Southern boy" like Jimmy Carter on the theory that "if you can't beat 'em, join 'em." There was a great deal of truth in 1976 G.O.P. Vice Presidential Nominee Robert Dole's assertion that Carter was nothing more than a "Southern-fried McGovern," and that the Democratic Liberals were trying to pull a fast one on the Rednecks. No wonder, four years later, when the Georgia Peanut Farmer ran for reelection, disgruntled Wallaceites helped vote Carter right out of office.3/

Yet in all fairness, Carter unwittingly became a prisoner (and ultimately a victim) of the Myth itself. For on the domestic front, ever since the days of Franklin Roosevelt, the Democratic Party (as the traditional home of American Liberalism) had been touted as the party of prosperity. And any Democratic President who assumed office in January, 1977 would have been expected to bring back 1960's-style prosperity, even though, as I pointed out in Chapter Thirteen, such prosperity had been purchased largely at the rest of the World's expense-a pleasant state of affairs which ended abruptly in 1973-74 with the advent of the International Economic Revolution. Moreover, despite the high inflation, high unemployment, sluggish growth, and dwindling opportunities for upward social mobility, the Carter Administration's economic track record looked more or less satisfactory when compared with the record of its two immediate Republican predecessors, Nixon and Ford. But any Democratic President in Carter's shoes would have been judged by the same, unreasonable yardstick of the affluent 1960's--the Kennedy-Johnson Years--when the United States enjoyed her great moment in the sun, if you will.

In addition to restoring 1960's-style prosperity, Jimmy Carter was expected to advance the cause of social reform in the New Deal - Fair Deal - New Frontier - Great Society tradition. And any Democrat assuming the White House in January, 1977 would have been forced to stock his Administration with a sizeable number of dynamic, eager young Liberals, itching for the chance to move the country once again in a pronounced Leftward direction. (In truth, it would be difficult to imagine how any modern day Democratic Administration could even function effectively without making use of the nation's tremendous pool of Liberal political talent.) Yet, at the same time, Carter realized that the country's mood was growing increasingly Conservative. Indeed Carter had won the 1976 Democratic Presidential Nomination by carefully preaching a judicious mixture of reform and retrenchment. The Georgia Peanut Farmer had managed to walk a tightrope between these two conflicting impulses by cloaking his Liberal reforms in more politically acceptable, Conservative garb. However, once established in the Oval Office, Carter had to face the realities of governing the nation—especially the fact that as President he automatically became the de facto leader of a political party (the Democratic) which itself was a prisoner of the Myth. And by refraining from embarking upon a major new crusade for social reform, Carter ran afoul of many traditional elements in the Democratic coalition. The net result for Carter was a vacillating, day-to-day Administration, which lacked a clear, consistent, ideological orientation (either Left, Center, or Right), and thus an Administration which pleased almost nobody, while angering nearly everyone in sight.

The New Right Returns

As American Liberalism collapsed like a house of cards during the late 1970's, the New Right emerged as the nation's most creative, dynamic political force. And while the resurgent New Right still retained many of its salient characteristics from the 1960's, naturally with the passage of time a new generation of political leaders, organizers, and intellectuals took their rightful place alongside (indeed sometimes superseded) older veterans of the Movement. Moreover, during the interim New Rightists had discovered how to infuse additional energy into their Movement by mastering new, ultra-modern, sophisticated political techniques.4/

Interestingly enough, the Goldwaterites themselves back in 1964 had pioneered many of today's most important campaign techniques. For example, the Goldwaterites were the first to raise vast amounts of money by soliciting large numbers of small donations from individual citizens, the first to perfect direct-mail political advertising, and the first to capture control of a major American political party at the grass roots level through state and local party caucuses. Soon afterwards the Goldwaterites' innovations of 1964 were temporarily overshadowed by the New Left's "Street Politics" of the late 1960's. But in the long run, the Goldwaterites' earlier innovations, not the New Left's "Politics of Confrontation," wound up having the most profound impact upon the way American politics is conducted today.

Then too, the fallout from the Watergate Scandal accidentally gave the New Right yet another great boost. For the 1974 Federal Election Campaign Act took the so-called "Fat Cats" out of Presidential politics--a development which redounded to the New Right's benefit, since they were already well equipped to raise good-size warchests through countless small contributors. Furthermore, the moral effects of Watergate revolutionized political campaigning at every level of American government. The demand for full disclosure of the sources of campaign funds, coupled with the unpopularity of "Big Money," made it imperative for candidates (yea, for political movements and single issue crusades) to raise their funds from a wide variety of sources (preferably small donations from private citizens), so as to create the illusion of broad "popular" support, and thus avoid the odium of appearing beholden to a few, well-heeled "Fat Cats." Of course, in this regard the New Right suddenly found itself admirably situated, since the key element in broad based political fundraising--the lengthy mailing lists--were a natural outgrowth of their legendary obsession with organizational details, as well as their long experience with direct-mail solicitation.

In addition to helping New Right candidates for public office, the revolution in political fundraising also greatly helped lobbyists representing the various New Right pressure groups. Before Watergate the typical New Right lobbyist, more often than not, was some heavyset, cigar-chomping, corporate gladhander (a la Washington cartoonist Herblock's devastating caricatures), who could offer politicians suitcases full of money but precious little else. However, as a result of the post-Watergate, grass roots, political fundraising revolution, New Right lobbyists, representing a virtual plethora of corporate or special interest political action committees, suddenly began wielding enormous clout as they stalked the corridors of Congress and state legislatures across the land. For behind these lobbyists now stood a broad-based, well-disciplined army of citizens who could be accurately identified and catalogued by ultra-modern, sophisticated surveying and computer technology, and then rapidly mobilized to vote, contribute money, write letters, walk precincts, attend political rallies, etc.

Furthermore, because these mailing lists became worth their weight in gold, the men who controlled access to these lists (or who knew how to utilize these lists effectively) acquired great power within the New Right Movement. Examples of these new, political "super-technicians" included direct-mail fundraising wizard Richard A. Viguerie (who got his start as George Wallace's 1968 American Independent Party fundraiser), Paul Weyrich of the influential Committee For the Survival of a Free Congress, John T. "Terry" Dolan of the National Conservative Political Action Committee, and Howard Phillips of the Conservative Caucus.

The post-Watergate climate also encouraged political movements to upgrade the image of their public relations and lobbying efforts in order to project a new veneer of respectability. Accordingly, the New Right began emulating the Left's longstanding subsidization of public issue research through various tax-exempt "think tanks" such as the Heritage Foundation, established in 1973 by Colorado brewer Joseph Coors and political organizer Paul Weyrich. Then too, in addition to these tax-exempt "public education" foundations like Heritage, the New Right opened a number of so-called "public interest" law firms, such as the Pacific Legal Foundation and the Washington Legal Foundation, in order to give a more impartial, less overtly partisan flavor to its lobbying activities.

The Discovery of Populism

As a result of the New Right's phenomenal success in obtaining campaign funds and political support from grass roots sources, the Movement's leaders gained a better appreciation for the common people-- Mr. and Mrs. Average Citizen, if you will. In other words, at this somewhat belated date, the New Right finally discovered the virtues of good, old-fashioned, American Populism.

This late-1970's style, New Right Populism, assumed several forms. First, the Movement (in true Populist tradition) celebrated the honest, down-to-earth qualities found in America's strong, vigorous, Southern and Western "frontier" areas, while, at the same time, rejecting the effete, decadent East. Next, these modern day, New Right Populists continued the traditional Populist attack upon the "Non-Producing Classes"--that is, those groups who sponge off the "real wealth" created by hard-working independent businessmen, laborers, and farmers. Currently, in the New Right's eyes, the most notorious parasites (often government subsidized parasites at that) are the members of the so-called "New Class," which author Alan Crawford has identified as "professors and education administrators, research scientists working on government grants, federal bureaucrats, planners in the public and private sector, consultants and public relations experts, national newscasters, and network journalists, writers, and critics." Incidentally, this "New Class" just so happens to be centered primarily in the nation's largest cities (another old Populist bugaboo) particularly the big Eastern cities (a double bugaboo). And lastly, New Right Populists denounce both the privileges and power of non-elected elites (especially Liberal-oriented government bureaucrats and judges) who are felt to be completely out of touch with the more Conservative public opinion.5/

Now, of course, a few New Right elements (in particular, the Southern Rednecks and the Forgotten Rightists) had always entertained these traditional Populistic sentiments. But with regards to the great majority of New Rightists, this sudden, wholesale embrace of Populism represented a dramatic reversal of the Movement's longstanding antipathy towards "the people" at large. One recalls the New Right's open disdain for "the rabble," as expressed throughout Chapter Three. And one recalls the "ancient Roman Senator" pretensions of a Barry Goldwater or a Robert Welch as they battled valiantly to preserve the American Republic from the onslaught of popular democracy.

Nevertheless, even strongly held beliefs sometimes change. Consequently, by the late 1970's the New Right was pleasantly surprised to discover that "the people" could often be trusted to vote Conservative. So a crusty, old Reactionary like Howard Jarvis used the Populist inspired initiative process to enact a drastic property tax limitation measure in California in June, 1978. In fact, "the people" in many cases had become the New Right's reliable ally in the common fight against Liberal legislatures, bureaucrats, and the courts. Moreover, by the later 1970's, up-and-coming New Right politicians, such as Utah Senator Orrin Hatch, Nevada Senator Paul Laxalt, North Carolina Senator Jesse Helms, Georgia Congressman Larry McDonald, California Congressman Robert Dornan, and Maryland Congressman Robert Bauman (until his political downfall as the result of a homosexual scandal), all deliberately eschewed the stuffy, Goldwateresque, "Old Roman" image in favor of a more folksy, Populist approach.*

Finally, in keeping with its new-found appreciation for Populism, the New Right stepped up its efforts to mobilize America's Conservative-oriented, churchgoing population. Ironically, it was Democrat Jimmy Carter himself back in 1976 who had first focused national attention upon the Fundamentalist Protestant, "Born Again" Movement. But in the years after 1976, the New Right reaped the benefits from the "Born Again" phenomenon, as Ministers like the Reverend Jerry Falwell of Lynchburg, Virginia (the founder of the Moral Majority), brought a New Right, Fundamentalist Protestant version of the gospel into millions of American homes on a weekly basis via the electronic medium of television.

---

*Note-- Many New Right intellectuals, especially those who came of age, so to speak, in the 1970's (such as author Kevin Phillips, and syndicated columnists John D. Lofton, Jr. and Patrick Buchanan) loudly sang the praises of the virtuous masses while reviling the elites. Yet, if the American people suddenly began voting Liberal once again, these New Right intellectuals (along with most other New Right leaders) would no doubt quickly rediscover their traditional objections to Populism.

New Tactics

In conjunction with their acceptance of Populism, New Rightists adopted a more flexible, less dogmatic approach to politics. Gone, at least for a while, were the days when a Barry Goldwater could stand before the 1964 G.O.P. National Convention to accept the Republican Presidential Nomination and then proceed to read all but the true believers out of the Party: "Any who join us in all sincerity, we welcome. Those who do not care for our cause we do not expect to enter our ranks in any case." Instead, by the late 1970's the New Right was willing to seek common ground with all sorts of other individuals and groups who, for one reason or another, just so happened to be in agreement with the New Right on a given issue. Thus, by dropping their earlier demand that all potential allies also become true believers in their Movement, New Rightists began attracting support from a wide variety of sources. And by focusing primarily upon selected issues, New Rightists began achieving, at long last, many of the goals which had often eluded them in the past.6/

A perfect illustration of the New Right's new ability to attract broad-based support for its policies can be found with regards to the Tax Limitation Movement which swept across the nation in 1978-79. For years the Tax Limitation Crusade had been the exclusive province of the New Right—in particular, Reactionary Wealth. But a New Rightist like Howard Jarvis managed to persuade California voters to approve his Proposition 13 by an astonishing 2 to 1 margin, which clearly indicates that on a given issue the New Right's appeal could now cut across party lines, indeed across ideological lines.

In similar fashion, New Rightists also enlisted widespread public support for a number of other economic issues including attempts to limit the overall growth of government, to reduce government spending, to restrict the power of public employee unions, to abolish government-inspired affirmative action programs (i.e., reverse discrimination in both government and private industry) so as to base hirings and promotions strictly on merit, to relax previously stringent environmental standards in order to foster growth and development (particularly in the Western states, home of the so-called Sagebrush Rebellion), to lessen government regulation of business, and to increase competition generally throughout the economy.

Indeed, perhaps more than anything else, the American people's desire to return to a free market economy served to give the New Right a certain degree of intellectual respectability, as well as a measure of support, even amongst its staunchest enemies. For many Liberals reluctantly came to the inescapable conclusion that the nation's economic problems could not be solved simply by redistribution of wealth alone, and that increased economic growth and productivity had become essential.

Likewise, with regards to a number of social issues (especially the New Right's pet "family issues"), groups such as Blue Collar Catholic Democrats and Orthodox Jews often joined forces with the New Right on selected issues of mutual concern. These issues included the Right-to-Life Movement which sought to prohibit abortions; the anti-Homosexual Crusade (featuring singer Anita Bryant); the anti-pornography, anti-sexual permissiveness campaign; the opposition to school busing, as well as the attempt to ban offensive public school textbooks and return American education back to the good old days of readin', writin', and 'rithmetic; the efforts to prevent the creation of a Federal Department of Education coupled with actions designed to return control of the public schools to local authorities; and the agitation to restore the death penalty and to crack down hard on crime generally.

Finally, in foreign affairs, one need not necessarily have been a card-carrying New Rightist to have opposed either the Carter Administration's "giveaway" of the Panama Canal, or the "one-sided" S.A.L.T. II Treaty negotiations with the Soviet Union. And even many fervent Liberals eventually came around to the New Right's viewpoint that the Soviet military buildup during the 1970's (both nuclear and conventional) represented a distinct threat to American security, which required a substantial increase in U.S. defense spending. In fact, the unwarranted Soviet military build-up in the face of a decreasing U.S. military presence, effectively laid to rest the notion that the Soviet's participation in the arms race was merely a defensive reaction to the possibility of American aggression. Clearly, the Soviets were pursuing the arms race for its own sake.

Nominal Allies: Libertarians and Neo-Conservatives

As the decade of the 1970's wore on, and as the various shortcomings of American Liberalism became increasingly apparent, many thoughtful men and women, unwilling to cast their fortunes with the New Right, instead sought refuge in two alternative movements--Libertarianism and Neo-Conservatism. Indeed, the curious relationship between the New Right and both these movements deserves a closer examination, since all three took issue with contemporary American Liberalism, but from somewhat different perspectives.

On the one hand, a good many members of the New Right felt favorably disposed towards the Libertarians. New Rightists in particular appreciated the Libertarian anti-big government, pro-free enterprise philosophy (while simply ignoring the Libertarians' unpalatable stance on various social issues). In fact, on more than one occasion, Ronald

337

Reagan himself has characterized his own economic philosophy as "Libertarian." Then too, over the years Reagan has made a point of enlisting a number of young economic advisors who have also characterized themselves as "Libertarian," or "Libertarian Conservative" (whatever that means).

However, Libertarians themselves are rather annoyed by New Rightists who claim to be Libertarians, but then reject the other half of the Libertarian philosophy--i.e., the strong commitment to individual freedom of choice in social, sexual, and cultural matters. Moreover, since the rank and file New Rightists still heartily applaud the forcible suppression of unorthodox social, sexual, and cultural ideas, I doubt whether the New Right as a movement will ever evolve into authentic Libertarianism, at least within the remainder of the twentieth century. (In my opinion, a widespread American Libertarian Movement would more likely develop from disenchanted Welfare State Liberals.)

On the other hand, New Rightists, by and large, were less than thrilled with the appearance of the so-called "Neo-Conservatives." True, both groups shared a strong commitment to the free enterprise system, as well as a healthy skepticism of Liberal social programs. Yet, from the New Right's perspective, several key factors precluded any genuine cooperation between the two groups.

First, New Rightists considered the Neo-Conservatives to be relatively late converts to the cause of Conservatism, and, as such, doubted the depth of their commitment. After all, nearly every contemporary Neo-Conservative had once come from a staunch, Liberal background. Few, if any, Neo-Conservatives had been Goldwaterites back in 1964. In fact, most Neo-Conservatives had been violently anti-Goldwater, and had come around to the Rightist point of view, not because Barry Goldwater had helped them see the light, but rather, as author Peter Steinfels emphasizes, because they recoiled against the turmoil of the late 1960's--especially the agitation of the New Left. As with regards to the Neo-Conservatives' newly discovered appreciation for the free enterprise system, one keen observer, former Treasury Secretary William Simon, may well have placed the matter in its proper focus, when he saw fit to describe them as nothing more than "liberals with economic common sense."7/

Secondly, not only did New Rightists question the Neo-Conservatives' commitment to conservatism, but they also suspected quite strongly that the Neo-Conservatives were simply cowbirds placed within their midst as part of a cunning Liberal scheme to sabotage a genuine Radical Conservative Movement. In essence, this line of reasoning went as follows: The Neo-Conservatives had decided to rescue American Liberalism from its own worst excesses, as well as from its contamination with New Leftism, both of which had angered the American people. Thus, the Neo-Conservatives, aware of the nation's drift to the Right, sought to head off a real Right-wing movement by creating its own "in-house" opposition to Liberalism itself. This ploy would safely channel the country's growing Rightist sentiment in a "constructive" direction. In short, unable to stem completely the Rightist tide (nor in favor of halting this tide altogether), Neo-Conservatives attempted to become its leaders. And, for good measure, the Eastern Liberal Establishment-oriented National News Media painted the Neo-Conservatives as "thoughtful" critics of American Liberalism, in direct contrast with the New Right's alleged "unreasonableness." No wonder, syndicated columnist and former Nixon Speechwriter Patrick Buchanan concluded that "we are better off with these guys [the Neo-Conservatives] as adversaries."8/

Furthermore, as author Alan Crawford has pointed out, the New Rightists distrusted the Neo-Conservatives precisely because its members had been so closely aligned with America's Eastern Intellectual Community (which, of course, has long been one of the New Right's prime targets). In fact, many New Rightists saw the Neo-Conservative Movement as an insidious maneuver by the Liberals to keep Rightist opposition clearly in the hands of the intellectual elites, while in the process conveniently aborting the budding, Right-wing Populist revolt brewing out in the Southern and Western hinterlands.9/

Third, a good many New Rightists felt, perhaps quite correctly, that, to a considerable degree, the Neo-Conservative Movement was dominated by Jewish intellectuals, who used it as a vehicle for the protection of strictly Jewish interests. Thus, Patrick Buchanan once labeled the Neo-Conservatives as the "Commentary crowd," in obvious reference to the American Jewish Committee's publication, Commentary, which serves as a forum for Neo-Conservatism. Buchanan remarked that "This Commentary crowd...didn't come around to our way of thinking, until the Soviet threat to Israel became apparent." Then too, New Rightists believed that Eastern Jewish Intellectuals had sought to curtail a genuine Right-wing Populism because of their traditional fear that such a mass movement might very well wind up becoming a hot-bed of anti-Semitism.10/

Reagan Prepares for 1980

By all calculations, the Carter Administration (which assumed office in January, 1977) should have been able to remain in power right through January, 1985. After all, ever since 1897, the political party (either Republican or Democrat) which had regained control of the White House, had always managed to get reelected to at least one additional term. Indeed, such a two-term tradition seemed firmly established in twentieth century American politics. Thus, from the perspective of January, 1977, it appeared likely that, barring a major upheaval, Jimmy Carter would win reelection in November, 1980. And if New Rightists

339

had really believed the old saying that "History repeats itself," they might well have considered skipping 1980 (in order to avoid another 1964-style Goldwater debacle against an incumbent Democratic President), and set their sights on 1984 instead. For the year 1984, from the perspective of 1977, looked like a much better chance for the New Right to make its move: the country would finally be ready for a return to Republican rule after eight years under the Democrats; the difficult issues of Vietnam and Watergate would, by this time, have been more or less forgotten; a new generation of younger New Rightists would emerge (one of whom would no doubt make a solid Presidential contender); and the Electoral College would now reflect the Census of 1980, which would serve to add greater weight to the Southern and Western states—already the area of the New Right's strongest support.

Nevertheless, the New Right's triumph actually wound up taking place in November, 1980—four years earlier than when might have been expected. True, the utter exhaustion of American Liberalism, as well as the political ineptitude displayed by Jimmy Carter on many occasions, both played an important role in the New Right's victory. But we must also recognize that Ronald Reagan (and the New Right Movement behind him) took an enormous gamble in 1980—a gamble which paid off handsomely, but which, had it backfired, would have saddled the Movement with yet another 1964 Goldwater-type fiasco (as alluded to a few moments ago). For Reagan, like his predecessor Goldwater, played a high stakes game by challenging an incumbent President of the nation's majority party. Moreover, Reagan entered the 1980 Campaign as a sixty-nine year old man, who was not a fresh face, but a well-known public figure strongly identified with Vietnam and, to a lesser degree, with Watergate. Consequently, a Reagan defeat in November, 1980 would have seriously injured the Movement (just as Goldwater's 1964 fiasco had done), and would probably have paved the way for a G.O.P. Moderate to pick up the pieces in 1984 (just as Nixon had done in 1968). However, politics remains a strange, unpredictable blend of timing and chemistry. And this time around in 1980, everything fell into place for Reagan and the New Right.

Specifically, what fell into place for Reagan and the New Right in 1980 was the issue of inflation, which became the major theme of the Presidential Campaign against Jimmy Carter and the Democrats. It boiled down to a simple case of a politician and a movement having the right issue at the right time.

Interestingly enough, Reagan basically restated Barry Goldwater's long forgotten message of 1964 on the subject of inflation—i.e., that inflation is much more than the phenomenon of rising prices. Rather, inflation reflects a deeper lack of consensus in society—an unwholesome state of affairs where everyone only looks out for his own selfish interest, and where everyone is engaged in a mad scramble against his neighbor for a piece of an ever-shrinking pie. Indeed, the impending breakdown of a sense of "community" in American life (of which inflation would merely be one symptom) was one of Goldwater's central campaign themes back in 1964. And Reagan in 1980, like Goldwater before him, promised to bring inflation under control, not just because of the economic hardships it created, but because inflation was destroying the American peoples' sense of community with one another.

As a matter of fact, as early as 1974, when Richard Nixon fell from power and the New Right reemerged from the shadows, Reagan had been warning about the evils of inflation, and how it must be brought under control at all costs. However, Reagan's message was not very popular back in 1974 (especially among the working classes) since the country was in the midst of a severe recession, and most Americans at that time were still adverse to fighting inflation with high unemployment and high interest rates. Even as late as 1976 Reagan would have easily lost a two-man race with Jimmy Carter, precisely because the working classes had not yet come to view inflation as their primary concern.

Nonetheless, after 1976 a good portion of the working classes did come around to Reagan's way of thinking. And not only did many working people begin to see inflation in a new context, but they also realized that Reagan was correct when he blamed the Federal Government for deliberately creating the inflation. Here was the benevolent welfare state of F.D.R. and J.F.K. finally being unmasked as the enemy of its own hard-pressed citizens. No wonder, for example, the working classes in California responded enthusiastically to a New Rightist like Howard Jarvis who insisted that because of inflation and skyrocketing taxes "the Government itself has gone into the business of manufacturing poor people." And another New Rightist summed up the sentiments of countless Americans when she charged that "the American people are being mugged by their own government!"11/

Reagan Captures the 1980 G.O.P. Presidential Nomination

Unlike 1968 or 1976, Ronald Reagan got a good head start in his campaign for the 1980 G.O.P. Presidential Nomination. Moreover, unlike 1968 or 1976, Reagan apparently wanted the Nomination this time around. In addition, as I mentioned earlier, Reagan had the winning issue for 1980 (inflation) which he skillfully wove together with other popular themes such as government retrenchment, lower taxes, a restoration of a sense of community among the American people, a renewed moral commitment, etc. And Reagan spread his effective message everywhere he went, aided by a special foundation, Citizens For the Republic, established specifically for Reagan's benefit using the surplus funds left over from Reagan's unsuccessful 1976 Primary Campaign. Citizens For the Republic paid much of Reagan's traveling expenses between 1977 and 1980, thus allowing him the luxury of campaigning virtually non-stop during this period, and, incidentally, allowing him to circumvent the rather strict campaign financing restrictions. Then too, Citizens For the Republic raised additional money of its own, which it then strategically dispensed to a number of G.O.P. candidates around the country in 1978. Reagan's personal appearances plus his foundation's generous campaign contributions ultimately produced a sizeable collection of political I.O.U.'s—all redeemable in 1980.12/

When the 1980 G.O.P. Presidential Primary Season eventually rolled around, Reagan had a relatively easy time of it. After all, the New Right had, in actuality, controlled the Republican Party at the grass roots level ever since the Goldwater Revolution of 1964. Consequently, New Rightists had the power to secure the Presidential Nomination for one of their own, if only they cared to mobilize their full resources on his behalf. And this they chose to do for Ronald Reagan in 1980, unlike both 1968 and 1976 when a sizeable percentage of New Rightists supported Richard Nixon and Gerald Ford respectively.

Without question, Gerald Ford would have once again been Reagan's strongest opponent in 1980 if the former President had been willing to slug it out with Reagan in the primaries. Instead, Ford decided to hang back and wait for a deadlocked G.O.P. Convention in July to turn to him. This, of course, never came to pass. Meanwhile, as the National News Media was frantically searching for someone other than Ford to stop Reagan, the former-California Governor easily brushed aside the two most likely alternative candidates for the assignment— Moderates George Bush, a former-Ambassador to the United Nations (who later wound up on the G.O.P. ticket as Reagan's Vice President), and Tennessee Senator Howard Baker. And for good measure, Reagan trounced Illinois Liberal Republican Congressman John Anderson, who, when he found that he could make no headway against Reagan as a Republican, organized an Independent candidacy in time for the November, 1980 General Election. (Anderson eventually garnered 7% of the popular vote in a three-way, Carter-Reagan-Anderson race.)

In truth, with Ford effectively out of the running, only some other candidate acceptable to the New Right could have furnished a serious threat to Reagan in 1980. For a brief time, a few New Rightists, South Carolina Senator J. Strom Thurmond included, had championed the Presidential candidacy of Texan John Connally, on the theory that Reagan was much too old and, hence, could not win against the Democrats in November. But aside from John Connally's association in the public's mind with Watergate, the former-crony of Lyndon Johnson was not fully trusted by rank and file New Rightists. That left Illinois Representative Phil Crane, a past Chairman of the American Conservative Union, who, in addition to a bland personality, was dogged by rumors of alleged sexual misconduct, and young, New York Representative Jack Kemp, who thought about challenging Reagan, but after

342

carefully surveying the situation, decided to wait for some future opportunity.

All told, perhaps the most newsworthy event of the otherwise uneventful 1980 G.O.P. Primary Season occurred when Reagan, on the eve of the New Hampshire contest, unceremoniously fired his National Campaign Manager John Sears, the man who had earned the New Right's undying enmity by arranging the infamous Richard Schweiker Vice Presidential Gambit back in the Summer of 1976. (See Chapter Thirteen.) Thus, while Sears was ostensibly dismissed for purely campaign related reasons, New Rightists chose to interpret his dismissal as a reaffirmation of Reagan's commitment to the principles of their Movement.

Carter vs. Reagan

The 1980 General Election pitted Republican challenger Ronald Reagan, a healthy, well-preserved, sixty-nine year old, former-California Governor against Democratic incumbent President Jimmy Carter, a fifty-six year old, political leader beset by severe problems both at home and abroad. Furthermore, considering the fact that the majority of the American people were no longer willing to accept "politics as usual" (and, hence, were ripe for a drastic change), Reagan should have won the Election hands down. Nonetheless, although Carter trailed badly throughout most of the campaign, as the November 4th Election Day drew near, many Democrats began remembering the Myth of F.D.R. and J.F.K., and began thinking seriously of returning to the fold.

However, at the last moment two events broke against Carter. First, the as-yet unresolved Iranian Hostage Crisis sparked a flurry of eleventh hour negotiations designed to secure the release of the fifty-two American captives by Election Day. No doubt, a great diplomatic triumph would have boosted the President's stock substantially, although it will forever remain a matter of historical speculation whether or not such a coup, by itself, would have turned the contest around. Nevertheless, it seems certain that the President's failure to reach such an agreement with Iran played a major role in insuring his defeat.

Second, Carter proved unable to turn the Election around during the major candidates' one and only joint, televised, Presidential debate. The Democratic incumbent failed miserably in his attempt to paint Reagan as a dangerous, Reactionary Radical, just as the Democrats had done so successfully against Barry Goldwater back in 1964. (See Chapter Nine.) That is not to imply that Carter failed for lack of effort. In fact, the President emptied his bottomless bag of tricks trying to connect Reagan with Goldwater's 1964 positions on civil rights, Social Security, and nuclear weapons, but to no avail. For as far as the majority of

343

American voters was concerned, Carter was running against Reagan in 1980, not against Goldwater in 1964. Besides, new political realities had set in; and what had happened way back in 1964 was now basically irrelevant to the urgent problems of the hour.*

On Tuesday, November 4, 1980 (one week after the Presidential Debate) Reagan scored a landslide victory, capturing 51% of the popular vote against only 41% for Carter and 7% for Independent John Anderson. Moreover, Reagan swept Carter 489 to 49 in the Electoral College—the latter carrying only half a dozen small states: his native Georgia, Hawaii, Maryland, Minnesota, Rhode Island, and West Virginia. In addition, the G.O.P. captured control of the U.S. Senate for the first time since 1952 and sharply reduced the Democratic majority in the U.S. House of Representatives. All in all, the New Right had finally achieved a measure of national political power.

---

*Note—Incidentally, the single most significant moment of the 1980 Carter-Reagan Debate occurred when veteran newspaper reporter Harry Ellis of the Christian Science Monitor, one of the four journalists serving on the panel of questioners, asked the candidates how inflation could ever be brought under control since it was due, in large part, to external factors beyond American control—i.e., the O.P.E.C. oil price increases. Now it remains a mystery whether Mr. Ellis' questions was innocently phrased in such a manner, or whether he was deliberately attempting to give the President a platform from which he could continue to maintain the illusion that his Administration was busy fighting the inflation which it had absolutely no part in bringing about. At any rate, Carter did use Ellis' question as a springboard to perpetuate this elaborate fiction regarding inflation. To Carter's answer, and to the underlying assumptions (whether intended or not) behind Ellis' question, Reagan, in turn, offered a stern, devastatingly effective rebuke:

> Mr. Ellis, I think this idea that has been spawned here in our country that inflation somehow came upon us like a plague and therefore it's uncontrollable and no one can do anything about it, is entirely spurious and it's dangerous to say this to the people.13/

The heretofore best kept secret in America—that the Federal Government itself was the major cause of inflation—had at last become common knowledge. The game was up, so to speak, and, as a result, Jimmy Carter and the Democrats were doomed.

344

CHAPTER FOURTEEN - Notes

1. American historian Richard Hofstadter predicted as much when he noted in his 1948 book The American Political Tradition that "Roosevelt is bound to be the dominant figure in the mythology of any resurgent American liberalism." Richard Hofstadter, The American Political Tradition (New York: Alfred A. Knopf, 1948), p. 347.

2. Los Angeles Times, August 13, 1980.

3. Witcover, Marathon, p. 535.

4. An excellent survey of the groups and individuals comprising the contemporary New Right can be found in Alan Crawford's, Thunder on the Right.

5. Ibid., p. 171.

6. Goldwater, Where I Stand, p. 16.

7. Peter Steinfels, The Neo-Conservatives (New York: Simon and Schuster, 1979);
Simon, A Time For Truth, p. 134.

8. New Guard, (June, 1976), p. 14.

9. Crawford, Thunder on the Right, p. 7.

10. New Guard, (June, 1976), p. 14.

11. Personal recollections from May, 1978.

12. Crawford, Thunder on the Right, p. 60.

13. New York Times, October 29, 1980.

CHAPTER FIFTEEN

THE NEW RIGHT IN HISTORICAL PERSPECTIVE

The Lost Opportunities

In order to assess briefly the significance of Ronald Reagan's 1980 victory in historical terms, we must once again return to three important themes which have already been developed throughout the course of this book: (a) the failure of Senator Robert Taft to secure the 1952 G.O.P. Presidential Nomination, (b) the New Right's disastrous allegiance to a trio of national political leaders--Richard Nixon, Barry Goldwater, and George Wallace--who, during the period 1960-76, caused the Movement grave harm, and (c) the failure of Governor Reagan to secure the 1968 G.O.P. Presidential Nomination. Only by contrasting Reagan's 1980 triumph with each of these three aforementioned events, can we hope to place Reagan's recent Election in some sort of meaningful historical context.

To begin with, although New Rightists are certainly celebrating Reagan's 1980 Election as a victory in their continuing struggle to preserve and defend the so-called "American Way of Life," obviously such a victory (if indeed it can be called one) comes rather late in the day. Clearly, the traditional American Way of Life has undergone serious erosion over the past several decades. And it goes without saying that this erosion would not have been nearly so pronounced by the year 1980 (nor as difficult to repair) had a strong Conservative, like Reagan, been elected to the White House at some earlier date. New Rightists have known this fact for decades, which is why, for example, they retain such bitter memories concerning Senator Robert Taft's defeat in 1952 at the hands of Eisenhower. (See Chapter Two.) For while they no doubt look upon Reagan's 1980 triumph with satisfaction, so much water has passed under the bridge in those twenty-eight intervening years that New Rightists will always be haunted by the idea that 1952 was the great opportunity which somehow got away.1/

Then too, in a roundabout way, the Reagan of 1980 is the political heir to the Robert Taft of 1952. (See Chapter One.) Yet between the Taft and Reagan Eras, the American Right found time to follow the treacherous, deceitful Richard Nixon, the flippant, impolitic Barry Goldwater, and the racist, demagogic George Wallace. Consequently, while the American Way of Life was disintegrating all around them, New Rightists supported three grossly inadequate leaders, each of whom, in his own inimitable fashion, managed to inflict enormous damage on the Movement. As with the lost opportunity of 1952, Reagan's 1980 victory can never make up for the precious time wasted during the Nixon-Goldwater-Wallace Era (1960-76).

Finally, with regards to Reagan himself, the former California Governor probably reached the White House a dozen years too late to save what still remained of the traditional American Way of Life. Had Reagan captured the 1968 G.O.P. Presidential Nomination (instead of Nixon) and had then gone on to beat Humphrey and Wallace in November, the United States would have entered the 1970's with a strong, Right-wing National Government. Perhaps some of the events of the 1970's, which so disillusioned the American people (i.e., the U.S. defeat in Vietnam, the double-digit inflation, the crushing tax burden, etc.), would never have come to pass. Surely, the trauma of Watergate would have been totally avoided.

Despite the turmoil of the 1960's, this exciting, prosperous decade was, in some respects, the nation's Periclean Age. But the debilitating 1970's permanently altered (one might say killed) the American people's traditional buoyant spirit. Simply stated, America was just not the same optimistic society in 1980 that it had been back in 1968. True enough, Reagan campaigned in 1980 stressing the twin themes of restoration and revitalization. The G.O.P. Standard-Bearer even went so far as to proclaim his Election as a glorious opportunity for a "New Beginning." Yet, most likely, Reagan is beating a dead horse—for the New Right's cherished American Way of Life can no longer be resurrected. Political rhetoric alone cannot work such a miracle.

The New Right in the 1980's

The New Right has made a number of significant adjustments to the new political realities of the 1980's. Indeed, Reagan captured the Presidency in November, 1980 precisely because many millions of American citizens (who were emphatically not New Rightists) wound up voting for him anyway—some, no doubt, enthusiastically. Of course, Reagan did represent the only viable alternative to another four years of Jimmy Carter. Nevertheless, Reagan's widespread support in 1980 reflects the fact that both he as well as the Movement itself have undergone substantial changes with the passage of time.

For instance, the New Right has managed to broaden its hitherto rather narrow political base. Traditionally, the Movement has concentrated upon protecting the dominant economic and social position of the American Male W.A.S.P., and faithfully serving his interests, while too often rejecting the legitimate aspirations of minority groups, women, and youth. Moreover, the Movement had retained an unmistakable, rural-small town flavor. Thus, by stubbornly ignoring the existence of urban America, the New Right had cut itself off from the mainstream of modern intellectual life, had fallen far behind the Left in the recruitment of high caliber political talent, and, incidentally, had earned the undying enmity of the powerful, sophisticated National News Media. In short, the dominant W.A.S.P. elements controlling the New

348

Right are finally coming to grips with the fact that their once-Waspish America has become a culturally, ethnically, racially, religiously, and sexually pluralistic society.

Then too, the 1964 Goldwater Revolution brought into national political prominence the Sunbelt Nouveau Riche--a new class of men who simply hated the Eastern region of the country and everything that the East represented. Now it goes without saying that such openly expressed, sectional antipathy flies in the face of what constitutes good, sound, national politics (which the impolitic Goldwaterites learned the hard way back in 1964). However, the passage of time gradually took some of the rambunctiousness out of the New Right. (The Reaganites of 1980 were not nearly as passionate as the Goldwaterites of 1964 had been.) So by the 1980's, while still prone to occasional, almost perfunctory, outbursts of anti-Eastern rhetoric (i.e., the bumper stickers in natural-gas producing Southern states which read "Freeze a Yankee"), most Sunbelt Nouveau Riche New Rightists have now reconciled themselves to the fact that American-style politics often requires compromise and accommodation. And having adjusted to this political fact of life, Sunbelt Nouveau Riche New Rightists have at last become ready to play a meaningful, responsible role in national affairs.

Perhaps the clearest indication of this necessary adjustment could be seen in the attitude of the Reagan camp in the days immediately following their candidate's November, 1980 Presidential victory. For when some unreconstructed New Rightists went so far as to proclaim that the newly elected Reagan was "their" President (and owed his victory to them alone), the Reagan camp took pains to set the record straight: Reagan intended to be President of all the American people--not just President of the true believers.

Furthermore, the New Right is only just now developing a capacity for ideological flexibility. Actually, this transformation should have come about long ago. For the United States underwent extraordinary economic, political, social, and cultural changes during the 1960's and 1970's; and the New Right spread its limited resources too thin by frantically attempting to plug up every single leak in the dike. Objectively speaking, many features of American life were surely not worth saving: Jim Crow, male chauvinism, sexual prudery, strict dress codes and personal grooming standards. Instead, the New Right should have devoted its full attention to saving the essentials: the American work ethic, the free enterprise system, the fiscal integrity of the United States Government, the safety of American streets from violent crime, and the defense of Western Civilization from the menace of World Communism.

The New Right's most significant philosophical adjustment concerned the welfare state itself. As of late, New Rightists have taken a stand, not against the mere existence of the welfare state, but rather against its all too frequent abuses. In 1976 Reagan failed to make this distinction absolutely clear in the American public's mind, and paid the price accordingly, especially in the early Presidential primaries against Gerald Ford. (See Chapter Thirteen) Determined not to repeat his 1976 mistake, Reagan campaigned in 1980 on a platform endorsing the welfare state, although, naturally he substituted the euphemism "safety net of social services" for the term welfare state. Incidentally, the euphemism "safety net" was coined by New York's up-and-coming Republican Congressman Jack Kemp in his fascinating little book, An American Renaissance.2/

Finally, during his first State of the Union Address as the nation's new Chief Executive, President Reagan drew yet another useful distinction—this time between the welfare state (i.e., the "safety net") and the redistribution of society's wealth. These two concepts are not identical, even though the political Left has traditionally linked the welfare state and redistribution together. (In some sense, the Left has used the welfare state as an excuse to pursue a policy of redistribution.) Nevertheless, while the welfare state often has enormous popular appeal, the idea of redistribution often does not. Thus the two concepts can be legitimately separated from one another as, for instance, in the British Tory Welfare State. And an American Conservative Welfare State, without the accompanying redistribution of wealth, was the position of both Robert Taft in 1952 and Ronald Reagan in 1980. The New Right could have spared itself a tremendous amount of grief if only it had bothered to make these vital distinctions absolutely clear right from the beginning. But, tragically, Barry Goldwater was sandwiched in between the eras of Taft and Reagan.

Not long ago, Barry Goldwater published his political memoirs, With No Apologies. Indeed, it is quite fitting that the Arizona Senator—the one man most responsible for the New Right's problems over the past two decades—should have selected such a title. For With No Apologies sums up perfectly both the life of a man and of a movement which were proud, stubborn, and, above all else, positively unwilling to admit that they had ever made so much as one, single, major mistake.3/

As a matter of fact, Goldwater is probably correct; both he and the New Right have nothing whatsoever to apologize for, either to themselves or to anyone else. They made a determined effort to save their version of the American Way of Life, and, in keeping with their character, went down in flames in the process. Furthermore, they failed to preserve their culture, not because they neglected to make the effort, but rather because their best effort simply wasn't good enough to succeed. Both Goldwater and the New Right lacked sufficient intellectual and political resources to carry the day.

Curiously though, of all the American people, the New Rightists possessed the strongest sense of the continuum of history. (See Chapter Three.) Appropriately, Goldwater's memoirs published in 1979 contained a passage restating the traditional New Right concern regarding the bitter lessons of history:

> History is the recital of the rise and fall of nations. If in our minds we mark the dissolution of empire by some singular military defeat, we are misreading history. In every case the climactic act has been preceded by internal failures, by a lessening of devotion to the principles and beliefs which created and sustained the rise to power and prominence. Great nations do not disappear into the dustbin of history without broadcasting in advance the direction they are taking.4/

Yet, ironically, this time around, the New Rightists (unlike their Ancient Roman counterparts) knew in advance that their way of life was crumbling. And, when all was said and done, New Rightists still proved much too inept to prevent it from happening all over again right before their very own eyes.

1. Political analyst Samuel Lubell revealed that a survey conducted by him during the 1952 General Election Campaign led him to conclude that Taft would have beaten Stevenson, although by a much narrower margin than did Eisenhower. Samuel Lubell, The Future of American Politics, 2nd Ed. (Revised) (Garden City, New York: Doubleday Anchor Books, 956), p. 250.

2. Jack Kemp, An American Renaissance (New York: Harper & Row, 1979).

3. Barry M. Goldwater, With No Apologies (New York: William Morrow and Company, Inc., 1979).

4. Ibid., p. 294.

BIBLIOGRAPHY

Books and Pamphlets

Adelson, Alan. SDS. New York: Charles Scribner's Sons, 1972.

Adler, Bill, ed. The Kennedy Wit. New York City: The Citadel Press, 1964.

Adorno, Theodore W., et. al. The Authoritarian Personality. New York: Harper, 1950.

Allen, Gary. Richard Nixon: The Man Behind the Mask. Boston: Western Islands Publishers, 1971.

Allen, Richard V. Peace or Peaceful Coexistence? Chicago: American Bar Assocation, 1966.

Amrise, Michael. The Awesome Challenge. New York: G.P. Putnam's Sons, 1964.

Apter, David, ed. Ideology and Discontent. New York: The Free Press of Glencoe, 1964.

Archer, Jules. 1968: Year of Crisis. New York: Julian Messner, 1971.

Auerbach, M. Morton. The Conservative Illusion. New York: Columbia University Press, 1959.

Austin, Anthony. The President's War. Philadelphia: J.B. Lippincott Company, 1971.

Bacciocco, Edward J., Jr. The New Left in America. Stanford, California: Hoover Institution Press, 1974.

Barrett, Russell H. Integration at Ole Miss. Chicago: Quadrangle Books, 1965.

Barron, Bryton. The Untouchable State Department. Springfield, Virginia: Crestwood Books, 1962.

Bealle, Morris A. 1960 Washington Squirrel Cage (The Story of the Roosevelt, Truman and Eisenhower Raw Deals in Satire). Washington, D.C.: Columbia Publishing Company, 1960.

Beaty, John. The Iron Curtain Over America. Barboursville, West Virginia: Chestnut Mountain Books, 1962.

354

Bell, Daniel. The Radical Right. Garden City, New York: Doubleday & Company, Inc., 1963.

Bell, Jack. Mr. Conservative: Barry Goldwater. Garden City, New York: Doubleday & Company, Inc., 1962.

Bell, Jack. The Johnson Treatment. New York: Harper & Row Publishers, 1965.

Bell, Leland V. In Hitler's Shadow: The Anatomy of American Nazism. Port Washington, New York: Kennikat Press, 1973.

Benson, Ezra Taft. A Nation Asleep. Salt Lake City, Utah: Bookcraft, Inc., 1963.

Benson, Ezra Taft. Cross Fire, The Eight Years With Eisenhower. Garden City, New York: Doubleday & Company, Inc. 1962.

Benson, Ezra Taft. The Red Carpet (Socialism--The Royal Road to Communism). Salt Lake City, Utah: Bookcraft, Inc., 1962.

Bowen, Robert O. The Truth About Communism. Northport, Alabama: Colonial Press, 1962.

Boyarsky, Bill. The Rise of Ronald Reagan. New York: Random House, 1968.

Boyer, William W. Issues, 1968. Lawrence, Kansas: The University Press of Kansas, 1968.

Bozell, L. Brent. The Warren Revolution. New Rochelle, New York: Arlington House, 1966.

Brandon, Henry. Anatomy of Error. Boston: Gambit Incorporated, 1969.

Brodie, Bernard. War and Politics. New York: The MacMillan Company, 1973.

Brooke, Edward. The Challenge of Change. Boston: Little Brown and Company, 1966.

Broyles, J. Allen. The John Birch Society (Anatomy of a Protest). Boston: Beacon Press, 1964.

Buckley, William F., Jr. The Governor Listeth. New York: G.P. Putnam's Sons, 1970.

uckley, William F., Jr. The Jeweler's Eye. New York: G.P. Putnam's Sons, 1968.

Buckley, William F., Jr. Dialogues in Americanism. Chicago, Illinois: Henry Regnery Co., 1964.

Buckley, William F., Jr. Rumbles Left and Right. New York: G.P. Putnam's Sons, 1963.

Buckley, William F., Jr. The Committee and Its Critics. New York: G.P. Putnam's Sons, 1962.

Buckley, William F., Jr., Up From Liberalism. New York: McDowell, Obolensky, 1959.

Buckley, William F., Jr., and Bozell, L. Brent. McCarthy and His Enemies: The Record and Its Meaning. Chicago: Henry Regnery, Co., 1954.

Bundy, Edgar C. Apostles of Deceit. Wheaton, Illinois: Church League of America, 1966.

Bundy, Edgar C. Collectivism in the Churches. Wheaton, Illinois: Church League of America, 1958.

Burdick, Eugene, and Wheeler, Harvey. Fail-Safe. New York: McGraw Hill, 1962.

Burlingame, Roger. The Sixth Column. New York: J.B. Lippincott Company, 1962.

Burnham, James. Suicide of the West. New York: The John Day Company, 1964.

Cain, Edward. They'd Rather Be Right: Youth and Conservatism. New York: the MacMillan Company, 1963.

Caldwell, Taylor. A Pillar of Iron. Garden City, New York: Doubleday & Company, Inc. 1965.

Cannon, Lou. Ronnie and Jesse. Garden City, New York: Doubleday & Company, Inc. 1969.

Carney, Francis M. and Way, Frank H., Jr. Politics, 1968. Belmont, California: Wadsworth Publishing Company, Inc., 1967.

Carney, Francis M. and Way, Frank H., Jr. Politics, 1964. Belmont, California: Wadsworth Publishing Company, Inc., 1964.

356

Cash, Kevin. Who the Hell is William Loeb? Manchester, Ne[w] Hampshire: Amoskeag Press, Inc., 1975.

Chodorov, Frank. The Income Tax, Root of All Evil. New York: The Devin-Adair Company, 1954.

Chomsky, Noam. At War With Asia. New York: Partheon Books, 1969.

Clabaugh, Gary K. Thunder on the Right. Chicago: Nelson-Hall Company, 1974.

Cohen, Martin A. The John Birch Society Coloring Book. Chicago: Serious Products Company, 1962.

Cook, Fred J. Barry Goldwater--Extremist on the Right. New York: Grove Press, Inc., 1964.

Cooper, Chester L. The Lost Crusade. New York: Dodd, Mead & Company, 1970.

Cooper, John Charles. The Turn Right. Philadelphia: The Westminster Press, 1970.

Cosman, Bernard. Five States For Goldwater. University, Alabama: University of Alabama Press, 1966.

Cosman, Bernard and Huckshorn, Robert J. Republican Politics. New York: Frederick A. Praeger, 1968.

Courtney, Kent and Phoebe. The Case of General Edwin A. Walker. New Orleans, Louisiana: Conservative Society of America Publications, 1961.

Crawford, Alan. Thunder on the Right: The New Right and the Politics of Resentment. New York: Pantheon Books, 1980.

Cummings, Milton C., Jr. The National Election of 1964. Washington, D.C.: The Brookings Institution, 1966.

Dalfiume, Richard M. American Politics Since 1945. Chicago: Quadrangle Books, 1969.

DeLove, Sidney L. The Quiet Betrayal. Chicago, Illinois: Normandie House Publishers, 1960.

deToledano, Ralph. The Winning Side: The Case for Goldwater Republicanism. New York: G.P. Putnam's Sons, 1963.

es, Martin. <u>Martin Dies' Story</u>. New York: Bookmailer, Inc., 1963.

Donner, Frank J. <u>The Un-Americans</u>. New York: Ballantine Books, 1961.

Donovan, Frank R. <u>The Americanism of Barry Goldwater</u>. New York: Macfadden-Bartell Corporation, 1964.

Donovan, Robert J. <u>The Future of the Republican Party</u>. New York: The New American Library, Inc., 1964.

Draper, Hal. <u>Berkeley: The New Student Revolt</u>. New York: Grove Press, Inc., 1965.

Draper, Theodore. <u>Abuse of Power</u>. New York: The Viking Press, 1967.

Driscoll, James G. <u>Elections 1968</u>. Silver Springs, Maryland: The National Observer, 1968.

Dudman, Richard. <u>Men of the Far Right</u>. New York: Pyramid Publications, Inc., 1962.

Edwards, Lee. <u>Reagan, A Political Biography</u>. San Diego: Viewpoint Books, 1968.

Epstein, Benjamin R., and Forster, Arnold. <u>The Radical Right (Report on the John Birch Society and its Allies)</u>. New York: Random House, 1966.

Epstein, Benjamin R., and Forster, Arnold. <u>Danger on The Right</u>. New York: Random House, 1964.

Epstein, Benjamin R., and Forster, Arnold. <u>Cross-Currents</u>. Garden City, New York: Doubleday & Company, Inc., 1956.

Evans, Medford. <u>The Usurpers</u>. Boston: Western Islands Publishers, 1968.

Evans, M. Stanton. <u>The Future of Conservatism</u>. New York: Holt, Rinehart and Winston, 1968.

Evans, M. Stanton. <u>The Lawbreakers</u>. New Rochelle, New York: Arlington House, 1968.

Evans, M. Stanton. <u>The Politics of Surrender</u>. New York: The Devin-Adair Company, 1966.

Evans, M. Stanton. <u>The Liberal Establishment</u>. New York: The Devin-Adair Company, 1965.

358

Evans, M. Stanton. The Fringe on Top. New York: American Feature Book, 1962.

Evans, M. Stanton. Revolt on the Campus. Chicago, Illinois: Henry Regnery Company, 1961.

Evans, Rowland, and Novak, Robert. Lyndon B. Johnson and the Exercise of Power. New York: The New American Library, 1966.

Faber, Harold, ed. The New York Times Election Handbook, 1968. New York: The New American Library, Inc., 1968.

Flynn, John T. The Decline of the American Republic. New York: The Devin-Adair Company, 1955.

Frady, Marshall. Wallace. New York: The World Publishing Company, 1968.

Franke, David, ed. Quotations From Chairman Bill (The Best of William F. Buckley, Jr.). New York: Pocket Books, 1971.

Frommer, Arthur, ed. Goldwater from A-Z--A Critical Handbook. New York: Frommer Pasmantier Publishing Corporation, 1964.

Furer, Howard B. Lyndon B. Johnson--1908-. Dobbs Ferry, New York: Oceana Publications, Inc., 1971.

Furgurson, Ernest B. Westmorland. Boston: Little, Brown and Company, 1968.

Galloway, John. The Gulf of Tonkin Resolution. Cranbury, New Jersey: Fairleigh Dickinson University Press, 1970.

Garett, Garet. The People's Pottage. Boston, Western Islands Publishers, 1965.

Geyelin, Philip. Lyndon B. Johnson and the World. New York: Frederick A. Praeger, 1966.

Gilden, George F., and Chapman, Bruce K. The Party That Lost Its Head. New York: Alfred A. Knopf, 1966.

Goldman, Eric F. The Tragedy of Lyndon Johnson. New York: Alfred A. Knopf, 1969.

Goldwater, Barry M. With No Apologies. New York: William Morrow and Company, Inc., 1979.

Goldwater, Barry M. The Conscience of a Majority. Englewood Cliffs, New Jersey: Prentice-Hall, Inc., 1970.

Goldwater, Barry M. Where I Stand. New York: McGraw Hill Book Company, Inc., 1964.

Goldwater, Barry M. Why Not Victory? (A Fresh Look at American Foreign Policy). New York: McGraw Hill Book Company, Inc., 1962.

Goldwater, Barry M. The Conscience of a Conservative. Shepherdsville, Kentucky: Victor Publishing Company, Inc., 1960.

Goldwin, Robert A., ed. Left, Right and Center. Chicago: Rand McNally & Company, 1965.

Gordon, Rosalie M. Nine Men Against America (The Story of the Supreme Court and Your Liberties) America's Future pamphlet, New Rochelle, New York, 1961.

Goulden, Joseph C. Truth is the First Casualty. Chicago: Rand McNally & Company, 1969.

Guttmann, Allen. The Conservative Tradition in America. New York: Oxford University Press, 1967.

Halberstam, David. The Best and the Brightest. New York: Random House, 1972.

Halberstam, David. The Making of a Quagmire. New York: Random House, 1965.

Haley, J. Evetts. A Texan Looks At Lyndon (A Study in Illegitimate Power). Canyon, Texas: Palo Duro Press, 1964.

Halle, Louis J. The Cold War As History. New York: Harper & Row Publishers, 1967.

Hargis, Billy James. Communist America--Must It Be? Berne, Indiana: Economy Printing Concern, 1960.

Hargis, Billy James. The Real Extremists--The Far Left. Tulsa: Christian Crusade, 1964.

Hargis, Billy James. The Facts About Communism and Our Churches. Tulsa: Christian Crudade, 1962.

Hart, Jeffrey. The American Dissent--A Decade of Modern Conservatism. Garden City, New York: Doubleday & Company, Inc., 1966.

360

Hartke, Vance. The American Crisis in Vietnam. Indianapolis, India The Bobbs-Merrill Company, Inc., 1968.

Hartz, Louis. The Liberal Tradition in America. New York: Harcourt, Brace, 1955.

Hass, Eric. The Reactionary Right. New York: New York Labor News Company, 1963.

Hazlitt, Henry. The Foundations of Morality. Princeton, New Jersey: Van Nostrand, 1964.

Heirich, Max. The Beginning: Berkeley, 1964. New York: Columbia University Press, 1968.

Hess, Karl. In a Cause That Will Triumph. Garden City, New York: Doubleday & Company, Inc., 1967.

Hess, Stephen, and Broder, David S. The Republican Establishment. New York: Harper & Row Publishers, 1967.

Hilsman, Roger. To Move A Nation. Garden City, New York: Doubleday & Company, Inc., 1967.

Hofstadter, Richard. The Paranoid Style in American Politics and Other Essays. New York: Alfred A. Knopf, 1965.

Hofstadter, Richard. Anti-Intellectualism in American Life. New York: Alfred A. Knopf, 1963.

Hofstadter, Richard. Social Darwinism in American Thought. Boston: Beacon Press, 1955.

Hofstadter, Richard. The Age of Reform. New York: Vintage Books, 1955.

Hofstadter, Richard. The American Political Tradition. New York: Alfred A. Knopf, 1948.

Hoopes, Townsend. The Limits of Intervention. New York: David McKay Company, Inc., 1969.

Hoover, J. Edgar. J. Edgar Hoover on Communism. New York: Random House, 1969.

Hoover, J. Edgar. Masters of Deceit. New York: Henry Holt and Company, 1958.

361

well, Millard L. An Answer to Goldwater. New York: Vantage Press, 1961.

Hunter, James T. Our Second Revolution. Caldwell, Idaho: The Caxton Printers, Ltd., 1968.

Hutchins, Lavern C. The John Birch Society and United States Foreign Policy. New York: Pageant Press, Inc., 1968.

Jacobs, Paul, and Landau, Saul. The New Radicals. New York: Random House, 1966.

Janson, Donald, and Eismann, Bernard. The Far Right. New York: McGraw-Hill Book Company, Inc., 1963.

Javits, Jacob K. Order of Battle: A Republican's Call To Reason. New York: Atheneum Publishers, 1964.

Johnson, Lyndon B. The Vantage Point. New York: Holt, Rinehart and Winston, 1971.

Johnson, Lyndon B. My Hope for America. New York: Random House, 1964.

Jones, Bill. The Wallace Story. Northport, Alabama: American Southern Publishing Company, 1966.

Jones, J. Harry. The Minutemen. Garden City, New York: Doubleday & Company, Inc., 1968.

Jordan, Winthrop D. White Over Black: American Attitudes Towards the Negro, 1550-1812. Chapel Hill, North Carolina: University of North Carolina Press, 1968.

Kalb, Marvin, and Able, Elie. Roots of Involvement. New York: W.W. Norton & Company, Inc., 1971.

Kemp, Jack. An American Renaissance. New York: Harper & Row, 1979.

Kendall, Willmoore. The Conservative Affirmation. Chicago: Henry Regnery Company, 1963.

Keniston, Kenneth. Young Radicals. New York: Harcourt, Brace & World, Inc., 1968.

Kessel, John Howard. The Goldwater Coalition. Indianapolis, Indiana: The Bobbs-Merrill Company, Inc., 1968.

Kilpatrick, James J. The Southern Case For School Segregation. n.p.: The Crowell-Collier Press, 1962.

Kilpatrick, James J. The Smut Peddlers. Garden City, New York: Doubleday & Company, Inc., 1960.

Kilpatrick, James J. The Sovereign States. Chicago: Henry Regnery Company, 1957.

Kirk, Russell. The Intemperate Professor. Baton Rouge: Louisiana State University Press, 1965.

Kirk, Russell. The American Cause. Chicago: Henry Regnery Company, 1957.

Kirk, Russell. Beyond the Dreams of Avarice. Chicago: Henry Regnery Company, 1956.

Kirk, Russell. Academic Freedom. Chicago: Henry Regnery Company, 1955.

Kirk, Russell. A Program For Conservatives. Chicago: Henry Regnery Company, 1954.

Kirk, Russell. The Conservative Mind. Chicago: Henry Regnery Company, 1953.

Kirk, Russell and McClellan, James. The Political Principles of Robert A. Taft. New York: Fleet Press Corporation, 1967.

Klein, Alexander, ed. Natural Enemies. Philadelphia & New York: J.B. Lippincott Company, 1969.

Knebel, Fletcher, and Bailey, Charles W., II. Seven Days In May. New York: Harper and Row, 1962.

Kraslow, David, and Loory, Stuart H. The Secret Search For Peace in Vietnam. New York: Random House, 1968.

Lachicotte, Alberta. Rebel Senator (Strom Thurmond of South Carolina). New York: The Devin-Adair Company, 1966.

Lasky, Victor. J.F.K., The Man and the Myth. New York: The MacMillan Company, 1963.

Lauter, Paul, and Howe, Florence. The Conspiracy of the Young. Cleveland, Ohio: The World Publishing Company, 1970.

363

Leipold, L. Edmond. Ronald Reagan: Governor and Statesman. Minneapolis, Minnesota: T.S. Denison & Company, 1968.

LeMay, Curtis E. with Kantor, MacKinlay. Mission With LeMay: My Story. Garden City, New York: Doubleday & Company, Inc., 1965.

Lewis, Joseph. What Makes Reagan Run? New York: McGraw-Hill Company, 1968.

Linington, Elizabeth. Come To Think Of It. Boston: Western Islands Publishers, 1965.

Lipset, Seymour Martin, and Wolin, Sheldon S. The Berkely Student Revolt. Garden City, New York: Doubleday & Company, Inc., 1965.

Lipset, Seymour Martin, and Raab, Earl. The Politics of Unreason. New York: Harper and Row Publishers, 1970.

Lokos, Lionel. Hysteria 1964. New Rochelle, New York: Arlington House 1967.

Lora, Ronald. Conservative Minds in America. Chicago: Rand McNally & Company, 1971.

Lubell, Samuel. The Future While It Happened. New York: W.W. Norton & Company, Inc., 1973.

Lubell, Samuel. The Hidden Crisis in American Politics. New York: W.W. Norton & Company, Inc., 1970.

Lubell, Samuel. White and Black: Test of a Nation. New York: Harper & Row Publishers, 1964.

Lubell, Samuel. Revolt of the Moderates. New York: Harper & Brothers, 1956.

Lubell, Samuel. The Future of American Politics. New York: Harper & Brothers, 1951.

Luce, Phillip Abbott. The New Left. New York: David McKay Company, Inc., 1966.

MacNeil, Neil. Dirksen: Portrait Of A Public Man. New York: The World Publishing Company, 1970.

Mailer, Norman. Miami and the Siege of Chicago. New York: The World Publishing Company, 1968.

Manion, Clarence. The Conservative American: His Fight For Natio.
Independence and Constitutional Government. New York: Tr
Devin-Adair Company, 1964.

Mannheim, Karl. Essays on Sociology and Social Psychology. London:
Routledge & Kegan Paul, Ltd., 1953.

Markham, Charles L. The Buckleys. New York: William Morrow &
Company, Inc., 1973.

Mattar, Edward Paul, III. Barry Goldwater (A Political Indictment).
Riverdale, Maryland: Century Twenty-One Limited, 1964.

May, Ernest R. Lessons of the Past: The Use and Misuse of History in
American Foreign Policy. New York: Oxford University Press,
1973.

May, Henry F. The End of American Innocence. New York: Alfred A.
Knopf, 1959.

Mayer, George H. The Republican Party. 2nd ed. New York: Oxford
University Press, 1967.

Mazo, Earl, and Hess, Stephen. Nixon: A Political Portrait. New
York: Harper & Row, 1968.

McDowell, Charles, Jr. Campaign Fever. New York: William Morrow
and Company, 1965.

McDowell, Edwin. Barry Goldwater: Portrait of an Arizonan. Chicago,
Illinois: Henry Regnery Company, 1964.

McEvoy, James III. Radical or Conservatives? Chicago: Rand McNally &
Company, 1971.

McGinniss, Joe. The Selling of the President, 1968. New York: Trident
Press, 1969.

McInerny, Timothy A. The Private Man. New York: Ivan Obolensky,
Inc., 1962.

McMillen, Neal R. The Citizens' Council. Chicago, Illinois: University
of Illinois Press, 1971.

McReady, Stanhope T. Birch Putsch Plans For 1964. n.p.: Domino
Publications, 1963.

Menashe, Louis, and Radash, Ronald, ed. Teach-Ins: U.S.A. New York:
Frederick A. Praeger, 1967.

365

eyer, Frank S. The Conservative Mainstream. New Rochelle, New York: Arlington House, 1969.

Meyer, Frank S., ed. The African Nettle. New York: The John Day Company, 1965.

Meyer, Frank S., ed. What Is Conservatism? New York: Holt, Rinehart and Winston, 1964.

Meyer, Frank S. In Defense of Freedom. Chicago: Henry Regnery Company, 1962.

Meyer, Frank S. The Moulding of Communists. New York: Harcourt, Brace and Company, 1961.

Michie, Allan A., and Ryhlick, Frank. Dixie Demagogues. New York: The Vanguard Press, 1939.

Miles, Michael W. The Odyssey of the American Right. New York: Oxford University Press, 1980.

Mille, Michael V., and Gilmore, Susan. Revolution at Berkeley. New York: The Dial Press, 1965.

Morgan, Thomas, ed. Goldwater Either/Or (A Self-Portrait Based Upon His Own Words). Washington, D.C.: Public Affairs Press, 1964.

Morris, Robert. Disarmament: Weapons of Conquest. New York: Bookmailer, 1963.

Morris, Robert. No Wonder We Are Losing. New York: Bookmailer, 1958.

Murphy, George, and Lasky, Victor. Say...Didn't You Used to be George Murphy? New York: Bartholomew House, 1970.

Murphy, Reg., and Gulliver, Hal. The Southern Strategy. New York: Charles Scribner's Sons, 1971.

Murray, Norbert. Legacy of an Assassination. New York: Pro-People Press, 1964.

Nash, Gary B., and Weiss, Richard. The Great Fear: Race in the Mind of America. New York: Holt, Rinehart and Winston, 1970.

Nash, George H. The Conservative Intellectual Movement in America Since 1945. New York: Basic Books, Inc., 1976.

Nenoff, Stephen. Who Are The Fellow Travellers? Denton, Texas Southern Patriotic Breeze Publications, n.d.

Newberry, Mike. The Yahoos. New York: Marzani and Munsell, 1964.

Newfield, Jack. A Prophetic Minority. New York: The American Library, 1966.

Newman, Edwin S. The Hate Reader. Dobbs Ferry, New York: Oceana Publications, Inc., 1964.

Nixon, Richard M. Six Crises. Garden City, New York: Doubleday & Company, Inc., 1962.

Noebel, David A. Communism, Hypnotism and the Beatles. Tulsa: Christian Crusade Publications, 1965.

Novak, Robert. The Agony of the G.O.P. 1964. New York: The MacMillan Company, 1965.

O'Brien, Lawrence F. No Final Victories. Garden City, New York: Doubleday & Company, Inc., 1974.

O'Neill, William L. Coming Apart: An Informal History of America in the 1960's. Chicago: Quadrangle Books, 1971.

Overstreet, Harry and Bonaro. The Strange Tactics of Extremism. New York: W.W. Norton & Company, Inc., 1964.

Porter, Kirk H., and Johnson, Donald Bruce, ed. National Party Platforms 1840-1960, Supplement 1964. Urbana: The University of Illinois Press, 1965.

Putnam, Carleton. Race and Reason: A Yankee View. Washington, D.C.: Public Affairs Press, 1961.

Rafferty, Max. Max Raferty on Education. New York: The Devin-Adair Company, 1968.

Rafferty, Max. What They Are Doing To Your Children. New York: New American Library, 1964.

Rafferty, Max. Suffer Little Children. New York: The Devin-Adair Company, 1962.

Rafferty, Max, and Stoops, Emery. Just a Minute, Junior. West Orange, New Jersey: Economics Press, 1963.

aywid, Mary Anne. The Ax-Grinders. New York: MacMillan & Company, Inc., 1962.

Reagan, Ronald. The Creative Society. New York: The Devin-Adair Company, 1968.

Reagan, Ronald, with Hubler, Richard G. Where's the Rest of Me? New York: Duell, Sloan and Pearce, 1965.

Redekop, John Harold. The American Far Right--A Case Study of Billy James Hargis and Christian Crusade. Grand Rapids, Michigan: W.B. Eerdman's Publishing Company, 1968.

Rickenbacker, Edward V. Rickenbacker. Englewood Cliffs, New Jersey: Prentice-Hall, Inc., 1967.

Roberts, Charles. LBJ'S Inner Circle. New York: Delacorte Press, 1965.

Rockwell, George Lincoln. This Time The World. New York: Parliament House, 1963.

Rockwell, Willard F. The Rebellious Colonel Speaks. selected papers arranged by Alfred Lief. New York: McGraw-Hill Company, 1964.

Romney, George. The Concerns of a Citizen. New York: G.P. Putnam's Sons, 1968.

Rosenstone, Robert A. Protest From the Right. Beverly Hills California: The Glencoe Press, 1968.

Rossiter, Clinton. Constitutional Dictatorship. New York: Harcourt, Brace & World, 1960.

Rossiter, Clinton, Marxism, The View From America. New York: Harcourt, Brace & World, 1960.

Rossiter, Clinton. Parties and Politics In America. Ithaca, New York: Cornell University Press, 1960.

Rossiter, Clinton. Conservatism in America. New York: Alfred A. Knopf, 1955.

Rostow, Walt W. The Diffusion of Power. New York: The MacMillan Company, 1972.

Rovere, Richard H. The Goldwater Caper. New York: Harcourt, Brace & World, 1965.

Rovere, Richard, and Schlesinger, Arthur M., Jr. The General and t. President. New York: Farrar, Strauss and Young, 1951.

Rusher, William A. Special Counsel. New Rochelle, New York: Arlington House, 1968.

Sale, Kirkpatrick. SDS. New York: Random House, 1973.

Salinger, Pierre. With Kennedy. Garden City, New York: Doubleday & Company, Inc., 1966.

Santayana, George. The Life of Reason: Reason in Common Sense. New York: Charles Scribner's Sons, 1905.

Schechter, William. Countdown '68. New York: Fleet Press Corporation, 1967.

Schlafly, Phyllis. Safe-Not Sorry. Alton, Illinois: Pere Marquette Press, 1967.

Schlafly, Phyllis. A Choice Not An Echo: "The Inside Story on How American Presidents Are Chosen." 3rd ed. Alton, Illinois: Pere Marquette Press, 1964.

Schlafly, Phyllis, and Ward, Chester. The Betrayers. Alton, Illinois: Pere Marquette Press, 1968.

Schlafly, Phyllis, and Ward, Chester. Strike From Space (How the Russians May Destroy Us). New York: The Devin-Adair Company, 1966.

Schlesinger, Arthur M., Jr. A Thousand Days. Boston: Houghton Mifflin, 1965.

Schoenbrun, David. Vietnam. New York: Atheneum Publishers, 1968.

Schomp, Gerald. Birchism Was My Business. Toronto, Ontario: The MacMillan Company, 1970.

Schurmann, Franz; Scott, Peter Dole; and Zelnik, Reginald. The Politics of Escalation in Vietnam. Boston: Beacon Press. 1966.

Schwarz, Frederick Charles. You Can Trust the Communists. Englewood Cliffs, New Jersey: Prentice-Hall, 1960.

Scott, Hugh. Come to the Party. Englewood Cliffs, New Jersey: Prentice-Hall, Inc., 1968.

369

...tt, Peter Dole. The War Conspiracy. Indianapolis, Indiana: The Bobbs-Merrill Company, Inc., 1972.

Sensing, Thurman. The Case Against the Welfare State. Nashville, Tennessee: n.d.

Sexson, Paul A., and Miles, Stephen B., Jr. The Challenge of Conservatism. New York: Exposition Press, 1964.

Shadegg, Stephen. What Happended to Goldwater. New York: Holt, Rinehart and Winston. 1965.

Shadegg, Stephen. Barry Goldwater: Freedom is His Flight Plan. New York: Fleet Publishing Company, 1962.

Sherwin, Mark. The Extremists. New York: St. Martin's Press, 1963.

Simon, William E. A Time For Truth. New York: McGraw-Hill, 1978.

Skousen, W. Cleon. The Naked Communist. 8th ed. Salt Lake City, Utah: The Ensign Publishing Company, 1961.

Smith, Anita. The Intimate Story of Lurleen Wallace. Montgomery, Alabama: Communications Unlimited, Inc., 1969.

Smith, George Henry. Who Is Ronald Reagan? New York: Pyramid Books, 1968.

Smoot, Dan. The Invisible Government. Boston: Western Islands Publishers, 1962.

Sobel, Lester A., ed. South Vietnam. vol 1. New York: Facts on File, Inc., 1966.

Sobel, Lester A., ed. South Vietnam. vol 2. New York: Facts on File, Inc., 1969.

Sorensen, Theodore. Kennedy. New York: Harper & Row Publishers, 1965.

Staebler, Neil, and Ross, Douglas. How to Argue With a Conservative. New York: Grossman Publishers, 1965.

Stang, Alan. It's Very Simple (The True Story of Civil Rights). Belmont, Massachusetts: Western Islands Publishers, 1965.

Stavins, Ralph; Barnet, Richard J.; and Raskin, Marcus G. Washington Plans An Aggressive War. New York: Random House, 1971.

Steffgen, Kent H. Here's the Rest of Him. Reno, Nevada: Forsigh. Books, 1968.

Steinfels, Peter. The Neo-Conservatives. New York: Simon & Schuster, 1979.

Stevens, Bryan W. The John Birch Society in California Politics. West Covina: The Publis Society, 1966.

Stone, I. F. In a Time of Torment. New York: Random House, 1967.

Stormer, John A. None Dare Call It Treason. Florissant, Missouri: Liberty Bell Press, 1964.

Suall, Irwin. The American Ultras. New York: New America, 1962.

Synon, John J., ed. George Wallace: Profile of a Presidential Candidate. Kilmarnock, Virginia: Ms. Inc., 1968.

Taylor, Telford. Grand Inquest. New York: Ballantine Books, 1961.

Thimmesch, Nick. The Condition of Republicanism. New York: W.W. Norton & Company, Inc., 1968.

Thurmond, Strom. The Faith We Have Not Kept. San Diego: Viewpoint Books, 1968.

Tindall, George Brown. The Disruption of the Solid South. Athens, Georgia: University of Georgia Press, 1972.

Topping, John C.; Lazarek, John R.; and Linden, William H. Southern Republicanism and the New South. Cambridge, Massachusetts: The Ripon Society, 1966.

Tower, John G. A Program for Conservatives. New York: Macfadden-Bartell Corporation, 1962.

Turner, William W. Power on the Right. Berkeley, California: Ramparts Press, 1971.

Vahan, Richard. The Truth About the John Birch Society. New York: Macfadden-Bartell Corporation, 1962.

Viorst, Milton. Fall From Grace. New York: The New American Library, 1968.

Voss, Earl H. Nuclear Ambush: The Test Ban Trap. Chicago: Henry Regnery Company, 1963.

371

Walker, Brooks R. The Christian Fright Peddlers. Garden City, New York: Doubleday & Company, Inc., 1964.

Wallace, George C. Hear Me Out. Anderson, South Carolina: Droke House Publishers, 1968.

Warshaw, Steven. The Trouble in Berkeley. Berkeley, California: Diablo Press, 1965.

Welch, Robert. The New Americanism (and Other Speeches and Essays). Belmont, Massachusetts: Western Islands Publishers, 1966.

Welch, Robert. The Politician. 5th ed. Belmont, Massachusetts: Belmont Publishing Company, 1964.

Welch, Robert. The Time Has Come. Belmont, Massachusetts: The John Birch Society, 1964.

Welch, Robert. The Neutralizers. Belmont, Massachusetts: The John Birch Society, 1963.

Welch, Robert. A Brief Introduction to the John Birch Society. Belmont, Massachusetts: John Birch Society, 1962.

Welch, Robert. The Blue Book of the John Birch Society. 7th ed. Belmont, Massachusetts: The John Birch Society, 1959.

Welch, Robert. The Life of John Birch (In the Story of One American Boy, the Ordeal of his Age). Chicago, Illinois: Henry Regnery Company, 1954.

Whalen, Richard J. Catch the Falling Flag. Boston: Houghton, Mifflin Company, 1972.

White, Clifton F., and Gill, William J. Suite 3505: The Story of the Draft Goldwater Movement. New Rochelle, New York: Arlington House, 1967.

White, Theodore H. The Making of the President, 1960. New York: Atheneum Publishers, 1961.

White, Theodore H. The Making of the President, 1964. New York: Atheneum Publishers, 1965.

White, Theodore H. The Making of the President, 1968. New York: Atheneum Publishers, 1969.

Wicker, Tom. JFK and LBJ. New York: William Morrow & Compa Inc., 1968.

Widener, Alice. Behind the U.N. Front. New York: The Bookmailer, 1962.

Wills, Garry. Nixon Agonistes. Boston: Houghton Mifflin Company, 1970.

Wills, Garry. The Second Civil War. New York: New American Library, 1968.

Windchy, Eugene G. Tonkin Gulf. Garden City, New York: Doubleday & Company, Inc., 1971.

Witcover, Jules. Marathon: The Pursuit of the Presidency, 1972-1976. New York: Viking Press, 1977.

Witcover, Jules. White Knight: The Rise of Spiro Agnew. New York: Random House, 1972.

Witcover, Jules. The Resurrection of Richard Nixon. New York: G.P. Putnam's Sons, 1970.

Wolin, Sheldon S., and Schaar, John H. The Berkeley Rebellion and Beyond. New York: Vintage Books, 1970.

Wood, Rob, and Smith, Dean. Barry Goldwater. New York: Avon Book Division, 1961.

Workman, William D., Jr. The Case For The South. New York: The Devin-Adair Company, 1960.

American Legion Magazine, 1962-1968.

American Mercury, 1960-1968.

American Opinion, 1960-1968.

America's Future, 1962-1968.

Beacon-Light Herald, 1960-1965.

Challenge to Socialism, 1962-1968.

Christian Economics, 1962-1968.

Citizen, 1962-1969.

Commentary, 1960-1968.

Common Sense, 1961-1968.

Counterattack, 1962-1968.

Cross and the Flag, 1960-1968.

Dan Smoot Report, 1963-1968.

Daughters of the American Revolution Magazine, 1960-1968.

Defender, 1960-1968.

Destiny, 1960-1968.

Economic Council Letter, 1962-1968.

Fiery Cross, 1966-1968.

Human Events, 1959-1969.

I. F. Stone's Weekly, 1960-1968.

John Birch Society Bulletin, 1960-1962.

Liberty Letter, 1966-1968.

Life, 1960-1968.

Life Lines, 1968.

Look, 1960-1968.

Los Angeles Times, 1960-1968.

Manion Forum Yearbook, 1962-1968.

National Defender, 1963-1968.

National Program Letter, 1963-1969.

National Review, 1955-1968.

National Review Bulletin, 1962-1968.

New Guard, 1961-1968.

News and Views, 1963-1968.

Newsweek, 1960-1968.

New York Times, 1960-1968.

Report to America, 1960-1967.

Rockwell Report, 1962-1967.

Sons of the American Revolution Magazine, 1960-1968.

Storm Trooper, 1964-1968.

Through to Victory, 1966-1968.

Time, 1960-1968.

Tocsin, 1963-1967.

Top of the News with Fulton Lewis, Jr., 1960-1968.

U.S.A., 1963-1968.

U.S. News and World Report, 1960-1968.

Washington Report, 1965-1968.

Weekly Crusader, 1963-1968.

INDEX

INDEX

For additional information on specific entries, see also end-of-chapter footnotes where indicated in the text.

380

C (Cont'd)

Coors, Joseph, 1, 334

Coughlin, Father Charles, x, 7, 16, 17, 106

Council on American Relations, 131

Counterattack, 226

Courtney, Kent, 106, 225

Courtney, Phoebe, 106

"Coxey's Army," 272

Crane, Phil, 342

Cranston, Alan, 317, 318

Crawford, Alan, 334, 339

Crime, 35, 36, 53, 57, 59, 60, 63, 88–90, 126, 157, 162, 187, 209, 213, 249–50, 253, 269, 273, 337, 349

Crommelin, John G., Jr., 105

Cross and the Flag, x, 5, 26, 61, 78, 104, 164, 253

Cuba, 33–35, 214, 233, 238, 312

Cuban Missile Crisis, 154, 190–91, 224–25, 226

Czechoslovakia, 269

D

Daley, Richard, 327

Dallas, 147–48

Dallas Morning News, 226

D (Cont'd)

Danger on the Right, 19, 32

Danzig, David, 14

Daughters of the American Revolution (DAR), 3, 125

Davis, Elmer, 9

Davis, Jefferson, 179

De Armand, Fred, 86

Death penalty, 337

Declaration of Independence, 48

Decline and Fall of the Roman Empire, The, 55, 59, 101, 182. See also Rome, fall of

de Courcy, Kenneth, 75, 83, 135

"Deep Throat," 314

Defenders of American Education, 48

Defender, The, 21, 58, 59, 103, 150, 164, 203

Defense, 10, 16, 192, 337

Demagoguery, 207, 209, 213, 272–73, 275

Democracy, 47–51; and civil rights, 161–62, 186

Democratic Party, 274, 288, 299, 331

Democrats, 1, 2, 5, 27, 33, 275, 276, 340

390

392

403

78732